27

The IDG Books *Creating Cool* Series Advantage

We at IDG Books Worldwide created *Creating Cool 3D Web Worlds with VRML* to meet your growing need for quick access to the most complete and accurate computer information available. Our books work the way you do: They focus on accomplishing specific tasks — not on learning random functions. Our books are not long-winded manuals or dry reference tomes. In each book, expert authors tell you exactly what you can do with new technology and software and how to evaluate its usefulness for your needs. Easy to follow information, comprehensive coverage, and convenient access in language and design — it's all here.

The authors of IDG books are uniquely qualified to give you expert advice as well as to provide insightful tips and techniques not found anywhere else. Our authors maintain close contact with end users through feedback from articles, training sessions, e-mail exchanges, user group participation, and consulting work. Because our authors know the realities of daily computer use and are directly linked to the reader, our books have a strategic advantage.

Our experienced authors know how to approach a topic in the most efficient manner, and we know that you, the reader, will benefit from a "one-on-one" relationship with the author. Our research shows that readers make computer book purchases because they want expert advice. Because readers want to benefit from the author's experience, the author's voice is always present in an IDG book.

In addition, the author is free to include or recommend useful software in an IDG book. The software that accompanies each book is not intended to be a casual filler but is linked to the content, theme, or procedures of the book. We know that you will benefit from the included software.

You will find what you need in this book whether you read it from cover to cover, section by section, or simply one topic at a time. As a computer user, you deserve a comprehensive resource of answers. We at IDG Books Worldwide are proud to deliver that resource with *Creating Cool 3D Web Worlds with VRML*.

Brenda McLaughlin
Senior Vice President and Group Publisher

Internet: YouTellUs@idgbooks.com

CREATING COOL 3D WEB WORLDS with VRML

Paul M. Summitt
Mary J. Summitt

CREATING COOL 3D WEB WORLDS WITH VRML

Paul M. Summitt

Mary J. Summitt

IDG Books Worldwide, Inc.
An International Data Group Company

Foster City, CA ♦ Chicago, IL ♦ Indianapolis, IN ♦ Braintree, MA ♦ Dallas, TX

Creating Cool 3D Web Worlds with VRML

Published by
IDG Books Worldwide, Inc.
An International Data Group Company
919 E. Hillsdale Blvd.
Suite 400
Foster City, CA 94404

Library of Congress Catalog Card No.: 95-81940

ISBN: 1-56884-796-3

Printed in the United States of America

10 9 8 7 6 5 4 3 2 1

1E/QW/RS/ZV

Distributed in the United States by IDG Books Worldwide, Inc.

Distributed by Macmillan Canada for Canada; by Computer and Technical Books for the Caribbean Basin; by Contemporanea de Ediciones for Venezuela; by Distribuidora Cuspide for Argentina; by CITEC for Brazil; by Ediciones ZETA S.C.R. Ltda. for Peru; by Editorial Limusa SA for Mexico; by Transworld Publishers Limited in the United Kingdom and Europe; by Al-Maiman Publishers & Distributors for Saudi Arabia; by Simron Pty. Ltd. for South Africa; by IDG Communications (HK) Ltd. for Hong Kong; by Toppan Company Ltd. for Japan; by Addison Wesley Publishing Company for Korea; by Longman Singapore Publishers Ltd. for Singapore, Malaysia, Thailand, and Indonesia; by Unalis Corporation for Taiwan; by WS Computer Publishing Company, Inc. for the Philippines; by WoodsLane Pty. Ltd. for Australia; by WoodsLane Enterprises Ltd. for New Zealand.

For general information on IDG Books Worldwide's books in the U.S., please call our Consumer Customer Service department at 800-762-2974. For reseller information, including discounts and premium sales, please call our Reseller Customer Service department at 800-434-3422.

For information on where to purchase IDG Books Worldwide's books outside the U.S., contact IDG Books Worldwide at 415-655-3021 or fax 415-655-3295.

For information on translations, contact Marc Jeffrey Mikulich, Director, Foreign & Subsidiary Rights, at IDG Books Worldwide, 415-655-3018 or fax 415-655-3295.

For sales inquiries and special prices for bulk quantities, write to the address above or call IDG Books Worldwide at 415-655-3200.

For information on using IDG Books Worldwide's books in the classroom, or ordering examination copies, contact Jim Kelly at 800-434-2086.

For authorization to photocopy items for corporate, personal, or educational use, please contact Copyright Clearance Center, 222 Rosewood Drive, Danvers, MA 01923, or fax 508-750-4470.

 is a trademark under exclusive license to IDG Books Worldwide, Inc., from International Data Group, Inc.

About the Authors

Paul M. Summitt is Director of Broadcasting at Pittsburg State University. He has been teaching for ten years. Paul is currently working toward a doctorate degree in communication. Paul enjoys researching his family genealogy, watching movies, and eating brownies (though he doesn't like chocolate).

Mary J. Summitt has a B.S. in broadcasting and may one day finish her master's degree. She is the owner of a research and publishing company. Mary enjoys reading, researching various topics, watching movies, and eating brownies (she does like chocolate).

Mary and Paul were the principal writers of the user manual for VR Basic. They are both interested in cyberspace and virtual reality. They hope to buy a sailboat one day and sail off to far away places.

Welcome to the world of IDG Books Worldwide.

IDG Books Worldwide, Inc., is a subsidiary of International Data Group, the world's largest publisher of computer-related information and the leading global provider of information services on information technology. IDG was founded more than 25 years ago and now employs more than 7,700 people worldwide. IDG publishes more than 250 computer publications in 67 countries (see listing below). More than 70 million people read one or more IDG publications each month.

Launched in 1990, IDG Books Worldwide is today the #1 publisher of best-selling computer books in the United States. We are proud to have received 8 awards from the Computer Press Association in recognition of editorial excellence and three from Computer Currents' First Annual Readers' Choice Awards, and our best-selling ...*For Dummies*® series has more than 19 million copies in print with translations in 28 languages. IDG Books Worldwide, through a joint venture with IDG's Hi-Tech Beijing, became the first U.S. publisher to publish a computer book in the People's Republic of China. In record time, IDG Books Worldwide has become the first choice for millions of readers around the world who want to learn how to better manage their businesses.

Our mission is simple: Every one of our books is designed to bring extra value and skill-building instructions to the reader. Our books are written by experts who understand and care about our readers. The knowledge base of our editorial staff comes from years of experience in publishing, education, and journalism — experience which we use to produce books for the '90s. In short, we care about books, so we attract the best people. We devote special attention to details such as audience, interior design, use of icons, and illustrations. And because we use an efficient process of authoring, editing, and desktop publishing our books electronically, we can spend more time ensuring superior content and spend less time on the technicalities of making books.

You can count on our commitment to deliver high-quality books at competitive prices on topics you want to read about. At IDG Books Worldwide, we continue in the IDG tradition of delivering quality for more than 25 years. You'll find no better book on a subject than one from IDG Books Worldwide.

John J. Kilcullen

John Kilcullen
President and CEO
IDG Books Worldwide, Inc.

Dedication

To Catherine Heisinger, Mary's mother, whose extreme support, enthusiasm, and devotion have enabled Paul and Mary to reach for the stars.

Credits

Senior Vice President
and Group Publisher
Brenda McLaughlin

Acquisitions Manager
Gregory Croy

Acquisitions Editor
Ellen L. Camm

Brand Manager
Melisa M. Duffy

Managing Editor
Andy Cummings

Editorial Assistants
Nate Holdread
Tim Borek

Production Director
Beth Jenkins

Production Assistant
Jacalyn L. Pennywell

Supervisor of Project Coordination
Cindy L. Phipps

Supervisor of Page Layout
Kathie S. Schnorr

Production Systems Specialist
Steve Peake

Pre-Press Coordination
Tony Augsburger
Patricia R. Reynolds
Theresa Sánchez-Baker

Media/Archive Coordination
Leslie Popplewell
Kerri Cornell
Michael Wilkey

Project Editor
Pat Seiler

Technical Reviewers
Mark Owen, Vice President,
WebForce
Barbara Singer, Vice President
of Engineering, InterVista

Graphics Coordination
Shelley Lea
Gina Scott
Carla Radzikinas

Production Page Layout
Shawn Aylsworth
Linda M. Boyer
Maridee V. Ennis
Angela F. Hunckler
Jill Lyttle
Michael Sullivan

Proofreaders
Kathleen Prata
Christine Meloy Beck
Gwenette Gaddis
Dwight Ramsey
Carl Saff
Robert Springer

Indexer
Liz Cunningham

Book Design
Theresa Sánchez-Baker

Cover Design
Three 8 Creative Group

Acknowledgments

The people at IDG have been fantastic. Special thanks to **Ellen Camm** for believing in us, **Andy Cummings** for his support, and **Pat Seiler** for her skillful editing (that hopefully made us look reasonably intelligent <g>). The others at IDG Books, names too numerous to mention in this small space, should know that we really appreciate their efforts.

The members of the VRML community made us feel a part of this new frontier. Special thanks to **Mark Pesce** and **Tony Parisi** for making themselves available to answer questions. A very special thanks to **Mark Owen**, without whose help and technical editing, we might never have met so many wonderful software developers and the VRML specification would not be as easy to understand as it is. Thanks also to **Barbara Singer** for her efforts on the technical edit.

Thanks to all the software developers who took time to help make the CD-ROM as good as it is. We can't thank the employees of 3DWeb, Caligari, Chaco, CompuServe, InterVista, MicronGreen, Microsoft, Paper Software, ParaGraph, Viewpoint, Virtus, and WebMaster enough for their long hours and diligent efforts.

Thanks to **Bernie Roehl** and **Keith Rule** for your time and efforts.

To **Doug Faxon**, **Dennis McKenzie**, and **Todd Porter**, thanks for your contributions. To our friends in CyberForum, thanks for listening to Paul's ramblings.

Many thanks to **Phil Utykansi** and **Eliot Jacobsen** at Viewpoint Datalabs for giving us such great cover images and for being such a great team to work with. Special thanks to Syndesis for helping Viewpoint Datalabs with VRML translations.

Sincere thanks and appreciation to **Marian Wallace** for making her last cover with IDG Books one of the best! Your professional efforts (*always* "above and beyond") will be missed.

Thanks to our kids, **Cathy**, **Michael**, and **Jaclyn**, for understanding how little time is left in the day when you both work and write.

John Gwinner, of VisNet, "you are, and always will be, [our] friend."

*(The Publisher would like to give special thanks to **Patrick J. McGovern**, without whom this book would not have been possible.)*

Web Pages Used in This Book

We'd like to thank the following for featuring their Web pages in our book. You can find these pages at the following URLs:

On the cover

Cover images provided by Viewpoint Datalabs International, Inc. For More information, call 1-800-DATASET.

Throughout the book

SlipKnot
File://LocalHost/D:/SLIPKNOT/SLIPKNOT.HTM

CompuServe's Home Page
http://www.compuserve.com

Doug Faxon's Home Page
http://www.sonic.net:80/~dfx/doug/

WWW User Survey
http://www.gatech.edu/pitkow/survey/survey-1-1994/graphs/results-gen

W3 Consortium
http://www.w3.org

Cello Internet Browser
file://localhost/D:/CELLO/default.htm

NCSA's Home Page
http://www.ncsa.uiuc.edu/SDG/Software/WinMosaic/HomePage.html

Netscape Home Page
http://home.netscape.com/

Flaxon Alternative Interface Technologies (FAIT) Home Page
http://www.sonic.net/~dfx/fait/

James E. Pitkow's Home Page
http://www.cc.gatech.edu/gvu/people/Phd/James.E.Pitkow.html

3DSite
http://www.lightside.com/3dsite/ad.html

NCSA VRML Home Page
http://www.ncsa.uiuc.edu/General/VRML/VRMLHome.html

NAVFlyer's download site
ftp://yoda.fdt.net/pub/users/m/micgreen

WebMaster
http://www.webmaster.com:80/vrml/wvwin/

Planet 9 Studios
http://www.hyperion.com/planet9/

WaxWeb
http://bug.village.virginia.edu/

Hotwired
http://www.hotwired.com/

Contents at a Glance

Table of Contents

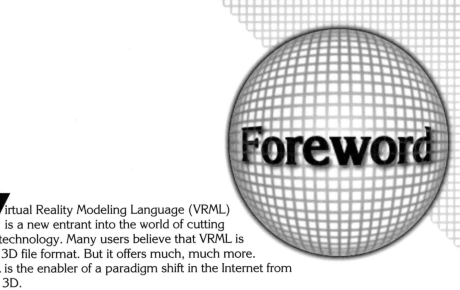

Foreword

Virtual Reality Modeling Language (VRML) is a new entrant into the world of cutting edge technology. Many users believe that VRML is just a 3D file format. But it offers much, much more. VRML is the enabler of a paradigm shift in the Internet from 2D to 3D.

Here's a brief history. Spurred by the tremendous growth of the Internet and the World Wide Web, an increase in CPU power, improved display adapters, cool 3D editing tools, and other technology breakthroughs, VRML has emerged as the necessary tool for creating a completely abstract and continuous Cyberspace.

VRML continues on a road started 20 years ago when we first played Pong — then the computers were all mainframes and UNIX was in development at Bell Labs. No one considered 3D modeling on a computer at that time; it just wasn't possible.

And while the Internet (ARPANet) was still text based and obscure, the first IBM and Apple personal computers arrived around 1980. By 1985 we had 286s with EGA screens on the high-end PCs. Techies started thinking about 3D graphics, but were understandably scared off by the million dollar machines required to create or manipulate them.

But the staggering advances in processing power in the past few years enabled 2D and 3D graphics to permeate the computing landscape. VRML was then a logical inevitability — the starting point for a true global village.

The WWW made the Internet navigable in a more intuitive manner. Though capable of expressing textual, pictorial, and increasingly, audio and video data, the Web's roots remain in text. That its depth of navigation is purely symbolic is its limitation. There is no there.

Humans, however, are not 2D creatures. Humans are superb visualizers and navigate in 3D on an everyday basis.

The new Internet will have a third dimension, but more importantly, all three dimensions will be discretionary. No longer will the dimensions of the Internet be limited only to what is appropriate for the presentation of textual data. Each dimension will be chosen to represent whatever best suits the intended function or purpose: physical distances, time, philosophical point of view, color, speed, style — the choices are limited only by imagination and ingenuity. Movement along these dimensions will be smooth and continuous.

Much as they do in the real world, these environments will supply spatial, functional, and thematic character. Users will be able to get around by relying on their visual and spatial memory much more easily then relying on literal and rote memory. The new Internet will be easy to navigate!

Three-dimensionality is not an incremental improvement. It will give rise to an explosion of new possibilities for content providers and a quantum increase in richness of experience for users.

VRML, while still in its infancy, has the ability to enable people to use the Internet for direct interaction with other people in an interactive multimedia environment, in pairs, in small or large groups, or en masse, publicly or privately, in person or in anonymity. The Internet will become a network of people, not just of information.

By showing you how to use VRML to create cool 3D Web worlds, this book takes us a step closer to that reality.

Tony Parisi
Co-creator of VRML

Introduction

Introduction

During the early 1980s, a young science-fiction writer living in Canada became interested in watching how players reacted to playing video games in the video arcades. He realized that the players had come to "believe" that the space behind the screen was real. The young writer was William Gibson. He called the space behind the screen *cyberspace*.

Gibson's first book, *Neuromancer*, was released in 1984 by Ace Books. The setting for Gibson's book was cyberspace. Gibson described cyberspace as "a consensual hallucination" created by "data abstracted from the banks of every computer in the human system."

Gibson's concept of "wrapping yourself in media and not hav[ing] to see what's really going on around you" perfectly describes putting on a head-mounted display (HMD) and experiencing a virtual world. The first description of *Neuromancer's* main character's stepping into this virtual world is a very colorful description of what entering a World Wide Web (WWW) of virtual reality (VR) might be like in the very near future.

This futuristic World Wide Web of virtual reality may have its beginnings in the new proposed Internet standard known as *Virtual Reality Modeling Language* or *VRML* (pronounced *ver'-mel*). This book is about how you can become a part of this future.

Virtual Reality on the Internet

Just as film technology was one of the forerunners of television technology, VR technology is one of the forerunners of the multitude of multimedia technologies that will exist in the future. Television has been called a window that you can look through into another world. VR has been called the door that you can step through into another world. An important difference between these two technologies is that with VR you are not restricted to simply experiencing worlds that others create. With VR, you can create the world that *you* want to experience. Using an Internet standard such as VRML, you can enable others to experience the world you have created.

We don't think that this concept of users' creating their own worlds has been examined as thoroughly as it should be. With other forms of media, such as books, radio, film, television, and most computer games and programs, other individuals create and produce the worlds that you experience. You have little choice in most of these worlds. Even in so-called "interactive" computer games, what you see and hear and the choices that you are offered are determined and "programmed" in advance for you. Even with the multiple channels offered by the newer cable technologies, what is the choice among so many clones? As a friend once said, "Where's the choice in five different brands of Cheerios? You're still eating Cheerios."

VR changes who's in control of the alternative worlds, the alternative *realities* if you will, that you experience. VR enables you, the user, to create and choose the virtual worlds that you want to experience. It enables you to make any decisions that you want within that world. As mentioned earlier, you don't have that choice in other media, such as television or film. You have to experience those worlds in the order that the producers want you to experience them. Creating your own virtual worlds is much different. *You* make all the choices. *You* choose the hardware. *You* choose the software. *You* choose the world to be created. The most important factor here is that *you* choose.

What This Book Is about

This book is about making some of these choices. We believe that the act of selection restricts your future choices. For example, the act of deciding upon a particular computer platform restricts your future choices of software. As philosopher Michael Heim has suggested, the choice of a specific word-processing program structures your mind in such a way as to reduce your choices. VRML attempts to reduce these restrictions. VRML has been proposed as the Internet standard for creating virtual worlds across computer platforms. VRML is cutting-edge programming that will provide multiuser interactive simulations over the global Internet hyper-linked to the World Wide Web.

These ambitions are not without pitfalls, however. At the end of June 1995, only four platforms were able to enter the virtual worlds awaiting exploration on the Web by using WebSpace, a Web browser with VRML capabilities from Silicon Graphics Incorporated (SGI) and Template Graphics Software (TGS).

These four platforms were SGI, Windows NT Intel, Sun Solaris ZX/TZX, and IBM AIX. WorldSpace for Windows 3.1, which is the dominant platform in the United States, was behind schedule, as was the DEC Alpha version of the program. MIPS and PowerPC Windows NT versions were in development, as were versions for all other Sun systems, except the Solaris mentioned previously. Portal, another Web browser with VRML capabilities for Windows 3.1, was behind schedule also. InterVista's WorldView, a Web browser with VRML capabilities for Windows 3.1, became available just before the end of June.

What to expect

In the months following June, individuals and companies have worked diligently to make the VRML virtual reality an on-line Internet reality. This book documents this progress and tells you how you can use VRML to create your own cyberspace.

What not to expect

One important thing to keep in mind as you learn about VRML is that it cannot create the kinds of virtual reality experiences that you might expect from what you have seen in the media. In other words, don't expect to be able to use VRML to create a *Lawnmower Man* experience. Some day, that kind of technology may be available, but today's technology enables us to create only the very simple kinds of worlds that you learn about in this book.

Although there is a great deal of hype about virtual reality out there, the software on the CD-ROM that's included with this book is truly cutting edge. Much of it is still in the beta stage. Several of the software developers were working right up to the last minute before this book's deadline to get us the most up-to-the-minute version of their software. We hope that future editions of this book, as well as other future projects we undertake discussing and using virtual reality, will have this same cutting-edge flavor.

We've divided the book into four parts, as described in the following sections.

Part I: Understanding Background Concepts

Part I has four chapters. In order to best understand the potential of VRML, you need to have a basic understanding of four separate concepts and technologies: the Internet itself, the World Wide Web, HTML and HTTP, and virtual reality.

Chapter 1: The Internet begins with what the Internet is. In order to best describe the Internet, we take a snapshot view of what the Internet is, or was, at the time of this writing. Because the Internet is in a constant state of evolution and never appears the same from one day to the next and from one user to the next, this chapter focuses on what has existed, what does exist, and what may exist on the Internet in the future. We take a brief look at the history of the Internet to find out where it came from and how it came to be what it is today, for the benefit of those of you who aren't familiar with how the Internet came about. You also hear from some of the people who use the Internet and learn why they find it as useful as they do. We take a short look at what you need in order to access the Internet. We also discuss the setup and operation for the commercial software on the CD-ROM included with this book that enables you to access the Internet.

Chapter 2: The World Wide Web begins with a look at the Web's history: how it came into being, where it is now, and where it may be going in the future. You examine the advantages and disadvantages of some of the more popular Web browsers. We then provide a brief discussion of the setup and operation of the Web browser that's on the CD-ROM that will enable you to start "surfing the Net." We even tell you about some of what we think are the more interesting places to visit on the Web. At this point, you'll be ready to learn how to create your own Web space, known as a *home page*.

Chapter 3: HTML and HTTP explains how and why the HTML and http standards are so important in the history, as well as operation, of VRML. You look at the concept of standards on the Internet and see why standards are important. An HTML viewer and editor have been included on the CD-ROM, and we discuss installing and operating this software before moving on to virtual reality.

Chapter 4: Virtual Reality on the Internet examines the basics of virtual reality and world-making. We begin by considering the differences between VR and other forms of media. In order to best understand virtual reality, we take a look at the human senses and how technology interacts with these senses in terms of quality and quantity and vividness and interactivity. Vividness is explained in terms of breadth and depth, and interactivity is examined in terms of speed, range, and mapping. VRML isn't the only possible method of doing virtual reality on the Internet, and in this chapter you learn about 3DGopher, DIS, and other methods that could have become possible standards. We compare these alternatives with VRML and look at the advantages and disadvantages of each possibility. We explain how to install the VRML viewing software included on the CD-ROM. You then go on a guided tour of some of the Internet locations where 3D virtual worlds already exist, seeing the interconnections that exist between HTML and VRML.

Part II: What Is VRML?

At this point in the book, you'll have gotten your feet wet concerning the Internet, the Web, and VR. We think that it is important for all of us to be working from similar experiences and background information in order to move into the next part of the book. Part II deals with virtual reality on the Web in the form of VRML, the virtual reality modeling language.

Chapter 5: Defining VRML explains what VRML is and compares it with HTML to find out how they differ. You also find out what VRML's creators defined as its purpose. Finally, you finish Chapter 5 with a look at VRML's mission statement.

Chapter 6: The Development of VRML Technology describes how VRML came about. VRML Version 1.0 is credited, to a large degree, to three individuals: Mark Pesce, Tony Parisi, and Gavin Bell. Although VRML was born in the spring of 1994 at the First International Conference on the World Wide Web held in Geneva, the behind-the-scenes efforts on the part of these three individuals during late 1993 prior to the conference are also discussed. In this chapter, we look at who Pesce, Parisi, and Bell are. We also look at the events that have transpired since the conference, both before the announcement of VRML's creation in April 1995 and since that time.

Chapter 7: The Future of 3D and Virtual Reality on the Web discusses the future of creating worlds with VRML. The chapter includes a discussion with virtual reality programmer Bernie Roehl on his views of the future of VR on the Internet.

Part III: How Does VRML Work?

Viewing virtual worlds on the Web is a relatively simple process. The VRML world has the extension .WRL and a MIME type of x-world/x-vrml that tells the Web server to notify the Web browser that a VRML world is being transmitted. (These are nothing more than identifiers for the browser to know what is being interpreted.) On being received, and actually during the transmission, the VRML document is then parsed, or read and interpreted, by the VRML viewer.

This part of the book looks at the technology behind three-dimensional graphics on the Web. We begin with a look at the basics of three-dimensional graphics.

Chapter 8: The Basics of 3D Graphics helps you to understand how VR and 3D graphics programming works in general. It begins by looking at two-dimensional computer representations. This chapter contains quite a bit of programming code. We start with an extremely simple programming language, QuickBASIC, and show how to create two-dimensional representations.

Because you can use different approaches to achieve similar results, we discuss the creation of the same application in a variety of programming languages. You're not expected to have all of these programming languages in order to learn something from the examples. We hope that by reading through the code for both simple and complex examples, you can see how you might achieve the results you're looking for by using the tools that you have.

As we work through the DOS and Windows two-dimensional examples using QuickBASIC, Visual Basic, and Visual C/C++, we'll be laying the groundwork for the examples of three-dimensional programming that the chapter concludes with. We work through the same application several times so you can see how different paths lead to similar results.

Chapter 9: VRML and Networking describes how networks operate. You also learn how some people hope to use VRML and consider your own expectations for VRML. We conclude the chapter by looking at the platform requirements of VRML.

Chapter 10: Setting Up the VRML Viewers describes the VRML viewers and helps you to begin the process of examining and choosing which viewer you want to use. Keep in mind that this technology is so new that most of the VRML applications on the CD-ROM that accompanies this book were still in the beta stage when this book went to press.

You walk through the installation of the provided software and look, somewhat, at how it operates. Then you take a cruise on the Web and view some of the worlds that are available.

Chapter 11: Setting Up and Using the VRML Editors gives you a look at some of the world-building applications that are available, and you learn how to install the software that's provided on the CD-ROM. Again, this technology is so new that much of the software we'll be discussing was in the beta stage when this book went to press.

Our method for this chapter is to show you how to build the same VRML world, a simple cube, in each of the applications that's on the CD-ROM. This process will give you an idea of which application is easier for you to use.

Chapter 12: The VRML Version 1.0 Specification provides you with the VRML Version 1.0 specification. Although the specification was finalized in May 1995, different interpretations of the same information led to clarifications during the following months. This chapter shows you the original specification.

Chapter 13: Learning VRML Version 1.0 Specification Basics takes a closer look at the VRML Version 1.0 specification and attempts to clarify some of the ambiguity in certain nodes. Each node of the specification is described, its syntax is discussed, and examples are provided from VRML worlds.

Chapter 14: VRML Sample Worlds enables you to look at a few specific VRML worlds to see how they are constructed. Beginning with a simple world and working your way through to a more complex one, you see how some of the various nodes operate within the virtual world.

Part IV: Where to Go from Here

The fourth part of the book builds on what you learned in the preceding chapters. There are two chapters in Part IV.

Chapter 15: VRML On-Line Sources lists on-line sites where you can update your software, get more information about the software, or keep abreast of the changing VRML community. Some of the sites provide information about behaviors, some about specific software, and others about the individuals involved in the creation of VRML.

Chapter 16: Glossary defines terms to make it easy for you to refer to information about specific concepts as you read through the book.

Appendix: The Creating Cool 3D Web Worlds with VRML CD-ROM

This appendix introduces you to VisNet's VisMenu and to the VR interface that it creates. The appendix includes a list of the worlds, files, programs, and applications that are on the CD-ROM.

Whom This Book Is for

We hope that anyone interested in virtual reality, beginner to expert, will be able to pick this book up and learn something of value. The book, however, is aimed at users from the novice-to-intermediate experience level.

Conventions Used in This Book

Some text in this book looks different from the rest of the text or is on a line by itself. This section explains some of the conventions we've used to make things clearer for you.

Things that you should type appear in bold, like this: Type **CUBE.WTP** for the filename.

When you should press an arrow key, the following symbols are used: ↑ for the up-arrow key, ↓ for the down-arrow key, → for the right-arrow key, and ← for the left-arrow key.

Internet addresses appear in computer font, like this: `hotmetal@sq.com`.

Listings of computer code and other things that appear on screen look like the following line. Notice that things that can change (variables) appear in italic.

```
<A HREF-"URL"> your words</A>
```

When you need to press the spacebar a certain number of times, you see something that looks like this: `<5 spaces>,` and when you need to press the Tab key, you see something that looks like this: `<Tab>`.

Occasionally, this book's pages are not wide enough to accommodate the number of characters that need to be on a given line of code. To solve this problem, we have used the ∟ symbol to denote that the line continues with the characters that follow this symbol.

Figures Used in This Book

We've included screen shots of what some of the images you'll be seeing online will look like. The problem is that no two-dimensional, black-and-white screen image representation (or even the two-dimensional color images provided in the color insert in the middle of the book) can do justice to the three-dimensionality of the color images you can see when you load the CD-ROM into your computer. Look to the figures for guidance, not for the final say on how the image will look.

Icons Used in This Book

Icons appear in the margin to draw attention to material that you should pay special attention to. Here is what those icons mean:

This icon points out programs that are on the *Creating Cool 3D Web Worlds with VRML* CD-ROM at the back of this book. Some of the programs are demos or beta versions that enable you to sample and compare programs before deciding which ones you want to purchase.

This icon tells you to pay particular attention to important information.

Where you see this icon, you'll find ideas that can make your life easier and save you time and frustration.

If you don't pay attention to the information that's marked with this icon, you may be asking for serious problems.

Programming Languages Used in This Book

At a quick glance, you may be surprised at our choice of programming languages for some of the examples in this book. This is not a programming language instruction manual. The programs we've created here are for demonstration and example purposes only, so we've chosen languages that most readers are likely to have on hand. The examples help to demonstrate how basic 2D and 3D graphics are created.

At the time this book was written, QuickBasic 4.5, Visual Basic 3.0 Professional Development System, and Visual C/C++ 1.52 were the most up-to-date versions of these 16-bit software packages available. With the advent of Windows 95, the 16-bit environment may be fading, and 32-bit may be on the rise. Future editions of this book will be geared toward this 32-bit environment and will use the associated programming tools.

The Creating Cool 3D Web Worlds with VRML CD-ROM

The CD-ROM that has been included with this book provides an experience that you may never have had before. The user interface for the CD-ROM is a virtual reality experience itself. VisNet's VisMenu program was used to create a virtual city that represents the software provided on the CD-ROM. By the way, we are so impressed with VisMenu that we arranged to include a version of it on the CD-ROM for you to change and use in any way you wish.

We can't go into detail here about all of the software on the CD-ROM, but you'll find example and demonstration programs, product demos, conversion routines, VRML .WRL files, VRML viewers, VRML creation tools, communication software, and a variety of other applications that will make your excursion into Internet virtual reality one of the most comprehensive possible.

Keep in mind that the software that is a demo or a beta program is subject to the kinds of limitations and restrictions that are normal for these types of applications. We've provided Internet addresses for all of the companies that produce this software, and coupons at the back of the book provide information about upgrading to the full versions of many of these applications.

Time to Move On

As you read this book, we cannot stress enough that you should beware of the hype that has surrounded virtual reality and VRML in the recent past. In some ways, you may be disappointed in what the actual capabilities of this technology are. Its potential, however, reaches past the stars.

On-line virtual worlds, such as Virtual SOMA and PSU World, may come into existence, enabling you to visit neighborhoods and communities around the world from the comfort of your own home. Information can be provided with the simplicity of a mouse click from a three-dimensional interface.

To us, the most important aspect of VRML has been the openness of the VRML community to working together in its creation. Worlds that are more than the simplicity of the individual parts can be created jointly by this community. You can be a part of this community. You can contribute your visions of how three-dimensional cyberspace can look.

Now, read on. It's time to start building your virtual future.

PART I
UNDERSTANDING
BACKGROUND CONCEPTS

The Internet

The Internet has changed the way we think, the way we do business, the way we gather information, and the way we entertain ourselves. Although this book is about using VRML for virtual reality and 3D graphics, the first thing we want to do is make sure that you are familiar with the Internet itself.

In the next few pages we're going to look at the Internet, starting with its origins and finishing up by exploring some of the capabilities of the Internet software on the CD-ROM that's included with this book.

The Origins of the Internet

Where did the Internet come from? It's not that somebody just said, "Let there be an Internet," and there was one. This wonderful cyberspace where you can meet everyone from college professors and military planners to cyberpunks and computer geeks was, like Rome, not built in a day. The beginnings of the Internet have few philanthropic origins. As with many modern technologies, it grew out of fear and terror.

The birth of the Internet

Those who were not in their teens or older during the fifties and sixties have a hard time understanding the true terror that existed for the average American then. At home, civil rights appeared to endanger that which many white males felt they had worked for and earned. (For more information on the fears generated during this time frame see *The Politics of Unreason: Right-Wing Extremism in America, 1790-1977*, by S. Lippsett and E. Raab, published by The University of Chicago Press, 1978.) Overseas, Africa, the Middle East, and Southeast Asia seethed with discontent.

The fifties saw America fight to a draw with a China-supported North Korea. The sixties saw Protestant America threatened by an alleged Catholic puppet as president. Not so many years later, America mourned the assassination of that same president. Before the end of the decade, America was almost torn apart by a police action that president had begun. And over all of these threatening situations loomed the biggest threat of all, nuclear war with the Soviet Union. Today, with the fall of the Berlin Wall, the reunification of the two Germanys, and the dismemberment of the Soviet Union, these fears might appear unjustified.

For our parents and grandparents, however, these fears were real and had to be dealt with on an almost daily basis. Many homes had bomb shelters in the backyard or basement. Of course, now everyone calls them storm shelters, but during that time frame, many people had bomb shelter mentalities. This bomb shelter mentality is what gave birth to the Internet.

ARPANET

Born of paranoia that was created by Cold War fear mongering, the Internet evolved from a series of research experiments that were begun in the late 1960s. Underlying this research was the fear that a thermonuclear strike might knock out the military's ability to communicate with its units. The U.S. Department of Defense began funding research on computer networking to improve military communications in just such an event. One of these funded research agencies was the *Advanced Research Projects Administration (ARPA)*. ARPA's project was a wide area network called *ARPANET*.

Keep in mind that the defense department wanted a communications network that wouldn't be knocked out by a Soviet initial strike on the United States. Early computer networks were extremely vulnerable. Just one nonfunctioning computer in the network might cause the whole network to fail. ARPANET's goal, therefore, was to remain decentralized, providing no central computer to be knocked out. It achieved this goal by using a set of computer protocols called Transmission Control Protocol/Internet Protocol (TCP/IP). These protocols created what might be called a "self-healing" network in that if information could not get to its destination through one route, it would automatically be sent through another route.

The communication taking place between the computer sending the information and the computer receiving it requires a minimum of information from the individual computers. The network is not responsible for this communication. The sending computer encloses the information to be sent in an Internet Protocol (IP) packet and addresses the packet to the receiving computer. This concept makes each and every computer on the network an equal, or peer, no matter what platform is being used. This equality of platforms is an important issue that is at the heart of the original VRML concept. We return to the peer issue several times during the remainder of this book. For now, we continue our look at ARPANET.

By the early 1980s, ARPANET had become the prototype Internet with a grand total of about 200 computers on the network. The Computer Science Network (CSNET), a project funded by the National Science Foundation (NSF), was quickly added to ARPANET. The defense department chose this fledgling Internet as its primary communications network in 1983, connecting all military sites to ARPANET and raising the total number of computers connected to the Internet to 562. By 1984, a total of 1,024 computers were on the Internet.

NSFNET

A new network (NSFNET) was established by the National Science Foundation (NSF) in 1985 to link its five supercomputer centers across the country. NSFNET, which used the same communication protocols as ARPANET, was quickly hooked into ARPANET. Due to lack of capacity, this coalition didn't work. ARPANET was shut down quietly in 1986.

Because of the nature of the Internet, a network of networks, no one really noticed that ARPANET had been shut down. The organization was gone, or in the process of being dismantled, but the ghost in the machine continued, and, as a result, some people think that ARPANET was not shut down until as late as 1990.

In 1987 a contract was awarded to Merit Network Inc. to manage and upgrade a new network. NSF helped fund and install a new, high-speed network that used 56,000 bit per second (56 Kbps) telephone lines in 1988. That year, 28,174 computers were on the Internet. The next year, that number jumped to 80,000. The following year, the number climbed to 290,000.

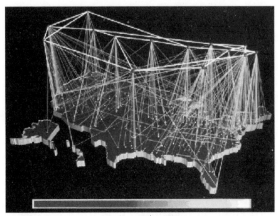
In 1992, a new network was constructed to fill the needs of the expanding number of Internet users. That network forms the main component of the Internet as it stands today. Figure 1-1 shows what the Internet looked like in July 1995. You can download this file from CompuServe's Internet New Users Forum under the name INMAP.GIF.

Figure 1-1: A 3D view of the Internet in July 1995.

Although the statistics report the number of *computers* connected to the Internet, it is estimated that more than 30 million people use the Internet at the time of this writing. At the current hookup rate, every person on this planet would have access to the Internet by the year 2003. In 1994 almost two and a quarter million computers were on the Internet, and estimates in early 1995 place that number at more than four million.

Looking at the Internet Today

What does the Internet look like? That depends on your hardware, your software, and your service provider. Although there may be some similarities between the user interfaces, different providers stress different aspects in order to differentiate their products. The quality of your monitor hardware and the speed of your connection also affect what the Internet looks like.

The graph in Figure 1-1 shows a particular aspect of the Internet at one point in time. It's just like your old grade school pictures. The child in those photographs doesn't exist anymore. The fact of the matter is that you, as that specific child, did not exist sixty seconds after that photograph was taken. You changed.

Think of the Internet as a child. It's growing and changing. Every second of every hour of every day, things on the Internet change. While surfing the Internet doing research for this book, we found several examples of these changes. For example, many, if not most, of the addresses listed in Patrick Vincent's chapter on Internet resources in *Free $tuff from the Internet* (1994, Coriolis Group Books) will take you straight to the information you're looking for. Some of the addresses, however, are only partially correct, requiring you to look in directories that are different from the ones that are listed. Some addresses don't even exist anymore. The reason for this discrepancy is that the Internet is constantly changing, and directories are moved, renamed, or even deleted. Neither the author nor the book publisher is at fault. If you don't find something in the location that's given for it, look around. With a little determination, you should be able to find what you need. Resource location is one of the biggest challenges the Internet faces. VRML technology can help to solve this problem.

Accessing the Internet

In order to access the Internet, the most important thing you need is a connection to the Internet. Connections are available in several different forms, from a full connection by way of a local area network (LAN), such as you'd find at your local college or university, to a limited dial-up connection that uses some sort of terminal emulation software package.

Regardless of what type of Internet connection you have, the organization that provides the connection is known as your *service provider*. Service providers offer many different types of services. There are advantages and disadvantages not only with each provider but also with each service offered. Over the years, we've had a number of different services and service providers ranging from connections through universities to our current service provider, CompuServe (CIS). We're pleased with both the services provided and the resources available to new users on CIS. There are many ways to connect to the Internet through CompuServe. Later in this chapter, we discuss installing and using the CompuServe software that is contained on the CD-ROM that's included with this book. First, however, we look at other ways that you can access the Internet.

Charles Cottle on the Internet

Charles Cottle, Director of User Training and Support Services in the Division of Technology and Information Resources at the University of Wisconsin at Whitewater, says that the Internet is an integral part of most things he does. During an on-line interview concerning Internet topics, we asked him what the future has in store for the Internet, based on what he has seen so far. Cottle's reply was "Anarchy — which I like."

Using a basic telecommunications program

Most colleges and universities have an Internet connection that you can gain access to by taking a course through the institution. Student fees generally include a charge for computer access. The computer services or academic computing organization on campus can give you the dial-up access number for the university's system. You also need to know what baud rate the system operates at (you need a minimum of 14.4K for most of the things we discuss later in this book) and what settings to use for such things as parity, data bits, and stop bits. You will be given a user name and a temporary password. (Don't forget to change your password once you're online.) One more thing that you need to know is what type of file transfer protocols the system's computers use. These protocols range from simple Kermit protocols to more advanced, and faster, x-modem, y-modem, and z-modem protocols. After you have all that information, all you have to do is type the dial-up access number into your own computer's telecommunication software, and you're set.

But wait! What telecommunication software do you need? At the University of Missouri at Columbia, Academic Computing provides students with a special version of ProComm Plus. Figure 1-2 shows how ProComm (DOS) can be configured to access your service provider. You also can use programs such as Q-Modem, QuickLink II Fax, or even the Telcom package that comes with Windows.

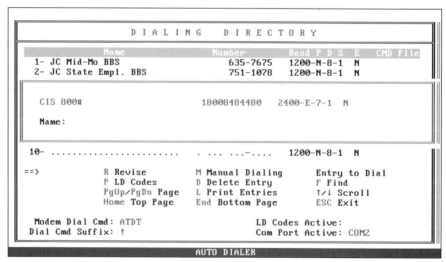

Figure 1-2: Configuring ProComm (DOS) settings to access the service provider.

After you configure the telecommunications software to access your service provider, you simply dial in, following your software user manual's directions. Figure 1-3 shows how you can use QuickLink II Fax for Windows to access your service provider.

The system's mainframe computer will prompt you for your user name and then your password. At the proper prompt, type your user name and then the password that you received from your service provider. You're now on the provider's mainframe computer, and accessing the Internet is just a few simple keystrokes away. The four ways to access the Internet are via e-mail, FTP, Gopher, and telnet. The following sections describe how to use these four tools with the basic telecommunications programs.

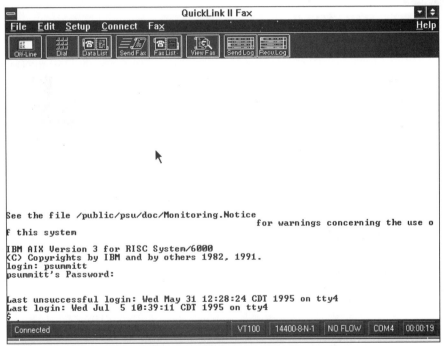

Figure 1-3: Using QuickLink II Fax for Windows to access the service provider.

Ed Brent on the Internet

Dr. Brent is a professor of sociology at the University of Missouri at Columbia and owner of a computer research and development firm. When, during an on-line interview about his work on the Internet, we asked how and why the use of the Internet has changed the way he works, Brent replied, "I spend too much time on it because it is addictive. Yet, it provides a sometimes very useful source of information. It greatly facilitates communicating with and collaborating with colleagues around the world. I talk with some people in other states and other countries more often than I speak with my departmental colleagues down the hall."

Electronic mail

Service providers' mainframes have several programs that can send electronic mail, or e-mail. Check with your service provider to find out which mail program is available for your use.

The mainframe at Pittsburg State University in Kansas has the Elm mail system available for student, faculty, and staff use. This system enables users to send messages and files, with special formatting, through the Internet if users know the address of the person they want to send mail to. Figure 1-4 shows Paul's screen as he checks for electronic mail at his office.

You also can send files to someone over the Internet by using uuencode and uudecode. If you want to send a binary code file as electronic mail to someone, you need to convert it to ASCII using *uuencode*, and the person you're sending it to needs to convert it back using *uudecode*. You can obtain the uuencode and uudecode programs from the Internet Resources Forum libraries on CompuServe.

One problem with Elm is that you need to read and write messages online. This is all right if you don't have to pay for the on-line connection time. It can be relatively expensive, however, if you have to pay these charges. Therefore, we recommend using a program that enables you to read and respond to messages offline, such as WinMail or PC Eudora. Both of these programs are on the CD-ROM that's included with *Internet Gizmos for Windows* by Joel Diamond, Howard Sobel, and Valda Hilley (IDG Books Worldwide, 1995). Other programs that provide this capability are available from many local BBSs and in the Internet Resources Forum on CompuServe.

The CompuServe software provides easy off-line mail capabilities, as seen in Figure 1-5.

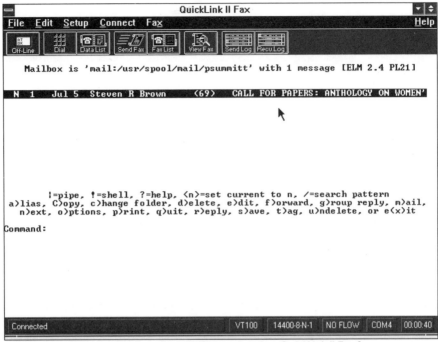

Figure 1-4: Checking Paul's mail on PittState.edu using QuickLink II Fax for Windows. Paul's address there is psummitt@PittState.edu.

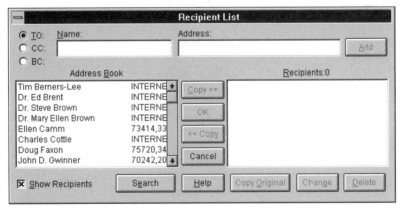

Figure 1-5: WinCIM's mail manager is easy to use and enables you to read and compose messages offline.

Electronic mail addresses

Electronic mail addresses are easy to understand after you know what their different parts signify. They use the following format:

username@service.organization type

Here are a couple of examples:

`psummitt@PittState.edu`

`76270.551@CompuServe.com`

These two addresses represent our e-mail addresses at Pittsburg State University and on CompuServe. The basic formatting of the address is simple. First comes the user name or user number. In the case of Paul at PSU, the user name is `psummitt`. On CompuServe, our user number is `76270.551`. Next comes the at symbol or @. This symbol is followed by the service the individual can be reached at, `PittState.edu` and `CompuServe.com`. The `edu` suffix means that Pittsburg State University is an educational organization. The `com` suffix means that CompuServe is a commercial or business organization. Other suffixes include `gov`, nonmilitary government organizations; `mil`, military units of the army, navy, and so on; `org`, other organizational types; and `net`, network resources. There are also extensions for users in other countries, such as `fr` for France, `de` for Germany, and `uk` for the United Kingdom. Knowing a user's e-mail address gives you quite a bit of information about the person and the type of Internet access the person uses.

WinCIM and NetLauncher, which are on the CD-ROM that accompanies this book, offer very good capabilities. Sending messages to other CompuServe users, to Internet addresses, and to users of other services, such as America Online or Prodigy, is relatively easy. Diamond, Sobel, and Hilley provide an excellent introduction to using the mail manager shown in Figure 1-5 in Chapter 9 of *Internet Gizmos for Windows*.

Using e-mail is easy. Simply determine who you want to send a message to and find out what that person's e-mail address is. Then, using the mail manager of your choice, type your message and send it. That's all there is to it.

FTP

FTP stands for File Transfer Protocol. You use FTP to quickly transfer large files from one computer to another on the Internet. It is one of the standardized methods of transferring files, and its name has become a verb, as in "ftp that file." There are specific FTP servers, as with most services on the Net, and these servers contain specific types of files. With just about any telecommunication package and an Internet connection, you can use FTP to download files to your computer.

Table 1-1 is a short list of FTP commands that should help you download files if you're connecting to the Internet by using programs such as ProComm, Q-Modem, and QuickLink II Fax.

Table 1-1	A Short List of FTP Commands
Command	**When to Use It**
ASCII	This command is usually the default mode. It sets FTP to ASCII mode for text files. If you're in this mode and you try to download a binary file, such as a program, without first using the BINARY command, the program file will be corrupted and unusable.
BINARY	If you're downloading an executable program file, a graphics file, or an audio file, you need to set FTP to the binary mode.
BYE	When you're ready to leave FTP, this command exits the program and returns you to your service provider.
CD	Stands for *change directory* on the computer that you are connected to. This command is similar to the DOS CD\ command, but notice that it has no backslash. In order to change from the current directory to your Mail directory, for example, you type **CD MAIL**, rather than **CD\MAIL**.
GET	This command tells FTP to retrieve a specific file from the computer you're connected to and store it on your computer.
OPEN	You use this command to establish a connection with a remote computer.

The following example shows how to use the OPEN and GET commands to download files by using FTP and a standard telecommunications program. In this example, you connect through FTP to the National Center for Super-computing Applications (NCSA) at the University of Illinois and download a free copy of the Web browser Mosaic.

```
>ftp
>open ftp.ncsa.uiuc.edu
>cd Mosaic
>cd Windows
>get wmos20a7.zip.
```

That's all there is to it. A copy of Mosaic transfers from NCSA's computer to yours. Keep in mind that a preconfigured copy of CompuServe's version of SPRY Mosaic is on the CD-ROM that's included with this book.

In the following example, you use the Internet connections available on CompuServe to ftp an updated Internet growth chart to your computer. The first thing you need to do is install the WinCIM software from the CD-ROM that accompanies this book.

Included on the CD-ROM is WinCIM Version 1.4, CompuServe Information Manager for Windows. This version requires at least 2MB of RAM, Microsoft Windows Version 3.1 running in enhanced mode, and at least 6MB of free disk space. A Hayes-compatible modem is highly recommended.

We've used WinCIM 1.4 with Windows 95 and had no problems. You can install it by using the VisMenu interface and simply double-clicking on the WinCIM installation building, or you can follow these simple instructions.

Installation is simple:

1. **From the Windows Program Manager, choose Run from the File menu.**

2. **Type the letter of your CD-ROM drive (for example, on one of our computers the CD-ROM drive is drive D, and on another it is drive E), followed by SETUP.EXE.**

   The following is what we would type for one of our computers.

   ```
   E:SETUP.EXE
   ```

3. **Follow the instructions that appear.**

It's that easy.

WinCIM is installed. If you're not already a CompuServe user, the program will help set up your new account. Otherwise, you're now ready to ftp that Internet growth chart we were discussing earlier.

1. **Run WinCIM.**

   Your screen should look very similar to Figure 1-6.

2. **Click on the Internet services icon.**

   This action connects you to CompuServe and brings up the Internet services menu. You should see a screen that looks very similar to Figure 1-7.

Figure 1-6: WinCIM's opening screen. You're now ready to ftp that file.

Figure 1-7: WinCIM's Internet Services window. Notice the arrow that's ready to select the FTP icon.

3. **Click the FTP button at the bottom of the window.**

    A window appears, asking for the site that you want to connect to.

4. **Type** munnari.oz.au.

    WinCIM makes the connection and goes into terminal mode.

5. **Type** cd ~big-internet.

6. **Type** get nsf-netnumbers-9305.ps.

    A copy of the file will transfer from the remote computer to yours.

You're now up to speed on FTP. Next, we take a quick look at Gopher.

Gopher

Gopher is a menu-driven information search application that's available on the Net. You can use its menus to find a wide variety of information. Gopher is a text-only service. Figure 1-8 shows how you can connect to Gopher by using QuickLink II Fax.

Figure 1-8: Connecting to Gopher by using QuickLink II Fax.

Although Gopher cannot show you graphics, you can use Gopher to find out where the information that you want is located. Then, if the information you're looking for is a graphics file, you can use FTP to obtain a copy of it.

Contrary to popular opinion, Gopher is not named for its capabilities to "go-fer" things. The program was developed at the University of Minnesota, where the football, basketball, and other sports teams are called the Gophers.

You can use Gopher with most telecommunications programs and an Internet connection. Check with your service provider to find out whether Gopher is available for your use.

Table 1-2 lists useful Gopher commands.

Table 1-2	A Short List of Gopher Commands
Command	**When to Use It**
↑	The up-arrow key moves you to the preceding line on the menu.
↓	The down-arrow key moves you to the next line on the menu.
→ or Enter	Use the right-arrow key or the Enter key to enter the current item on the menu.
← or u	Use the left-arrow key or the lowercase *u* to exit the current item on the screen.
PgDn, >, +, or the spacebar	Press PgDn, >, +, or the spacebar to move to the next page, if there is one, of the current menu.
PgUp, <, -, or b	Press PgUp, <, -, or lowercase *b,* to move to the preceding page, if there is one, of the current menu.
Numbers	Type any number to move to that specific line of the menu.
m	The lowercase *m* moves you back to the main menu.
q	The lowercase *q* quits Gopher with a prompt that asks whether you're sure you want to leave Gopher.
Q	The uppercase *Q* quits Gopher with no prompt, unconditionally.

Telnet

Finally, you need to know something about telnet. Telnet is a method of accessing, or logging into, a computer that is connected to the Internet without dialing into the system that the computer is a part of. An example is calling up the mainframe at PSU and then telnetting to CompuServe or vice versa.

Table 1-3	A Short List of Telnet Commands
Command	**When to Use It**
CLOSE or c	If you start telnet without telling it what computer to hook up to, this command terminates the connection and leaves you in the telnet command mode. You also can use CLOSE to both terminate a session that you're having with a remote computer and quit telnet. (The effect is the same as using the QUIT command.) You can use the lowercase c for the close command.
Enter	Pressing the Enter key while you are in the telnet command mode returns you to your active remote session. If you don't have an active session, you exit telnet.
OPEN	This command connects you to the remote computer when you're at the `telnet>` prompt.
QUIT	You use this command to leave telnet.

Steve Brown on the Internet

Dr. Brown is a professor of political science at Kent State University and moderator of the Q-Method discussion list on the Internet. Q-Method is a research methodology used in communication, psychology, journalism, and several other fields. During our on-line interview concerning his use of the Internet, Dr. Brown had several interesting things to say about the Internet, society, and education.

Question: How much do you use the Internet?

Brown: I sign onto my account virtually daily. I receive somewhere in the neighborhood of 20 to 100 messages per day . . . At the office, I typically leave the computer on throughout the day and often respond to new incoming messages as they arrive.

Since I am mainframe-oriented, I am almost always involved in writing manuscripts, creating syllabi, authoring memos, etc., so that incoming messages are part of a kind of seamless flow . . . I also try to incorporate Internet use into those classes of mine that lend themselves to it.

Question: Do you think the Internet has changed higher education?

Brown: Although I wouldn't deny that some fundamental changes have been wrought, the Internet . . . has mainly accelerated processes that were previously in slow motion, hence has not changed things as much as put them on fast-forward. Some superficial . . . changes include the fact that virtually all students are now keyboard adept; their term papers are therefore now typed rather than written longhand, and spellcheckers assure fewer misspellings: The nonchange is reflected in the fact that the papers contentwise say little more than they did a generation ago, and this is also reflected in many Internet lists: The technology *for* communicating has at least temporarily raced ahead of the capacity *to* communicate, and so the airwaves are filled with much information of low quality and with a short shelf life.

One temporary social impact has been that the new generation of scholars has leapfrogged over their predecessors, who know little about computers. It's the young ones that are impacting our department right now, and I suspect this is the case across all disciplines, from physics to art. (This has always been the case to some extent, but technological advances have temporarily accelerated the process . . .) A negative consequence of this temporary status advantage of the new generation of scholars is that they are relatively cut off from whatever wisdom and knowledge is possessed by their elders, who are seen as more irrelevant than usual (and therefore more easily ignored) because of their lack of technical skills . . .

Another socio-educational impact which the Internet has facilitated is the loosening of authority structures, in part by removing some of the signs and symbols of authority. It is now harder to tell whether you are responding to a seasoned professor or a college sophomore since all you have to go on in most cases is text plus a username on the FROM line of the header. This is a two-edged sword: People no doubt now respond more to content than to the status of the author; on the other hand, there has been an infusion of irrelevancies (by professors as well as sophomores!) that has polluted various Internet lists and has probably driven away some good minds.

Another consequence, related to the above, is that information can be produced and retrieved with a speed that cheapens it, almost like the effect that supply has on price . . . There is a general trend for people to be less discerning about sources of information — note the variety of sources (Internet or otherwise) of advice about health, from medicine to spiritualism — and the Internet will likely continue to contribute to this poorly-differentiated mass due to the ease with which discussion lists and networks can be created.

(continued)

(continued)

By the same token, the ease with which communication can take place has created new possibilities for dissemination capable of rivaling traditional print media (i.e., books and journals) and undermining the stranglehold that markets have over them. Witness the outbreak of electronic journals such as the *Electronic Journal of Communication*, the *Electronic Journal of Sociology*, and *Post-Modern Culture*. These represent "free" sources of information, which is a price that McGraw-Hill and Macmillan can't afford. In a Marxian sense, this development is beginning to narrow the alienation gap between producers (i.e., academics) and the fruits of their labors. Until recently, academics (as institutionalized in universities) could not really afford the journals and books which they themselves were producing: The Kent State University Library budget, for example, has gradually declined as the availability of information has increased; however, on-line e-journals are easily affordable and accessible, and they solve many economic problems (e.g., article length) associated with the print media.

There is a sense, however, in which the Internet will likely not change education much, and that is in terms of the status structure within the academy and the structure between the academy and the remainder of society. The elite schools (with the likely exception of technical havens such as MIT and Cal Tech) did not seem to be the first to gravitate towards these new technologies, but once the handwriting was on the wall, so to speak, they quickly expended the resources necessary to reassert their superiority. Hence, the revolutionary potential of the new technology has largely been absorbed into (and therefore serves to reinforce) preexisting respect structures within the university system. By the same token, business and (more recently) government has plunged headlong into the information revolution where they can be expected to have their impact as well. I doubt the government will tolerate these rival sources of power and influence, or that business will tolerate a "free" flow of information if it can somehow be turned to profit.

Question: Based on what you've seen, what do you think the future has in store for the Internet?

Brown: This is a very difficult question. So far the changes have been mainly technological—i.e., new technical possibilities have been opened up, but this has had little impact as yet on content . . . However, information paves the way for more communication, just as communication paves the way for more information.

Insofar as emerging patterns of influence are concerned, I would expect the Internet to both promote and benefit from a more technically sophisticated public, and that information elites will grow stronger and stronger. There will be more pressure to expand the Internet to currently inaccessible corners of society: Eventually, an on-line computer will be as essential, affordable, and available as a telephone. In the short run, there will be haves and have-nots, and once the have-nots have what the haves have now, the haves will have better versions — i.e., I do not think the new technology will really prove revolutionary except insofar as it moves the entire social structure toward greater sophistication while maintaining the structure intact.

As the Internet becomes more and more comprehensive, it will absorb more and more resources . . . Those who integrate the Internet into their work and take advantage of its resources will likely benefit in terms of grants and personal income, much of which will translate into departmental influence and the demand for commitment of even greater resources in Internet-related directions.

The human side of the Internet development has mainly taken the form of a skills revolution, i.e., of developing dexterity at the keyboard and of developing and internalizing rules and procedures for accessing information. This has given the edge to males over females and to students with self confidence who already have rudimentary problem-solving abilities (mainly the offspring of middle and upper-middle class families). Incorporation of the laggards will mean increasing inducements (e.g., efforts to make the Internet more user friendly) and increasing coercion (e.g., in the form of mandatory class assignments). The pressure to join the computerized society will be unremitting, and those who fail to develop the necessary skills will fall even farther behind.

It is already apparent that those achieving technical mastery are vouchsafed a degree of respect and awe not enjoyed by the less skilled, and the reciprocal impact of the Internet and respect structures will likely continue to enhance both: Those enjoying respect due to computer mastery will be targets of emulation, and will be turned to for recommendations not only about future technical acquisitions (e.g., more Internet terminals) but also about a variety of technology-irrelevant topics. The Internet will remain advantaged so long as its unofficial sponsors continue to receive respect.

Finally, we cannot overlook the multifaceted spiritual dimension. Insofar as the Internet induces awe among the legions of neophytes and ignorant (but admiring) nonusers, it will benefit from religious sentiments, and knowledgeable insiders will be deferred to in the same way as priests. To the extent that the Internet becomes host to nonconsensual activities (gay rights and abortion bulletin boards, pornographic http sites, etc.) AND the electronic public is widened to include intolerant segments of the public (e.g., the evangelical right, militia groups, violent segments of the animal rights movement, etc.), the Internet may itself be drawn into moral and ethical question, in which case pressure may mount for government to license and censure.

The technical means have taken a quantum leap, but like a dog that's finally caught up with the car it's been chasing, we don't really know what to do with them. One would hope that the new possibilities would be turned mainly to good. With the past as our guide, however, the best prediction is that the future will produce a mixed result.

Putting What You've Learned into Practice

Before you move on to Chapter 2, we want to make sure that you know how to use the tools that we've discussed so far. If you haven't already done so, turn back to the instructions for installing the WinCIM software, earlier in this chapter, and install it on your computer. Go ahead. Do it now. We'll wait.

All right. You've got it installed? Now you're ready to do some practice exercises that will give you not only more experience working with the WinCIM software but also more information about the Internet so that you'll know more about the system you'll be using.

In this section, we walk you through four exercises: examining CompuServe's billing procedures, ftping a file from an Internet remote computer, downloading a file from one of the CompuServe forums, and sending an e-mail message. Keep in mind that the last three of these exercises will add charges to your CIS bill because you'll be leaving CompuServe's Basic Services and using the Extended Services in order to perform them.

If some of the directions in the following exercises seem too simplistic, forgive us. Remember, our intention is to bring every reader up to speed as quickly as possible so that everyone is working from the same experience level. You're under no obligation to do the exercises if you already know how to perform these tasks. However, you should go ahead and download the two files we discuss here.

Exercise #1: Examining your charges

Begin with the Windows Program Manager on your screen. It should look something like Figure 1-9, but instead of a Communication Group you'll have a CompuServe Group.

1. **Double Click the CompuServe Group Icon.**

   You see the CompuServe Group. Your screen looks similar to ours, as seen in Figure 1-10.

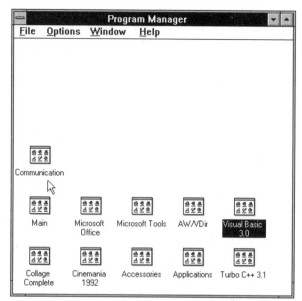

Figure 1-9: The Windows Program Manager on one of our computers.

Figure 1-10: WinCIM's program icon on one of our computers.

2.   **Double-click the WinCIM icon to start the program.**

If you have a sound card and you installed WinCIM's sound capabilities during the setup procedure for the program, a young lady's voice tells you that you're now accessing CompuServe. This software feature is relatively new, and it took us a little while to get used to it. Soon you'll have something that looks similar to Figure 1-6 again (See Figure 1-11).

You should have a little dialog box asking whether you want to connect to CompuServe or continue in WinCIM without connecting to CompuServe. That dialog box doesn't appear in the figure. You can disable this function, as we have, by clicking the Show at Startup check box at the bottom of this dialog box. WinCIM will record your changes as it closes the dialog box and won't show the dialog box at startup again.

Figure 1-11: The Services dialog box.

Along the top of your screen is the desktop ribbon that shows pictures of the services and features that are available for your use. You can customize this ribbon, but that is beyond the scope of this book. Look at the lower-right corner of the Services dialog box and find the Member Service icon.

3. Click the Member Service icon to bring up the Member Services dialog box as shown in Figure 1-12.

Figure 1-12: The Member Services dialog box.

This screen offers you a series of menu choices.

4. Double-click **Rates & Pricing Information** to bring up an explanation of CompuServe's service charges in another window, as shown in Figure 1-13.

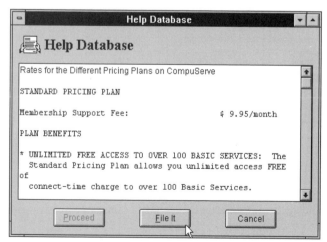

Figure 1-13: The Help Database screen provides an explanation of CIS's connection charges.

5.   Click the File It button at the bottom of this explanation window to save the explanation to disk so that you can read it later when you're offline and not incurring any charges.

6.   Click the Cancel button at the bottom of the Help Database box to leave this area of CompuServe.

   The Services Window should now be on your screen again.

7.   **Click the Internet icon.**

   Your monitor should now look like Figure 1-14.

You've now accessed CompuServe and gotten information on the charges that are currently being billed for these services. Your next step is to learn how to ftp a file.

Figure 1-14: Returning to the Internet Services Window.

Exercise #2: Ftping another file

The next step is to ftp a file. Follow these directions carefully:

1.   **Click the FTP option at the bottom of the Internet menu box.**

     Your screen looks similar to Figure 1-15.

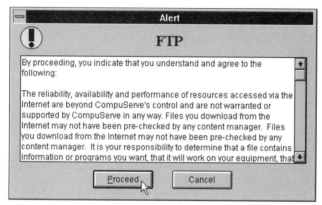

Figure 1-15: The FTP Alert dialog box.

At this point, CIS warns you that you're about to access a remote computer.

2.   **Click the Proceed button at the bottom of the screen.**

     Your screen now looks similar to Figure 1-16.

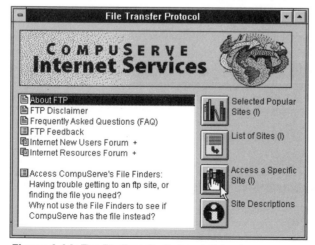

Figure 1-16: The File Transfer Protocol dialog box.

3. Click the Access a Specific Site icon.

    Another dialog box (Figure 1-17) comes up now asking for the name of the site you want to access.

Figure 1-17: The Access a Specific Site dialog box.

4. In the Site Name box, type nic.merit.edu.

5. Type internet/resources/cruise.dos in the Directory box.

6. Click OK at the bottom of this dialog box, as well as the next.

7. Click the file meritcrz.zip and then the Retrieve button.

    Now sit back and relax while a copy of this file is transferred to your computer. When it's finished, you're ready to move on to the next exercise.

8. Click the Close button at the bottom of the File Transfer Protocol and Internet dialog boxes to close them.

Exercise #3: Downloading a file from a CIS Forum

Your next step is to learn to download a file from one of the CompuServe forums.

1. **Click the Go icon (the one on the desktop ribbon that looks like a traffic light).**

   You see the Go dialog box where you can access the various CompuServe services directly by name.

   You should have something similar to Figure 1-18 on your screen.

Figure 1-18: The Go dialog box.

2. **Type** gernet **in the Go dialog box that appears.**

3. **Click OK.**

   You go to the forum that you selected — the Deutsches Computer+ Forum.

4. **Go ahead and join the forum when the screen prompts you to.**

   You have to join in order to have access to the libraries.

   Along the right side of the screen is another vertical double ribbon of icons. The third one down on the right is the search library icon (See Figure 1-19).

5. **Click the Search Library icon.**

   The Search for Files dialog box appears (See Figure 1-20), asking for the name of the file that you are searching for.

6. **Type** wwwfaq.zip **in the File Name box.**

7. **Click the Search button at the bottom of the dialog box.**

   The file WWWFAQ.ZIP is displayed in the next window that appears.

8. **Click the Retrieve button and wait while a copy of this file is transferred to your computer.**

9. **After it has been transferred, click the Exit Forum icon, the second icon from the right on the desktop ribbon (the one where the man is leaving through the door) as shown in Figure 1-20, and exit this forum.**

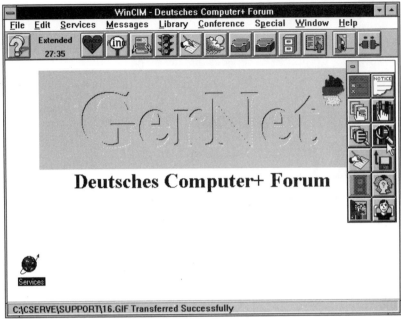

Figure 1-19: The Search Library icon.

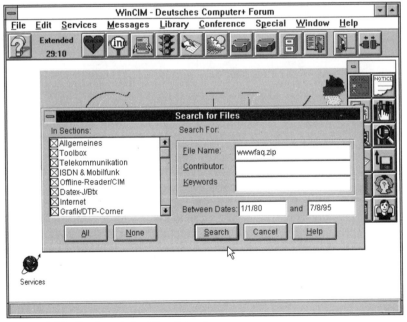

Figure 1-20: The Search for Files dialog box.

Exercise #4: Sending an e-mail message

Finally, you send an e-mail message.

1. **In the Services dialog box, choose Create Mail from the Mail menu.**

    The Create Mail dialog box appears, followed by the Recipient List dialog box that asks whom you wish to send mail to (See Figure 1-21).

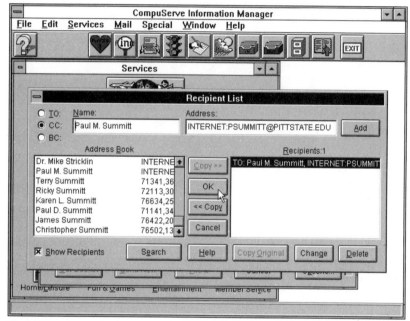

Figure 1-21: The Recipient List dialog box appears when you choose the Create Mail option.

2. **Type** Paul M. Summitt **for the name and** INTERNET:psummitt@PittState.edu **for the address.**

3. **Click Copy and OK.**

4. **Write a short note telling Paul what you think of the book so far and then click the Send Now button at the bottom of the dialog box.**

    WinCIM posts a message at the bottom of the screen in the message bar telling you that your mail was sent successfully.

5. **Click the Exit button on the desktop ribbon, and you're done.**

You've performed all the exercises for this chapter in record time. There will be more exercises at the end of Chapter 2. So far you're doing great!

**Moving
On**

In this chapter we've provided an introduction to the history of the Internet and a look at some of the things that make up the Internet. You've read comments from users and critics. You've also been exposed to and learned how to use some of the more basic tools for accessing the Internet. In the next chapter, we introduce you to the World Wide Web, some of the people responsible for it, some users, and some of the tools you need to create your own cyberspace.

The World Wide Web

In Chapter 1 you looked at what the Internet is. Some estimates indicate that the Internet contains more than three million programs and files that are available for viewing and downloading. But how do you access these files? FTP, telnet, Gopher, and e-mail are four methods that you can use, but when you consider that the Internet contains all types of documents, graphics, videos, sounds, and other types of files, these four access methods seem somewhat lacking in ability.

The best means of accessing files may be the World Wide Web, which is one of the newest services available on the Internet. Sometimes known affectionately as either the WWW or the Web, it could be the beginning of William Gibson's vision of cyberspace. It has been referred to as "the most important advance in publishing since the printing press" and as "a productivity drain" that has been "over-hyped" by the media. Will the Web become the foundation for cyberspace or just another dead-end technology that's soon overwhelmed by something newer and more hip? Who knows?

Just Exactly What Is the Web?

As with many other areas and services of the Internet, the Web is very much under construction. It's considered the fastest-growing part of the Internet and has been called the future of the Internet. For many users, the Web is the most exciting part of the Internet. The simplest definition of the Web might be that it is a system or method for accessing information on the Internet.

The Web consists of a multitude of documents, graphics, videos, and other multimedia resources that are scattered throughout the Internet. These resources, which are linked together through hypertext, exist in a collection of computers that are in many geographical locations around the world. Each of these hyperlinked documents is called a *page*. Each page can consist of various combinations of text, graphics, digitized sounds, video animations, more hypertext links to other documents and pages, and now, virtual environments. A page will often be too large to fit on the screen at one time.

The Web manages to link all these documents together by using *URLs* (pronounced both as *U-R-L* and *earl*). URL stands for *Uniform Resource Locator*. A URL specifies the exact location for a specific Internet resource. The following examples show some of the ways that URLs are written:

➡ http://www.sonic.net/~dfx/doug/index.html

➡ http://www.w3.org

➡ http://sunsite.unc.edu/boutell/faq/www_faq.html

 Before you go any further, you need to know what a *FAQ* file is. FAQ stands for *frequently asked questions*. The many FAQ files cover a myriad of topics. You downloaded the WWW FAQ in Chapter 1. Take some time to read it now. Then return to the discussion of URLs.

If you look carefully at these addresses, you'll realize that they look a great deal like FTP addresses. The reason for this resemblance is that FTP addresses are URLs.

The first part of the URL is the access method. The four most common access methods are

Prefix	Method
ftp	File Transfer Protocol
gopher	Gopher
http	HyperText Transfer Protocol
telnet	telnet

Chapter 1 introduced you to three of these methods. The http prefix in the example addresses means that the documents at these locations are hypertext documents that have hypertext links to other documents. The two slashes (/ /) after the colon indicate that what follows is the computer address of the specific file. It's very similar to the e-mail addresses discussed in Chapter 1.

How do you view Web pages?

To view, or read, these hypertext Web pages, you use a program that's called a *Web browser*. Web browsers are intuitive graphical programs that send specific commands to an individual computer site that you want to connect to and then display the information that's contained in the page that you are currently accessing.

Numerous browsers are available, depending on the platform you are using. Some of the more popular browsers include Netscape Navigator, Chameleon, SlipKnot (Figure 2-1), Cello, InternetWorks, NetCruiser, WinWeb, and the various forms of Mosaic. All of these browsers belong to the *graphical browser* family.

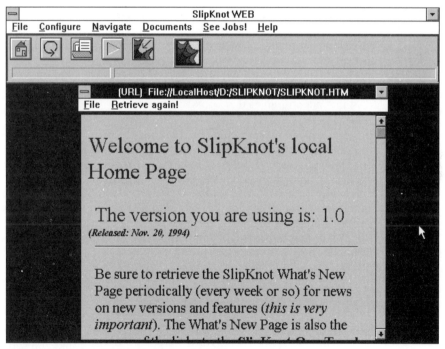

Figure 2-1: Using SlipKnot to access the Web.

The three basic types, or families, of browsers are

➡ Line-mode browsers

➡ Full-screen browsers

➡ Graphical browsers

The line-mode browser requires you to type a command for which you get some information. You type another command, and you get more information. Sounds rather non-user-friendly, doesn't it? You're right. It is non-user-friendly. You can think of it as being much like FTP.

The full-screen browser, on the other hand, is much like Gopher. The browser puts a menu on your computer screen. You move the cursor up and down on the screen and select a highlighted link, and then you press Enter. The next document then appears on your screen.

The final kind of Web browser, the graphical browser, enables you to look not only at text, but also at pictures, movies, and animations, and to listen to sounds. What you see on your computer screen looks more like a page from a magazine than like a Gopher menu. You also can use your mouse to point-and-click on the hypertext link to access the page.

 We're interested only in the last type of Web browser, the graphical browser. Later in this chapter we compare the various graphical browsers that are available for the PC platform. We also explain how to install and operate the SPRY Air Mosaic software from CompuServe (Figure 2-2) that is included on the CD-ROM that accompanies this book.

As we suggested earlier in the chapter, the browser first views, or reads, these hyperlinked, hypermedia, and hypertext documents. It then displays them on the screen of your computer. What are hypermedia and hypertext? *Hypertext* is text that contains connections to other text. *Hypermedia* is any medium, audiovisual or textual, that contains connections to other media. The browser sometimes also can access files by using FTP, Gopher, and other, ever in-creasing, ranges of methods. You look at some of the capabilities of browsers later in this chapter when you learn about the advantages and disadvantages of different browsers for the PC platform.

What does the browser read?

Each document, or page, that's available on the Web is written in a language called *HTML*, or HyperText Markup Language. HTML is like the source code for the Web. Figure 2-3 shows a screen shot from the home page of Doug Faxon, a musician, recording studio engineer, Web page architect, and long-time virtual world builder who lives in San Francisco. Listing 2-1 shows what this page looks like in HTML.

Figure 2-2: CompuServe's Web Home Page as seen using SPRY Air Mosaic.

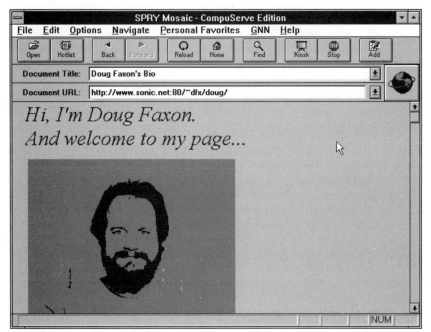

Figure 2-3: Accessing Doug Faxon's home page on the Web by using SPRY Air Mosaic.

Listing 2-1: Doug Faxon's Home Page in HTML

```
<html>
<head>
<title>Doug Faxon's Bio</title>
</head>
<body>
<body background="blue.gif">
<center><h1><i> Hi, I'm Doug Faxon.<br>
And welcome to my page...<br></i></h1>
<img src="doug1.gif">
<hr>
</center></h2>
<b>
I've been quite busy of late. Some of the things I've been
involved in include:
<ul type=square>
<li>Taking Ann Lynnworth's <a href="http://www.sonic.net/~ann/
htmlsmnr.html"> <i>Infobahn Construction Workshop</i></a> course,
learning how to build Worldwide Web pages and basically catching
up on all this Internet stuff.
<li>Recording an album with Clark Hansen when time permits, which
unfortunately hasn't been as often as I'd prefer, lately.  The
album will be called <a href="visptrl.html"><i>"Vision Patrol"</
i></a> when it comes out.
<li>Continuing work on the HUGE job of documenting the activities
of my cousin, <a href=http://www.sonic.net/~dfx/fait/> <i> The
Evil Doctor Flaxon </i> </a>.
<li>Spending time with my current loves, <a
href="carla.html">Carla</a> and <a href="simone.html">Simone </
a>(they're mother and daughter, folks - I don't have <i>that</i>
much energy), who keep me from retreating from the world alto-
gether and becoming a full-time techno-geek.
<li>Preparing to delve into Superscape VRT, a Virtual Reality
environment design tool I snagged at <a href="http://www.
mecklerweb.com/"> Mecklermedia</a>'s VR95 conference in May.
<li>Trying to keep up with a steady influx of email, both from
the 'net as well as from <a href="ciscyber.html">Compuserve's
Cyberforum</a>, where I still have many friends that share my
passionate interest in Virtual Reality.
<li>Trying to generate business opportunities by combining the
various talents listed above.
<center><h2><a href="webpages.html">Need A Web Page?</a></h2></
center>
<a href=mailto:"dfx@sonic.net">Email me here...
</b>
</body>
</html>
```

Doug is a human being of many talents. He's the owner and proprietor of DFX Studios, a music production facility, and of Inflaxonation, a publishing company devoted, as Doug says, "to all things Flaxon" (things related to Doug's "evil cousin"). During the Web tour later in this chapter, you visit Dr. Flaxon's home page so you can better understand this typographical error, turned joke, gone wild. You also get to see some of the Flaxon imagery that talented artist David Lee Ingersoll has created.

Compare what you see in Figure 2-3, with the beginning of the HTML code for Doug's home page. The listing begins with `<html>`, which signifies that this file is an HTML file. A few lines later, you see the following:

```
<center><h1><i> Hi, I'm Doug Faxon.<br>
And welcome to my page...<br></i></h1>
<img src="doug1.gif">
```

This code is the HTML code for what appears in Figure 2-3. The picture of Doug is contained in `doug1.gif`. In Chapter 3, we go into more depth on the history of HTML and how it works so that you can understand how HTML and HTTP both help and hinder VRML. For right now, however, we move on to how the Web came into being.

The History of the World Wide Web

In order to understand how to best use a tool, it is sometimes good to have a general understanding of how that tool came about. We think this applies to HTML and HTTP.

CERN

The Web began as an effort to create collaborative documents. It was born in 1989 at the European Center for Particle Physics (known by its French acronym, *CERN*). CERN's purpose was to enable scientists to publish hypertext documents and make them available over the Internet. Its current purpose, as stated in the WWW FAQ (contained in `wwwfaq.zip`, the file you downloaded from the GERNET forum on CompuServe during the exercises contained in Chapter 1), is "to build a distributed hypermedia system."

Hyperlinked documents enable you to follow the information, ideas, and themes you're interested in from one page to the next. This capability is available no matter what computers these documents are stored on and no matter where in the world those computers are located. Doug Faxon's home page includes two examples of hyperlinking. Listing 2-1 contains the following code fragments:

```
<li>Continuing work on the HUGE job of documenting the activities
of my cousin, <a href=http://www.sonic.net/~dfx/fait/> <i> The
Evil Doctor Flaxon </i> </a>.
```

```
<li>Preparing to delve into Superscape VRT, a Virtual Reality
environment design tool I snagged at <a href="http://www
mecklerweb.com/"> Mecklermedia</a>'s VR95 conference in May.
```

In the first code fragment, by clicking on the text `The Evil Doctor Flaxon`, you will be hyperlinked to another page located on the same computer. Clicking on the text `Mecklermedia` in the second example, however, hyperlinks you to a `mecklerweb.com` document located on another computer. In this hypertext environment, you choose what ideas you want to follow. If you choose "The Evil Dr. Flaxon," you will get quite different information than if you choose "Mecklermedia."

One of the interesting aspects of how the Web became possible is that Tim Berners-Lee, the WWW project leader and possibly one of the most influential people in the world as to how the Web looks, made the HTML protocols publicly available. The result is that HTML quickly became the de facto standard on the Internet. We look more at the concept of Internet standardization in Chapter 3.

Who uses the Web?

No discussion of the Web as it exists today would be complete without talking about who uses the Web. In the past, and probably still today, Web demographics have been skewed toward the technologically friendly, thirty-something, Anglo-Saxon male. How do we know that? Because of the Graphics, Visualization, and Usability (GVU) Center's World Wide Web User Surveys. The GVU Center is affiliated with Georgia Tech's College of Computing. The center has done three Web surveys in the past. You can access these surveys and take part in future surveys at the following URL:

```
http://www.cc.gatech.edu/gvu/user_surveys/User_Survey_Home.html
```

The first Web survey took place in January 1994, and the second survey followed in October 1994. The third survey took place in April 1995. Future surveys are planned every six months beginning October 10, 1995, and continuing every April 10 and October 10.

The first survey was divided into five parts: general, HTML, HTTP, Mosaic, and usage. The results from the general survey indicate that 56 percent of those taking part in the survey were between the ages of 21 and 30. A large percentage, 94 percent, were male, and 69 percent were located in North America. Table 2-1 shows part of the overall results for the general survey.

Table 2-1: Results from the General Survey of the First World Wide Web User Survey, January 1994

(Not all questions from the survey are included in this table.)

Question 1: Primary Platform

Mac	PC	UNIX	VMS	Other
3.6%	4.94%	88.46%	2.47%	0.01%

Question 2: Primary Browser

Cello	Lynx	Mosaic	Other	Samba
0.08%	1.95%	97.22%	0.38%	0.30%

Question 6: Location

Asia	Australia	Europe	N. A.	S. A.
0.75%	2.04%	28.43%	68.63%	0.15%

Question 7: Occupation

Under-graduate	Admini-strative	Business	Faculty	Graduate	Professional	Other
14.4%	2.86%	3.99%	7.07%	21.6%	44.7%	5.64%

Question 9: Age

<20	21–25	26 – 30	31–35	36–40	41–50	50+
6.32%	28.27%	26.93%	16.22%	10.71%	7.66%	1.93%

Question 10: Gender

Female	Male
5.1%	94.9%

Figure 2-4 shows the age breakdown for the first survey. Compare that with the graph in Figure 2-5 from the third survey. As you'll recall, the third survey took place just a little over a year after the first. In the third survey, the average age had risen to 35. Whereas 56 percent of those responding to the first survey were between the ages of 21 and 30, only a little more than 30 percent were in that age group for the third survey.

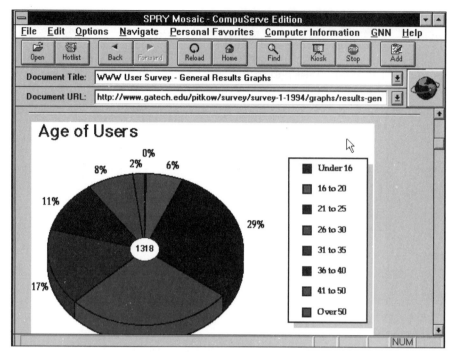

Figure 2-4: The graph of the results of the question on the age of users from the first survey.

In the first survey, there was practically no gender breakdown because males made up almost 95 percent of the respondents. This changed somewhat in the third survey, with males making up 82 percent of the respondents. The conclusions of the survey suggest that females are being integrated into the Web user population more quickly than into other parts of the Internet world.

And, just as the Web and Internet are constantly changing, so are the demographics, or characteristics, of the average user as more on-line services are added. Responses to the gender question suggest a linear trend and indicate that as early as 1997, the male/female ratio could be even. The survey also suggests a trend toward older users on the Web.

All of the information concerning these surveys and the data contained in them are copyrighted 1995 by the Georgia Tech Research Corporation (GTRC) and the Graphics, Visualization, and Usability Center. This information is used within the applicable copyright restrictions. We are grateful to Jim Pitkow and both the GTRC and the GVU Center for allowing us to include this information.

Jim asked that we remind you that the URL for these surveys is `http://www.cc.gatech.edu/gvu/user_surveys/`. You learn more about Jim in the exercises at the end of this chapter when you visit his home page at `http://www.cc.gatech.edu/gvu/people/Phd/James.E.Pitkow.html`.

The W3 Consortium

Before we move on to the future of the Web, we need to mention the people who will be responsible for that evolution, the W3 consortium. This group is an industry consortium led by the Laboratory for Computer Science at the Massachusetts Institute of Technology. Its twofold goal is to promote standards and to strive for interoperability among Web products. You can learn more about this group at `http://www.w3.org` and in the discussion of standards for the Internet that is found in Chapter 3.

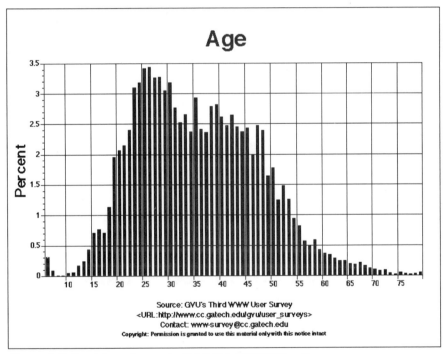

Figure 2-5: Breakdown for age in GVU's Third WWW User Survey.

The Future Evolution of the World Wide Web

The evolution of the Web includes many facets, not the least of which is the main topic of this book. VRML is not the first, nor will it be the last, of the exciting new technologies that you will be seeing on the Web. This section covers some of these new innovations and their interconnections to VRML.

When Ed Krol wrote the first edition of *The Whole Internet: User's Guide and Catalog* in 1992, graphical browsers were unheard of. Krol discussed the need for browsers that could access files other than just simple text files. Now, using a graphical browser is the only way to go, and graphical browsers will quickly be replaced or upgraded to include VRML capabilities. It's amazing how fast the Internet and the Web change.

Already, other limitations that Krol discussed in 1992 are being overcome on the Web. For example, you can now link your home page to other documents, as you saw in Doug Faxon's home page.

In the not too distant future, William Gibson's vision of cyberspace may become a virtual reality, if you will pardon the pun. The hyped versions of the information superhighway and representations of virtual reality in films and television programs such as *Disclosure* and "Earth 2" may soon become the norm on the Web.

Accessing the Web

So, you now know something about the history of the Web. The question now is how do you access the Web?

The Web versus other Internet tools

Before the development of the Web, the most user-friendly information presentation systems were Gopher and WAIS. As we've discussed previously, Gopher is text based. All information, including menus, documents, and any indexes, is presented as text.

WAIS stands for *Wide Area Information Servers*. Although WAIS is a very powerful method for retrieving information from databases that are available on the Internet, it is still text based. Everything is either an index or a document returned from an index.

You can use the Web to access both Gopher and WAIS. You also have the added advantage of being able to access hypertext documents that include not only textual information but also audio, video, and other graphical forms of information. Gopher menus are represented as lists of links, and Gopher documents become hypertext documents without links to other documents. WAIS indexes become searchable pages, and WAIS documents become hypertext documents with no links to other documents.

But in order to utilize the advantages that the Web offers, you must have another software package, called a *Web browser*.

A comparison of the available Web browsers

As we suggested earlier in this chapter, some of the more popular browsers include Netscape Navigator, Chameleon, SlipKnot, Cello, InternetWorks, NetCruiser, WinWeb, and the various forms of Mosaic. Although we use CompuServe's SPRY Air Mosaic at home and Paul uses Netscape Navigator at work, we realize that not everyone needs or wants either of these two browsers. With that in mind, we cover the more popular Web browsers in this section. Each browser has its own advantages and disadvantages, but we won't deny a certain bias. We begin alphabetically with Cello.

Cello

When Cello was developed at the Cornell University School of Law, it was one of the first graphical browsers available. Figure 2-6 provides a look at Cello.

Version 2.0 of Cello should be available by the time you read this. Version 1.01a, which dates from early 1994, has a few inconveniences. First, it doesn't allow multiple downloads. Version 2.0 should. Second, the toolbar on Cello Version 1.01a is rather simple. There are buttons for Back, Stop, and Home but nothing more. Version 2.0 is supposed to have buttons for searching and copying. It may also have buttons for other activities. Third, when you start downloading a page, Cello lists how much of the page has been received but not how much is left to receive. Finally, you can't enter a URL on the toolbar; you have to click your way through a series of menus.

We don't want to give the impression that there's nothing right about this package. Probably its strongest plus is its price. You can download it for free — and it is a 16-bit application, so using it on older machines is no problem. Setting it up is easy, also. All you have to do is configure the TCP/IP stack, and the program is ready to run.

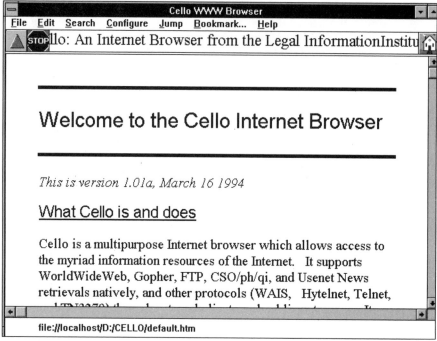

Figure 2-6: Using Cello to access the Web.

If you are interested in Cello, you can use the skills that you learned in Chapter 1 to download it by anonymous FTP from `ftp.law.cornell.edu`, in the `pub/ LII/Cello` directory. Unless you just want to check it out yourself or practice your FTP skills, however, we suggest that you pass on Versions 1.01a or 2.0 of Cello, even if they are free. We think that the package included on the CD-ROM is much stronger.

Chameleon

Internet Chameleon 4.1 is a commercial all-in-one package. It includes both Windows and HTML on-line help files as well as printed documentation. Another 16-bit application, it will run on some of the older machines and is extremely easy to set up. Even the act of setting up your Internet account with one of five default service providers is automated.

Unfortunately, the program is glitchy and, we suspect, full of bugs. Another problem is that you have no way of knowing whether a page is loading until after it loads.

Overall, we think that the price is a little steep for what you get and the headaches you have to put up with. Pass on this one and download one of the others if you don't use the browser package on the CD-ROM.

Internet Works

InternetWorks is another all-in-one commercial package. One of the interesting aspects of this package is its innovative navigational methods. For example, InternetWorks opens with its own locally stored table of contents. Instead of the normal history log, it has a row of tabs across the bottom of the screen. To top it all off, it has a card catalog instead of the traditional hot list. You can also use the side-by-side windows to view multiple pages at the same time.

Of course, as with any other package, there also are inconveniences to deal with. For example, when you move from one page to another, the first page disappears, and you are left looking at nothing but the incoming byte counter.

If you decide to ignore our advice and look for a Web browser other than the software included with the CD-ROM, Internet Works would probably be one of our second choices.

Mosaic

Several versions of Mosaic are available, both commercial and free. We examine four versions here (NCSA Mosaic 2.009a, Enhanced Mosaic 2.0, Mosaic in a Box 1.0, and CompuServe's SPRY Air Mosaic) and discuss SPRY Air Mosaic, which is included on the CD-ROM that's included with this book, more fully in the next section of the chapter.

Patrick Vincent's *Free $tuff from the Internet* (1994) is another source of excellent information on using Mosaic. See the chapter titled "The Tightwad's Guide to Mosaic."

Advantages, which apply to all of the versions of this program that we cover, include a preinstalled hot list that can be organized as menus and, depending on the speed of your modem or Internet connection, excellent performance. One disadvantage is that you can't continue surfing on to another page until the page you've started downloading is finished, including its graphics.

Generally, all versions of Mosaic are extremely easy to use, but a constant complaint has been the lack of documentation. We don't think that this complaint is justified (especially after seeing the quality of some of the documentation that comes with other browsers). When we downloaded NCSA Mosaic 2.009a, the zipped file included an installation and configuration guide. Also, when you run the program, you open on NCSA's home page (`http://www.ncsa.uiuc.edu/SDG/Software/WinMosaic/HomePage.html`), where you find Mosaic's on-line documentation. Spend a little time looking at the information provided there.

NCSA Mosaic 2.009a

This version of Mosaic is free, and you can download it from ftp.ncsa. uluc.edu by using anonymous FTP. The file is in the /Mosaic/Windows directory. NCSA Mosaic is a 32-bit program that requires the Win32s extensions to run. If you don't have them already, you can download these Win32 files at the same time that you're downloading the browser. Figure 2-7 illustrates what this program looks like when accessing the Web.

Enhanced Mosaic 2.0

Spyglass is expected to release Enhanced Mosaic 2.0, its commercial version of Mosaic, and may very well have done so by the time you read this. The performance and security of what we consider to be an already excellent program is supposed to be exceptionally enhanced. The price for this version of Mosaic will depend on the licensee.

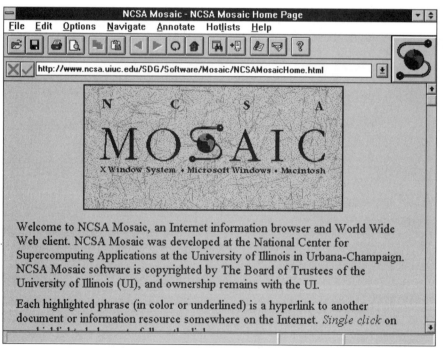

Figure 2-7: Using NCSA Mosaic to access the Web.

Mosaic in a Box 1.0

Automatic setup, the ImageView graphics utility, and outlined hot lists are just a few of the features that are available in this commercial package of Mosaic.

Mosaic in a Box has a default service provider (CompuServe), and unless you're planning to use another provider, installation, setup, and getting online are a snap. ImageView is an excellent graphics utility that enables you to view, edit, and save graphics either online or offline.

CompuServe's SPRY Air Mosaic

SPRY Air Mosaic is the Web browser that's on the CD-ROM that comes with this book (See Figure 2-8).

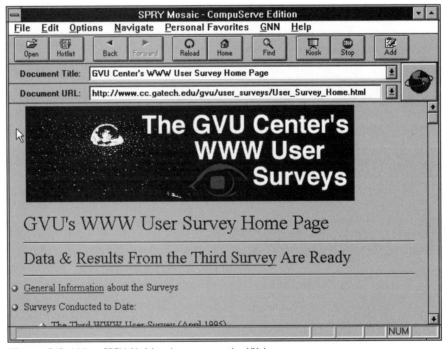

Figure 2-8: Using SPRY Air Mosaic to access the Web.

We chose this browser for several reasons:

➡ We've been happy with CompuServe as our service provider for most of the past ten years.

➡ Air Mosaic comes with both on-line documentation, in the form of Windows Help files, and printable user documentation in .WRI format that you can print out by using the Windows Write program.

➡ You can configure Air Mosaic to work with another service provider if necessary.

We provide more details about this program later in the chapter.

NetCruiser

NetCruiser Plus 1.52, a commercial package, works with only Netcom, another Internet service provider. Another disadvantage is that you can't leave a page until it finishes loading. NetCruiser Plus does, however, completely automate the installation and setup process. We recommend passing on this one completely.

Netscape Navigator

According to the GVU Center's World Wide Web User Surveys, Netscape Navigator is the most used browser on the Web. This is understandable because of the price and the fact that it's free for academic, nonprofit, and evaluation use. Paul uses it on his university office computer. It was given to him along with his Internet account when he had the computer hooked into the Internet. Of course, the free version doesn't come with technical support or documentation. Figure 2-9 illustrates accessing the Web using Netscape Navigator.

Still, for the commercial version, price and performance are strong factors to consider when you are evaluating this piece of software. As with SPRY Air Mosaic, you can speed things up by turning off the graphics when loading a page. Then, if you decide that you want to see the graphics, a simple click of a button on the toolbar will reload the page with graphics.

It also offers some of the best security available in any of the browsers.

SlipKnot

We occasionally use this relatively easy-to-use browser to access the university's Internet connection from one of our home computers. SlipKnot, shown in Figure 2-10, was designed to use with slower modem connections and requires no SLIP, PPP, or TCP/IP services from the service provider.

Figure 2-9: Using Netscape Navigator to access the Web.

Figure 2-10: Using SlipKnot to access the Web.

SlipKnot can retrieve documents (including embedded graphics and pictures) in the background while you browse documents in the foreground. In addition, you can save entire documents to user-defined folders for later off-line display. Up to five documents can be on the screen at one time. Finally, one of Slip-Knot's primary advantages is its capability to upgrade itself automatically to the most recent version when you connect to the SlipKnot home page.

SlipKnot is not without limitations, however. One limitation is that it can't display interactive forms, although a future release should contain this capability. In its current release, it can use only the HTTP and FTP protocols to access documents; it does not support Gopher and several other protocols, including Mailto. Again, these capabilities are supposed to be added in a future release. SlipKnot does have a terminal window, however, from which you can access Gopher or the service provider's mail program, such as Elm. From this terminal window, you can access any UNIX operation that you would usually use with any terminal communications program.

SlipKnot is available for download on CompuServe's Internet Resources forum. Just use WinCIM to access the forum and perform a library search (as you did in Chapter 1) for the keyword `slipknot`.

WinWeb

WinWeb is another of the free browsers, and it is available for download by anonymous FTP at `ftp://einet.net/einet/pc/winweb/winweb/zip`. If you obtain it this way, you will not have support and documentation; the program is also available commercially.

You need a TCP/IP stack, because WinWeb doesn't come with one; but otherwise, WinWeb is ready to go. The program opens with Einet's (another Internet service provider) home page that includes a wonderful index of Web sites to visit. You can navigate by using WinWeb's hot lists or its simple toolbar. As with some of the other browsers, you can't leave a page until it finishes loading, and you can't download more than one page at a time.

Taking a Closer Look at SPRY Air Mosaic

SPRY Air Mosaic is provided on the CD-ROM, and now you are going to learn more about it. Figure 2-11 provides a look at using the browser to access the Web.

Figure 2-11: Using SPRY Air Mosaic to look at CompuServe's home page.

Installing SPRY Air Mosaic

Follow these instructions to install the SPRY Air Mosaic software that is included on the CD-ROM that accompanies this book.

1. **Place the CD in your drive and then choose Run from the File menu.**

    You see the Run dialog box (See Figure 2-12).

Figure 2-12: The Run dialog box.

2. Type X:AIRSETUP (where X represents your CD-ROM drive) in the Command Line box and press Enter.

3. Follow the on-screen directions, and you'll soon have your Web browser installed and the setup complete.

You're now ready for a quick, down-and-dirty, tour of the Web.

A short guided tour of the Web

All right, you've finished installing the software. Now for some fun.

1. From the Program Manager (See Figure 2-13), which now includes a CompuServe icon, double-click on the CompuServe icon.

   You have the CompuServe icon if you accepted the defaults during setup of the CompuServe software. On our computer (we didn't accept the defaults), the CIS software is located in the Communication group, as shown in Figure 2-13.

2. In the next window, double-click on the Spry Mosaic icon, as in Figure 2-14.

   The browser connects to CompuServe. It takes a minute or so to connect, depending on the connection, so just relax. Soon, the program begins to retrieve information (as you can tell by looking at the message bar at the bottom of the screen). After a few moments, text appears on the screen, and you notice in the message bar that more information is being retrieved. A few moments more and you'll have something that may look very much like Figure 2-15 on your screen.

   Take a few moments to browse around and down this page. It has plenty of information about what's going on at CompuServe. Get the feel of the program. We have a hunch that you'll be spending a great deal of time with it.

3. Play around and explore for a few minutes by clicking on some of the highlighted words and watching where the program takes you or by checking out the Hot Lists (clicking on one of the menu items that interest you).

   The Hot List topics range from sports to science and beyond. When you click on one of the Hot List menu items, more information is accessed, and another page replaces the one that you were looking at.

4. When you have seen enough, choose Exit from the File menu.

5. Reopen the Internet Dialer and hang up so that you disconnect from the service.

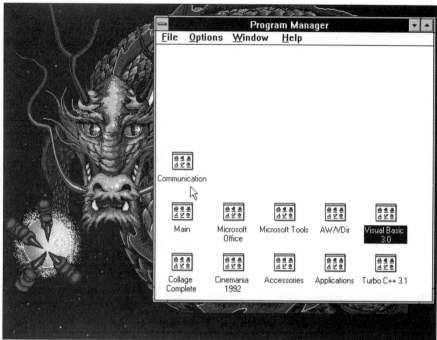

Figure 2-13: Double-click on the icon of the program group where SPRY Air Mosaic is located.

Figure 2-14: Double-click on the SPRY Mosaic icon.

Figure 2-15: CompuServe's home page on the Internet.

Putting what you've learned into practice

Now that you're familiar with the software, you can use it to explore the Web.

Exercise #1: The Evil Dr. Flaxon

As we promised earlier in this chapter, you are now going to have the opportunity to explore the world of the Evil Dr. Flaxon, Doug Faxon's evil cousin.

1. **Start Spry Air Mosaic just as you did during the guided tour.**

2. **When you arrived at CompuServe's home page, click once on the Document URL box.**

   The URL in the box (`http://www.compuserve.com`) is highlighted.

3. **Backspace to delete this URL.**

   Don't worry. It's still in your hot list. It's just removed from the box for the time being.

4. **Type** http://www.sonic.net/~dfx/fait/ **and press Enter.**

   After a moment, your screen looks similar to Figure 2-16.

   We suggest that you read this page carefully and keep in mind that Dr. Flaxon is a joke gone wild. The entire Dr. Flaxon myth comes exploding from the imagination of Doug Faxon. For more information on how Dr. Flaxon came into being, surf over to Doug's home page at the URL `http://www.sonic.net/~dfx/doug/` and read the reference to Dr. Flaxon that's found on the Cyberforum page.

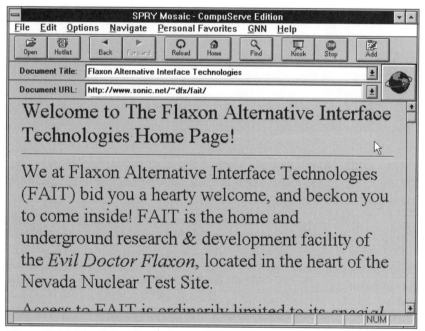

Figure 2-16: The Flaxon Alternative Interface Technologies (FAIT) Home Page: the home of the Evil Dr. Flaxon.

5. **Scroll down the page by clicking the downward-pointing arrow on the lower-right side of the screen until you come to the list shown in Figure 2-17.**

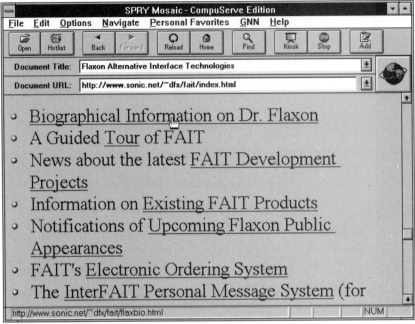

Figure 2-17: A menu of options available on FAIT's home page.

6.   Notice that the pointer is a hand when you move the mouse over the page itself; use it to click the blue highlighted option that reads **Biographical Information on Dr. Flaxon.**

Now you can see what the evil Dr. Flaxon looks like (See Figure 2-18). Do you notice a slight family resemblance to Doug?

7.   **Scroll down and read the fictional history of this evil genius.**

When you come to the bottom of the page, at the end of this imaginary tale, you see a blue highlighted area reading HOME and NEXT.

8.   **Click NEXT to take a tour of FAIT's facilities.**

As you read this page you'll notice two highlighted areas for Secure Entrances and a Secret Drive-in Entrance. We suggest that you look at these interesting and humorous areas.

As you return to the tour and keep reading, you'll come down to the blue highlighted words *Caustic Hot Tub* (See Figure 2-19).

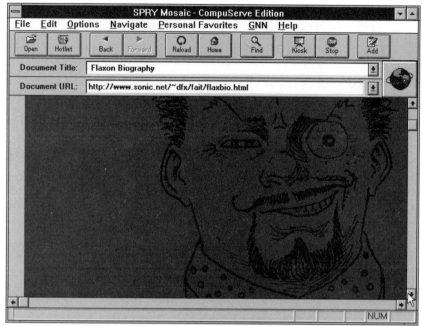

Figure 2-18: An illustration of what the Evil Dr. Flaxon looks like.

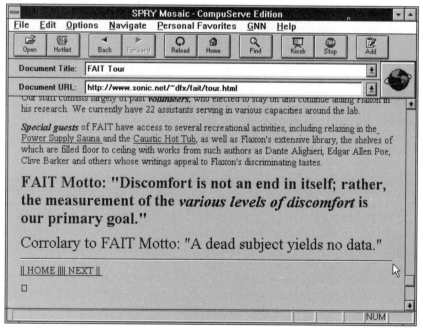

Figure 2-19: Part of the FAIT Tour page.

9. Click on the highlighted area to see some of the artwork created by David Lee Ingersol.

   Ingersol has created about 90 percent of the Flaxon imagery so far, according to Doug. Figure 2-20 shows Ingersol's Caustic Hot Tub.

10. Click on NEXT in the lower-left of the hot tub page to proceed to the FAIT Space Shuttle Adventure page, as shown in Figure 2-21.

11. Scroll through this material and read the imaginative description of this FAIT product.

    You'll also want to look at the graphic of the minor glitch that FAIT ran into in testing the adventure with volunteers.

12. Click the blue highlighted word NEXT at the bottom of the page to go to the product list shown in Figure 2-22.

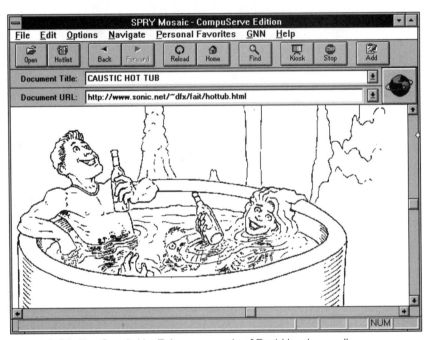

Figure 2-20: The Caustic Hot Tub: an example of David Lee Ingersol's artwork that can be viewed in the FAIT Tour.

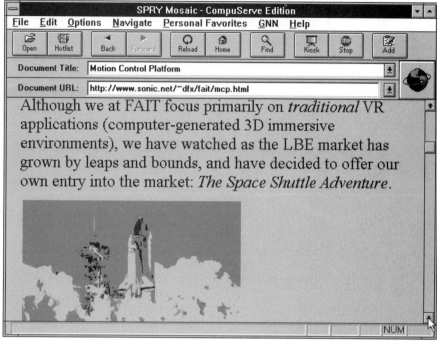

Figure 2-21: FAIT's Space Shuttle Adventure.

Figure 2-22: The FAIT Product Listing.

13. **Click on some of the products and enjoy the imagination that went into devising them.**

   We haven't had the courage to look at some of them yet. You be the judge of what you want to look at.

   On the next page is a list of upcoming events where you may be able to meet the Evil Dr. Flaxon. Doug has warned us that Dr. Flaxon is always on the lookout for possible victims — we mean *volunteers* — for his experiments.

   The next page (See Figure 2-23) is an order form for some of the products shown during the tour. You also can leave a message or comment on this page.

   The next page gives you the e-mail addresses of some of FAIT's employees. You can even send a message to the Evil Dr. Flaxon from here.

   Finally, the last page of this series is a list of Dr. Flaxon's favorite Web sites. You'll notice that these sites all have something to do with horror, so be careful not to become one of Flaxon's victims, er, *volunteers.*

 One final note before moving on to the next exercise. If you want to keep the FAIT home page URL in your hot list of favorite Web sites, click the Add icon in the toolbar at the top of the page.

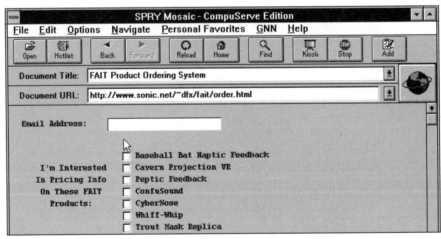

Figure 2-23: The FAIT product order form.

Exercise #2: The home page of James Pitkow

In the next, and final, exercise for this chapter, you look at the home page of James Pitkow, a Ph.D. candidate at Georgia Tech. Jim is responsible for helping to make the Web surveys available via the Web.

1. **Click the Document URL box.**

2. **Backspace to remove the contents.**

3. **Type** http://www.cc.gatech.edu/gvu/people/Phd/James.E.Pitkow.html **and press Enter.**

   After a few moments, the text and graphics for Jim's home page appear on your screen (See Figure 2-24).

Besides some interesting background information concerning Jim, you see a list of options that enable you to view pictures that Jim finds important in his life. Take a few minutes to look through this material.

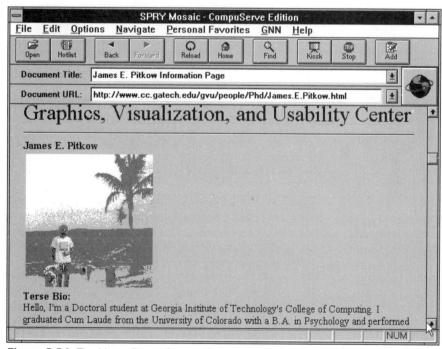

Figure 2-24: The Home Page of James E. Pitkow.

Leaving SPRY Air Mosaic

That's it for the exercises in this chapter. Now all you have to do is exit the browser and disconnect from CompuServe.

1. **From the File menu, choose Exit.**

    You return to the Program Manager, but you're still connected to CompuServe.

2. **Reenter the CompuServe Internet Dialer program by double-clicking on the icon at the bottom of the screen.**

3. **Click the Hang-Up button in the upper-left corner, and then choose Exit from the File menu.**

    You are disconnected and returned to the Windows Program Manager.

In addition to giving you some experience with SPRY Air Mosaic, we hope that these exercises have given you some idea of what can be done with HTTP and the Web. You can create hyperlinked pages that enable other users to look at artwork, text, and pictures or to listen to audio clips. You can even listen to a couple of radio stations on the Web.

The exercises teach skills that will enable you to build your virtual world on the Internet. There are two more chapters of basic background and foundation information to cover, and then you'll be ready to start building your own virtual world.

Moving On

In the past several pages you've had the opportunity to explore the Web using the software provided on the CD-ROM. We've discussed a variety of other Web browsers that are available if you should decide to use a different service provider.

The next chapter gives you a basic introduction to the history of HTML and HTTP and explains their importance to what you do with VRML later in this book. You look at the concept of standardization on the Internet and the Web and at what standardization means to VRML. Finally, we introduce you to a little HTML programming by discussing the HTML editor and viewer that's provided on the CD-ROM that accompanies this book. Then you can try your hand at creating your own Web page.

Well, we need to quit talking about what we're going to do and get on with it. Keep in mind the old film and television adage, "Producers produce!"

The CompuServe Internet Club

Because you may be spending quite a bit of time surfing the Internet and the Web, you may want to consider adding the Internet Club package to your CompuServe membership charges. Basic membership gives you 3 hours of Internet connection per month. The charge is $2.50 for every hour above the 3 free hours.

If you spend more than 9 hours a month surfing the Web, the Internet Club is a much better deal. You get 20 hours free each month, and the charge is only $1.95 for each hour over 20. Membership in the Internet Club is $15 extra per month, so your CIS basic bill is about $25 each month.

These rates were correct in August 1995. Go online to check for the current rates.

HTML and HTTP

You know that HTML stands for *Hypertext Markup Language* and that HTTP stands for *Hypertext Transfer Protocol*. That's all well and good, but what do the terms *Hypertext Markup Language* and *Hypertext Transfer Protocol* mean? And what can you do with HTML and HTTP? After all, information becomes valuable only when you can do something with it.

In Chapters 1 and 2, you learned about the tools and skills necessary for gathering information on the Net. In this chapter, you learn how to do something with that information. We begin with a brief explanation of what HTTP and HTML do and how they do it. Then we examine the history of both the language and the protocol and look at the issue of standardizing languages and protocols on the Web.

After all that, we get into the meat of the chapter — using HTML. Don't expect this chapter to be the be-all-and-end-all explanation of how to use HTML to create a Web page. Plenty of other books do that. (*Creating Cool Web Pages with HTML* by Dave Taylor, IDG, 1995, is one that you may want to take a look at.) All we want to do in this chapter is give you enough background and skills so that you can create a Web page into which you can later incorporate a VRML virtual world.

In order to do that, we look at some of the HTML editors available and examine their strengths and weaknesses. We talk about where and how you can get these editors and explain how to install and use the editor that's on the CD-ROM that comes with this book. Then we explain how to create a simple Web page, and you create one of your own.

A Short Discussion of HTTP, HTML and SGML

We begin with HTTP because this protocol is what makes all of the technology of the Web possible. When we discuss URLs in Chapter 2, we say that HTTP is the way that the computers and servers on the Web talk to each other. HTTP is how Web documents are transferred across the Internet. When you use `http:`, you're telling your browser that you want to connect to a Web document.

HTML

The World Wide Web is based on HTML. HTML was developed to create a method of taking plain ASCII text and encoding complex hypermedia document control strings that focus the document more on structure than on appearance. Another important consideration is that these documents need to be accessible by a wide variety of platforms so that anyone who accesses the Internet can access the documents, using no matter what computer, operating system, or network.

HTML looks a lot like the industry standard *Standard Generalized Markup Language*, *(SGML),* which is found mainly on high-end workstations. The creators of HTML were probably extremely familiar with SGML because you can use HTML in conjunction with SGML. HTML, however, doesn't take full advantage of the full SGML capabilities. We don't get into SGML here because it's not necessary.

The different versions of HTML

Currently, three different versions, or levels, of HTML coexist on the Web. These three versions are 0.9, 1.0, and 2.0. Version 3.0 is waiting in the wings but hasn't been finalized.

Versions 0.9 and 1.0

Versions 0.9 and 1.0 use codes to control headings, lists, and character formatting. Just about any browser can read these codes. The commands are relatively easy to learn, and you use them later in this chapter to create your Web page. Of course, for the full implementation of graphics, sounds, and VRML worlds, you have to learn codes that are found in Versions 2.0 and 3.0.

Version 2.0

Version 2.0 of HTML adds commands for menus and interactive forms. The SPRY Air Mosaic browser that's included on the CD-ROM is capable of reading Version 2.0's commands. (Figure 3-1 shows the interactive form that you saw during your tour of FAIT's home page in the exercises for Chapter 2.)

Most browsers can interpret Version 2.0's menu and form commands, but you'll remember from Chapter 2 that, of the browsers we introduced you to, SlipKnot Version 1.0 can't interpret them. Some users won't see your menus or forms if you use these commands.

Version 3.0

Version 3.0 of HTML is not finalized as of this writing. It is supposed to support many new functions, including background bitmaps and the capability to create tables. A *background bitmap* is a graphic image displayed behind the HTML information. You can see an example of a background bitmap on WebMaster's home page. (The URL for WebMaster is in Chapter 15.) Some of the more recent Web browsers are supposed to have implemented many of Version 3.0's features, but don't expect that all browsers will be able to handle these new features.

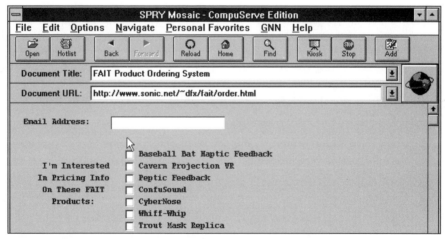

Figure 3-1: An example of an interactive form from FAIT's home page.

The Issue of Standardization

The issue of standardization on the Internet is a controversial one. Standardization is a mixed blessing: It can make more things available to more people and, at the same time, restrict creativity and stifle growth. It is, at its very essence, conformity. In the case of the Internet, standardization requires all users to conform to the specifications set by the Internet's governing body.

At the same time, however, standardization is an arbitrary concept. When there are many standards for a language, none of them can be called a standard, and the very word *standard* becomes confusing. HTTP and HTML are the de facto standards for the Web. Yet, as you shall see, there are three concurrent versions of HTML and a fourth waiting in the wings. Each may be a version of the standard, but which is the standard if each version adds to and takes away from the previous version?

To top it all off, as of early 1995, all three of the concurrent versions of HTML had been proposed to the W3 consortium for approval as the standard. None, however, had been approved by the consortium or any other Internet governing body. However, it can take years to get through this process…especially with VRML. Many of the VRML Version 1.0 products will be reference implementations and facilitate a quicker approval time.

VRML is touted as the standard for virtual reality programming on the Internet. VRML Version 1.0 was announced in November 1994. Version 2 is expected by December of 1995. Already, there are expectations of a second standard when relatively few users have been able to take advantage of the first standard.

We suggest that, with both HTML and VRML, the possibility of standardization may stifle creativity. Standardization produces a restriction on the diversity in thinking.

Turn, for a moment, to the definition of technology. A *technology* is a structured way of doing things. Therefore, accepting any program, language, or application as the standard method of doing things means that you've accepted that technology. A technology structures the way you look at the world.

There are, however, arguments in favor of standardization. The masses benefit from standardization. The individual benefits from diversity. Standardization allows for mass produced items that make the lives of the masses easier and more "normal." There are standards for just about everything from nuts and bolts to modems and phone lines. Standards create commonality.

How is a standard created? There are basically two ways.

The first is a de facto standard known as the "industry" standard. This is the standard that results when the marketplace determines the standard. Often, the "best" solution does not win. An example of this can be seen in the standardization of home VCRs. Sony's Beta format is considered by many professionals to be a higher quality product than the VHS format. However, VHS, which was lower in quality but also cheaper in price, quickly became the standard for home video recorders. The "industry" standard does not, therefore, always represent the highest quality but, more often than not, the ability of one corporation to flood the marketplace with lower quality, less expensive products.

The second way that a standard can be created is by a "standards making" body. Here, an organization is set up for the purpose of writing a standard and making that standard available for public review. Although this method generally takes a long time, it can be sped up, or even reversed, by organizations that have an interest in the outcome of the standardization process.

An example of this might be the standardization process for color television. The standard for black and white television was the NTSC (National Television Standards Committee) standard of 525 lines of resolution. This resolution is a low standard compared with the standards used by the rest of the world. (The British standard is 625 lines of resolution.) When color television was being considered, there were two dominant alternatives. One came from CBS, and the other came from NBC, the creator of the original NTSC standard.

CBS offered a non-NTSC-compatible standard that was, at first, accepted by the standardization body. The strongest negative associated with the CBS alternative was its lack of compatibility with the NTSC standard. Otherwise, many thought that its color rendition and resolution were superior to the alternative that NBC offered.

Within a short time, the standardization body reversed itself and accepted NBC's alternative. The main reason given for the reversal was that NBC's alternative was compatible with the television sets that most people already had.

By the way, this argument was not sufficient to prevent this same standards governing body from moving the entire FM broadcast spectrum, the frequencies assigned for FM radio broadcast, when it wanted to create new frequencies and make them available for different uses. This action had the effect of almost killing FM broadcasting as a medium, something that NBC favored because FM endangered NBC's AM broadcasting holdings.

As you can see from these examples, standardization does not always provide the user with the best option.

The problem here, to our way of thinking, is that a standard, by its very definition, presents the possibility of limiting the imagination and, therefore, creativity.

At present, the VRML community resembles the Greek democracies, with all their strong points and their weak points. These democracies are noted for their high levels of creativity, a phase that the VRML community has been in for more than a year.

But even the Greek democracies, in times of extreme stress, gave way to periods of complete authoritarianism for the good of the community. Authoritarianism is low in creativity but extremely high in productivity. The VRML community is currently in a time of extremely high stress. There is the real danger of fragmentation, and fragmentation means that no one, programmer or user, wins. A proposal has been made creating the VRML Architecture Group (VAG) and charging it with the responsibility of determining the future of VRML.

Another analogy to the history of broadcasting can be made to support this regulatory organization. During the 1920s there was no central governing body to control the use of the broadcast frequencies. The result was anarchy on the air. The public grew tired of the noise on the radio channels and quit buying receivers. During this time period, there was little advertising, and stations were supported through the sale of receivers. Station owners turned to the government to regulate them.

The government did not want to get involved with broadcasting again because it had had its fill of broadcasting during World War I when it had taken possession of all radio transmitters in the country. It had just been within the past few years that the government had managed to extricate itself from the broadcasting quagmire.

It quickly became apparent, however, that for the good of the public, and more importantly, for the good of commerce, regulation and standardization were required. A temporary body called the Federal Radio Commission was set up in 1927. It was thought that this organization would be able to straighten out the mess within a year. The body was still in operation in 1934 when it was replaced by a permanent body called the Federal Communications Commission.

Complete freedom for broadcasting created complete anarchy. No standard was in place, and the public rebelled by not listening. Broadcasting survived and flourished for a time under regulation and standardization. The Web has also survived and flourished under the standardization surrounding HTML.

The time for a strong standard and a strong standards body for VRML is here. The VAG provides such a body. At the same time, however, it provides for the elasticity that individual creativity also requires. The good of the entire VRML community, not just individual corporate entities, requires it.

Using HTML

For this short HTML tutorial, we stick predominantly with Version 0.9 and 1.0 commands. These commands can be divided into eight basic categories: structural commands, text-flow commands, heading commands, character-formatting commands, list-formatting commands, special character escape sequences, in-line graphic commands, and anchor commands. In the following sections, you look at each of these categories and see some examples of the commands.

Structural commands

Structural commands define the parts of the Web document that you are creating. HTML commands are called *HTML tags.* When you start a part of your page with a tag, you need to close that part of your page with a tag. Table 3-1 shows some examples.

Table 3-1: Examples of Structural Commands

HTML Tag	Closing Tag	What the Command Does
\<HTML\>	\</HTML\>	Opens and closes an HTML Web file
\<HEAD\>	\</HEAD\>	Opens and closes formatting information
\<BODY\>	\</BODY\>	Defines the body of an HTML document

Other structural commands will be of interest and use to you, but these three commands are probably the most important ones. You learn how to use these tags when you start creating your Web page, later in this chapter.

Text-flow commands

You use text-flow commands to format the information within the HTML document. These commands do not require a closing tag. Table 3-2 shows some examples of text-flow commands.

Table 3-2: Examples of Text-Flow Commands

HTML Tag	What the Command Does
\<P\>	Indicates the end of a paragraph
\<BR\>	Forces a line break
\<HR\>	Draws a horizontal line across the window

There are other text-flow commands, but these three are the ones that you will probably use the most.

Heading commands

Heading commands define headings and subheadings within your page. As with structural tags, heading tags must have a beginning and an end. Table 3-3 shows the six levels for heading tags.

Table 3-3: Heading Commands

HTML Tag	Closing Tag	What the Command Does
<H1>	</H1>	Opens and closes Heading level 1
<H2>	</H2>	Opens and closes Heading level 2
<H3>	</H3>	Opens and closes Heading level 3
<H4>	</H4>	Opens and closes Heading level 4
<H5>	</H5>	Opens and closes Heading level 5
<H6>	</H6>	Opens and closes Heading level 6

The type size and typeface for the display of each heading level depends on the browser that you are using to access the document. The main thing here is that heading level 1 is always the largest type size and heading level 6 is always the smallest type size. Heading tags terminate the current paragraph, as you see when you create your Web page.

Character-formatting commands

This group of commands has two basic subcategories. The first one deals with physical characteristics, and the second one deals with logical characteristics. Again, these tags are always in pairs. Table 3-4 shows some of the character tags for physical characteristics.

Table 3-4: Examples of Character Commands for Physical Characteristics

HTML Tag	Closing Tag	What the Command Does
<B>	</B>	Creates **bold** text in a document
<I>	</I>	Creates *italicized* text in a document
<U>	</U>	Creates underlined text in a document

These commands have no effect on the formatting of anything outside of the opening and closing of the command. They operate much like the formatting of your word processor in that they don't change spacing or indentation.

The second subcategory of character-formatting commands includes a larger number of tags, and these character tags for logical characteristics are more abstract than the tags for physical characteristics. Table 3-5 illustrates some of the tags for logical characteristics.

Table 3-5: Examples of Character Commands for Logical Characteristics

HTML Tag	Closing Tag	What the Command Does
`<ADDRESS>`	`</ADDRESS>`	Provides contact information for the author of the HTML document
`<CITE>`	`</CITE>`	Opens and closes citation information
`<SAMP>`	`</SAMP>`	Opens and closes sample outputs of commands

Currently, many browsers interpret these character-formatting tags for logical characteristics the same way as they interpret the character-formatting tags for physical characteristics. In other words, some browsers may simply interpret the address tag to mean to apply bold or italic to the material. The logical subcategory, however, should provide information about the nature of the text as well as just its appearance. At this point in time, there's no way to tell what any given browser is going to do with commands in the logical subcategory. Despite this problem, many HTML trainers suggest using the logical subcategory rather than the physical one whenever possible.

We don't suggest that you use multiple categories on the same text. In other words, although it might be fine to make a certain text bold and italic in your word processor, it's not a very good idea to do that with HTML. There's really no telling what the browsers will do with your text if you do.

List-formatting commands

List-formatting commands create three basic styles of lists for your Web page. The three styles are ordered lists, unordered lists, and definition lists. Table 3-6 provides examples of the commands for these three styles and explains each type of list.

Table 3-6: Examples of List-Formatting Commands

HTML Tag	Closing Tag	What the Command Does
`<OL>`	`</OL>`	Opens and closes an ordered list where each item is numbered
`<UL>`	`</UL>`	Opens and closes an unordered or bulleted list
`<DL>`	`</DL>`	Opens and closes a list of definitions

Individual items within ordered and unordered lists are marked with the `<LI>` tag. This tag is placed only as an opening tag before each item inside the list.

Individual items inside definition lists are marked with `<DT>` and `<DD>` tags defining them as terms or definitions, respectively. Again, these tags are placed only as opening tags for the terms or the definitions.

Special character escape sequences

In order for HTML to be compatible with a wide variety of platforms, most documents are created so as to display using the lowest common denominator of ASCII. Sometimes, however, especially in electronic publishing, you may need to use special symbols. These symbols are referred to as *special character escape sequences*. An escape sequence enables you to use non-ASCII symbols by encoding them into the HTML document. Some of these symbols and their codes are shown in Table 3-7.

Table 3-7: Examples of Commands for Special Character Escape Sequences

Escape Sequence	Displays As
`&lt;`	<
`&gt;`	>
`&amp;`	&
`&quot;`	"
`&#169`	©
`&#174`	®

A large number of escape sequences are available. You can find the entire list of escape sequences in the HTML 2.0 specifications, which are available on the Web at `http://info.cern.ch`, as well as at other locations.

In-line graphics commands

Graphics are not actually embedded into HTML documents. Instead, the <IMG> tag is used to reference them in the document. The graphics are stored in a separate file either on the same computer as the HTML file or on any address-able Web server. The basic format of the <IMG> tag is

```
<IMG SRC="URL" [ALIGN=TOP/MIDDLE/BOTTOM] [ALT="text"]>
```

When this tag is viewed by the browser, the image stored at the location speci-fied by the URL is retrieved into the document and aligned according to the optional alignment parameters. The default alignment parameter is BOTTOM. Another optional parameter is the ALT parameter. You use the ALT parameter to specify the text to be displayed in place of the image when the document is being viewed by character-only browsers or if Web sites have text–only filters.

Usually, the graphical browsers discussed in Chapter 2 can handle a variety of different image formats, including JPEG and CompuServe .GIF files.

Anchor commands

You use anchor commands to designate and code *hyperlinks,* the default blue underlined words (can be any RGB setting) or, in some cases, bitmapped graphics, that the user clicks on to get from one document to another docu-ment or to another location within the same document.

The basic form of an anchor tag is

```
<A HREF-"URL"> your words</A>
```

where *your words* is what the user sees. The URL is the location of the hyper-link. This URL can be absolute, relative, or local:

➡ The URL is *absolute* if it contains the full hostname and filename of the document that you want to be displayed.

➡ The URL is *relative* if the path to the document is the same as the path to the original document.

➡ The URL is *local* if the file is on the machine that is running the browser instead of on the server.

Using a Simple HTML Editor

If you're willing to memorize all the commands we mentioned previously, as well as several hundred more, you can use any text editor that saves your files in ASCII format and allows the HTML extension (.HTM for PCs) to create a Web page.

Another option is to download the specifications for one of the four versions of HTML that is currently available. But then you need to keep this 190+ page document next to you as you create the Web page on your computer.

For obvious reasons, we prefer to use one of the various HTML editors that are available in commercial, shareware, or public domain versions. In the following section, we examine five of these editors and tell you how to use the one that's on the CD-ROM that accompanies this book.

Several HTML editors are distributed on the Internet for free; some of them also come in commercial versions. These editors enable you to load and edit HTML files on your computer. The following sections describe five editors and give the locations where you can download them.

Editors that you can download

At the time we wrote this chapter, the locations and filenames of the programs were correct. Keep in mind that anything online can change from one minute to the next. In searching for these files, we found that they were no longer located in many forums where they were supposed to have been at one time. If you have this problem, use the PC File Finder that's available online with CompuServe and search on the program name, *not* on the filename.

HoTMetaL

HoTMetaL is an excellent SGML tool for the beginner to use for learning to create HTML documents. It requires Windows 3.1 or above. Although the program says that it requires at least 4MB of memory, with 8MB recommended, it would not run on a 20 MHz 386SX with 6MB. It did run nicely, however, on a 66 MHz 486DX2 with 16MB.

This program comes in both commercial and freely distributed versions. You can order the commercial version from the following address:

SoftQuad Inc.
56 Aberfoyle Cresent
Toronto, Ontario
CANADA M*X 2W4
phone 416-239-7105
e-mail: hotmetal@sq.com

SoftQuad provides no support for Version 1.0, which is a freely distributed, public domain edition. You can download this version from CompuServe under either of the filenames, file sizes, and forums listed in Table 3-8.

Table 3-8: Where to Find HoTMetaL

Filename	File Size	Forum
HOTMETAL.ZIP	1,350,061 bytes	PCEFORUM
HOTMETAL.ZIP	1,358,061 bytes	ERUFORUM

HTML Assistant

HTML Assistant was created in Visual Basic and, as with HoTMetaL, is also available in both a freeware version and a commercial version. The commercial version is called HTML Assistant Pro.

This program is basically a text editor with additions that enable you to use it to create a Web page. The features of the program vary depending on what version you have. You can subscribe to a free e-mail newsletter for the program by sending an e-mail message to harawitz@fox.nstn.ns.ca. In the subject field, place the single word subscribe; you also can place comments in the content field of the message.

You can download the freeware version of the program from one of the libraries and forums on CompuServe that are listed in Table 3-9.

Table 3-9: Where to Find HTML Assistant

Filename	File Size	Forum
HTMLAS.ZIP	206,616 bytes	PCEFORUM
HTMLAS.ZIP	167,678 bytes	INETRESOURCE
HTMLAS.ZIP	206,616 bytes	WUGNET
HTMLAS.ZIP	206,616 bytes	EURFORUM
HTMLAT.ZIP	206,616 bytes	EURFORUM
HTMLASST.ZIP	206,616 bytes	MUTFORUM

The program is not WYSIWYG (what-you-see-is-what-you-get) because it uses Mosaic or an OLE (Object Linking and Embedding) link to Cello in order to view files. One last thing you need to be aware of is that Version 1.0, the downloadable version, is limited to editing files that are less than 32K.

You can purchase the commercial version of HTML Assistant by contacting Brooklyn North Software Works by phone at 902-835-2600 or by e-mail at `harawitz@fox.nstn.ns.ca`.

HTML Writer

HTML Writer, like HTML Assistant, was created with Visual Basic. HTML Writer is an easy-to-use, easy-to-learn, Windows-based text editor that was created for using HTML to build and edit Web pages. Table 3-10 shows where you can find HTML Writer.

Table 3-10: Where to Find HTML Writer

Filename	File Size	Forum
HWR9B4.ZIP	252,141 bytes	PCEFORUM
HW9B4A.ZIP	252,141 bytes	PCUKFORUM
HWR9B4.ZIP	252,141 bytes	EURFORUM
HTMLWR.ZIP	252,018 bytes	WUGNET
HTMWRT.EXE	242,286 bytes	GERWIN

According to the author, Kris Nosack, HTML Writer is *donationware*. In other words, there are no restrictions on the program's use. You're free to use it as long as you want and as much as you want without ever feeling a pang of guilt because you haven't paid for it. If, however, you want to thank the author, you can send him five or ten dollars. His address is 376 North Main Street, Orem, Utah 84057.

You also can reach Mr. Nosack and sign up to be on the mailing list to receive the HTML Writer newsletter at `html_writer@byu.edu`.

One final note, HTML Writer has its own home page, which is located at the following address: `http://wwf.et.byu.edu/~nosackk/htmlwrit.html`.

CU_HTML.DOT

CU_HTML.DOT is a template that enables you to create HTML documents from inside Word for Windows. You use a WYSIWYG screen and can generate the resulting HTML file directly from Word. You can use your spell checker and grammar checker, as well as any of the other tools in Word that you've grown accustomed to.

This add-on template comes with no support. The copyright for this software is owned by the Computer Services Centre of The Chinese University of Hong Kong. You can download the most up-to-date version of this template from `ftp.cuhk.hk` under the filename `CU-HTML.ZIP`. You can download other versions of this template as well as other word processor add-ons from the forums listed in Table 3-11.

Table 3-11: Where to Find Word Processor HTML Add-Ons

Filename	Word Processor	File Size	Forum
GTHTML.ZIP	WinWord 6.0	40,040 bytes	INETRESOURCE
TAGWIZ.ZIP	WinWord 6.0	471,868 bytes	INETRESOURCE
ANTHTM.ZIP	WinWord 6.0	99,831 bytes	WINMAG
WORDIA.ZIP	WinWord 6.0	1,093,313 bytes	WINMAG
WORDIA.ZIP	WinWord 6.0	1,041,040 bytes	IBMCOM
TXTSTY.ZIP	Ami Pro	6,772 bytes	LOTUSWP
AMIWEB12.ZIP	Ami Pro 3.0	56,359 bytes	LOTUSWP
INTASSIS.ZIP	WinWord 6.0	1,120,360 bytes	UKSHARE
WORDIA.EXE	WinWord 6.0	1,120,361 bytes	WINMAG
WORDIA.ZIP	WinWord 6.0	1,120,361 bytes	GERWIN
AMIWEB.ZIP	Ami Pro 3.0+	105,236 bytes	WUGNET
CUHTML.ZIP	WinWord 2.0 or 6.0	69,970 bytes	WUGNET
WORDIA.ZIP	WinWord 6.0+	1,041,040 bytes	EURFORUM

Web Weaver

Web Weaver is an editor that automates the process of creating and editing HTML documents. The program requires Windows 3.1 or above and VBRUN300.DLL. You can find Web Weaver in the locations provided in Table 3-12.

Table 3-12: Where to Find Web Weaver

Filename	File Size	Forum
WEBWEA.ZIP	39,359 bytes	PCEFORUM
WEBWEA.ZIP	77,474 bytes	PCUKFORUM
WEBWEA.ZIP	77,475 bytes	EURFORUM

Microsoft Internet Assistant for Word for Windows 6.0

What HTML editor you choose is a matter of what features you want and need for your application. We prefer integrated software whenever possible, so we use Microsoft Internet Assistant for Word for Windows 6.0. This program enables us to create and view Web pages in the word processing program that we're accustomed to using. In addition, its built-in browser capability enables us to go online from inside Word for Windows.

When you use Microsoft Internet Assistant for Word 6.0, you don't have to learn or even see the HTML codes for the documents that you are creating. The program includes a built-in browser that uses Word as its viewing screen, so you can cut-and-paste from any Web page to which you're connected to the page you're working on and also link your computer to other pages. Advanced HTML features require that you edit the codes by hand, using the edit mode that's available in the add-on program.

When you are using Internet Assistant, one thing that you need to remember to do is to create a title field. Internet Assistant lets you create a document without entering a title field, but all browsers require a title field.

We originally downloaded the program under the filename WORDIA.EXE from the WINMAG forum on CompuServe. You can install it from the CD-ROM that's in the back of this book.

Installing Microsoft Internet Assistant for Word for Windows 6.0

Installing Microsoft Internet Assistant is easy. There are two ways to install this software. The first method is to double–click on the Microsoft Internet Assistant for Word building in the VIS menu. If you're installing from the CD-ROM, follow these steps:

1. Change to the CD-ROM drive (either drive D or drive E on our machines) while in the File Manager.

2. Double-click on the WORDIA subdirectory.

3. Double-click on the file SETUP.EXE.

   The Microsoft Internet Assistant installation begins. From this point, you simply sit back and answer the questions the program asks. When the installation is complete, you are given the choice of starting Word or exiting.

4. Choose Exit.

5. Exit File Manager.

If you've downloaded the most recent version of this software, follow these steps:

1. Create a temporary subdirectory (TEMP) from inside the File Manager.

2. Copy WORDIA.EXE from your WINCIM download subdirectory to the new TEMP subdirectory.

3. Double-click on WORDIA.EXE.

   WORDIA.EXE is a self-extracting file, and it will take a few moments, depending on the speed of your computer, to extract all the files.

4. Double-click on the file SETUP.EXE, as seen in Figure 3-2.

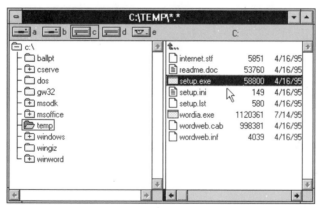

Figure 3-2: If you've downloaded the program and run the self-executing file in the TEMP directory as suggested, you're now ready to run Microsoft Internet Assistant's SETUP.EXE.

The Microsoft Internet Assistant installation begins. From this point, you simply sit back and answer the questions the program asks. When the installation is complete, you are given the choice of starting Word or exiting.

5.   Choose Exit.

6.   Exit the File Manager.

Exploring Microsoft Internet Assistant

Before using Microsoft Internet Assistant to create your own Web page, you
need to take some time to get to know how the program add-on works. Start
Microsoft Word for Windows. After Word has loaded, you'll notice a few minor
differences in your desktop (See Figure 3-3).

1.   Choose Open from the File menu.

2.   Make sure that you're in the Internet subdirectory under WinWord
     and click the DEFAULT.DOC file (See Figure 3-4).

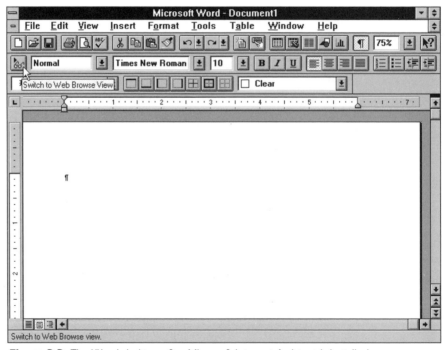

Figure 3-3: The Word desktop after Microsoft Internet Assistant is installed.

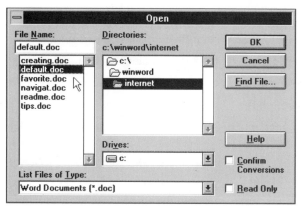

Figure 3-4: Open default.doc in the winword \ internet subdirectory.

3. **Click OK.**

   Word opens the document and switches to the Web browser view of
   the document. Your screen looks similar to Figure 3-5.

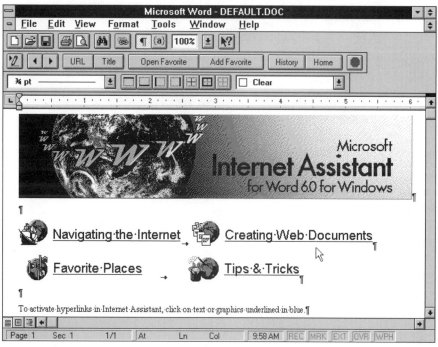

Figure 3-5: The Web browser view of Word with Microsoft Internet
Assistant installed.

You have four choices: Navigating the Internet, Creating Web Documents, Favorite Places, and Tips & Tricks. The text is blue and underlined to indicate that the items are hypertext links.

4. **Click Navigating the Internet to select that page.**

   You see something that is similar to Figure 3-6.

5. **Read through the material on the screen.**

   Don't expect to understand all of it yet. Just read it to familiarize yourself with it.

6. **After you've read the document, choose DEFAULT.DOC from the Window menu.**

   Again you're confronted with the screen presented in Figure 3-5.

7. **Click Creating Web Documents.**

   You see something that is similar to Figure 3-7.

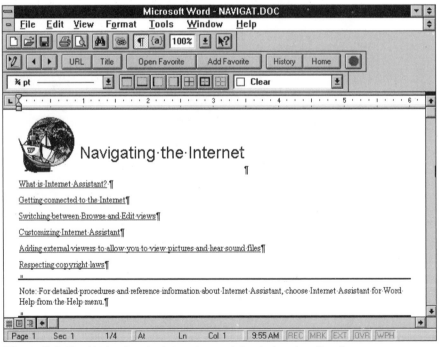

Figure 3-6: The Navigating the Internet page is loaded and waiting for your next command.

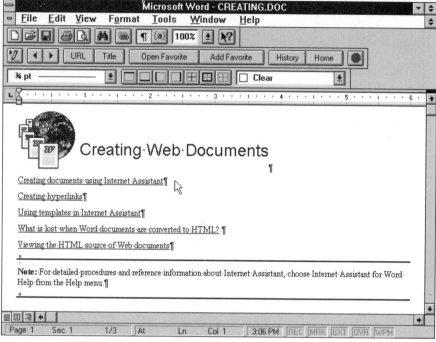

Figure 3-7: Use the Creating Web Documents page to obtain information about Internet Assistant that isn't included in this chapter.

8. **Read through this material and then switch back to DEFAULT.DOC again.**

9. **Click Favorite Places.**

   You see the Favorite Places page (See Figure 3-8), which explains how to add locations to your Favorite Places list and how to remove them from the list.

10. **After you've read this document, switch back to DEFAULT.DOC.**

11. **Select Tips & Tricks to look at the final part of this document (See Figure 3-9).**

12. **Read the Tips & Tricks page.**

   As you read through this document, you'll notice that if you're connected to the Internet, you can use InternetWorks to access it. This document also has information on how to create what Microsoft calls a "local web."

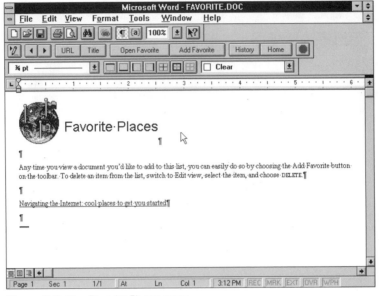

Figure 3-8: The Favorite Places page.

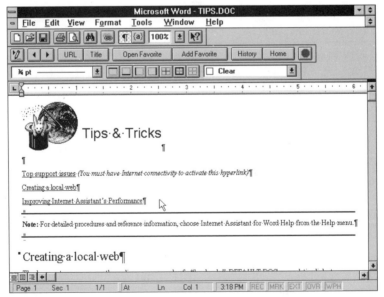

Figure 3-9: The Tips & Tricks page explains how to improve Internet Assistant's performance.

TIP Keep in mind that if you need information on detailed procedures, all you have to do is choose Internet Assistant from the Help menu on the desktop menu bar.

Putting What You've Learned into Practice

This exercise is the only one in this chapter. It walks you through the process of creating a home page for yourself by using Microsoft Internet Assistant for Word 6.0. If you're using a different editor, follow the directions and translate them into the commands necessary for your editor.

1. **Start your engine.**

   Well, anyway, start your HTML editor. In our case, and yours if you've decided to follow our suggestion, you're already in Microsoft Word for Windows and using Internet Assistant. Remember, you can start Internet Assistant either by clicking the icon with the eyeglasses at the upper-left end of the toolbar (See Figure 3-10) or by choosing the Browse Web option from the File menu (See Figure 3-11).

   You're now presented with DEFAULT.DOC (See Figure 3-12).

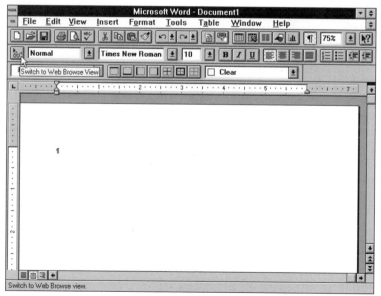

Figure 3-10: Click the icon with the eyeglasses to start Internet Assistant.

2. Choose New from the File menu, as in Figure 3-13, to create a new HTML file.

    You're confronted with a blank page, the scourge of every writer (See Figure 3-14).

    Don't forget, Internet Assistant will not stop you if you forget to create the document title field, which is required by all browsers. So the solution is to get into the habit of creating the title field first.

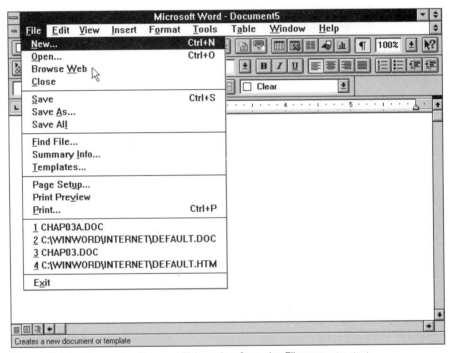

Figure 3-11: Choose the Browse Web option from the File menu to start Internet Assistant.

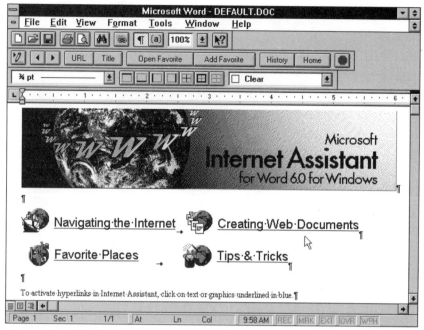

Figure 3-12: The Web browser view of Word with Microsoft Internet Assistant installed.

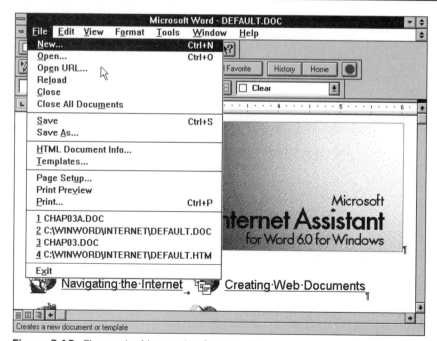

Figure 3-13: Choose the New option from the File menu to create a new HTML document.

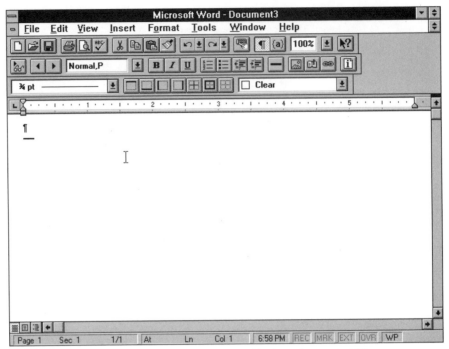

Figure 3-14: Don't let the blank page scare you. You're going to start filling it up now.

3. **To create a title field, you first click on the Title button on the desktop.**

   You see a dialog box that asks you to enter the information that you want to include in the title (See Figure 3-15).

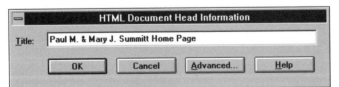

Figure 3-15: Enter the name of your home page in the HTML Document Head Information dialog box.

4. **Enter a title for your home page.**

   Be sure to use your own name instead of ours in this dialog box.

These two simple steps, clicking the Title button and entering the title information, created the following HTML code in the document:

```
<HTML>
<HEAD>
<TITLE> Paul M. & Mary J. Summitt Home Page</TITLE>
</HEAD>
```

Those of you who are using Internet Assistant need not worry that there still doesn't seem to be anything on your page. Remember, one of the advantages of this program is not having to deal with the code directly. Instead of concerning yourself with the mechanics of the operation, you can apply your creative energies to the aesthetics of the document. Let the computer and the program worry about the manual labor.

Some, if not most, browsers will pick up this title field and display it on the screen of anyone who accesses your page. But some browsers ignore this field, so you want to make sure that anyone accessing your Web page will know whom it belongs to. The first thing that you need to do is define the body of the document. Internet Assistant defines the body automatically. If you are using a different HTML editor, press Enter and then type the following after the </HEAD> statement:

```
<BODY>
```

Now you need to tell the person accessing your page who it belongs to, no matter what browser they're using. You want everyone to see the name of your page, so use the <H1> command.

In Internet Assistant, you change the style in the style drop-down box in the upper-left side of the desktop. Currently, the style should be set to Normal, P.

5. **Change the Style from Normal, P, to Heading 1, H1, as shown in Figure 3-16.**

6. **Type the same information as you did for the title field.**

    We typed "Paul M. & Mary J. Summitt Home Page." You need to use your own name.

7. **Press Enter.**

8. **Select the style for the next line.**

    Choose Heading 2, H2.

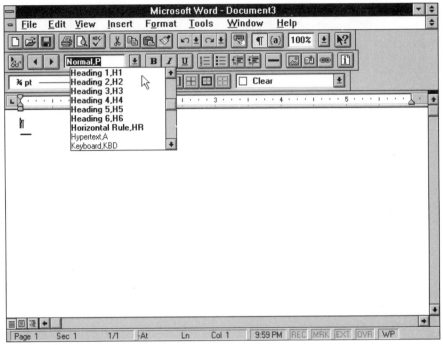

Figure 3-16: Change the style for your first paragraph to Heading 1, H1.

9. **Type anything you want.**

We typed "Home of VREvolution" for our virtual reality programming and consulting company.

The page isn't blank anymore. Ours looks like Figure 3-17.

But there's not much there yet. You'll want to add a picture of yourself or a graphic that illustrates what your company does or sells. For this example, just pick a .GIF file that you have lying around. We selected a screen capture from Intel's 3DR demo. The .GIF file is shown in Figure 3-18.

The first thing you need to do at this point is save the HTML file. Choose Save As from the File menu. Name the file HOMEPAGE.HTM. Make sure that your cursor is on the third line. (In our case, this line is directly below Home of VREvolution.) To insert the file, select the Picture button, as shown in Figure 3-19.

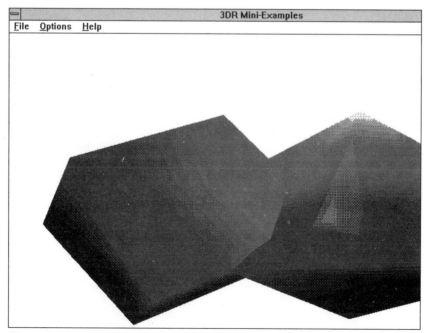

Figure 3-17: Our page isn't blank anymore. Is yours?

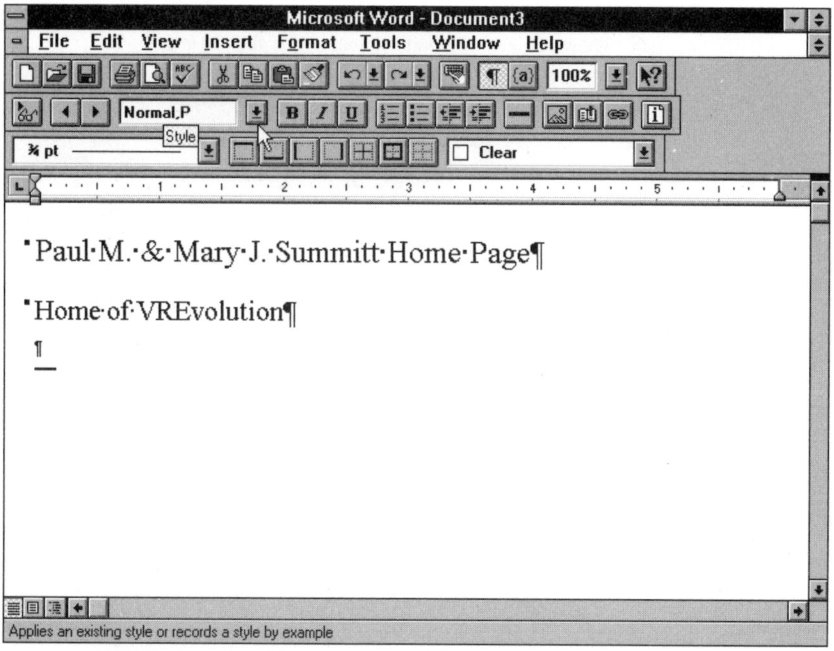

Figure 3-18: The .GIF file for our home page.

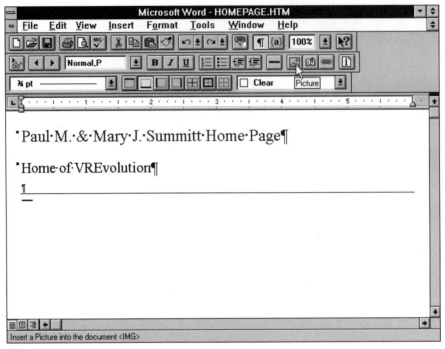

Figure 3-19: Select the Picture button in the toolbar.

The Insert Picture dialog box appears (See Figure 3-20), asking you for the name of the .GIF file that you want to include. It is important that the .GIF and .HTM files be located on the same drive and in the same directory. Notice also, that at the bottom of the Insert Picture dialog box you can designate text to be displayed if the graphic can't be viewed by someone who is using a character-only browser.

Congratulations! You've created a basic home page. You can look at ours (See Figure 3-21) by loading HOMEPAGE.HTM into your browser. Listing 3-1 is the entire HTML code for HOMEPAGE.HTM, so you can see exactly what the program looks like.

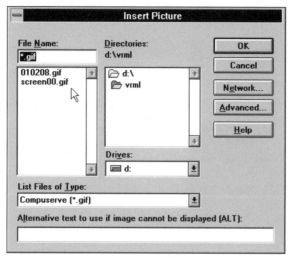

Figure 3-20: The Insert Picture dialog box, where you choose
the .GIF file that you want to load into your document.

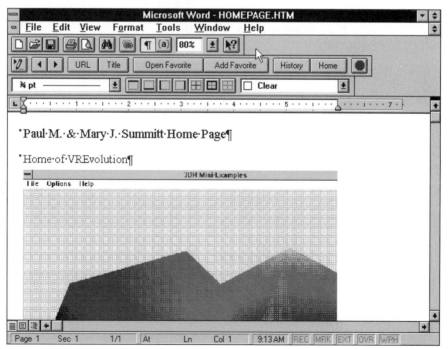

Figure 3-21: Paul and Mary's home page with the graphic from
the .GIF file.

Listing 3-1: HOMEPAGE.HTM

```
<!doctype html public "-//IETF//DTD HTML//EN">
<HTML>
<HEAD>
<TITLE>Paul M. & Mary J. Summitt Home Page</TITLE>
<META NAME="GENERATOR" CONTENT="Internet Assistant for Word
1.0Z">
<META NAME="AUTHOR" CONTENT="Paul M. Summitt">
</HEAD>
<BODY>
<H1>Paul M. &amp; Mary J. Summitt Home Page</H1>
<H2>Home of VREvolution</H2>
<P>
<IMG SRC="screen00.gif" ALIGN="BOTTOM"><HR>
</BODY>
</HTML>
```

Now, we don't want you to think that this home page is some kind of fantastic HTML document — because it's not. It's simple. It's basic. And it was done in a reasonable amount of time with a reasonable amount of effort. You'll notice that there are several HTML commands in Listing 3-1 that we never said anything about in the exercise. That's the beauty of Internet Assistant. It enables you to plan your work and format it without having to memorize a lot of code and commands.

We make some modifications to this home page later in the book. Right now, however, you have the template started for the home page for your virtual world using VRML.

Moving On

In this chapter, you looked at HTML and saw how a Web page is constructed. You learned about several software options in addition to those on the CD-ROM. You then joined us in creating a simple Web page using Microsoft's Internet Assistant for Word 6.0. We return to the page that we created when we show you how to move from HTML to VRML and back in Chapter 14.

Right now, we're moving on to Chapter 4, where you'll be introduced to virtual reality.

Virtual Reality on the Internet

We begin this chapter by looking at the evolution of communication from its beginnings in the oral tradition, through the written or literary tradition, to the visual tradition, and into what Paul calls the interactive tradition. In the interactive, we find virtual reality.

We then look at what virtual reality (VR) is. We look at how VR has been produced on the PC by using such programs as VRBASIC and REND386. We also explain the difference between VR and other forms of media and how the human senses come into play.

Next, we look closer at the issue of standardization, and then we close Chapter 4 by looking at several VRML samples that are available on the Internet.

What Is Virtual Reality?

In order to understand the significance of virtual reality and its place in communication, you need to examine the philosophical history of communication in general. VR will be, and is at times, a controversial area in communication. Today, with the ability to manipulate photographic images and the future possibilities of this, as represented by fictional films such as *Rising Sun*, what is reality, real, or the truth, becomes questionable from one minute to the next. Anyone trying to understand VR needs to have a grasp of these aspects in order to use and create virtual worlds.

Introduction

We don't mean to be melodramatic but, . . .

In the beginning, was the spoken word. This spoken word was powerful enough to bring worlds into being and separate the light from the dark.

> And God said, Let there be light: and there was light.
>
> *Genesis 1:3* (King James Version)

The spoken word even had the ability to create life.

> And God said, Let the earth bring forth grass, the herb-yielding seed, and the fruit tree yielding fruit after his kind, whose seed is in itself, upon the earth: and it was so.
>
> *Genesis 1:11* (King James Version)

According to communication theorist Neil Postman in his book *Amusing Ourselves to Death,* truth is the very essence of the spoken word for people who are tied to oral tradition. Even during the beginning of what Postman calls the *literary tradition,* reading can be seen as simply a method of training the student for public speaking.

When we talk here about the oral and the literary traditions, we're talking in terms of communication. Literary should be seen as dealing with the skill of writing. Literary, therefore, has nothing to do with art. Both the Bible and such works as the *Iliad* and the *Odyssey*, while today seen in written form and considered literature, came to us from the oral tradition of communication.

Another point you should keep in mind is that literacy has to do with the mastering of a skill within a specific tradition. Our current terminology tends to suggest that a literate person is one who is well read; yet children, who have read very little, tend to be more visually literate than their parents. An individual, therefore, can be literate within one tradition and illiterate within others.

As time moved forward (an interesting concept in and of itself in that the word *forward* suggests some positive aspect), the written word slowly engulfed the spoken word. The effect of this new literary tradition on society and the individual was to change the way people thought. In fact, it changed the very structure of both language and thought. Before this change, truth was seen in the spoken word of the individual (that is, "a man's word is his bond"); under the literary tradition, legal contracts were required. Truth lay in the written word rather than in the spoken word.

These changes in language and in the very structure of our thoughts continued in the transition from the literal to the visual tradition. Once again, the locus of truth moved — this time from the written word to the visual image. Now, seeing is believing. This concept can be substantiated by the analysis of surveys of where people get their news. Within the past twenty years, we have seen the trend move from newspapers, the written word, to television, the visual image. To some, if you see it on TV, it has to be true.

All of this is not to imply that these traditions cannot coexist, side by side, to a certain extent. People still talk. We still take the word of friends as being truthful to an extent. Some people still read (you, dear reader, are an example one of these literary literates). The question, however, is where does truth exist for the individual? Research studies have shown that today the masses get the majority of their information from television and find it the most believable of the available media. This, despite TV news reenactments and dramatizations. Heavy users of television believe the world to be a much more dangerous place than crime statistics actually show it to be. This is because, for these individuals, truth lies in the visual, in the televised. The television is their tool for information gathering.

The tools that people use to gather information structure how they think about the information. When you think in the oral tradition, it affects how you think. When you think in the literary tradition, that tradition affects how you think. Despite objections concerning individuals who read or about believing what our friends say, currently the masses believe what they see on television. But it's not over. This alteration, or restructuring, in our thinking, continues today with society's transition into what Paul calls, for lack of a better phrase, the *interactive* tradition.

Paul's academic papers on virtual reality and communication

Paul has discussed virtual reality and communication, as well as the transition to the interactive tradition, in previous academic papers. Some of these papers, as well as some research studies, are available for download in the CyberForum libraries on CompuServe.

We're now moving into a time when experiencing will be the locus of truth. This is not to imply that we have not experienced reality in the past. It does suggest a change in the definition of reality. Each of us experiences our own reality, and, therefore, each of us has his or her own truth. Many times we group together as communities and accept similar concepts as being reality and truth. In the future, however, as diversity becomes accepted as the norm, truth may be found in our interactive experience of the reality, virtual or otherwise.

We need to look at an example of the difference between the visual and the interactive in order to understand this concept. In television news, the viewer is guided by an authoritarian media to see and hear what that dictatorship wishes the viewer to see and hear. Yes, these are strong terms, but just try to look at something on television that the director and other television professionals have not prepared for you to see. Understand that everything you see and hear is preordained by these individuals. The camera operators determine what the director has to choose from as far as visuals are concerned. The audio operators determine what the director has to choose from as far as sounds are concerned. The producer determines what stories will be seen in the newscast and how it will be presented. The viewers themselves have little choice because these determinations are made by unseen authoritarians. Of course, the viewer can turn the television off, choosing between what the authoritarians have selected and nothing. The simple truth is, however, that the majority doesn't.

In the interactive, the viewer determines where the stories come from and who tells those stories. A multiplicity of voices becomes heard and the owners of those voices seen. The viewer determines from what vantage point to view a disaster, or whether to see disasters at all. So, just as the literary replaced the oral and the visual "conquered" the literary, we suggest that the interactive will devour the visual as more and more people discover that they don't have to take the prepackaged content of the television medium.

This new interactive tradition has at its nucleus a technology known as virtual reality. Most people know very little about VR other than what they've read or seen in the media. Imagine basing your perception of what VR is on what you've seen in films such as *Lawnmower Man* or *Total Recall.* The simple fact is that this new medium is far too important for you to base your perceptions of it on such fictional accounts as these. Many people, however, have accepted these presentations as truth.

Before we go much further, we need to look at what VR is and examine how the long-term use of VR could change the way we think about and see the world. First, we need to define some things. ·

Defining virtual reality

Because VR has William Gibson's idea of cyberspace at its core, it is important to define the concept of cyberspace at this point. Other terms used to describe this notion are *cyberia, virtual space, virtual worlds, dataspace, the digital domain, the electronic realm, artificial reality,* and *the information sphere.*

VR, to us, represents one way of defining cyberspace. We must now turn our attention to defining VR.

For our purposes, we'll define *virtual reality* as an electronic communication medium and an extension of the human senses through which we expand our capability for actual experience. By "extension of the human senses," we mean that VR can be seen in a similar context as the telephone. The telephone extends the range of our ears by enabling us to hear voices from many miles away. Virtual reality can extend all of our senses in ways that we're just now beginning to contemplate.

To many people, the technology is the thing. They're wrapped up in the new toys. They are sometimes referred to as *console cowboys, techno-weenies,* and *compu-nerds.* As you've seen in the Web surveys discussed in Chapter 2, that stereotype doesn't necessarily represent the actuality of the current Web users.

The machinery is not the medium of communication. The machinery is not the technology. The machinery is just a manifestation of the technology. Technology is the *structure* of how things get done, not the mechanical tools used in getting things done. You don't need to be concerned about examining the tools of the technology. What you need to examine is how communication takes place within those tools and what effect those tools have on the communication that's taking place. Philosopher Roberto Eco suggests that each technology is nothing more than a grouping of semiotic codes and systems. Yet, many definitions of VR have tended to describe it in terms of the machinery, the tools.

For example, virtual reality has been described by some as simulations that can be experienced using head-mounted displays (HMDs) and gloves.

Others, basing their definitions on films such as *Lawnmower Man*, have portrayed VR as alternative worlds composed of computer-generated images that required HMD's, data-gloves, and data-suits for human interaction. Even artificial reality pioneer Myron Krueger suggests that the term implies a requirement for an HMD and a glove.

As you can see, people often define cyberspace and virtual reality in terms of tools. However, you need to examine the concepts of cyberspace and virtual reality in more than just a "machine" context. You need to look past the machines to the communication that takes place between the users of those machines and the programmers of those tools. The interaction with the technological device of the television is not what should interest us, just as it is not the interaction with the technological device of the computer or the goggles and glove that should be examined. The communication interaction takes place between the programmer and the user, not between the machine and the user.

For many people this is a rather difficult concept to accept. We need to look at an example in order to grasp this more fully. Paul is at work one day and needs to tell Mary something. He picks up the phone and calls home, but Mary has gone to the store so the answering machine answers the call. Paul leaves the message that he will be late getting home that night. When Mary gets home, she listens to the message.

Question: Who is the message from? Paul? Or the answering machine? The answer is that the message is from Paul. It is not the answering machine that will be getting home late that night.

Communication does not need to be instantaneous to occur between humans, even when occurring within a computer program. It is not the computer that is asking you whether you want to install the software on the CD-ROM to your hard disk. This is a direct question asked by the programmers who put the software and CD-ROM together.

Just as when we ask someone how they are doing and expect a specific answer, the programmer is asking a specific question and expecting a range of specific answers. The computer is not asking anything. The question comes from the programmer, just as the message that he was going to get home late came from Paul.

In defining virtual reality, some people have focused on the process of communicating. When discussed in terms of technology as machine, VR can be defined as an environment in which VR, the experience, takes place. VR, as environment, is an electronic communications medium, not the machine. This definition of VR makes it clear that VR refers to an experience, rather than a machine. This virtual experience is determined and defined across the dimensions of vividness and interactivity.

VR defined by vividness and interactivity

A *vivid environment* is one in which information is available in abundance to one of the human senses. The larger the amount of information available to that specific human sense, the more vivid the environment. If you add to this the idea that several senses can be presented with stimuli, or information, simultaneously (sensory breadth) and that the definition, or resolution, of that stimulus can be high or low (sensory depth) the concept of vividness becomes more easily understood.

Interactivity, on the other hand, is the degree to which an individual can take part in changing the form and content of the mediated, or virtual, environment in real time. Several academic researchers have looked into the interaction between the individual and the machine, but little research has been done on facilitating communication in media that is highly interactive.

According to the preceding definitions, most modern media are low in sensory breadth (because they rely on one, or at most two, of the human senses), low in sensory depth, and provide little opportunity for interaction.

A telephone conversation can be viewed as a form of virtual reality. The person you are communicating with is there but, at the same time, somewhere else. The telephone is high in interactivity but low in vividness due to its low breadth and low depth. A letter is another low-end example. Here, interactivity is extremely low as are breadth and depth. The higher the level of interactivity, and sensory breadth and sensory depth, the more real the situation is to the user. Vividness and interaction are factors that help to determine and influence how real the user believes the experience to be.

An extension of the interactive concept is the application of stress to the user. Research has suggested that the higher the perceptual and cognitive stress level that is placed on users, the more willing they are to accept low vividness in their perceptions of the real. Understanding these ideas gives you a beginning understanding of the concept, rather than the hype, of virtual reality.

There is not enough space here to cover all of these concepts as deeply as they need to be covered, so we will leave these topics for another time, another place, and perhaps, another book.

Virtual reality as a medium of communication

What are the media?

What is a medium?

A *medium* is a means of effecting or conveying something (as in the means of transmission of a force, or effect) or a channel of communication. These channels of communication include public presentations, such as speeches, poetry readings, and stage drama, as well as the more commonly thought of electronic media, such as radio, television, film, and the telephone. Currently, virtual reality is similar in purpose and form to these electronic media. VR doesn't just provide representations of events to an audience. VR, in its current form, has a determining role in what you see and how you make sense of it.

Communication research has shown that people spend about seven years of their lives watching television. What happens if people use VR in the same manner that they currently use TV and computers? Some people could spend as much as 20 or more years inside virtual reality! Why do people spend this much of their lives with television, and why would they spend considerably more time with VR?

Virtual reality will shape our attitudes, beliefs, and behaviors just as much or more as other forms of mass media have. VR, therefore, has more potential, because of the vividness factors and the potential amount of time that will be spent inside of it, for both empowerment or enslavement, than television or any other previous medium of communication.

Conclusions in regard to the definition of VR

Keep in mind that today VR, and perhaps VRML, is mainly hype and hyperreal. It's generally understood among communication researchers that an important purpose of the media is to extend our knowledge of our environment beyond people, places, objects, and events that we have direct contact with, and, therefore, can directly experience. This is exactly what the various forms of virtual reality do, except that in virtual reality the user can directly experience and have interaction with these simulations of reality.

It has been suggested that reality itself is hyperrealistic. Einstein suggested that reality is part of the theory that one uses to understand the world, not part of the world itself. If this concept of reality is true, then VR is more capable of enslaving the user than television could ever hope to be. The more of your human senses that are engaged by an event, the more real that event will seem to you. Add perceptual and cognitive stress, and the user will probably accept any experience as real.

Empowerment of the user can come if interactivity is increased. The question of interactivity and behaviors hasn't really been dealt with in the Version 1.0 specifications of VRML. Users can manipulate the world they enter, but few can create their own worlds.

At present, users are as dependent on VR programmers for their virtual worlds as they are on TV programmers (program creators as well as those who schedule the programs) for their television programming.

Some programmers realize this power they possess to manipulate and enslave VR users. It is our hope that the creation of VR software and languages such as VRML will enable users to create their own worlds so that users can be empowered rather than enslaved by this new technology.

The Human Computer

The human body is the most sophisticated computer on this planet at this point in time. It has at least five data input devices from which you constantly gather information. The central processing unit that you call your brain then accesses and evaluates this information. This is an on-going, never-stopping process.

The five basic data input devices are hearing, sight, touch, smell, and taste. Most of the information that you use to make decisions must come through these five data input devices. Hearing and sight are the two data input devices that dominate.

Hearing

We look at hearing first. The reason for choosing hearing first is historical. As we discussed earlier in this chapter, human societies traveled through an oral tradition first in regard to the location of truth. Hearing was believing. We suggest that because of this, hearing must have been the dominant input device at one time in human history. In order to discuss this human data input device properly, we must first look at sound itself.

Sound

Sound is the result of an object's vibrating back and forth. The vibrations create waves in the material around the object, and those waves move outward and away from the object. The energy of the original object's vibration causes the individual molecules of the material to move, not the material itself. In moving, the molecules collide and bounce off other molecules, creating a chain reaction that passes a portion of the energy of the original object's vibration along to the next molecule.

One of the best known examples of this effect is called the *ripple effect.* As an example, when you drop a small stone into the center of a pool of water, you see waves extend from the point of impact in all directions, each wave having the same intensity as every other wave.

These waves are examples of sine waves. You probably learned about sine waves in your junior or senior high school math classes. SINEWAVE.BAS, the sine wave file that's in the BASIC\CODE subdirectory on the CD-ROM that accompanies this book, shows an example of the ripple effect. This example uses the BASIC programming language; it will run using either GWBASIC or QBASIC (one of which should have come with your computer), or you can run SINEWAVE.EXE, which can be found in the BASIC\DEMO subdirectory.

Listing 4-1, the program for the sine wave, was written and compiled using Microsoft QuickBasic 4.5. Although Basic is not a language you would want to try to write 3D programs with (in fact, one would be foolhardy to even try; Paul knows), it is useful for learning structured programming techniques. Your computer has a version of BASIC in the DOS subdirectory. We have used this language for this example because it is one that you have readily available. You can load and run the following .BAS file into it, or you can load the .BAS file into your word processor if you just want to look at it. You can run the .EXE version of the program from the DOS prompt or by choosing Run from the File menu in the Windows Program Manager.

Listing 4-1: SINEWAVE.BAS

```
10 REM  This is a simple BASIC program to demonstrate a sine wave
20 WORD = 0
30 FOR TIME = 0 TO 40 STEP .25
40 AMOUNT = INT(26 + 25 * SIN(TIME))
50 PRINT TAB(AMOUNT);
60 IF WORD = 1 THEN 100
70 PRINT "SINE"
80 WORD = 1
90 GOTO 120
100 PRINT "WAVE"
110 WORD = 0
120 NEXT TIME
130 END
```

Figure 4-1 shows what a sample run of this basic program looks like.

```
                                                      WAVE
                                                    SINE
                                                 WAVE
                                            SINE
                                       WAVE
                                  SINE
                            WAVE
                      SINE
                WAVE
            SINE
        WAVE
SINE
WAVE
 SINE
   WAVE
       SINE
            WAVE
                  SINE
                        WAVE
                              SINE
                                    WAVE
                                         SINE
                                             WAVE
```

Figure 4-1: A sample run of SINEWAVE.BAS.

Notice that the vertical wave moves from the top of the screen to the bottom of the screen. SINEWAV2.EXE, which is in the VB\DEMO subdirectory on the CD-ROM, turns the wave on its side horizontally and places it over a system of coordinates so that you can look at it more closely.

This demonstration program was written using Visual Basic 3.0 for Windows Professional Edition. Listing 4-2 shows the code (found on the CD-ROM in the VB\CODE subdirectory), and Figure 4-2 shows a sample run.

Listing 4-2: SINEWAV2.BAS (Code written by Paul M. Summitt and Todd Porter)

```
FRMABOUT.FRM
Option Explicit
Declare Function SetSysModalWindow Lib "User" (ByVal hWnd
↳As Integer) As Integer
Sub cmdOK_Click ()
Unload frmAbout
SineWaveForm.Cls
End Sub
```

(continued)

Listing 4-2 *(continued)*:

```
Sub drawsine ()
  Dim A, X1, Y1
  Dim count
  Dim MaxX
  MaxX = 50
  count = 300
  Dim tp%
  For X1 = 0 To MaxX Step .01
   count = count + 2
   tp% = DoEvents()
   Y1 = (Sin(X1) * 700) + 1000
    PSet (Y1, count), QBColor(Rnd * 15)
   If count > frmAbout.Height - 500 Then Exit For
  Next
End Sub
Sub Form_Load ()
Dim di%
  cmdOK.Enabled = False
  left = screen.Width / 2 - Width / 2
  top = screen.Height / 2 - Height / 2
  Show
  di% = SetSysModalWindow(frmAbout.hWnd)   'lock window
  drawsine
  cmdOK.Enabled = True
End Sub
SINEWAVE.FRM
Sub AboutItem_Click ()
  Load frmAbout
End Sub
Sub ClearItem_Click ()
  Cls
  SineWaveItem.Enabled = False
  LabelItem.Enabled = False
  pnlStat = "Click Demonstration to run Demo again."
End Sub
Sub Command1_Click ()
End Sub
Sub ContentsItem_Click ()
  R = WinHelp(SineWaveForm.hWnd, "/sinewave.hlp",
  HELP_INDEX, CLng(0))
End Sub
Sub ExitItem_Click ()
  End
End Sub
```

```
Sub Form_Load ()
left = screen.Width / 2 - Width / 2
top = screen.Height / 2 - Height / 2
pnlStat.Caption = "Click on Demonstration Menu item to get
L started."
End Sub
Sub Form_Unload (Cancel As Integer)
End
End Sub
Sub LabelItem_Click ()
  X0 = ScaleWidth / 2
  Y0 = ScaleHeight / 2
  CurrentX = 200
  CurrentY = 900
  Print "A"
  CurrentX = 200
  CurrentY = 1200
  Print "M"
  CurrentX = 200
  CurrentY = 1500
  Print "P"
  CurrentX = 200
  CurrentY = 1800
  Print "L"
  CurrentX = 200
  CurrentY = 2100
  Print "I"
  CurrentX = 200
  CurrentY = 2400
  Print "T"
  CurrentX = 200
  CurrentY = 2700
  Print "U"
  CurrentX = 200
  CurrentY = 3000
  Print "D"
  CurrentX = 200
  CurrentY = 3300
  Print "E"
  CurrentX = 2300
  CurrentY = 700
  Print "Compression"
  CurrentX = 2000
  CurrentY = Y0
  Print "[————————One Cycle————————]"
```

(continued)

Listing 4-2 *(continued)*:

```
CurrentX = 4000
CurrentY = 4000
Print "Rarefaction"
pnlStat = "Click File to Exit, Clear to run again, or Help"
End Sub
Sub mnuExit_Click ()
End
End Sub
Sub ShowGraphItem_Click ()
  Cls
  X0 = ScaleWidth / 2
  Y0 = ScaleHeight / 2
  Line (400, Y0)-(ScaleWidth - 200, Y0), QBColor(1)
  Line (400, 400)-(400, ScaleHeight - 600), QBColor(1)
  CurrentX = 500
  CurrentY = 25
  Print "y-axis"
  CurrentX = ScaleWidth - 750
  CurrentY = Y0 - 300
  Print "x-axis"
  SineWaveItem.Enabled = True
  pnlStat = "Now click on Sine Wave to draw Wave!"
End Sub
Sub SineWaveItem_Click ()
  Dim A, X1, Y1
  Dim count
  MaxX = 10000
  count = 410
  pnlStat = "Drawing Wave..."
  For X1 = 0 To MaxX Step .01
   count = count + 5
   tp% = DoEvents()
   Y1 = (Sin(X1) * 1500) + 2400
   PSet (count, Y1), RED
      If count > SineWaveForm.Width - 300 Then Exit For
      'label1 = count
  Next
  pnlStat = "Now Click Labels to name the parts of the wave"
  LabelItem.Enabled = True
End Sub
SINEWAVE.BAS
'   Help engine declarations.
'   Commands to pass WinHelp()
```

```
Global Const HELP_CONTEXT = &H1        ' Display topic identified by
└ number in Data
Global Const HELP_QUIT = &H2           ' Terminate help
Global Const HELP_INDEX = &H3          ' Display index
Global Const HELP_HELPONHELP = &H4     ' Display help on using help
Global Const HELP_SETINDEX = &H5       ' Set an alternate Index for
└ help file with more than one index
Global Const HELP_KEY = &H101          ' Display topic for keyword
└ in Data
Global Const HELP_MULTIKEY = &H201     ' Lookup keyword in alternate
└ table and display topic
Declare Function WinHelp Lib "User" (ByVal hWnd As Integer, ByVal
└ lpHelpFile As String, ByVal wCommand As Integer, dwData As
└ Any) As Integer
Type MULTIKEYHELP
  mkSize As Integer
  mkKeylist As String * 1
  szKeyphrase As String * 253
End Type
```

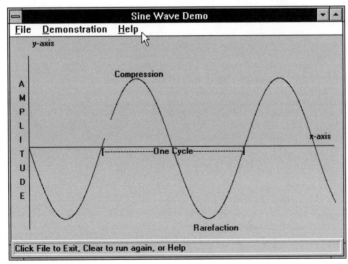

Figure 4-2: The sine wave as shown in SINEWAV2.EXE.

The Cartesian plane is named in honor of the French philosopher and mathematician René Descartes. Descartes is given credit for creating the system of designating the locations of individual points along the various x-, y-, and z-coordinates. This system created a new mathematics known as *analytic geometry*.

Place the sine wave on an x and y coordinate system, known as the *Cartesian plane,* as shown in Figure 4-3. Here the horizontal represents the x-axis, and the vertical represents the y-axis. Of course, horizontal and vertical are subjective terms, though they have been accepted as universals due to a common experience. The x-axis and y-axis are defined by the arbitrary zero point that you assign. This arbitrary zero point is defined by your subjective point of view. We discuss the concept of relativity in regard to coordinates a little later in the chapter, but for now go ahead and use the subjective concepts that you've come to accept as absolutes for horizontal (left and right) and vertical (up and down).

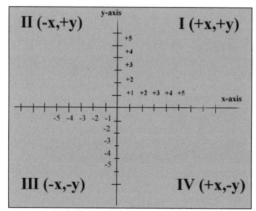

Figure 4-3: The x and y coordinate system for a Cartesian, 2-dimensional, plane.

The Cartesian plane can be divided into four quadrants:

➡ The upper-right quadrant, known as Quadrant I, where both x and y are positive

➡ The upper-left quadrant, known as Quadrant II, where x is negative and y is positive

➡ The lower-left known quadrant, known as Quadrant III, where both x and y are negative

➡ The lower-right quadrant, known as Quadrant IV, where x is positive and y is negative

At this point in the discussion, we're interested only in Quadrants I and IV. Figure 4-4 represents the new coordinate system that we'll use.

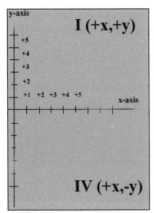

Figure 4-4: The new coordinate system
with only Quadrants I and IV included.

Assume that the sine wave represents a sound wave. The height of the wave is referred to as the wave's *amplitude,* which is measured from the zero point on the y-axis to either of the peaks, upper or lower. Think of amplitude as a measure of the wave's intensity or loudness. In sound, this measurement is expressed in decibels (dB). For each increase of about 10 dB, the perceived loudness is doubled. The intensity becomes painful to the human ear at about 120 dB.

The number of times that the complete wave passes a particular point each second is referred to as the wave's *frequency.* The frequency is measured on the x-axis, with each mark or number on the axis representing one second in time. Frequency is measured in units called hertz (Hz), or cycles per second. A cycle is measured from the zero point through the first, or positive, peak back down to the zero point, through the negative peak, and back to the zero point again. The human ear can perceive frequencies that range between 16 Hz and 20,000 Hz.

We used the word *perceive* in relationship to both amplitude and frequency. No two human beings hear things exactly the same way. The range of frequencies that an individual can hear is based on biological factors and life experience, and it differs from one person to another. Paul played in rock bands during his early years and then was exposed to the sound of weapons' being discharged while he was in the service. Whatever frequency range he was born with, the repetitious exposure to loud music and gunfire probably decreased it. There is no standard frequency hearing level, but there is a standard frequency range. This range was developed to take into account the variability between individuals. The result is an arbitrary standard for hearing that represents the variability that is inherent when comparing human beings. No one individual's hearing is average in a statistical sense. Each individual has a unique zero point that is then compared with the arbitrary zero point.

The human ear

Hearing, which is known as the *auditory system,* can be thought of as a highly evolved extension of the sense of touch. You can feel sounds. You do feel sounds. Look at Figure 4-5. Sounds are created by the vibrations of a human membrane known as the *eardrum.* We delve deeper into the sense of touch later in this chapter.

We can determine the location and estimate the distance of sounds because we have two ears. In effect, having two ears enables us to perceive sound as three-dimensional because of the differences in time between when a sound wave reaches the first ear and when that same wave reaches the other ear. This sound localization process enables you to know, for example, that the footsteps you hear are coming from behind you.

If you close your eyes for a moment and listen, you can "picture" the environment around you. Currently, for us, the warm purr of the computer is directly in

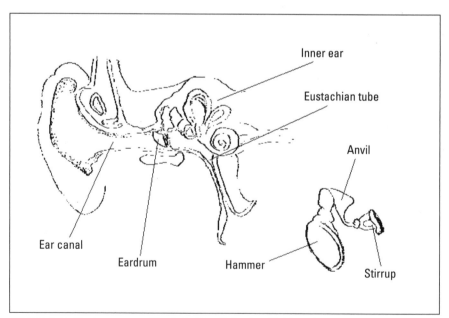

Figure 4-5: The human ear (illustrated by Catherine Heisinger).

front of us, with the keyboard keys clicking away, just below and slightly closer than the computer. Off to our left, *Glacier Bay* is playing on the stereo. The coffee pot is perking, making fresh coffee in the kitchen down the hall. The air conditioning just came on, as indicated by the small roar from the vent near the bay window behind us. With only one ear, you can't make location determinations such as these.

Hearing the virtual

The location of the sound source in relationship to your two ears is also important. The greater the difference between when sound reaches one ear and when it reaches the other ear, the better you can determine its location. A sound coming from directly above you, below you, in front of you, or behind you provides less location information.

Hearing, therefore, is an important aspect of the perceived reality around us. As we mentioned earlier, the oral tradition came first. Without hearing, primitive humans could not have survived in their environment.

When VR systems and their programmers ignore sound, therefore, the virtual experience that they provide is less realistic than when they take sound into account. Although hearing is a primary data input device for the human computer, if it were the only input device, we would be considerably hampered in our data-gathering abilities. We'll now turn to look at the sense of sight (pun intended).

Sight

The second tradition, the literary, deals with sight as the primary data input device. In reading, you use your eyes to scan the page and truth is created through this interaction. Truth, therefore, is located in the written word. The third tradition, the visual, also deals with sight as the primary data input device, but it incorporates hearing. The image provided by the television now becomes the source of truth, and "seeing is believing" becomes the battle cry of the masses. As with sound, we need to look at how human beings see in order to understand sight's implications for VR.

Light

You can think about light in three ways. One explanation of light is that it is made up of individual particles known as *photons*. This explanation comes from the fact that light appears to travel in straight lines or in rays. However, this explanation does not account for some of the other characteristics of light.

Considering light as a wave or a series of waves explains some, but not by any means all, of the remaining characteristics of light. The best way to explain light is to say that it is made up of both particles and waves. Any good high school physics or physical science text can provide a more detailed explanation of these two methods of considering light.

Color

Light is made up of frequencies just as sound is. Certain frequencies are too low for humans to see, while others are too high. Within the visible range of light for the human eye, certain frequencies represent specific colors. Lower frequencies tend toward the red, with a lower frequency of 430,000,000,000,000 Hz, and higher frequencies tend toward the violet, with an upper frequency of 750,000,000,000,000 Hz.

Anything outside of these upper and lower frequencies is not visible to the human eye. Once again, however, not every human's vision is the same. Some people are nearsighted, some are farsighted, and some are color blind. No two individuals perceive color in exactly the same manner. Again, we are dealing with comparing individual perceptions to an arbitrary range of acceptable standards.

Vision

Seeing occurs when light bounces off an object and is reflected into the human eye, so without light, vision is not possible. Look at the cross-section of the human eye provided in Figure 4-6.

The way the system works is that light reflected off the object you are looking at is bounced into your eyes. The amount of light that enters your eyes is determined by your eyelids and your pupils. The pupil is the circular black area in the center of each eye. Actually, the pupil sits in the middle of the iris and is an opening that's controlled by a group of muscles that expand and contract this hole. If the light level is high, the muscles contract the hole to allow less light in. If the light level is low, the muscles expand the hole to allow more light in.

The pupil is immediately behind the lens. The muscles around the lens change its shape so that you can focus on objects close by and then shift to objects far away.

The thickness and color of the lens has a lot to do with age. At first, babies can't shift focus at all. As the lens becomes more elastic and controllable, they can quickly change focus from one subject distance to the next. Later in life, as the lens grows thicker, the ability to change focus slows.

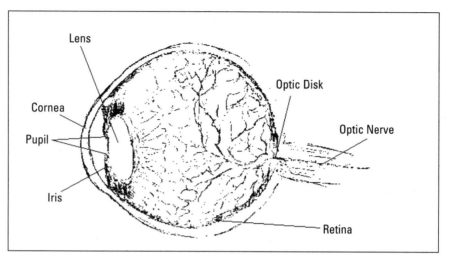

Figure 4-6: A cross-sectional view of the human eye (illustrated by Catherine Heisinger).

Another effect of age on the lens has to do with color. The lens is slightly yellow to begin with, so it absorbs some blue and violet (and some harmful ultraviolet) light frequencies and prevents them from reaching the retina. As humans grow older and the density of the lens increases, more of the blue and violet light frequencies are absorbed, causing a difference between age groups in the perception of the color of some objects.

Finally, light entering the eye falls on the retina. The retina is a thin layer of light-sensitive material that lines most of the interior of the eye. On the back side of the retina are the photoreceptors know as *rods* and *cones*. It is here that light is converted to electrical impulses that are then transferred to the brain through the optic nerve. How does it do that?

Rods are extremely sensitive to brightness, but they are sensitive only to black-and-white information. Cones, on the other hand, are less sensitive but provide information concerning color and detail. Cones come in three types. The first type senses blue wavelengths, the second senses green wavelengths, and the third senses red wavelengths.

Although each eye has millions of rods and millions of cones, each eye has more than 15 times as many rods in each eye as there are cones. Cones are highly concentrated at the rear wall of the retina where light is focused, but less concentrated away from this area. Rods, on the other hand are less concentrated in this area, but more concentrated away from this area.

This arrangement of rods and cones has a dramatic impact on sight. The area that you focus your eyes on is fully detailed, while material to the edges of your vision is out of focus. For example, when you look at the center of a page of text, you know that there are words at the top of the page, but those words are unreadable while you are focused on the words in the center of the page.

Focus also has a dramatic impact on the perception of what is real. When you look at a television or film screen, all of the picture is in focus. No part of that picture is out of focus unless it has intentionally been made out of focus for aesthetic reasons. Promoters of the new high-definition television formats claim that every blade of grass in a picture of a grassy knoll will be in sharp, clear focus. That, however, is not the way the human eye sees things.

Depth perception

With two eyes, judging distances and depth is, for the most part, simple. This is because of *parallax,* which means that each eye's view of the world is slightly different even though the separation between your eyes is only about 2 ^{1}/$_2$ inches. This slight difference in view is probably the most powerful cue for depth that you have available. Even with one eye, however, there are other visual cues that help you judge depth. These cues are static cues, motion cues, and physiological cues.

Static cues include interposition, shading, brightness, size, linear perspective, and texture gradient.

⇒ If one object blocks our view of another object, we know that the first object is closer than the second. This cue is called *interposition.*

⇒ *Shadows* and *shading* are other cues about the depth of an object. Shading also provides information about the physical features of an object.

⇒ The relative *brightness* and *sharpness* of an object provide cues to its distance. The farther away an object is, the duller and fuzzier it appears.

⇒ The *size* of an object is a cue that is based in large part on past experience. When you see an apple and a watermelon in a picture and both of them appear to be the same size, experience tells you that the apple is closer to you than the watermelon. What if the apple is just extremely large? Its size would throw off your ability to judge depth, wouldn't it?

⇒ *Linear perspective* is created because of the perception that the farther a building's edge is away from you, the shorter that side of the building is.

This convergence of the building's lines give you vital clues as to the depths involved. The cue, however, can also be deceptive if the lines are not actually uniform.

→ The closer to you an object is, the more well-defined the *texture* of the object is. The farther away from you the object is, the less well-defined the texture is. Texture is an extremely subtle, but powerful, cue.

Motion cues are only available when the objects that you are looking at are moving. Objects that are closer to you appear to move faster than objects that are farther away.

Physiological cues for judging depth include accommodation and convergence. They are both based on how the eye moves.

→ *Accommodation* refers to the effort necessary for the eye muscles to adjust the lens to focus on closer objects. These muscles are more relaxed when focusing on distant objects than when focusing on near ones. This type of cue, however, can often be incorrect.

→ *Convergence* is a reliable method for judging distances of less than 20 feet. The eye has to turn toward the nose in order to focus on any object that's less than 20 feet away. The closer the object, the more toward the nose the eye must turn. Convergence can provide reliable information, but not very powerful cues for depth.

Field of view

Although you can focus on only a small area, your field of view is between 180° and 270°. This is because each eye can provide a 90° view and can pivot to either side by about 45°. This peripheral vision is an important clue to the level of reality you are dealing with. One way of knowing that television and films are less real is because the field of view is small.

Joining hearing and sight

Presentations via media such as film and television, which have joined the oral and the visual together, provide engaging experiences. How many times have you said that you saw something, when what you really saw was a film or television representation of that something?

Did you *see* the McCarthy hearings in 1954? Did you *see* the first Mercury launch in 1961? Did you *see* the deaths of John F. Kennedy and the man accused of shooting him in 1963? Did you *see* the Tet offensive in Vietnam during February and March of 1968? Did you *see* Robert Kennedy's assassination in June of 1968? Did you *see* Neil Armstrong walk on the moon in July of 1969? Did you see O.J.'s attempted getaway and the subsequent trial? Did you see the Oklahoma City bombing? Did you *see* . . . Did you *see* . . . Did you *see* . . . Did you *see* the latest news on the television last night?

The answer to all of the questions, no matter what your age, is an emphatic No! You didn't *see* any of these events. What you saw was television, or television's representation of those events — interpreted, homogenized, selected, and fed to you just as your mother fed your first baby food to you.

This is the danger of one-way, producer-controlled, limited sensory media products.

Were the events represented *real?* Yes. Was what you saw *real?* Only to the level that you accepted it as real.

This is the important aspect of this discussion. *Real* lies with the individual. It is a product of that individual's perceptions interpreted through the various data input channels available at any given point in time.

But what happens when you add other data input channels to the mix? Does it become more real?

Touch

There are two basic systems of providing the sense of touch. The first has to do with the skin's use of *mechanoreceptors* to measure the amount of pressure and displacement that's caused by an object's pressing and/or moving against the skin. The second, called *proprioception,* involves the muscles' sending information to you concerning the size, weight, and texture of an object that you have picked up. Together, these two methods make up the *haptic system,* which is more commonly referred to as the sense of touch.

Mechanoreceptors provide you with information concerning the shape, texture, and temperature of an object. They do this by comparing the known quality of the skin to the unknown quality of the object. These kinds of tactile sensations are extremely difficult to create within a virtual environment.

Proprioceptive information is derived from the muscles and tendons, which provide information about the shape, force, and firmness of an object. Muscles move in response to the force required to hold an object. The simple act of holding an object tells you a great deal about the object's shape. A brick's shape is much different than that of an egg. The force required to pick up something also tells you a great deal about the object. Holding a brick requires less force than holding an egg. Finally, the object's resistance tells you a great deal about the object. A brick pushes back harder than an egg does.

These two systems work in conjunction with each other. However, age works against these systems. As you get older, you have fewer mechanoreceptors in their various locations in your body — another example of how and why people perceive things differently.

Have you ever felt cold? How about hot? These statements are subjective and have no objective relationship to the mathematical reality. They exist only within the individual reality. Walk into a room filled with 20 people, where the temperature is set at 72°, and you will have 21 subjective accounts concerning the warmth or lack thereof in the room. The objective mathematical reality is that the temperature is 72°. There are 21 subjective realities. Individuals exist within their subjective reality, created through their perceptions and historical interpretations of the mathematical reality. And these perceptions and historical interpretations are provided through their input data devices, which are known as the human senses.

Smell

Most of us don't even recognize most smells unless they are particularly pleasing or offensive. Even then, constant exposure to obvious smells dulls our ability to distinguish them. The sense of smell, then, becomes a product of the individual and the quality of difference. In other words, you smell something only when it's different. If you cannot see the source of a smell that is both new and different from what you are accustomed to, you can create visions of that object within your individual reality. At the same time, a picture of honeysuckle can recall memories of its smell within your individual reality.

The response to a smell, like responses to other stimuli, is subjective. Again, what smells pleasant or offensive is a subjective response. In many cases, these responses are created through a combination of the smell stimuli itself and past life experience. The reality of the smell, therefore, differs from one individual to the next.

Taste

The sense of taste can be seen as a highly refined extension of the sense of smell. At the same time, it has some of the qualities of the haptic system. All of the previous comments in relationship to the sense of smell and the sense of touch, therefore, are applicable to the sense of taste.

As before, we are dealing with individual perceptions rather than with universal objective realities. What tastes good to one person may taste terrible to another. Sweetness and sourness are also subjective qualities. With regard to the reality of any given experience of tasting something, judgments are extremely subjective and outside the realm of objective mathematical reality.

Virtual Reality as the Communication

Because any VR environment is based on an arbitrary interpretation and perception of some objective mathematical reality, the programmer's efforts should be stressed in the direction of providing some sort of commonality of experience for the user. What we mean by this is that a programmer who is creating a virtual world for the experience of others should look toward those common experiences that both the programmer and the users have had.

This approach is similar to the efforts taken by television and film producers and by advertising and marketing executives: Know who your audience is, know what you want to say to it, and know what you want the audience to do after it is exposed to your media message.

All communication is purposive and purposeful. There is a reason, conscious or unconscious, for the creation of every message — oral, written, visual, or VR.

You have the best chance of getting your message across if you know the audience, the message, and the result. Not knowing, or understanding, any one of these three factors can endanger your message.

Any communication can be described by using psychologist J. R. Kantor's 1959 formulation for a psychological event. Each act of communication is a psychological event for the individual who is receiving the communication. The formula is

$$PE = C(k, sf, rf, hi, st, md)$$

where C symbolizes that the event consists of an entire system of functions in interaction; k represents the uniqueness of the event itself; sf represents the communicative stimulus of the event; rf represents the choices of possible responses to the event; hi represents the history or life experience of the individual with this particular type of event; st represents the immediate setting or environment where the event takes place; and md represents the medium of interbehavior or the channel, or channels, through which the communication itself takes place.

With VR, the event can have every bit as much impact and reality as the individual desires, whether that desire is conscious or unconscious. The event therefore becomes part of the reality, through becoming part of the life experience.

Virtual Experience

Now we need to move into how we can achieve this virtual experience with the technologies available to us. One way we can achieve this is through DOS- and Windows-based virtual reality programs.

PC-based virtual reality

Several programs have been designed to create virtual worlds on a PC-compatible computer. In this section of the chapter, we look at some of these programs and some of the worlds created with these programs. To prepare for working with VRML in the next section of the book, we also discuss the levels of vividness and interactivity that are found in the programs.

Understanding the terms in this list will make it easier to understand the program descriptions that follow:

> A *library* is a collection of small object-file modules that are already written to do a specific function in other programs.

> *Render* is the process of converting a graphics image into an array of pixel colors for display.

> An *engine* is what runs the program's routine, so a *rendering engine* is the program's routine that displays the images on the screen.

> *Porting* means converting or translating a program from one platform to another, and *portable* means that a program can be ported.

2Morrow World Builder

2Morrow World Builder is Todd Porter's virtual world creation and viewing system (See Figure 4-7). You can use this program to build objects or worlds up to 4MB in size. A demo shareware version of 2Morrow World Builder is on the CD-ROM included with this book.

Figure 4-7: Exploring and creating virtual worlds with 2Morrow World Builder.

The demo version is an unregistered version with some of the features disabled. Your saved worlds can contain a maximum of five objects, and you don't receive the 2Morrow Object Modeler, which is a powerful CAD program that enables you to create objects. The registered version of this software does not have these limitations. A coupon in the back of this book tells you how to order it.

One last comment before we move on to the next software program. You can use 2Morrow World Builder to create worlds and then translate those worlds to VRML using one of the conversion programs that's on the CD-ROM included with this book. We discuss this possibility more fully in Chapter 11.

AVRIL

AVRIL 2.0 (See Figure 4-8), which was released in March 1995, is Bernie Roehl's most recent PC-based VR application. AVRIL stands for *A Virtual Reality Interface Library*. Written almost entirely in ANSI-C, the PC version includes some short assembly language routines to help handle some of the fixed-point math.

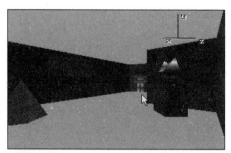

Figure 4-8: Looking at a virtual world using AVRIL.

This program represents Roehl's effort to create a VR program that can be ported to other platforms. Roehl has been writing software for more than 20 years. He currently works as a senior software developer and system administrator and as a freelance software developer.

According to the documentation, AVRIL was designed to be fast, portable, and easy to use. Its fast, polygon-based rendering engine and set of support routines make creating virtual worlds reasonably straightforward. You can find AVRIL under the filename AVRIL20.ZIP in the libraries of CYBERFORUM. AVRIL is free for noncommercial use. It includes a relatively simple and well-documented API (Applications Programming Interface) that makes it easier to develop applications.

This aspect of the program may be important for anyone who is interested in virtual world development on the PC because most current PC VR libraries are very expensive. Roehl says in the documentation that "AVRIL is intended to give everyone with an interest in VR an opportunity to develop some simple applications without having to invest huge sums of money."

Roehl has also written the excellent book, *Playing God* (1995), in which he discusses the construction of virtual worlds in great detail. A valuable asset that's available in both the book and the downloadable file is the C source code for the world renderer. Examining and studying this file can give you a considerable understanding of the requirements of creating virtual worlds and graphic design for the PC.

You can use AVRIL to create worlds and then translate those worlds to VRML using one of the conversion programs on the CD-ROM that's included with this book. We'll discuss this possibility more fully in Chapter 11.

REND386

REND386 was written by Bernie Roehl and Dave Stampe. Roehl wrote the program in C, and Stampe used assembly language to optimize the program's speed. The first version of the program was made available on the Internet at the end of January 1992. REND386 went through five generations before Roehl and Stampe each went on to separate projects.

REND386 Version 5.0 (See Figure 4-9) was included in the book *Virtual Reality Creations* (1993) written by Roehl, Stampe, and John Eagan. It included support for head-mounted displays (HMDs); the PowerGlove; and greater keyboard, joystick, and mouse controls, just to name a few. The Mattel PowerGlove is a low cost data glove that can be converted for use with some PC virtual reality programs.

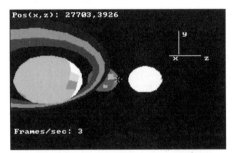

Figure 4-9: Exploring a virtual world with REND386.

The only negative thing about the book is that it doesn't include the source code to REND386. Several downloadable versions of both Version 4.0 and Version 5.0 are available at the locations listed in Table 4-1, and some of these files include the source code.

Table 4-1: Where to Find REND386

Filename	Forum
DEMO4.ZIP	CYBERFORUM
DEVEL4.ZIP*	CYBERFORUM
CREND.ZIP	CYBERFORUM
DEVEL5.ZIP	CYBERFORUM
JIREND.ZIP*	CYBERFORUM
JIREND.EXE	CYBERFORUM
EEDEMO.ZIP	CYBERFORUM

* signifies that the file includes source code

As a minimum, REND386 requires a 386SX, 20 MHz, IBM PC-compatible computer with about 800K of free hard disk space and at least 540K of free memory, VGA graphics, and a color monitor. We have operated REND386, Version 5.0, from a floppy disk for specific application purposes.

You can use this program to create worlds and then translate those worlds to VRML using one of the conversion programs on the CD-ROM that accompanies this book. We discuss this possibility more fully in Chapter 11.

Superscape VRT

Superscape VRT (*Virtual Reality Toolkit*) is a commercial VR package for the PC (See Figure 4-10). The minimum requirements for this software are a 386SX IBM PC-compatible computer, 8MB of RAM, a hard disk, VGA graphics, a color monitor, a Microsoft-compatible serial mouse, and DOS version 5.0.

Figure 4-10: Exploring a virtual world with Superscape VRT.

This program provides you with a graphical user interface that provides access to the four main operating areas: the shape editor, the world editor, the console editor, and the visualiser. The *shape editor* provides you with tools that enable you to create the objects you will place in your virtual world. You can then use the *world editor* to place the objects in the world and work on the various behaviors of the world. The *console editor* enables you to create special consoles for your virtual world. Finally, the *visualiser* enables you to access the world you are building in order to see how the world looks and behaves.

Superscape VRT also provides a programming language called Superscape Control Language (SCL). SCL allows for detailed control over the virtual world you are creating.

Virtual Reality Studio

Virtual Reality Studio is available in versions 1.0 and 2.0. We found a copy of Version 1.0 in a used bookstore for five dollars (See Figure 4-11). A full working copy of Version 1.0 is on the disk that's included with Linda Jacobson's *Garage Virtual Reality* (1994) and on the CD-ROM that's included with Ron Wodaski's *Virtual Reality Madness* (1993).

Figure 4-11: Exploring virtual worlds with Virtual Reality Studio 1.0.

The minimum hardware and software requirements for Virtual Reality Studio 1.0 are an IBM-compatible AT computer, DOS 2.0, and CGA graphics. Virtual Reality Studio can be used for creating self-executing demos and games for use with 286s and above.

Virtual Reality Studio also supports a mouse, a joystick, and an Ad Lib-compatible sound board. The Virtual Reality Studio Editor allows you to create and test your virtual worlds. You can use a mouse to move around the main View window as you create and edit.

Virtus WalkThrough VRML

Virtus WalkThrough VRML is another package that you can use to create virtual worlds on a PC (See Figure 4-12). You also can used it to create VRML worlds.

Virtus WalkThrough VRML is included on the CD-ROM in the Virtus building. Click on the building and VisMenu will begin the installation process.

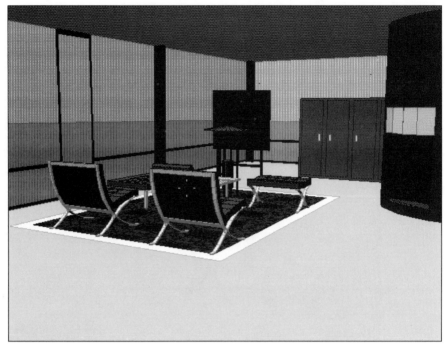

Figure 4-12: Exploring the possibilities of Virtus WalkThrough VRML.

Using Virtus WalkThrough VRML, you can create 3D environments that include both text and graphics. Chapter 11 includes a more detailed discussion of this software.

Vistapro

Vistapro (See Figure 4-13) is a commercially available, three-dimensional, landscape simulation program. A complete working copy of Version 1.0 of this software is available on the CD-ROM that's included with Ron Wodaski's *Virtual Reality Madness* (1993). A demo of Version 3.0 is available on the disk that's included with Linda Jacobson's *Garage Virtual Reality* (1994).

The minimum software and hardware requirements for Vistapro 1.0 include an IBM PC-compatible computer with at least 640K, DOS, a Microsoft-compatible mouse, VGA graphics, and at least 3MB of free space on the hard drive.

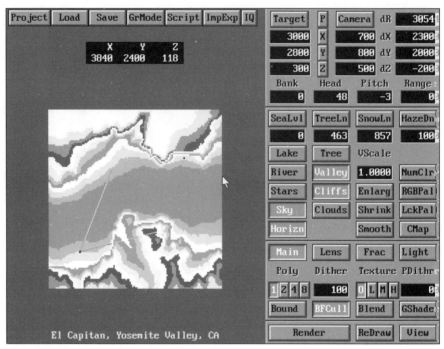

Figure 4-13: Exploring the virtual El Capitan, Yosemite Valley, California, with Vistapro.

VR386

VR386 (See Figure 4-14), written by Dave Stampe, is an expansion of the REND386 software. It has the same minimum hardware and software requirements as its predecessor. This program is sometimes referred to as REND386 Version 6.0.

This program is freeware and is downloadable from the libraries of CYBERFORUM on CompuServe. The file is named VR386.ZIP. VR386 also allows for the use of extended memory in creating worlds, which can be a tremendous advantage with extremely large worlds.

This is another program that you can use to create worlds and then translate those worlds to VRML by using one of the conversion programs on the CD-ROM included with this book. We discuss this possibility more fully in Chapter 11.

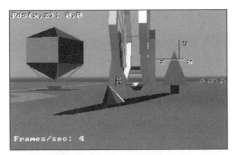

Figure 4-14: Exploring virtual worlds with VR386.

VRBASIC

VRBASIC (See Figure 4-15) is a commercial software package for the PC that's available from Waite Group Press.

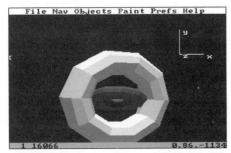

Figure 4-15: Exploring a virtual world using VRBASIC.

The program requires a 386 CPU, 25 MHz or higher, (although we have run it on a 386SX, 20 MHz, with a math coprocessor), at least 1.6MB of free hard drive space, VGA color graphics, MS-DOS 5.0 or higher, and 570K of free conventional memory. A demo of this program can be found in the CYBERFORUM libraries on CompuServe. The file is VRBDEMO.EXE.

This is another program that you can use to create worlds and then translate those worlds to VRML using one of the conversion programs on the CD-ROM that accompanies this book. We discuss this possibility more fully in Chapter 11.

VRCreator

VRCreator (See Figure 4-16) is a commercially available product from VREAM for IBM-compatible machines running DOS 3.3 or higher. It also requires a 386 CPU running at 25 MHz or higher, 4MB of RAM, 6MB of free hard drive space, VGA graphics, a mouse, a joystick, and an extended memory manager such as HIMEM.SYS and EMM386.SYS.

A demo of this program is available on the disk included with Tom Hayward's *Adventures in Virtual Reality* (1993).

World Development Tools

If you have some abilities to program using one of the various C/C++ programming languages, you can also use one of the world development tools that are available. We discuss some of these tools in this section. Although these products are not directly capable of creating VRML worlds, all of them, in conjunction with the specific programming language used, are capable of working with VRML.

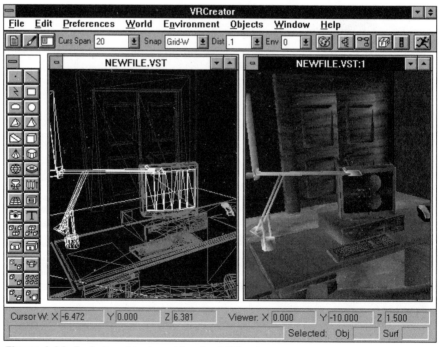

Figure 4-16: Exploring virtual worlds using VRCreator.

Autodesk Cyberspace Development Kit

Autodesk is one of the world's largest software companies. It is probably best known for its extremely successful computer-aided design (CAD) product, AutoCAD.

In late 1988, Autodesk assembled a virtual reality research team. In the spring of 1993, Autodesk released the Cyberspace Development Kit. The product was capable of running on a 386 PC with 8MB of RAM. It was not an application in and of itself but rather a tool for users to create their own applications and 3D spaces with development languages such as C/C++.

DIVE Laboratories Amber

At the time of this writing, another product was just being announced that may be of considerable assistance in the creation of virtual worlds and products for accessing those worlds. In late September 1995, Peter Rothman, president of DIVE Laboratories, announced the release of the WindowsNT version of the Amber virtual reality development system. Windows 3.1 and 95 versions of the software were to begin shipping during the first week of October and the SGI version on October 15.

Amber supports OpenGL under Windows NT and reads both VRML and NGG object files. This product is a toolkit for use with a C/C++ programming language. Currently, Microsoft Visual C/C++ 1.52 and 2.2 are required. Future versions for Borland compilers and for Microsoft Visual Basic are in the works.

Sense8 WorldToolKit

Sense8 Corp. was founded in 1990 by Eric Gullichsen and Patrice Gelband when they left Autodesk to pursue their own vision of what virtual reality could be. WorldToolKit, the company's flagship product, is not an applications software product, but rather a library of C computer language routines that you can use to create your own virtual reality applications.

The product is available on a number of platforms and will run on a 486 running Windows. A new product called World Up and a Visual Basic-compatible version of WorldToolKit are being released that will also allow for world development.

Vividness versus interactivity

Take another look at the figures in the past several pages. Look at the differences in graphics quality from one program to the next. Better still, if you can, buy or download these programs and experiment with them.

One thing you'll discover rather quickly is that there's a trade-off between the levels of vividness and the levels of interactivity that each program is capable of. Generally speaking, the higher the graphics quality, the lower the level of interactivity, and the opposite is also true.

With few exceptions (and those exceptions require high-end machines and expensive add-ons), the programs listed previously provide relatively low-end graphics. As this technology is still in its infancy, we can expect to see dramatic changes over the next short months. Windows 95 may be only the beginning of these improvements.

Depending on the software, the level of interactivity ranges from moderate to high. The REND386 family of VR systems, "crude" as far as graphics are concerned in the words of some, provides some of the highest interactivity available from programs aimed at the home PC.

And how does VR fare on the Internet in terms of vividness and interactivity levels? That's the subject of the next part of this chapter.

Virtual Reality on the Internet

Within days after the announcement of VRML's worldwide launch on April 3, 1995, more than 50 VRML sites sprang up around the Web. Within 30 days, this number had risen to several hundred. We delve into the history of VRML in Chapter 6.

VRML Version 1.0 provides a relatively low level of interactivity. Its creators say that they'll address this issue in Version 1.x, which is supposed to be ready in December 1995, and Version 2.0, which should be available in March 1996.

All is not well in the VRML world. Some complain that the language is hard to work with and that other, more vivid and more interactive alternatives were and are available. In the next section of this chapter, we look briefly at some of those alternatives. Then we discuss vividness and interactivity with a virtual reality pioneer.

Other Contenders for the Web VR Standard

The following contenders are just some of the systems that could have become the ancestor of VRML instead of Open Inventor. More information concerning these programs can be found at the URLs listed in Chapter 15.

DIS

Probably the most advanced and official standard is IEEE 1278, better known as the Distributed Interaction Simulation (DIS) protocol. Heavily used in U.S. military simulation systems, the DIS network library was developed for use on UNIX systems. The system has also been tested on SGI and SUN systems. The system was created by John Locke, David R. Pratt, and Michael J. Zyda of the Department of Computer Science at the Naval Postgraduate School in Monterey, California.

RenderWare

RenderWare is available from Criterion Software Ltd. in England. This software is an API for building 3D applications on several platforms, including DOS, Windows, and SunOS/Solaris. It is very popular but also very expensive.

The Object Oriented Geometry Language

OOGL is a language that was developed at the Geometry Center at the University of Minnesota. It has seen several years of extensive testing as a geometric visualization format in math, physical science, and engineering. There's a WWW interface called WebOOGL that you can download and check out. OOGL is a nonproprietary language that includes sophisticated graphics and support for hyperbolic geometry.

Manchester Scene Description Language

Created at the University of Manchester in England, the Manchester Scene Description Language enables the user to specify 3D objects. A C/C++ parser library is also available.

Java

Java is a new programming language from Sun Microsystems. Java works in conjunction with HTML, enabling developers to include Java programs called *applets* on Web pages. The applet is downloaded to the user's computer automatically and executed on the user's computer. Java brings a possibly richer level of interactivity to a Web page.

Jaron Lanier: Virtual reality on the Internet?

At the age of fourteen, Jaron Lanier managed to become a student in the chemistry department at New Mexico State University. Ten years later, he was helping to develop a new technology: virtual reality. Sought after by politicians on matters high-tech and featured prominently on the cover of financial magazines, Lanier is still, despite losing control of his company, VPL Research, and its patents in 1992, looking toward the cyberspace worlds of tomorrow. Now 34, Lanier travels widely consulting on and about cyberspace. We talked with him by phone in his home in San Francisco in July 1995.

Question: What's your take on the current status of virtual reality on the Web given things like VRML?

Lanier: First of all, VRML is a very exciting direction. If you go back to the start of virtual reality, the term *virtual reality* was actually a term I made up to try to indicate the notion of having a shared place that people could visit as opposed to just simulations for one at a time. The whole notion of virtual reality, at least the word *reality,* was to sort of convey this excitement of the possibility of networking with it.

So VRML is all very exciting. I think things are moving about as fast, I suppose, as they reasonably could be expected to. There might be a little bit of an overemphasis on the geometry of the environment as opposed to the functionality of the environment. What I mean by that is that VRML focuses really on the shape of the place. Experiencing virtual reality, that's not the most important part at all; the most important part is the interactivity. The functionality is the behavior of the imaginary places. With VRML, there's a lack there.

Another important thing is that what really makes virtual reality magical is that your body is in it. And your body can be different at different times. For instance, if you're a surgeon, your hand, instead of looking like a hand, might look like a surgeon's tool that's controlled directly by the movement of your fingers. In some cases that's actually an easier thing to do than picking up the tool. So another lack in VRML is that it doesn't take into account the body of the participants.

To me, VRML isn't quite at the virtual reality stage yet. It's more just virtual environments, but it's still a good start.

The other trend right now, as we speak, in the world of the Web, is the Java language. That, to me, is very important because it's starting to bring in this notion of behavior and functionality into Web pages. What I hope to see in the future is a merger of VRML type things with Java type things. These things would include the notion of the human body rather than just an out-the-window view of a world. Very, very important is that those things include really good authoring tools to enable programmers to work with them.

Question: Do you think the Hollywood special effects, such as were in *Johnny Mnemonic*, are what cyberspace will look like in the future?

Lanier: I think the hope of virtual reality is that rather than just having a particular appearance, it'll be like a giant dream convention for all humanity in which a million flowers are blooming. And so, I would think that that would be one future among millions of others. It's supposed to be a giant festival of the imagination so that particular sort of thing is one kind of place, and I think there will be many, many, many, many others as well.

Question: So you think there's going to be multiple realities then?

Lanier: Oh, absolutely!

Question: According to the last Web survey, doesn't NetScape hold about a 90 percent share of the browser units being used?

Lanier: Well, that'll be interesting to see. AOL might have quite an impact on that, you know. I've looked at the AOL browser lately, and it's, I think for a very large number of people, it'll be very effective.

As far as NetScape goes, I mean, it remains to be seen. Some of the things NetScape has talked about doing are offensive, I think. But, as far as what they've actually done so far, it's not offensive. So I think it just remains to be seen what happens with NetScape.

The point though, is that just because they're distributing the browser doesn't mean that they control the Web. HTML and the Web are not controlled by anybody.

Question: Authoring tools, which ones are you using right now? Which ones do you recommend?

continued

continued

Lanier: Right now, it's a real problem. The only ones I've ever really liked were the VPL ones, and I think that's just because I was there. I just think they got to a point where they were just great to use. I had some problems also, but they had that feeling of fluid creation that you get in an authoring tool.

Like PhotoShop has this wonderful feeling when you use it, and the VPL tools were the only ones that had that kind of feeling for virtual reality development. Right now, obviously, they're not supported and there's a problem there.

So, I'm not really sure what to recommend. I don't think you can use C-style programming for virtual reality and make a good fluid, wonderful world. I just don't think it works that way.

Putting What You've Learned into Practice

All right, now you're ready to dive into the Web and go surfing to find VRML. Turn on your computer, load up SPRY Air Mosaic or whichever Web browser you've decided to use, and we'll guide you to one of the most exciting VRML locations on the Web. Keep in mind that things on the Internet change on almost a minute-by-minute basis, and these pages may be anywhere from slightly to dramatically different when you access them than when we wrote this part of the book.

1. **Type** http://www.lightside.com/3dsite/ **as the Document URL and then press Enter.**

    At the bottom of the screen, SPRY Air Mosaic provides information about the status of the access request. It should begin loading the document quickly. In a few moments, you have something similar to Figure 4-17 on your screen.

    Look around a little bit. Notice the 3DSite graphic. When you first accessed the site, you saw a little Mosaic graphic, and you were able to watch as the browser retrieved the 3DSite graphic from www.lightside.com. Then the Mosaic graphic changed to the 3DSite graphic. The browser loads a default graphic until is can access the graphic listed. Just under the graphic are two blue underlined phrases.

2. **Click on the word 3DSite.**

At the bottom of the screen you'll notice that you are now loading ad.html. In a few minutes, after the graphics have loaded, your screen looks similar to Figure 4-18.

Explore this page. Notice the excellent graphic showing the constellations surrounded by multiple replications of the earth. Read through this material. When you've read it all, move on to the next step.

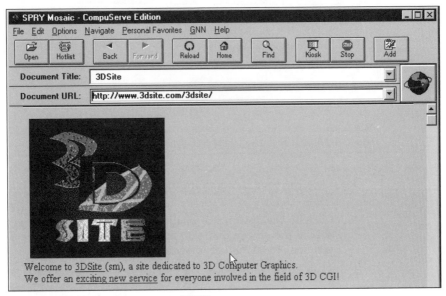

Figure 4-17: You've now accessed 3DSite.

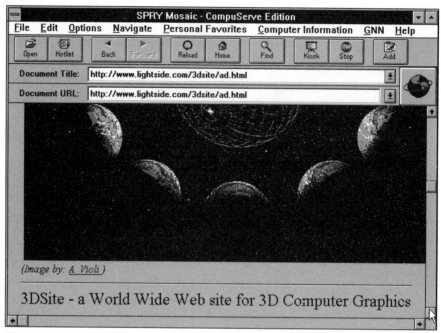

(Image by: A. Violi)

3DSite - a World Wide Web site for 3D Computer Graphics

Figure 4-18: 3DSite is one of the Web sites for 3D Computer Graphics.

3. Click the third button from the left in the toolbar, which is labeled Back.

4. Click on the downward-pointing arrow in the scroll bar at the right side of the screen until you are about midway down the page, where you see Model Market underlined and colored blue.

5. Click on Model Market.

A page that looks similar to Figure 4-19 loads.

Again, explore the page before you continue. Usually, several different types of 3D graphic projects are available. Your browser will be able to view some of the graphics, but not most of them. When you're finished looking around, go back to the top of the document again. Just under the graphic, you see Welcome to 3DSite's Model Market.

6. Click on Welcome to 3DSite's Model Market.

Read the page that appears. It looks similar to Figure 4-20.

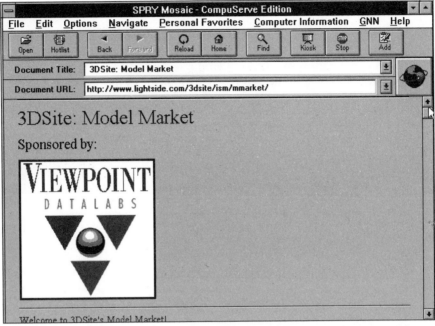

Figure 4-19: The Model Market provides a location for people to show their worlds.

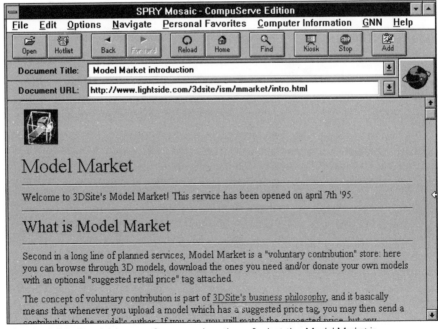

Figure 4-20: Read this page for an explanation of what the Model Market is.

7. Click the Back button to return to the page that looks like Figure 4-19.

8. Click the Back button twice to return to the page in Figure 4-17.

9. Click on the downward-pointing arrow in the scroll bar at the right side of the screen until you see CGI Information: Table of Contents.

    The phrase is underlined and highlighted in blue.

10. Click the phrase.

    A page loads that looks similar to Figure 4-21.

    Read through this information if you want.

11 Click on CGI and Animation Literature, References and Discussions.

    Again, read through the information on this page. Examine the various documents that are available for download or on-line reading.

12. Click on the Back button.

13. When the previous page has reloaded, move down the screen till you get near the bottom and then click on Virtual Reality Modeling Language (See Figure 4-22).

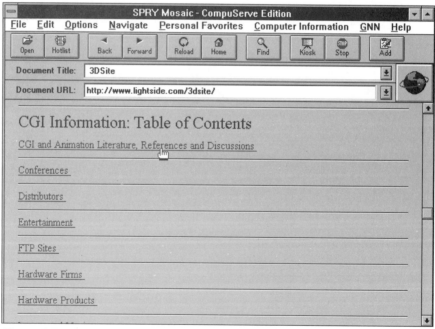

Figure 4-21: The CGI Information: Table of Contents page.

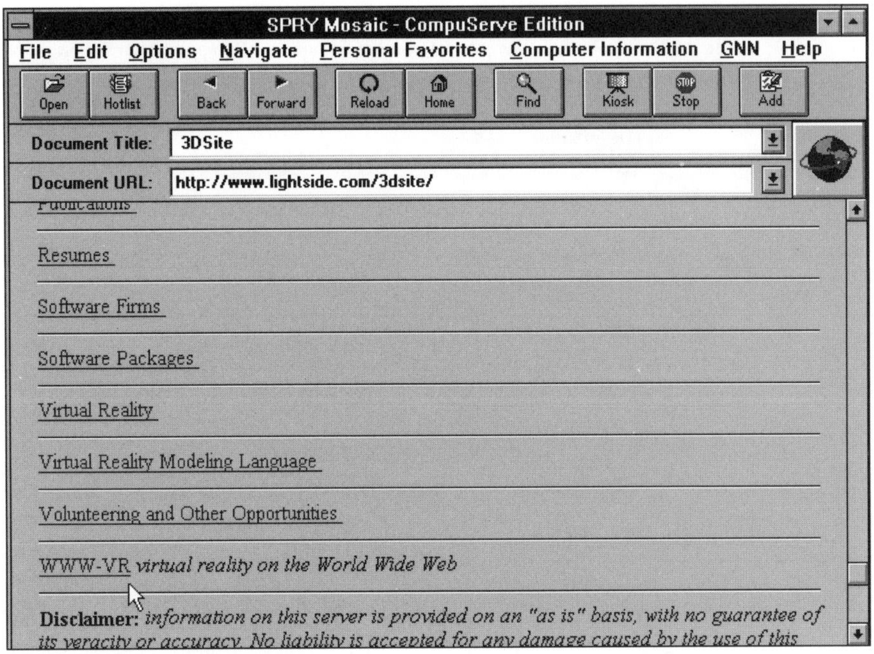

Figure 4-22: The Virtual Reality and Virtual Reality Modeling Language areas are of particular interest.

The new page looks somewhat like Figure 4-23. The URL is the important thing. You will probably want to add this URL to your Personal Favorites list right now.

14. **Click the Add button at the right end of the toolbar.**

That's all there is to it. If you choose Personal Favorites in the menu bar, you will be able to access this page quickly.

You'll want to explore this page fully. Actual VRML files, 3D file formats, information on upcoming events, mailing lists, reference material, and many other things are available here for your study and examination.

15. **Move down the page until you come to NewsGroups/Mailing Lists (See Figure 4-24).**

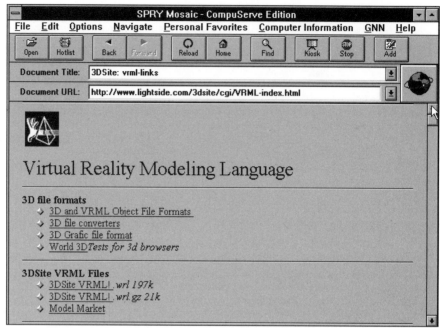

Figure 4-23: The Virtual Reality Modeling Language page has many interesting subjects.

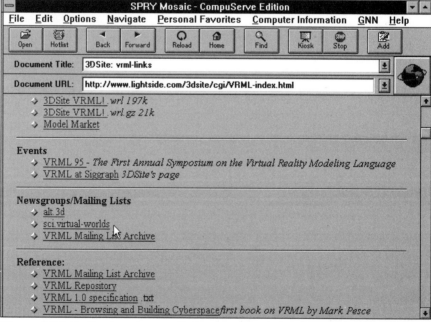

Figure 4-24: You'll enjoy what you find in the sci.virtual-worlds mailing list area.

You'll want to see the VRML Mailing List Archive later; for now take a look at `sci.virtual-worlds`.

16. **Click** `sci.virtual-worlds`, **which is highlighted and appears in blue.**

    The page that appears on your screen (See Figure 4-25) displays a listing of the available articles on the list that are about virtual worlds. As you get more involved in world building, you'll want to read some of these articles, so remember where they are. Oh, but you did add this to your Personal Favorites, didn't you?

    It's time to finish this tour. If you're anything like us, you've been online for 30 minutes to an hour already.

17. **Click the Back button to return to the page shown in Figure 4-24 and move down the page until you come to the listing of sites (See Figure 4-26).**

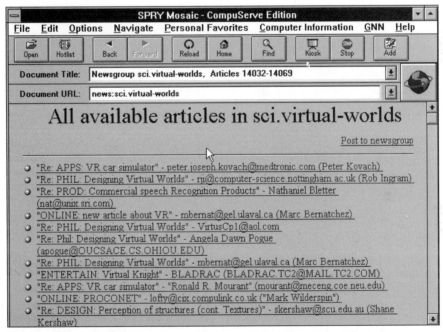

Figure 4-25: You'll want to read some of these articles later, so remember where you saw them.

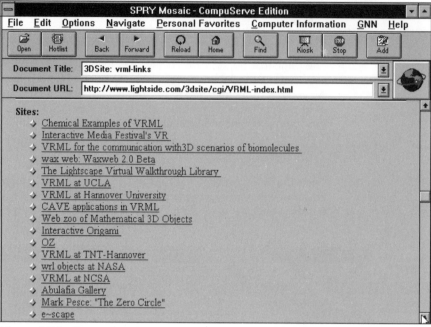

Figure 4-26: Choose the VRML at NCSA option.

18. **Click VRML at NCSA.**

    When the page finishes loading, you're at the National Center for Supercomputing Applications (See Figure 4-27). This page contains a great deal of information about how VRML works, what kinds of VRML software is available, and where to find VRML worlds. Read through the material, and don't worry if you're feeling a little bit of information overload at this point. It's normal. When you're finished reading this material, sign off.

19. **Choose Exit from the File menu.**

20. **Restore the Internet Dialer and hang-up the connection.**

In this exercise, you have used many skills that are involved in accessing the Web. You need these skills and more when you start building and accessing VRML worlds.

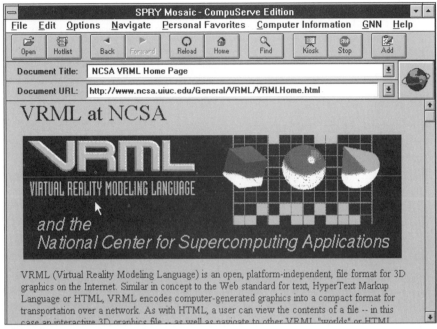

Figure 4-27: Visiting the VRML at NCSA site.

Moving On

This chapter began with a discussion of how human beings perceive reality and how virtual reality can be created. You saw that virtual reality is a medium of communication that is characterized by vividness and interactivity. You learned about various PC-based VR programs that can be used to build worlds that can be converted to VRML and about some of the world development tools that are capable of working with VRML.

You also saw VRML's "competition" — other systems that might allow virtual experiences. Virtual reality pioneer Jaron Lanier shared some of his thoughts on the current state of VR on the Web, and, finally, you explored virtual world sites on the Internet.

In Part I, you have become familiar with important concepts that you need to understand before moving on to Chapter 5, which begins Part II of this book, "What is VRML?"

PART II
WHAT IS VRML?

Defining
VRML

Virtual reality implies an interactive 3D environment. In this chapter, we look at how well VRML fulfills this expectation. We also revisit some of the expectations we discussed in Chapter 4 and consider how well VRML may or may not live up to them.

VRML

So, what is VRML? You find out in this chapter.

As we said in this book's Introduction, VRML stands for *Virtual Reality Modeling Language*. The *M* originally stood for *markup,* as in HTML, the *HyperText Markup Language*. In fact, VRML has been referred to as a virtual reality equivalent of HTML. It has also been called 3D for the masses and the new platform-independent standard for making sophisticated 3D viewpoint graphics available on the Internet. Basically, we can define VRML as a 3D scene description and layout language for use on the Internet and the World Wide Web.

VRML has been endorsed in industry and commercial magazines by Silicon Graphics, Digital, Intergraph, Netscape, NEC, Spyglass, NCD, Wavefront, Template Graphics, InterVista, and IBM. Software companies such as Caligari,

InterVision, Virtus, Inner Action, Silicon Graphics, VREAM, VR Lab, Template Graphics, InterVista, and ParaGraph are all either marketing VRML browsers or getting ready to market them.

So, we return to our earlier question, what is VRML?

In an article titled "VRML and the World Wide Web" in the June 1995 issue of *Dr. Dobbs Developer Update* (page 2), Joe Stewart, director of business development at Template Graphics Software (TGS), said that VRML "makes true 3D interaction on the World Wide Web possible." According to Stewart in this article, VRML is supposed to be platform independent, extensible, and have the ability to work using low-bandwidth connections (such as with a 14.4 Kbps modem).

VRML describes virtual worlds networked via the Internet. These worlds can be hyperlinked through the World Wide Web. Perhaps most importantly, VRML renders the world locally on your computer hardware. As a result, the levels of vividness and interactivity available through VRML are limited by your hardware's performance.

Keep in mind that we are discussing VRML in terms of its levels of vividness and interactivity. The performance of VRML, therefore, is largely dependent on your software and your hardware, not on the kind of Internet connection that you have. (This situation is much the same with HTML.) Of course, the speed of your Internet connection affects such interactivity aspects as download time, but if we accept a standard minimum of 14.4 Kbps, then any differences in vividness and interactivity will be created by the local platform and not by the Internet connection. Later in this chapter we return to the apparent restriction that this hardware and software dependence imposes on "3D for the masses." But first we examine how VRML and HTML are similar, yet different.

HTML and VRML: A Comparison

Chapter 3 examines HTML extensively. We need to return to what you learned there to compare HTML and VRML. As we do this, please remember, as we said in the Introduction, that you need to evaluate these programs based on what their creators' intent was rather than on what your expectations are.

HyperText Markup Language

HTML was created in 1989 at CERN. Tim Berners-Lee created the first Web server and browser at that time. HTML improved the connectivity and the interface of the Internet. It improved connectivity by allowing documents to be connected through semantic references. It improved the interface by allowing the inclusion of more than just the hyperlinking capability. For example, HTML can represent hypertext news, mail, documentation, hypermedia, menu options, database query results, graphics, and hypertext views of existing bodies of information. In this way, HTML begins to approach a standard document description format for the Internet.

As you learned in Chapter 3, HTML works by forming a union between HTTP, URLs, and the software on the computer that's accessing the Internet. This union allows access to information via the Web. Extensions to HTML's original syntax provide for the inclusion of still images, moving images, sounds, surveys, and tables in on-line documents.

The way HTML works is relatively simple. On a PC, after you're connected to the server, your Windows-based access software uses a *graphical user interface (GUI)*, a user interface system that relies on pictures and objects called *icons,* to specify some piece of specific information that you're searching for via its URL. The information is then transferred to your computer for interpretation and display.

That's it. After the transfer is complete, the server is done with most of its work. It simply sits there and waits for the next request from your computer. Your local computer, however, now has the job of interpreting and displaying the information selected. Your local browser software does all this work. After the information is displayed, you make choices about what embedded objects (other documents, still and moving images, sounds, surveys, tables, and so on) you want to see. Clicking these items sends a signal to the server that you want to access these items — starting the whole process over again.

HTML does a relatively good job of providing access to client software and documents that already exist on the Internet. The main problem with HTML is that finding things on the Internet is, for the most part, a matter of hit and miss. Of course, HTML was never designed to solve this resource discovery type of problem, so we really can't fault the protocol.

The result is, though, that if you don't already know the URL for a document, or it's not already hyperlinked to the page that you're on, finding it is extremely difficult. Finding most documents for which you don't have the URL, therefore, is many times simply an accident.

When we discussed the syntax of URLs in Chapter 2, you learned that a URL is a computer code. Understanding a URL is relatively easy when you're looking at it. Think of a URL as a zipcode. The problem is that, just as with zipcodes, remembering very many URLs for any length of time is practically impossible. That's because URLs are oriented to computers, not to humans.

At this point in time, there's really no way to visualize the Web (despite Hollywood's best attempts in such films as *Johnny Mnemonic*). The location of each document, its URL, is text based and textual in content. When you use your Web browser to access a document, as in Figure 5-1, you have to specify the exact URL that you want to access. If you mistype a URL, the browser gives you either the wrong document or a message that the URL doesn't exist.

A perfect example of a URL's lack of human orientation occurred while we were writing this chapter. After a phone conversation with Ashley Sharp of Virtus Corporation, Paul needed to access Virtus's Web page to download some information. In an effort to hurry the process, Paul typed the URL directly into the URL dialog box. What he typed was **http:/www.virtus.com**. Do you see the error?

When the browser reported that the server wouldn't grant him access, he called and left a message for Ashley telling her that the server wouldn't allow him in. A short while later, Paul tried to access another server by deleting part of the URL and retyping the new information. Again, Paul was denied access. After having about three servers deny him access, Paul took a long look at the URL.

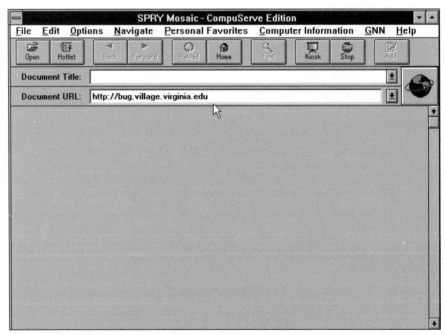

Figure 5-1: Because URLs are text based and textual in content, finding documents on the Web is difficult.

What he should have typed was **http://www.virtus.com**. Notice the two slashes, instead of just one, as he had typed before. Paul was extremely embarrassed when Ashley returned his phone call and he had to explain that his lack of access was not a server problem but his own pilot error. Don't worry about Paul. He'll live.

This lack of human orientation in HTML is problematic and less than satisfactory in many instances. From a standpoint of vividness and interactivity, HTML, while having the ability to be relatively vivid, is considerably lacking in interactivity. HTML is used for what has been referred to as *Web publishing.* The word *publishing,* however, implies a lack of changeability in the documents themselves.

Using your Web browser, access any page, anywhere, that represents the work of someone else and try to change that page. You can't do it. You can't change, subtract from, or add to that page in any way, shape, or form without the page author's permission. Yes, if you establish an account and place your own home page on the Web, you are adding to the Web as a whole. But you can't change anything there that doesn't belong to you. When you sign off the Web, the Web HTML world is just the same as if you'd never signed on to begin with (unless you've added your own page). Just look at Figure 5-2. So much for any HTML interactivity levels.

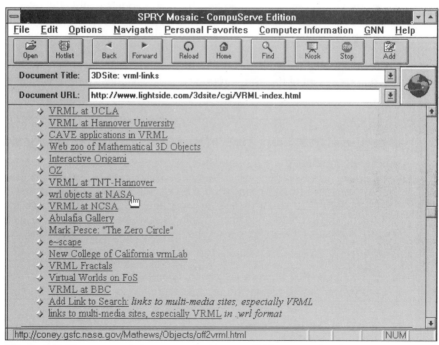

Figure 5-2: Try as you might, you can't change a Web page unless its creator authorizes you to change it.

The point here is that unless you are granted access to change a page, or you are changing a page that you yourself have created, you can only interact with HTML so far. The same is true to a large degree with VRML. There are some things that VRML allows you to do that we will see.

Virtual Reality Modeling Language

Making sense of our reality requires us to use our senses. As we said in Chapter 4, it is through the interpretation of the data gathered with our senses that our individual reality is created.

A URL is a location that doesn't really exist. It's a two-dimensional, virtual location. It might have height, and it might have width, but it has no depth. Because it is two-dimensional, we three-dimensional beings have difficulty seeing it as real.

If we can find a way to "sense" this two-dimensional, virtual location, then the location becomes "real" in our perceptions. This way of "sensing" must take place in a three-dimensional reality because we human beings are born into a three-dimensional navigational space in life.

Enter virtual reality technologies. VR technologies enable the user to "sense," and therefore experience, environments that don't exist. Through this experience, the environment becomes real to the user.

Virtual reality technologies are more than just high-level 3D graphics. The graphics level of the image represents the vividness part of virtual reality.

Bernie Roehl on the vividness/interactivity of virtual reality

I believe interactivity to be a critical issue. A beautifully rendered scene running at one frame per second is almost useless for most people. They'd rather have smooth movement with less detail. Certainly anything below about ten frames per second is choppy, and below five frames per second, it's not something that people will want to use.

Now, having said that, image quality is also important. My personal feeling is that so long as you're getting twenty frames per second or so, it's better to improve the graphics quality at the expense of higher frame rates. Below twenty frames per second, work on sacrificing graphics quality in order to improve the interactivity.

VR moves toward a more human-centered design of the user interface. In VR, the virtual space around the user becomes the computing environment. The computer, therefore, becomes more responsive to the user.

Defining virtual reality

One problem that faces us now is the definition of virtual reality. In Chapter 4, we said that virtual reality can be seen as an electronic communication medium and an extension of the human senses through which we expand our capability for actual experience. Another way of defining VR is as the experience of an environment by means of a communications medium.

In accepting this definition of VR, we realize that VR refers to an experience, rather than to a machine. This experience is determined through the individual's perceptions across the aforementioned dimensions of vividness and interactivity. Virtual reality exists in the mind of the user.

As we think you have probably already guessed, we prefer this last definition. Virtual reality, as all realities, exists in the mind of the individual (see Figure 5-3). What you are willing to accept as "real" is what is of primary importance. Dealing with the media-created hype that surrounds virtual reality, and to a large extent, VRML, is a challenge for us all, however.

VRML's purpose

In his presentation to the Developer's Day attendees at WWW95 in Darmstadt, Germany, Mark Pesce, one of VRML's creators, referred to VRML as "a three-dimensional equivalent of HTML."

The draft specifications for VRML Version 1.0 state that VRML "is a language for describing multiparticipant interactive simulations — virtual worlds networked via the global Internet and hyperlinked with the World Wide Web."

Pesce's presentation and the draft specifications for VRML place quite a demand on VRML as a language. In order to be the "three-dimensional equivalent of HTML," VRML must provide three things:

➡ A means for defining objects geometrically

➡ A means for defining scenes and locating objects within these scenes

➡ A protocol for linking objects within a scene with other files on the Internet

In order to meet the purposes and requirements of the draft specifications, VRML must provide a means for building multiuser, interactive environments that are accessible via the Web and the Internet. This requirement necessitates platform independence.

Figure 5-3: Reality exists in the mind of the individual user. (Photographer: Nick Vedros. Photograph courtesy of Pitsco, Inc., Pittsburg, Kansas.)

Platform independence

In his on-line document, "Extending WWW to support Platform Independent Virtual Reality," David Raggett of Hewlett Packard Laboratories asked whether an interchange format for virtual reality environments could be created that could be visualized on a variety of computer platforms.

Platform independence is one of the most important requirements placed on VRML. Defining platform independence in the context of 3D graphics require-ments, however, may be difficult. Realistic 3D graphics require extremely fast processing speeds. When we say "platform independence," are we suggesting that, as with the Internet itself, any computer platform should be able to access and use VRML?

Does this mean that anyone with an Atari 800XL and a TV or an 8088 and CGA graphics should be able to access and use VRML? These units, with the proper software, can access the Internet. Will they be able to access the virtual spaces that VRML can possibly bring to life?

Or, in defining platform independence, is the definition limited to include only those platforms that are deemed appropriate and of sufficient quality and power to attain the goals set for VRML as a language? If so, will those of us who own older technologies be relegated to a second-class citizenship on the Internet and be excluded from the Web and from virtual worlds placed there by what could be seen as 3D technological and economic dictatorships?

At the same time as we ask these questions, we also realize that older technologies will fade. No one seriously uses an Atari 800XL to communicate on the Internet anymore. The issue may become more serious to us all, however, when seemingly semimodern technologies, such as a 486, are made obsolete without major modifications by a new operating system such as Windows 95 or its successor.

Multiparticipant

Can a room exist in multiple locations at the same time? If it can, do different objects and individuals coexist in this virtual room that exists in multiple locations? The answers to these questions, and other questions of this nature, lie in the nature of the technology.

If we equate a telephone conversation with an experience in virtual reality, we may be able to determine the answers to some of these questions. In order to fully conceptualize this virtual experience, the phone conversation we will examine should be a conference call with individual participants in several locations, such as St. Louis, Chicago, New York, Miami, San Francisco, San Diego, and your location. Seven locations in all. To increase the virtual experience, each participant is using a speaker phone in the room in which they are located.

The first thing we must accept is that the phone conversation does not take place in any of these locations. Yet, each individual believes the conversation to be taking place in his or her specific location. William Gibson uses the concept of "consensual hallucination" to explain this phenomenon: Each participant unconsciously accepts and concedes to the hallucination that the conversation is taking place.

When the phone call is over, each participant leaves the experience with the perception that, not only did the conversation take place, but things were accomplished during the conversation. Each participant formed opinions, beliefs, and attitudes based on the experience. Yet, this conversation's location was in the ephemeral virtual world of cyberspace. Each physical room was different; yet the room where the conversation took place, that "consensual hallucination," was the same.

Now, the question arises concerning virtual spaces on the Web; will those spaces be the same for every user? The answer to this question lies with the answer to the question concerning platform independence.

If VRML is truly platform independent, each room cannot be the same. There will be differences in the method of access. There will be differences in the processor speed of the accessing computers. There will be differences in the graphics capabilities of the accessing platforms.

It's readily apparent that technological segregation is already occurring on the Web. Platform independence within the multiuser environment means that different platforms will present different views to the individual participants. The views may range from simple cartoon-level graphics to high-grade, photo-realistic graphics.

What kinds of differences in the experience for the individual participants might be created by this form of platform independence? Are there any methods that would help to minimize these differences? (For example, storing preestablished and platform-specific objects for the virtual environment on the user's site would increase the speed of the rendering and improve the standardization of the virtual objects.)

The alternative to these options is to restrict platform independence to those platforms that have sufficient processing power and graphics capabilities. Again, the technological and economic dictatorship rears in anticipation. The diversity of the quality of experience is perhaps preferred to this serpent.

Interactive

Interactivity is the key to making virtual spaces on the Web be more than simple 3D graphics displays. Without interactivity, 3D graphics are nothing more than artwork displayed in an on-line museum.

The way that the Internet works presents a challenge to bringing interactivity to virtual spaces. As we discussed previously, the Internet makes your computer do most of the work, including the graphics rendering. The server simply transfers information back and forth through the use of packets that the server routes through the best path possible to reach the local computer. Transferring the information takes time, and time is the enemy of interactivity.

We'll look first at on-line conferencing as it can take place today so that you can begin to get some concept of what these challenges represent. If you want to send a message, you must type it into the dialog box at the bottom of the screen. Nothing is sent to the on-line conference until you press Enter. At that time, depending on a number of factors — including how many people are taking part in the conference and the speed (baud rate) of the connection — a certain amount of time elapses before your message appears in the conference discussion.

Many things can have happened during this time lapse. In many cases, the discussion may have gone on to other topics. Multiple individual discussions can therefore erupt, causing confusion for new users. Listing 5-1 shows an example of the number of topics that can result from this time lapse.

Listing 5-1: The Form of an On-Line Conference

```
LO1/Seattle: D, do you think the artist can still be the culture-
bearer in a world with 500 television channels?
DL/DC: LO1: sure why not. Tell why One million channels
JI/LA: even with better tools, my creations will not rival
JW/Tampa: LO1! We're all culture-bearers. Technology is a subset
of culture. So, even programmers . . .
DL/DC: would change anything.
JI/LA: the artistic quality of, say LO2's.
LO1/Seattle: DL, I don't understand your artists<->programmers
point. Are you saying artists cannot be programmers and program-
mers cannot be artists? Bull.
JI/LA: I enjoy the synergism of working with artists to create
LO2: that's an opinion JI.
DL/DC: No. I said that both can be both.
JI/LA: new expressions with technology.
LO1/Seattle: OK. I agree there.
JI/LA: They can be both, but with training.
DL/DC: But more importantly, Artists WILL be programmers in the
future.
LO2: there is so much to do and we must work together as teams
DL/DC: That is the new paint brush. or one of them.
JI/LA: I am not skilled in art, or developed it.
```

As you can see, the direction of the conference conversations twists and turns, a product of the time delay. Many times, the thoughts of one specific speaker are separated by the thoughts of others because of this time delay. This is, however, an example of an extremely interactive on-line conference.

The time delay can affect experiences of virtual reality on the Net also, so it must be taken into consideration when planning a 3D VR experience.

Sandy Ressler discusses vividness, interactivity, virtual reality, and VRML

Sandy Ressler is the director of the Open Virtual Reality Testbed Office at the National Institute of Standards and Technology. As such, he operates the Open Virtual Reality Testbed site on the Internet. We've included the URL for this site in Chapter 15. Ressler was one of the cocreators of one of the first VRML worlds, the House of Immersion. We interviewed Sandy by phone in July 1995.

Question: Could you describe VRML in terms of vividness and interactivity?

Ressler: VRML is just a way of representing 3D objects and integrating them with the WWW. I mean, I don't think there's any interactivity. It's not that amazing in some sense. The trick is writing renderers that can display those models in real time on whatever platform you're on.

I don't see much of a difference between VRML and, for example, Open Inventor, since VRML is based on Open Inventor, which I think was a really good decision by the people that are dealing with it. There's the additional ability to associate URLs with objects. [Authors' note: VRML is not based on Open Inventor. The two share a common ASCII file format.]

Once regular Web browsers get more integrated with the association of URL's with objects and those kinds of things, it'll open up a lot of interesting possibilities. Again, sort of using spatial objects as ways of organizing and getting to information and visualizing information.

Question: It has been suggested that it ought to be called 3DML rather than VRML. From your comments, do we take it that you agree?

Ressler: I'm not sure what is meant by the lack of interactivity. Do they mean, like behavior, objects that can do things? Supposedly, that's just gonna be in Version 2.0. If it's called VRML or 3DML, either is fine with me. I think this name question is sort of silly Internet bandwidth wasting.

It depends on how much you object or not to the term *virtual reality*. If you want to get sort of really formal about it, VRML has nothing to do with virtual reality because the hooks we're dealing with, that's just good old-fashioned computer graphics. It's not virtual reality 'cause it doesn't deal with immersion or any of those issues. That's not to say it can't, but right now it's just 3D graphics.

I don't buy that VR won't work on the Internet. With VRML, like a lot of other things, there's some latency when you click on an image to bring the model over to your computer. There's a delay between the click and the model being on your machine.

But then the entire model sits on your machine and you don't have the bandwidth problems. You can travel around wherever you want.

Now, when you're talking about interacting with another person in a shared virtual world, then you get into some really hairy issues. Bandwidth, these kinds of things are a problem.

Right now, all of these things are in the future. In the current incarnation, all you've got is a sort of 3D modeling language. That's not to say that you can't add to that things like behavior and distributed worlds.

[Authors' Note: Interactivity in the virtual spaces created by VRML then, as we have seen, will be a challenge due to the inherent operation of the Web and the Internet themselves.]

VRML's mission statement

In the draft specifications of VRML Version 1.0, Mark Pesce provides a brief discussion of the development of the Internet. Here he divides the history of the Internet into three phases.

The first of these phases was the development of the TCP/IP protocol infrastructure. This development allowed for the storage of information. Storage can be seen as memory or, in other terminology, history or life experience. Memory alone, without accessibility, however, cannot provide the necessary information needed for decision making.

The second phase was the development of the Web. The Web provided a means of accessing the information through URLs. We've already discussed the problem of the lack of intuitiveness in URLs. All the memory in the world doesn't do you any good if you don't have some way of retrieving, or associating, the information stored there for use. But again, memory and association are of little value without the ability to perceive.

The ability to perceive, or sense, the environment around you enables you to make sense of it. You interpret the "real" world through your senses. The odor of cinnamon bread baking. The sounds of the oven door opening. The sight of steam rising from the warm bread. The crusty feel of the bread's outer layer. The taste of butter heaped on a slab of the bread. These five individual pieces of data alone are not enough to make the event real to you. It is the retrieval of memories and the association of those memories with the input data that creates the "real." Without the memory of what cinnamon smells like, you have no basis for the perception of the event. The same goes for the other senses. Without the memory of what opening an oven door sounds like, what steam looks like, what a crusty feel is, and what butter tastes like, the event has no context. The senses, by and of themselves, provide useless bits of data without context. It is the associations with similar past events that, in conjunction with current perceptions of the senses, create the reality of the event.

VRML is one of the first efforts to create a simulated environment, available on the Internet, that you can "sense" and make "sense" of. The degree to which VRML is capable of making the objects that populate these simulated environments realistic will determine the degree to which we, as users, will perceive the environment as "real" and therefore sensible.

VRML's relationship with Open Inventor

We need to cover one last topic in this chapter before we move on: VRML's relationship with Open Inventor. Open Inventor is an object-oriented 3D toolkit written in C++ and based on OpenGL. The toolkit is a product of Silicon Graphics Inc. (SGI), and Windows versions are available from Template Graphics Software (TGS). VRML and Open Inventor share a common ASCII file format. Other than this common file format, the two are separate entities, though they do share some similarities, and Open Inventor can be seen as an ancestor of VRML.

Moving On

This chapter covered quite a bit of information in a relatively short period of time. VRML, Virtual Reality Modeling Language, is a method of true 3D interaction with the World Wide Web. VRML deals with visually interactive material; HTML, on the other hand, deals with textual material.

VRML's purpose is to provide "a language for describing multi-participant interactive simulations — virtual worlds networked via the global Internet and hyperlinked with the World Wide Web." It works at making sense of the World Wide Web and making the Web sensible.

VRML shares a common ASCII file format with Open Inventor. Other than that, the rest of this relationship is hype and misinformation. Perhaps a closer examination of the history of VRML can help to shed more light on the relationship between VRML and Open Inventor.

The next chapter covers the history of VRML's development.

The Development of VRML Technology

The history of VRML technology includes the history of the Internet, the Web, VR technologies in general, and VRML. Because we discuss portions of these histories in earlier chapters, this chapter covers only the history of VRML. We point to instances and refer you to magazine articles and Internet documents. The history of VRML is what you make of it.

We have pieced together the history of VRML's development from original documents, magazine articles, and personal interviews. This chapter includes some of the highlights. We hope that this overview gives you a better understanding of the simultaneous events that occurred in the creation of VRML.

1993

Mark Pesce begins work on adding 3D worlds to the Web

In 1993, four years after Tim Berners-Lee created the first Web browser, the National Center for Supercomputer Applications (NCSA) released Mosaic. In October 1993, Mark Pesce discovered this Web browser.

Using Mosaic, Pesce found the beginnings of a potential global hypermedia world, a world-wide cyberuniverse similar to Gibson's matrix or Stephenson's metaverse. Still, there was a lack of three-dimensional experiences — those events and images that make up the "real." After creating his own Web site, Pesce turned to the task of adding three-dimensionality to the Web.

The source code that creates the Web is downloadable, and it would compile on Pesce's computer, so he set about modifying the code to create a 3D interface for the Web. Although he had conceived of the basic design, he realized that his designs would need more than HTML. He needed a new language, and he realized that he could not create it without help.

Building Labyrinth

By late 1993, Pesce had Tony Parisi, a software engineer, involved in the creation of a new program called Labyrinth. This program was designed to provide a 3D user interface to the World Wide Web. It was a beginning.

1994

Labyrinth unchained

By the middle of February 1994, Parisi and Pesce had a working alpha version of Labyrinth ready. The program consisted of a three-dimensional equivalent of HTML and another application that worked in conjunction with an HTML-based Web browser. Together, these applications allowed for the first 3D view of the Web. Now, if there were just something on the Web to view in 3D . . . Still, Labyrinth quickly generated a great amount of interest among people on the Web.

Pesce contacts Tim Berners-Lee

In February, Pesce discovered several articles concerning the use of virtual reality on the Web on the CERN (European Center for Particle Physics) home page. Many of these articles were written by Tim Berners-Lee, the father of the Web. These articles contained Berners-Lee's belief that a "perceptualized," or sensible, Web browser was an extremely important step forward in the evolution of the Web.

Pesce contacted Berners-Lee, who invited Pesce and Parisi to present their work concerning the 3D interface for the Web before the First International Conference on the World Wide Web in Geneva in the spring of 1994.

"Extending WWW to support Platform Independent Virtual Reality"

Early in 1994, David Raggett of Hewlett Packard Laboratories, who is one of the primary individuals behind the development of HTML, proposed extending the WWW to include virtual reality. His paper, "Extending WWW to support Platform Independent Virtual Reality," included his preliminary ideas. These ideas included the utilization of sound in creating the illusion in a virtual environment.

Most of the rest of Raggett's paper dealt with the common elements of the VR environment and the use of the Standard Generalized Markup Language (SGML) to specify the logical level, thereby leaving the local browser to fill in the detail according to the capabilities of the local platform. In other words, the VR environment is defined at some minimal level, and the local computer platform's browser adds specifics. This concept is similar to what is discussed in Chapter 5 about how the virtual environment is different depending on which platform you use to access it.

Raggett also discussed the possible use of the .DXF format for the storage of the VR objects, the use of URLs to dynamically extend the capabilities of the VR environment, and a sketch of his proposed Virtual Reality Markup Language (VRML), possibly the first use of this term. The .DXF file format, used by AutoCAD, holds a list of vertices along with various other properties.

Raggett's paper is available for download from the Internet. We found it while searching through the VRML history at http://www.vrml.com.

"Beam Me Up To My Avatar"

Hillary McLellan, an expert on virtual reality and education, wrote the article "Beam Me Up To My Avatar" for the March/April issue of *Virtual Reality World* (a VR magazine whose last issue was July/August 1995). The article begins on page 33.

Toward the end of the article, McLellan discussed "sensory combinatorics." This concept centers on the proper placement of sensors in a multisensory environment. She discussed the phenomenon that high-resolution audio can cause users to report graphics that are higher resolution than the virtual experience actually contains. High-resolution graphics together with low-resolution audio, however, shatters the illusion of the virtual environment. Audio, therefore, should be a important tool in the design of virtual environments.

The First International Conference on the World Wide Web

Those attending the First International Conference on the World Wide Web came from mostly academic backgrounds. At this point in time, the Web was commerce free and commercial free. This changed quickly.

Tim Berners-Lee delivered the keynote address on the subject of a constitution for cyberspace.

In 1991, comments had been made that cyberspace was peopled by outlaws. In just three short years, cyberspace had been colonized to the point where a group was calling for the civilization of cyberspace through a constitution.

The second speaker at the WWW conference was Dr. David Chaum. His topic was privacy and security on the Internet. Suddenly, the Internet and the Web were becoming private property that needs protection.

On the second day of the conference, Berners-Lee and David Raggett pulled together a "birds-of-a-feather" meeting to discuss virtual environments on the Web. At these conferences, a birds-of-a-feather (BOF) meeting is a gathering of people interested in similar topics. CERN, NCSA, and others were very interested in the possibilities of "perceptualizing" the Web's interface.

Several people attending the meeting described their individual projects aimed at building a three-dimensional interface for the Web. Raggett's proposals (discussed earlier in this chapter) helped to provide a focus for the group, and they agreed on the need for a virtual reality version of HTML. Raggett's term,

Virtual Reality Markup Language, (VRML), stuck. The group agreed to begin working on the specifications for VRML after the conference. Some participants also realized that a more "industry-driven" approach might be necessary for the development of VRML.

During this meeting, Mark Pesce met Brian Behlendorf, the UNIX system administrator for *WIRED* magazine. Behlendorf was excited about the possibility of a 3D Web language. With the blessing of the magazine, which donated the server space and bandwidth, it was decided to establish a mailing list for those interested in the development of VRML.

The VRML mailing list is established

The VRML mailing list (www-vrml@wired.com) was active within a month, with Pesce as its moderator. Within a week of its activation, the list had 1,000 members. Within a month, the list numbered over 2,000.

Proposing a VRML specification

Pesce set a very aggressive schedule for the development of a VRML, announcing his intention of having a draft version of the specification ready by the fall 1994 WWW conference. The first task was to set up requirements for VRML Version 1.0. The second was to search for existing technologies on which to base VRML.

Requirements for VRML are discussed

A set of assumptions quickly evolved as to what the requirements of VRML should be. In one of the initial VRML mailing list survey pages, the following requirements were mentioned as being needed, "no contest."

- Platform independence
- True 3D information (not prerendered texture maps à la DOOM)
- PHIGS-ish lighting and view model (*PHIGS* stands for *programmers hierarchical interface for graphics systems,* a software interface standard for graphics that includes data structures for high-level 3D applications.)
- The ignoring of unrecognized data types (to leave open future development)
- Hierarchical data structure
- Lightweight design

➡ The capability to use convex and concave objects

➡ Fill-in-the-detail support (pictures in a museum)

➡ A file format that is in the public domain

VRML Version 1.0 specifications list the language as being designed to meet three requirements:

➡ Platform independence

➡ Extensibility

➡ Ability to work well over low-bandwidth connections

The VRML Version 1.0 specification goes on to say that interactive behaviors, with the exception of the hyperlinking feature, would not be supported in the current version.

The VRML Working Specification, Revision 1.3.1, is posted on the Web

In June, Tony Parisi and Mark Pesce posted the Virtual Reality Markup Language (VRML) Working Specification, Revision 1.3.1, to the Web. This document discusses the world parser (a software engine that converts the geometry definitions provided by the VRML file and the visualized geometry). The document also presents the syntax for VRML.

"Multi-user virtual environments, part 1"

VRML was beginning to be noticed by the media. Jerry Micalski, in an article titled "Multi-user virtual environments, part 1" in the June 27, 1994, issue of *RELease 1.0,* discussed a variety of VR applications on the Net and concluded the article with VRML's mail list address.

Government Computer News

The U.S. government was also beginning to take notice. In a column titled "Roaming cyberspace, virtual reality heads want your body, too" in the July 11, 1994, issue of *Government Computer News,* Shawn McCarthy discussed the effort to build a Virtual Reality Markup Language. He also discussed how the Open Virtual Reality Testbed office at the National Institute of Standards and Technology was "listening in" to the VRML mail list.

Looking at existing technologies

A survey was conducted on the VRML mail list in August to assess what features to include in the baseline specification and which of the following proposals merited closer inspection:

- "Cyberspace Description Format" proposed by AutoDesk
- "A File Format for the Interchange of Virtual Worlds" by Bernie Roehl and Kerry Bonin
- "Labyrinth — VRML Specification" by Mark Pesce and Tony Parisi
- "Manchester Scene Description Language" from the University of Manchester
- "Meme" by Immersive System
- "OOGL," an object-oriented graphics language from the Geometry Center at the University of Minnesota
- "SGI Open Inventor"

The following three proposals were selected for further examination and discussion:

- "Cyberspace Description Format"
- "OOGL"
- "Open Inventor"

After about three months of discussion, the VRML list settled on the ASCII file format of Open Inventor. SGI agreed to place the data format in the public domain. QvLib, a C++ class library that can be used as a parser for VRML, was placed in the public domain by SGI also.

The group also decided that VRML Version 1.0 would not be highly interactive, but that it would be able to reproduce HTML's in-line graphics and anchor functions (as described in Chapter 3).

Release of the VRML Version 1.0 draft specification

Mark Pesce released the VRML 1.0 Specification (Draft) over the Web in November.

The Second International Conference on the World Wide Web

In Chicago, Gavin Bell presented the draft specification for VRML 1.0 to attendees of the Second International Conference on the World Wide Web. The specification needed some slight cleaning up, but it met the requirements set for it.

1995

A VRML launch date is set

The VRML standards group decided that April 3, 1995, would be the worldwide launch date for VRML and products built around it.

TGS and SGI announce VRML products

TGS (Template Graphics Software) and SGI jumped the gun on the VRML worldwide launch date and announce the first "Official VRML 1.0" product, WebSpace, a 3D/VRML browser. They also announced Open Inventor, with VRML support, as the first VRML 1.0 development toolkit.

The Third International Conference on the World Wide Web

Mark Pesce addressed the attendees of the Third International Conference on the World Wide Web, referring to VRML as the 3D equivalent of HTML. Speaking of future modifications to VRML, he said that work had already begun on adding sound and texture support. He promised that the draft specification for VRML Version 1.1 would be available in late June. It didn't make it.

The VRML Version 1.0 final specification

In early May 1995, Gavin Bell's document, "VRML Design Notes," evolved into the final specification for VRML 1.0.

"VRML and the World Wide Web"

The June issue of *Dr. Dobb's Developer Update* included an article by Joe Stewart, director of business development at Template Graphics Software. The article, "VRML and the World Wide Web," described how VRML works and included a small sample VRML file.

"Putting the *Space* in Cyberspace"

"Putting the *Space* in Cyberspace," by Linda and Erick Von Schweber, appeared in the June 13, 1995, issue of *PC Magazine*. It described three VRML-compatible products from TGS/SGI (WebSpace), InterVista (WorldView), and VREAM (WebView).

Some VRML events in July

TGS placed a VRML position statement on its Web page pledging TGS's support for the current and future VRML standards.

Macmillan placed the table of contents and a unedited sample chapter from Pesce's upcoming book on VRML on its Web page.

Interactivity magazine ran a two-page spread titled "Strolling through Cyberspace: VR finally comes to the Net via VRML" in the July/August 1995 issue.

Siggraph 95

For the majority of the history of VRML, we've been observers rather than participants. However, in August 1995 we attended the Siggraph conference in Los Angeles.

Sunday afternoon Gavin Bell and Mark Pesce took part in a workshop on VRML titled "VRML: Using 3D to Surf the Web." The workshop materials consisted, to a large degree, of previously released material that was available on the Web.

The VRML players

The Birds of a Feather meeting for VRML took place shortly after the workshop on VRML. During the break between the workshop and the meeting, we met some of the players.

Mark Pesce, the VRML evangelist, has the unenviable responsibilities of continuing to form a coalition of individuals and groups around the concept of VRML and preventing its fragmentation. When we talked with him, his comments on the wonders of cyberspace and the possibilities of VRML were interspersed and contrasted with remarks on the dangers of fragmentation for the VRML community and the politics of capitalism.

Mark Owen, vice president of WebMaster, associated with InterVista, introduced us to as many of the VRML players as possible during the course of the conference. Information about many of the VRML editors and browsers that we discuss and use later in this book came from some of the following people whom Owen introduced us to:

➡ Arnie Cachelin of NewTek Inc., who has designed a VRML editor and browser to be used with the Video Toaster. It will be shipped with each unit of LightWave that NewTek sends out.

➡ Mike Conduris, of 3D Web, who told us about Spinner, 3D Web's new 3D VRML layout tool for the Web.

➡ Michael McCue, CEO of Paper Software Inc., Woodstock, New York, who told us about Paper Software's new VRML product, WebFX.

➡ Stephan Pachikov, CEO and president of ParaGraph International, who demonstrated ParaGraph's Home Space Builder product at Siggraph.

➡ Raj Singh, vice president for sales for 3Dlabs, which makes the Glint video acceleration board.

The VRML Birds-of-a-Feather meeting

About 100 people attended the Birds-of-a-Feather meeting, with unknown numbers listening and watching via an Internet link. Mark Pesce spoke briefly about the history of VRML, and then he turned the audience's attention to where VRML is going. VRML Version 1.x, with its possible additions, was the first topic.

A discussion quickly developed about whether Version 1.x was really Version 1.1, Version 1.5, or what. Pesce explained that Version 1.x is a transitional version and that the group should try to clean up and solidify the specification for Version 1.x before adding behaviors and interactions — functions that are to be included in Version 2.0.

Pesce asked which specific functions interested the audience. Several of the replies mentioned functions that are considered to be under the realm of Version 2.0, so they were put off for the time being.

A spokesperson for the Geometry Center asked that the 4×4 matrix that is present in the current specification not be taken out of any future specification. Pesce seemed surprised that someone would think that something would be taken out of the specification and assured the questioner that it would remain.

Ben Delaney, editor of *CyberEdge Journal*, asked that those responsible for the creation of the next version of VRML not forget the "ignorant end-user."

Keeping track of what was Version 1.x and discussible and what was Version 2.0 and not discussible became extremely difficult. Brian Blau from AutoDesk spoke about AutoDesk's Cyberspace Developers Kit. Rick Kerry, of SGI, discussed Open Inventor. Tony Parisi spoke about things that can and can't be added to VRML. Gavin Bell discussed world scalability again.

VRML standards

The next topic was the need for a standards body. Pesce proposed a strong central standardization consortium with an office, a director, a secretary, and programmers. He also proposed a fee structure for membership so that the office and staff could be supported.

Others proposed a more decentralized organization with little power or authority. Still others proposed levels of authority and responsibility between the two extremes.

Demonstrations of VRML products

Several VRML products were demonstrated before the meeting closed. Many of the products are discussed in later chapters when you load them onto your hard drive and take them out for a test drive.

Tony Parisi's role

On Tuesday morning, we met with Tony Parisi to discuss his role in the history of VRML. Parisi is a software engineer, and he will be the first to tell you that 3D graphics is not his primary area. Despite this, if Mark Pesce is the father of VRML, Tony Parisi is the doctor who delivered the baby. Other doctors have improved the baby's health, but it was Parisi who made sure that it was alive.

In addition to answering questions about the VRML specification, Parisi stressed the need for a standards body for VRML. He fears that individual ambitions of some of the VRML corporate players can lead to fragmentation, which would mean that there would be a VRML standard in name only. "No one can be the NetScape of VRML yet. If they try, they could tear the whole thing apart."

Overview of the conference

Clearly, the VRML community is young, with all the problems that such a community faces. But it is a community, with people who are eager to share what they've learned with each other and work together to build 3D worlds on the Internet.

Moving On

This chapter describes how VRML came into being. You learned about Mark Pesce's and Tony Parisi's contributions to the creation of VRML. Mark Pesce began the process of developing VRML in 1993 when he decided that three-dimensionality was needed on the Web. From that time until the announcement of VRML in April 1995, VRML was the topic of magazine articles and conference workshops as interest in it grew. You also took another look at the issue of standardization and the standardization process.

You learned about the creation of the VRML mail list and the specification for VRML that grew out of this collaboration.

The discussions and exhibits at Siggraph 95 represented, pretty much, where the VRML world stood at the time we wrote this chapter. Where it may go from here is the subject of the next chapter.

The Future of 3D and Virtual Reality on the Web

In This Chapter

The future is 3D

Looking at the many possible futures of VRML

If the future is 3D, what is the future of 3D?

Creating worlds

Authoring VRML

Browsing the virtual Web

Building VRML's future

There are many possible futures in store for VRML. The decisions made during the current discussion concerning the potential capabilities of VRML Version 1.x and Version 2.0 will have a dramatic impact on which path VRML will follow into the future. If these discussions deteriorate into turf wars between the various platform advocates, the idealistic dream of a multiplatform virtual reality user interface for the Web will be lost. Instead, the Web will consist of competing proprietary language formats. Each of these proprietary formats will have advantages and disadvantages over the others, but the primary disadvantage of all of them will be the lack of compatibility for Web users.

Factors that Influence the Future of VRML

The June 1995 issue of *DV* (Digital Video) magazine contained an article written by Craig Lyn titled "The Future Is 3D." This article, beginning on page 26, was the first of a series of articles concerning the future of multimedia and the technologies that are going to make this future possible.

Lyn's article in *DV* brings out a point that is often overlooked in discussions of new technologies. The first applications of any new communication technology are usually in the areas of sex and violence. This has been true for video cassettes and for video games in the past and will more than likely be true for 3D technologies as well. The reason for this is probably that sex and violence are the most vivid and most interactive topics available for exploitation. To understand one of the possible paths that the future of VRML may take, perhaps we should begin by looking at where video games are going in regard to 3D levels of vividness and interactivity.

Vividness vs. interactivity in 3D video games

The problem facing video game producers is much the same problem facing those preparing the specifications for VRML: the choice between vividness and interactivity. Some games, such as Broderbund's Myst, provide extremely vivid 3D prerendered images that are linked together in a hierarchical manner. This hierarchical linkage, though, limits the level of interactivity.

Other games, such as Castle Wolfenstein, provide an extremely interactive environment at the cost of vividness. This low vividness is a result of repetitive textures with high pixilation. Rather than being 3D, therefore, the interactive environment is restricted to one of perhaps only two-and-a-half dimensions, at best.

Interactivity in applications for Windows

Another problem in game and VR programming concerns software. For the average computer user, real-time interactivity has been limited, generally, to DOS-based programs. The recent releases of Microsoft's WinG API (Application Programming Interface), Intel's 3DR API (which rumor has it Intel may abandon), and the new 32-bit applications for Win95, such as Direct Draw, have made this type of interactivity available to programs based on Windows. These *APIs* (interfaces used for accessing a programming library), as well as other proprietary tools, have made possible an expanded growth of animated applications that are based on Windows.

Games, just as VRML, must provide high-quality visuals on consumer-quality hardware in order to succeed. As a result of the more widespread use of hardware acceleration and the lowering of the hardware cost, the number of 3D applications in Windows has grown. These changes in hardware may have the same effect on the growth of VRML.

The three APIs used most often in game development are Argonaut Software's BRender, Criterion Software's RenderWare, and Microsoft's recently acquired Reality Lab. As with VRML, an advantage of using these APIs is that they are not platform specific. In fact, some programmers have turned to these APIs in creating their VRML browsers.

Tools for creating 3D worlds

In considering the future of VRML, we must first look at how the user will create worlds. Although creating a world by hand is possible (the creation of worlds by hand using a text editor and VRML node statements is discussed in Chapters 12 and 13), most users will use *CAD* (computer aided design), walkthrough, or specialized VRML editor programs to create worlds. (In Chapters 10 and 11, we examine several of these VRML tools and applications, and some of them are included on the CD-ROM that accompanies this book.)

HTML is about text. It's also about page design. As you learned in Chapter 3, you can write HTML and create Web pages from within your word processor or a simple text editor. These tools are appropriate for text and page design, but you cannot use most of them to create three-dimensional environments.

If the future is 3D, what is the future of 3D?

The future of VRML is intrinsically tied to the future of the Internet as a whole. HTML and the Web have changed the Internet. VRML will do the same, one way or another. Ed Brent, a professor of sociology at the University of Missouri and owner of a computer software company, has the following to say about the future of the Internet:

Continued growth, evolution, controversy, maturation: the Internet is a new technology. We should expect continued high growth for a while until it begins to reach saturation in the population. We should expect new uses and the abandoning of old ones as it becomes clear what can be accomplished effectively with the Net. As the technology and the infrastructure mature, we should expect solidification of norms for use, some formal regulations (we're beginning to see some already in the form of misguided attempts at censorship), and routinization.

Bernie Roehl on the future of VRML

In the short term, we'll have fairly simple worlds, most to provide context for socializing. Down the road the worlds will become more complex, and the level of interaction between participants will improve.

Initially, ordinary desktop computers, with an Internet connection, of course, will be enough. Eventually, 3D graphics accelerators, HMDs [head-mounted displays], gloves, and other input devices will become commonplace.

I think that one weakness of VRML is that there are many places where the spec is ambiguous, and there's a danger that not all VRML worlds will be compatible with all VRML browsers, at least initially.

It's important to distinguish between three things: 1. QvLib, a C++ class library which parses VRML; 2. VRML itself; and 3. the issue of scene graphs versus no scene graphs.

I've heard people saying they don't like QvLib, and a lot of us are writing our own parsers to use instead of QvLib. VRML itself isn't bad. It's the only real standard in existence for describing virtual worlds. But, there are a lot of unresolved issues related to it that need to be cleared up relatively soon. The issue of scene graphs is going to get more contentious, since it has such a profound effect on the behavior of objects in these virtual worlds.

One of the most important issues when dealing with VR over the Internet is "latency," or lag. Because of the packet-switching nature of the Net, it's possible to have delays of up to several "seconds" for an individual message traveling over the network. This obviously has a serious effect on interactivity. But there are two kinds of slowness: initial startup slowness, the result of slow modem lines, heavy loading on Web servers, etc.; and run-time slowness, the result of slow software or a badly-written browser. The rather enthusiastic debate on the VRML list right now is partly to do with run-time performance versus compatibility with Open Inventor.

I don't have a problem with the spec itself, apart from the way lights are handled. However, there are a lot of problems waiting in the wings when we try to implement behaviors in a way that everyone will be happy with. My only concern is that we address some of those issues early on. VRML itself is fine.

[Roehl has been writing software for more than 20 years. He currently works as a senior software developer and system administrator and as a freelance software developer.]

The tool of choice for publishing virtual worlds on the Web will provide ease-of-use with accessibility for the masses. Software companies currently provide a variety of alternatives to use in creating worlds. Some, such as AutoDesk's 3DStudio and Caligari's trueSpace2, are extremely sophisticated. Others, such as Virtus WalkThrough Pro and ParaGraph's Home Space Builder, are less expensive and, at the same time, less sophisticated. We look at some of these packages in Chapter 11.

Authoring tools for VRML environments are already beginning to appear from these companies as well as from others. Virtus has released a new version (2.5) of WalkThrough Pro that is VRML compliant, as well as WalkThrough VRML. ParaGraph has released Home Space Builder. Caligari has released a new product named Fountain. Virtual Presence has released G-Web. We also look at some of these packages in Chapter 11.

Tools for browsing the virtual Web

Browsing tools for VRML environments are also already beginning to appear from different software producers. TGS's WebSpace, InterVista's WorldView, VREAM's WebView, and Inner Action's Portal are currently available for a variety of platforms. We look at some of these viewers, as well as others, including VisNet's VisCIS, in Chapter 10.

Some browsers include world editing capabilities. The browser/editor combinations that enable users to view the creative works of others and create original creative works are expected to achieve dominance in the market.

A Possible Future for VRML

Each user wants different things from VRML. For some, the graphics are the thing. For others, the interactivity is foremost. If either side wins out, the other will go its own way.

Perhaps, for the vividness versus interactivity discussion, the same sort of negotiated commonality can suffice. VRML could serve as the core structure. Extensions to the core could provide for high vividness or high interactivity. All worlds could contain the same basic, generic underlying format. At the same time, the world would have the specifics of vividness or interactivity that the world's creator declared for this particular world in the extensions. In this manner, the same basic standard VRML file format can satisfy both the graphics enthusiast and the interactivity enthusiast.

However, adding these extensions to VRML has the practical effect of weakening VRML's overall effectiveness and importance as a standard. For this reason, we don't support this future for VRML.

Another Possible Future for VRML

Another variation of this future might satisfy the advocates of having various platforms: Restrain the VRML standard within the created worlds to object basics and allow the specific platform to provide the object specifics.

This is what happens between individuals anyway. When I use the word *tree* in a conversation, because of my past experience I see, in my mind, a large full-limbed, leaf covered oak tree. You, however, may, because of your past experience, see, in your mind, an evergreen tree of some type. Because of the combined commonality between you and me, communication takes place even in a generic form.

Communication between platforms using VRML would take place in a similar manner. If you specified a generic tree in the VRML .WRL file, the various platforms tasked with rendering the tree might add the specifics of the type of tree from a library of trees available on CD-ROM at the local platform. This selection would be based on a default option defined by either the user or the programmer.

HTML browsers already do something similar in that if you turn off the automatic loading of images when you are using SPRY Air Mosaic, the program places a generic image on the document in the place of the image not loaded from the server. This rather simplistic analogy gives us a starting point, but we will want slightly more specification of the object in VRML due to the visual nature of the 3D events.

These types of negotiated compromises can help to create a VRML standard that might, if not satisfying all concerned, at least provide an adequate platform for the exchange of virtual worlds on the Web.

Nowhere in William Gibson's cyberspace-related works does he imply that cyberspace always looks the same to each and every person entering it. Each of Gibson's descriptions of cyberspace is rich and colorful, providing different visions of cyberspace to each and every reader.

Perhaps we shouldn't expect our realities to always be objective and constant. The virtually real will be no more constant and standard than the subjectively real that exists with each and every one of us. Real has no future, for it exists only within the subjective perceptions of the individual for a split second of time. After that it is history, subject to modification by the individual. Before that it is anticipation and dream.

Moving On

This chapter began with an examination of the future in terms of 3D. It quickly became apparent that there are many possible futures for VRML. You learned about some of the possible futures, futures that included lessons learned from 3D video games and the programming of Windows applications. We discussed the creation of worlds and the authoring tools that would be required. We looked at the question of vividness vs. interactivity again and proposed another possible alternative future. Finally, we returned to William Gibson's vision of cyberspace and discussed how it will be you who will build VRML's future.

It's your turn now. In the past seven chapters, you've learned information and had experiences that have exposed you to the Internet, the Web, virtual reality, and VRML. Now you're going to move on to creating worlds. First you will build some basic worlds that will enable you to build more advanced worlds later. Chapter 8 begins this process by walking you through the transition from two dimensions to three dimensions. You also learn about the math that's involved in building worlds by hand.

PART III
HOW DOES VRML WORK?

File   Edit   View   Go   Bookmarks   Options   Directory   Help

The Basics of 3D Graphics

The first seven chapters of this book cover the Internet, the Web, virtual reality, and the history of VRML. If you jumped ahead to this chapter without reading the preceding seven, we suggest that you read them now so that you will have the foundation necessary for learning to create basic three-dimensional objects for the PC and transforming those objects into VRML worlds that you can exchange on the Internet.

Before you learn to create 3D objects, however, you need to learn the basic mathematical concepts on which creating 3D worlds is based. Along the way, you learn about two-dimensional calculations and how to make the transition to the three-dimensional calculations that go into creating a virtual world.

We begin this chapter by looking at the binary system, the basic language of all computers. Then we move on to the Cartesian coordinate system and its three-dimensional equivalent, the 3D coordinate system.

Armed with this information and a variety of programming languages and tools, you can create two-dimensional objects and then transform them into full-color three-dimensional objects. After these objects are floating in virtual space, you'll be ready to move into the realm of VRML, the Web, and the Internet.

Binary Mathematics: The Basic Language of All Computers

Whether you like it or not, you have to begin with math. As the heading states, binary mathematics is the universal language that all computers use. This language, however, has only two *letters,* or digits, in it. For a computer, everything is represented by multiples of two specific digits, 0 and 1. Everything the computer does is made possible because the computer manipulates these two digits. From these two digits, the computer can form and process many more complex numbers and symbols.

Binary mathematics

The language that computers use is called *binary mathematics.* Binary mathematics is a numerical system that's based on the powers of 2.

A *bit,* or *binary digit,* is the smallest unit of storage or measurement on a computer. It is one digit — either a *0* or a *1.* In binary math, 0 represents the absence of an electrical signal or indicates that something is off, and 1 represents the presence of an electrical signal or indicates that something is on.

Four bits is sometimes called a *nibble,* but that term is not used very much.

Eight bits is a *byte.* A byte is one of the basic units of data storage and manipulation on a computer. Because there are eight bits in a byte, a byte can represent any number from 0 to 255. Note that this means that a byte can represent 256 different numbers, zero being the first.

The next largest data storage and manipulation unit is the *word.* A word typically is equal to 2 bytes, or 16 bits. A word can represent values up to 65,536. Basically, a word is the number of bits that can be processed at a single time.

A number of early personal computers were known as *8-bit computers* because they used 8-bit words. The AT is capable of 16-bit words, and the newer operating systems enable 386 computers and above to use 32-bit words. The increase in capacity greatly increases the way they handle data.

 In this chapter, there are several example programs that were created using older languages, such as QuickBasic 4.5. The purpose of these example programs is not to teach you how to program with these languages but to demonstrate a principle we're discussing at a given point in time.

We've included the source code for these examples simply for your edification. QuickBasic is an excellent beginning for the study of structured programming techniques.

The QuickBasic program CRVTBASE.BAS converts base-10 numbers from 0 to 255 to binary and hexadecimal formats. Figure 8-1 shows what your screen looks like when the program opens.

The program doesn't do anything fancy and offers no graphic capabilities at all, but if you can't write this type of basic programming code, you may have difficulty in understanding how to use VRML. First, run the executable program CRVTBASE.EXE from the CD-ROM that accompanies this book. It's in the \QBASIC\PROGRAMS\ subdirectory. Try converting some numbers. When you are finished converting numbers, press N when you are asked whether you want to convert another, and the program will close. Then after you finish running the program and have a feel for what the program does, type Listing 8-1 into your QuickBASIC or QBASIC editor.

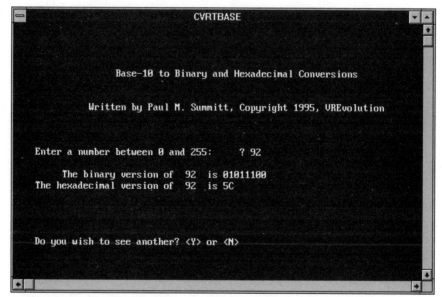

Figure 8-1: CRVTBASE.BAS enables you to convert base-10 numbers to both binary and hexadecimal formats.

Listing 8-1: A QuickBasic Program that Converts Base-10 Numbers to Binary and Hexadecimal

```
'<TAB>PROGRAM NAME:<TAB>CNVTBASE.BAS
'<TAB>PROGRAM PURPOSE:<TAB>To demonstrate base-10 to base-2
∟ conversions
'<TAB>PROGRAM DATE:<TAB>August 1, 1995
'<TAB>PROGRAM AUTHOR:<TAB>Paul M. Summitt
'<TAB>COPYRIGHT:<TAB>VREvolution, 1995
DECLARE SUB ASK ()
DECLARE SUB QUIT ()
DECLARE FUNCTION Bin$ (inVal&)
CLS
SCREEN 12
COLOR 15
LOCATE 5, 20
PRINT "Base-10 to Binary and Hexadecimal Conversions"
LOCATE 8, 15
PRINT "Written by Paul M. Summitt, Copyright 1995, VREvolution"
ASK
QUIT
END
SUB ASK
LOCATE 12, 5
PRINT "Enter a number between 0 and 255:<10 spaces>";
LOCATE 12, 43
INPUT inVal&
IF inVal& < 0 OR inVal& > 255 THEN
ASK
END IF
LOCATE 14, 5
PRINT "<5 spaces>The binary version of "; inVal&; " is ";
Bin$(inVal&)
PRINT TAB(5); "The hexadecimal version of "; inVal&; " is ";
HEX$(inVal&)
QUIT
END SUB
FUNCTION Bin$ (inVal&) 'This function supplies the binary
∟(base- 2) equivalent of a base-10 integer.
h$ = HEX$(inVal&)
outBin$ = ""
hVal% = INSTR("ABCDEF", hChar$)
IF hVal% <> 0 THEN
hVal% = hVal% + 9
```

```
ELSE
hVal% = VAL(hChar$)
END IF
curVal% = 0
FOR j% = 3 TO 0 STEP -1
IF 2 ^ j% + curVal% <= hVal% THEN
outBin$ = outBin$ + "1"
curVal% = curVal% + 2 ^ j%
ELSE
outBin$ = outBin$ + "0"
END IF
NEXT j%
NEXT i%
Bin$ = outBin$
END FUNCTION
SUB QUIT
LOCATE 20, 5
PRINT "Do you wish to see another? <Y> or <N> "
DO
ans$ = UCASE$(INKEY$)
LOOP UNTIL LEN(ans$) > 0 AND INSTR("YN", ans$) <> 0
SELECT CASE ans$
CASE IS = "Y"
LOCATE 14, 5
PRINT "<59 spaces>"
PRINT "<59 spaces>"
LOCATE 20, 5
PRINT  "<59 spaces>"
ASK
CASE IS = "N"
PRINT TAB(5); "Thank you for using the Conversion program."
END
END SELECT
END SUB
```

Although the full listing for CVRTBASE.BAS is on the CD-ROM in the \BASIC\ CODE\ subdirectory, we recommend that you type the code yourself. Yes, we know that it's a drag and it takes too long, and we know all the other excuses, but typing the code helps you understand the programming. If you just load the basic listing from the CD-ROM into your editor, you will miss part of the experience and lose out on the serendipitous knowledge that you might gain if you type it.

ASCII

We said earlier in the chapter that an 8-bit word can represent 256 different characters. The first 128 of these are used for the *American Standard Code for Information Interchange (ASCII)*. ASCII is used for data transmission between different kinds of computers. ASCII remains a standard between multiple platforms, and that's what makes it so powerful.

ASCII uses only the last seven digits of an 8-bit word. The first digit is either ignored or is used for checking accuracy during transmission from one computer to another or from one platform to another.

Table 8-1 lists examples of a few letters and numbers so you can see how ASCII represents them in an 8-bit word.

Table 8-1: Examples of ASCII Equivalents

Alpha-Numeric	Binary
1	00110001
2	00110010
3	00110011
4	00110100
5	00110101
6	00110110
7	00110111
A	01000001
B	01000010
C	01000011
D	01000100
E	01000101
F	01000101
G	01000111

The first 32 binary numbers are reserved for characters such as the space bar and the Enter key. You can get a general ideal of how the others lay out in the first 128 number sequences of ASCII by looking again at Table 8-1. For now the question arises, is that all there is?

We're glad you asked that question. The answer is no, that's not all there is.

HEX

Earlier in the chapter, we discussed how you can combine bits to form a byte, or a word. You also can combine words to form larger words and sentences, so to speak. When you put 2 bytes together, you have 16 bits. On some machines and operating systems, a 16-bit word is that specific computer's basic word.

Two bytes, 16 bits, are also called *hexadecimal*, or *hex* for short. Hexadecimal is base-16.

Most of us usually work and deal with base-10 during everyday business. Probably the reason for this is that when humans first learned to count, they used their ten fingers.

You'll notice that there is no digit to represent the number *ten*. The first ten digits in base-10 are 0, *1, 2, 3, 4, 5, 6, 7, 8,* and *9.* When you reach 9, you have to go back to 0 and add a *1* in front of it to represent one 10.

The same is true when you work with base-2, or binary. You have only two digits, *0* and *1.* When you get past the number 1 there is nothing else to do but use the 0 again and add a 1 in front of it to represent one 2.

Base-16 with hexadecimal uses letters of the alphabet in addition to numbers. Go back and run CVRTBASE.EXE again, and this time pay attention to the hexadecimal conversion. Start with the number *1* and walk your way through to the number *17.* Notice anything? In the hexadecimal system, *0* through *9* are used, and then the letters *A* through *F.* (*A* represents *10, B* represents *11, C* represents *12,* and so on, through *17.*) The number 25 would therefore be equal to 19 hexadecimal; one 16 and nine 1's. You will sometimes see a hexadecimal number ending with the letter *H.*

Investing in an inexpensive calculator that converts from decimal to binary to hexadecimal would probably be an excellent idea. You'll need it as you begin to do more and more programming for your virtual worlds.

Although binary is the language of choice, so to speak, of the computer, it is difficult for the human mind to comprehend. Hexadecimal represents a mid-point where conversions between base-10 and base-2 are made easier for humans to understand.

The Programming Languages Used in the Examples

In this chapter, we cover a great deal of material in order to prepare for programming cool virtual worlds with VRML. In this process, we use the following programming languages: Microsoft QuickBASIC (or QBASIC if that's all you have), Microsoft Visual Basic for Windows, and Microsoft Visual C/C++ for DOS and Windows.

You probably already have QBASIC because it came packaged with your DOS operating system. Most BASIC languages are similar enough, however, that if you are using a different BASIC language, you shouldn't have too much trouble getting our QBASIC programs to run with your specific BASIC language.

Visual Basic is a reasonably priced package that provides a more intuitive approach to BASIC programming. Visual Basic comes in two versions — Visual Basic for DOS and Visual Basic for Windows — and in professional versions of both of these packages. We are using Visual Basic Professional 3.0 for Windows to write the Visual Basic programs for this book. We have tested the source code under Visual Basic Professional 4.0 for Windows, and it works fine in that version also.

Many versions of the C and C++ languages are available, and you should choose the one that works best for you. If you talk to other programmers about which C/C++ *compiler* (a program that translates your programming code into a form, usually machine language, that the computer can better understand) to buy, many times you will get as many different answers as there are programmers. The four dominant C/C++ programming languages seem to be Borland C/C++, Microsoft C/C++, Symantic C/C++, and Watcom C/C++.

If you're just starting out with C/C++ programming, we suggest that you try to find an older copy of Borland Turbo C/C++ for DOS or Microsoft QuickC for DOS. We've used both, but we prefer QuickC because we found it easier to use. These two programming languages will enable you to write and create DOS C programs as easily as is possible when you are learning a new language.

After you've learned the basics of C programming, you can move up to Windows programming, using the various C/C++ programming languages. We occasionally still use Turbo C++, but we have moved most of our programming applications over to Microsoft Visual C/C++ because we find it easier to use.

All of the C and C++ programs in this chapter will run and compile under Visual C/C++. If you're using a different compiler, it shouldn't take too much time to rewrite and modify some of the code to run under your specific compiler.

Creating Two-Dimensional Worlds

Recently, we saw a rerun of an old *Star Trek: The Next Generation* episode on television.

In the episode, the *Enterprise* was caught in a two-dimensional entity and was swept along with the entity toward a gravitational anomaly that would tear the ship apart. The characters had to deal with the problem of communicating with an entity that existed in only two dimensions.

This is indeed a problem. Humans, existing since birth in a three-dimensional world, interpret everything from a three-dimensional perspective. An entity that had existed since birth in a two-dimensional world would interpret everything from a two-dimensional perspective. Where would the commonality be that would enable them to communicate?

The crew of the *Enterprise* solved its problem by looking at the situation from the two-dimensional entity's perspective. Everyone lived happily ever after, and the *Enterprise* continued its mission.

This is the route we're going to take in solving the challenge of creating virtual worlds in three-dimensions. We'll begin with creating two-dimensional images for our computer screens and then change our perspective and create three-dimensional images.

The Cartesian plane

In Chapter 4, we discuss the Cartesian plane and show the graphic representation of that plane that you can see again in Figure 8-2.

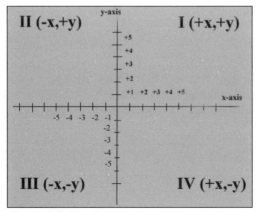

Figure 8-2: The Cartesian plane.

We will define the *origin* of the Cartesian plane as being the point designated by zero on the x-axis and zero on the y-axis. This definition is a completely arbitrary assignment.

If there is a physical point on that plane represented by the x-coordinate of +3 and the y-coordinate of +2, it is very easy for us to locate that point. From the intersection of the x- and y-axis, which represents the zero point on both axes, count three units to the right along the x-axis. Now, count up two units on the y-axis directly above the +3 point on the x-axis. This is the point located by the coordinates (3,2).

Now, keep in mind that this is all completely arbitrary. We've assigned the intersection as the zero point and called it the origin. Why did we choose this intersection as the zero point? Mainly because it made things simple. The point is that this intersection doesn't have to be the zero point. You can just as easily assign any other value to this point. Keep this in mind as you look at some of the programs that you'll be using.

Another thing that you need to consider in conjunction with this concept is that defining this point on the Cartesian plane actually requires three points. The third point is hidden in your perspective; in other words, it's based on your location as an observer. In order to define any point on a two-dimensional plane, the location of the observer must also be taken into account. We get into this concept more deeply when we start discussing plotting points in three-dimensional space.

Programming a Cartesian plane

The preceding paragraphs describe how to plot a point on the plane by hand. Now, get out your programming language, so that you can use it to plot a point on a 2D plane. Don't forget, the program listings are provided on the CD-ROM, but you'll get more experience and knowledge from actually typing the code and experimenting with it.

2DCPLANE.BAS

Load 2DCPLANE.EXE in the \QBASIC\PROGRAMS\ subdirectory on the CD-ROM. Run it once or twice and get a feel for how it works. Figure 8-3 shows what your screen looks like when the program opens.

```
                    The Cartesian Plane

              Program written by Paul M. Summitt
                 Copyright 1995, VREvolution


           1. Place a point on the Cartesian Plane
           2. Draw a line on the Cartesian Plane
           3. Draw an object on the Cartesian Plane
           4. Quit 2-D Cartesian Plane Program
?  █
```

Figure 8-3: 2DCPLANE offers the user a list of options to choose from.

Choose Option 4 in the program and press Enter to exit the program. All right, now it's your turn to type Listing 8-2.

Listing 8-2: 2DCPLANE.BAS

```
'<TAB>PROGRAM NAME:<TAB>2DCPLANE.BAS
'<TAB>PROGRAM PURPOSE:<TAB>To demonstrate placing a point, a
└line, and
'                             an object on a Cartesian Plane
'<TAB>PROGRAM DATE:<TAB>August 4, 1995
'<TAB>PROGRAM AUTHOR:<TAB>Paul M. Summitt
'<TAB>COPYRIGHT:<TAB>VREvolution, 1995
DECLARE SUB dataenter ()
DECLARE SUB ASK ()
DECLARE SUB graph ()
DECLARE SUB another ()
DECLARE SUB placepoint ()
```

(continued)

Listing 8-2: *(continued)*

```
DECLARE SUB mainmenu ()
DECLARE SUB drawline ()
DECLARE SUB drawobject ()
DECLARE SUB linedraw ()
DECLARE SUB drawbox ()
DIM SHARED xcord&, ycord&, xcord1&, ycord1&, xcord2&, ycord2&
SCREEN 12
mainmenu
END
SUB dataenter
LOCATE 12, 15
PRINT "<39 spaces>"
PRINT TAB(15); "<37 spaces>"
PRINT TAB(15); "<40 spaces>"
PRINT TAB(15); "<34 spaces>"
PRINT "<5 spaces>"
LOCATE 16, 1
PRINT "You have indicated that you wish"
PRINT " to enter and plot x- and y-"
PRINT " coordinates on the Cartesian Plane."
LOCATE 20, 1
INPUT "Type the x-coordinate:"; xcord&
<TAB>IF xcord& < -9 OR xcord& > 9 THEN
<TAB><TAB>dataenter
<TAB>END IF
LOCATE 21, 1
INPUT "Type the y-coordinate;"; ycord&
<TAB>IF ycord& < -9 OR ycord& > 9 THEN
<TAB><TAB>dataenter
<TAB>END IF
graph
placepoint
END SUB
SUB drawbox
LINE (xcord1&, ycord1&)-(xcord2&, ycord2&), 14, BF
LOCATE 12, 45
PRINT "Press spacebar to continue"; INKEY$
<TAB>WHILE spBar$ <> " "
<TAB><TAB>spBar$ = INKEY$
<TAB>WEND
LOCATE 12, 45
PRINT "<27 spaces>"
mainmenu
```

```
END SUB
SUB drawline
LOCATE 12, 15
PRINT "<39 spaces>"
PRINT TAB(15); "<37 spaces>"
PRINT TAB(15); "<40 spaces>"
PRINT TAB(15); "<35 spaces>"
PRINT "<5 spaces>"
LOCATE 16, 1
PRINT "You have indicated that you wish"
PRINT " to draw a line<13 spaces>"
PRINT " on the Cartesian Plane.<12 spaces>"
LOCATE 20, 1
INPUT "Type the first x-coordinate:"; xcord1&
IF xcord1& < -9 OR xcord1& > 9 THEN
dataenter
END IF
LOCATE 21, 1
INPUT "Type the first y-coordinate;"; ycord1&
IF ycord1& < -9 OR ycord1& > 9 THEN
dataenter
END IF
LOCATE 20, 1
PRINT "<40 spaces>"
LOCATE 20, 1
INPUT "Type the second x-coordinate:"; xcord2&
IF xcord2& < -9 OR xcord2& > 9 THEN
dataenter
END IF
LOCATE 21, 1
PRINT "<40 spaces>"
LOCATE 21, 1
INPUT "Type the second y-coordinate;"; ycord2&
IF ycord2& < -9 OR ycord2& > 9 THEN
dataenter
END IF
graph
linedraw
END SUB
SUB drawobject
LOCATE 12, 15
PRINT "<39 spaces>"
PRINT TAB(15); "<37 spaces>"
PRINT TAB(15); "<40 spaces>"
PRINT TAB(15); "<35 spaces>"
PRINT "<5 spaces>"
LOCATE 16, 1
```

(continued)

Listing 8-2: *(continued)*

```
PRINT "You have indicated that you wish"
PRINT " to draw an object (a box)<2 spaces>"
PRINT " on the Cartesian Plane.<12 spaces>"
LOCATE 20, 1
INPUT "Type the first x-coordinate:"; xcord1&
IF xcord1& < -9 OR xcord1& > 9 THEN
dataenter
END IF
LOCATE 21, 1
INPUT "Type the first y-coordinate;"; ycord1&
IF ycord1& < -9 OR ycord1& > 9 THEN
dataenter
END IF
LOCATE 20, 1
PRINT "<40 spaces>"
LOCATE 20, 1
INPUT "Type the second x-coordinate:"; xcord2&
IF xcord2& < -9 OR xcord2& > 9 THEN
dataenter
END IF
LOCATE 21, 1
PRINT "<40 spaces>"
LOCATE 21, 1
INPUT "Type the second y-coordinate;"; ycord2&
IF ycord2& < -9 OR ycord2& > 9 THEN
dataenter
END IF
graph
drawbox
END SUB
SUB graph
LOCATE 16, 1
PRINT "<32 spaces>"
PRINT "<28 spaces>"
PRINT "<36 spaces>"
LOCATE 20, 1
PRINT "<28 spaces>"
LOCATE 21, 1
PRINT "<37 spaces>"
VIEW (315, 235)-(629, 469)
WINDOW (-10, -10)-(10, 10)
PAINT (0, 0), 1
LINE (-9, 0)-(9, 0), 15
LINE (0, 9)-(0, -9), 15
FOR x1 = -8 TO 8 STEP 1
LINE (x1, -.5)-(x1, .5)
NEXT x1
```

```
FOR y1 = -8 TO 8 STEP 1
LINE (-.5, y1)-(.5, y1)
NEXT y1
END SUB
SUB linedraw
LINE (xcord1&, ycord1&)-(xcord2&, ycord2&), 14
LOCATE 12, 45
PRINT "Press spacebar to continue"; INKEY$
WHILE spBar$ <> " "
spBar$ = INKEY$
WEND
LOCATE 12, 45
PRINT "                              "
mainmenu
END SUB
SUB mainmenu
CLS
LOCATE 5, 29
PRINT "The Cartesian Plane"
LOCATE 8, 22
PRINT "Program written by Paul M. Summitt"
LOCATE 9, 25
PRINT "Copyright 1995, VREvolution"
LOCATE 12, 15
PRINT "1. Place a point on the Cartesian Plane"
PRINT TAB(15); "2. Draw a line on the Cartesian Plane"
PRINT TAB(15); "3. Draw an object on the Cartesian Plane"
PRINT TAB(15); "4. Quit 2-D Cartesian Plane Program"
INPUT choice
SELECT CASE choice
CASE IS = 1
dataenter
CASE IS = 2
drawline
CASE IS = 3
drawobject
CASE IS = 4
CLS
PRINT "Thank you for using the"
PRINT "2-D Cartesian Plane Program."
END
END SELECT
END SUB
SUB placepoint
PSET (xcord&, ycord&), 14
LOCATE 12, 45
PRINT "Press spacebar to continue"; INKEY$
WHILE spBar$ <> " "
```

(continued)

Listing 8-2: *(continued)*

```
spBar$ = INKEY$
WEND
LOCATE 12, 45
PRINT "<27 spaces>"
mainmenu
END SUB
```

The main purpose of typing this program is to become familiar with the graphics commands that place a point in 2D space, draw a line in 2D space, and draw an object in 2D space. Those commands are:

```
PSET (xcord&, ycord&), 14
```

Place a yellow point at the x and y coordinates.

```
LINE (xcord1&, ycord1&)-(xcord2&, ycord2&), 14
```

Draw a yellow line from the first x, y coordinates to the second x, y coordinates.

```
LINE (xcord1&, ycord1&)-(xcord2&, ycord2&), 14, BF
```

Draw a box using the first and second x, y coordinates as corners and fill this box with the foreground color selected, which is yellow.

The format for the PSET command in QBASIC is

```
PSET (x, y) color
```

where the point is defined by its x- and y-coordinates, and by a number representing the color that the point is to be displayed in. In the preceding example, the user-provided x-coordinate is located in the variable xcord& and the user-provided y-coordinate is located in the variable ycord&. The number 14 defines the color for the point to be displayed in as yellow.

The format for the LINE command in QBASIC is

```
LINE (x1, y1) - (x2, y2), color
```

where the line to be drawn is defined by its beginning point, described by (x1, y1), and its ending point, described by (x2, y2). The color is optional. In the example from the program, the user has provided x1 and y1 in the form of xcord1& and ycord1&. The user has also provided x2 and y2 in the form of xcord2& and ycord2&. The number 14 defines the color for the line to be displayed in as yellow.

Finally, the format for the LINE command in QBASIC that creates the box is

```
LINE (x1, y1) - (x2, y2), color, BF
```

where the box to be drawn is defined by two points, (x1, y1) and (x2, y2). These two points are defined by the user input in our program. The color again is yellow. The B tells QBASIC to create the box and the F tells QBASIC to fill the box with the default foreground color.

All right, you can create two-dimensional points, lines, and objects now. But that's not why you bought this book. You need to move past whatever BASIC program you're working with and on to more advanced languages.

2DCP2.BAS

In this section, we create a program similar to the 2DCPLANE program, but this time we use Visual Basic 3.0 for Windows Professional Development System. If you have Visual Basic 3.0, feel free to work along with us.

All the files necessary for this project are in the \VB\CODE\ subdirectory on the CD-ROM that accompanies this book. An executable version called 2DCP2.EXE is in the \VB\PROGRAMS\ subdirectory. Figure 8-4 shows what the computer screen looks like when you run 2DCP2.EXE. When you run the program from Windows, notice the differences between it and the preceding DOS version of the Cartesian plane program. We discuss these differences later in the chapter.

The Visual Basic version, like the QBASIC program, enables you to place a point, draw a line, or draw a box on the Cartesian plane. Begin by running the executable version of the program, 2DCP2.EXE, in the \VB\PROGRAMS\ subdirectory on the CD-ROM that comes with this book. Notice the Cartesian plane coordinate system in the program window.

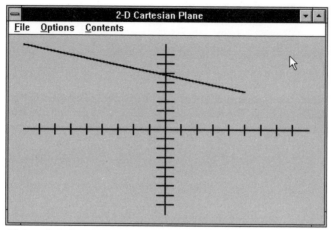

Figure 8-4: The Cartesian Plane in 2DCP2.EXE.

Follow these steps to place a point at a given location.

1.   **Choose Point from the Options menu.**

2.   **Enter an x coordinate and a y coordinate and click OK.**

     The point is placed at the x and y location that you've chosen.

Next, draw a line.

1.   **Choose Line from the Option menu.**

2.   **Enter coordinates for the beginning and ending points of the line and click OK.**

     The line is drawn in the window.

Now draw a box.

1.   **Choose Box from the Option menu.**

     You see a screen that is very similar to the one that you saw when you chose the Line option.

2.   **Enter the two x and y coordinates and click OK.**

     The program draws a box in the location that you specified.

After one more version of this 2D demonstration program, you'll be ready to make the transition from two dimensions to three dimensions. Exit Visual Basic and run your C compiler.

2DCP3.CPP

This final DOS version of the 2D examples was written using Microsoft C/C++. The program is relatively simple and should run with a minimum of changes if your are using a different compiler.

Basically, the C version is similar to the two preceding versions. The difference is that, with C++, as with Visual Basic for Windows, you can move easily into 3D programming.

Load your C/C++ compiler and enter Listing 8-3. The executable version of the program is in the \C\PROGRAMS subdirectory, and the code listing is in the \C\CODE\ subdirectory of the CD-ROM that comes with this book. Figure 8-5 shows what your screen looks like when 2DCP3.EXE opens.

Once again, run the program and play with the various options before you go on. You have three options, as with the two preceding versions of this program: place a point, draw a line, and draw a box. Practice these three tasks for a few moments and then look back at the other two programs again.

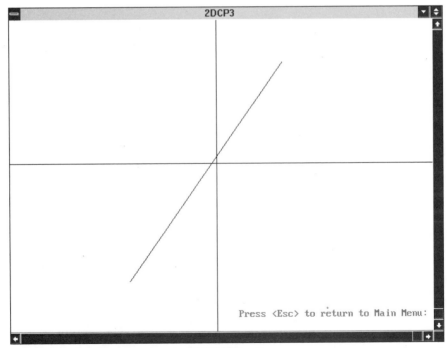

Figure 8-5: The Cartesian plane in 2DCP3.EXE.

Listing 8-3: 2DCP3.CPP

```cpp
// Program Name:   2DCP3.cpp
// Purpose: To demonstrate placing a point, drawing
// a line, and drawing a square on a two-
// dimensional Cartesian Plane
// Copyright: 1995, VREvolution
// Programmer: Paul M. Summitt
#include <iostream.h>
#include <graph.h>
#include <stdlib.h>
#include <stdio.h>
#include <bios.h>
struct videoconfig vc;
void coords(void);
void graph(void);
void mainmenu(void);
void placepoint(void);
void drawline(void);
void drawbox(void);
void keyboard(void);
void quit_prgm(void);
void graphics_setup(void);
// declare global variables
int C0=0,C1=1,C2=2,C3=3,C4=4,C5=5,
C6=6,C7=7,C8=8,C9=9,C10=10,C11=11,
C12=12,C13=13,C14=14,C15=15,mode_flag=0;
int x_res = 640,y_res = 480,x_zero=x_res/2,y_zero=y_res/2;
int sx,sy,x,y,x1,x2,x3,x4,y1,y2,y3,y4;
int color,index;
char response;
// M A I N   R O U T I N E
main()
{
graphics_setup();
_getvideoconfig(&vc);
mainmenu();
quit_prgm();
return(0);
}
// SUBROUTINE: coords()
void coords()
{
sx=sx*(x_res/640);
sy=sy*(y_res/480);
return;
}
```

```
// SUBROUTINE: mainmenu()
void mainmenu()
{
_clearscreen(_GCLEARSCREEN);
cout << "\n\n\n\n\t\t\tThe Cartesian Plane\n\n";
cout << "\t\tA. Place Point on the Cartesian Plane\n";
cout << "\t\tB. Draw Line on the Cartesian Plane\n";
cout << "\t\tC. Draw Rectangle on the Cartesian Plane\n";
cout << "\t\tD. Quit this program\n\n\n";
cout << "\t\t\tEnter A, B, C, or D: <3 spaces>";
cin >> response;
switch (toupper(response))
{
case 'A':
<x spaces> placepoint();
<x spaces> break;
case 'B':
<x spaces> drawline();
<x spaces> break;
case 'C':
<x spaces> drawbox();
<x spaces> break;
case 'D':
<x spaces> quit_prgm();
<x spaces> break;
default:
<x spaces> mainmenu();
<x spaces> break;
};
return;
}
// SUBROUTINE: placepoint()
void placepoint()
{
cout << "\nEnter the x-coordinate: <3 spaces>";
cin >> x1;
cout << "\nEnter the y-coordinate: <3 spaces>";
cin >> y1;
sx=x1;
sy=y1;
coords();
graph();
x=x_zero + (sx*32);
y=y_zero - (sy*24);
color = rand()%16;
_setcolor(color);
```

(continued)

Listing 8-3: *(continued)*

```
_setpixel(x,y);
keyboard();
mainmenu();
}
// SUBROUTINE: drawline()
void drawline()
{
cout << "\nEnter the first x-coordinate: <3 spaces>";
cin >> x;
cout << "\nEnter the first y-coordinate: <3 spaces>";
cin >> y;
sx=x;
sy=y;
coords();
x1=x_zero + (sx*32);
y1=y_zero - (sy*24);
cout << "\nEnter the second x-coordinate: <3 spaces>";
cin >> x;
cout << "\nEnter the second y-coordinate: <3 spaces>";
cin >> y;
sx=x;
sy=y;
coords();
x2=x_zero + (sx*32);
y2=y_zero - (sy*24);
graph();
_moveto(x1,y1);
_lineto(x2,y2);
keyboard();
mainmenu();
}
// SUBROUTINE: drawbox()
void drawbox()
{
cout << "\nEnter the x-coordinate for the upper left corner:
└<3 spaces> ";
cin >> x;
cout << "\nEnter the y-coordinate for the upper left corner:
└<3 spaces> ";
cin >> y;
sx=x;
sy=y;
coords();
x1=x_zero + (sx*32);
y1=y_zero - (sy*24);
cout << "\nEnter the x-coordinate for the upper right corner:
└<3 spaces> ";
```

```
cin >> x;
cout << "\nEnter the y-coordinate for the upper right corner:
⌐<3 spaces> ";
cin >> y;
sx=x;
sy=y;
coords();
x2=x_zero + (sx*32);
y2=y_zero - (sy*24);
cout << "\nEnter the x-coordinate for the lower left corner:
⌐<3 spaces> ";
cin >> x;
cout << "\nEnter the y-coordinate for the lower left corner:
⌐<3 spaces> ";
cin >> y;
sx=x;
sy=y;
coords();
x3=x_zero + (sx*32);
y3=y_zero - (sy*24);
cout << "\nEnter the x-coordinate for the lower right corner:
⌐<3 spaces> ";
cin >> x;
cout << "\nEnter the y-coordinate for the lower right corner:
⌐<3 spaces> ";
cin >> y;
sx=x;
sy=y;
coords();
x4=x_zero + (sx*32);
y4=y_zero - (sy*24);
graph();
_moveto(x1,y1);
_lineto(x2,y2);
_lineto(x3,y3);
_lineto(x4,y4);
_lineto(x1,y1);
keyboard();
mainmenu();
}
// SUBROUTINE: quit_prgm()
void quit_prgm()
{
_clearscreen(_GCLEARSCREEN);
_setvideomode(_DEFAULTMODE);
return;
}
```

(continued)

Listing 8-3: *(continued)*

```
// SUBROUTINE: graph()
void graph()
{
_clearscreen(_GCLEARSCREEN);
_settextposition(29,45);
_outtext("Press <Esc> to return to Main Menu: <3 spaces> ");
_moveto (0, y_res/2);
_lineto (x_res,y_res/2);
_moveto (x_res/2, 0);
_lineto (x_res/2,y_res);
return;
}
// SUBROUTINE: graphics_setup(void)
void graphics_setup()
{
VGA_mode:
if (_setvideomode(_VRES16COLOR)==0)
{
goto EGA_ECD_mode;
}
else
{
x_res=640;
y_res=480;
mode_flag=1;
_settextcolor(7);
_settextposition(30,30);
_outtext("640x480 16-color VGA mode");
return;
}
EGA_ECD_mode:
if (_setvideomode(_ERESCOLOR)==0)
{
goto EGA_SCD_mode;
}
else
{
x_res=640;
y_res=350;
mode_flag=2;
_settextcolor(7);
_settextposition(25,30);
_outtext("640x350 16-color EGA mode");
return;
}
```

```
EGA_SCD_mode:
if (_setvideomode(_HRES16COLOR)==0)
{
goto CGA_mode;
}
else
{
x_res=640;
y_res=200;
mode_flag=3;
_settextcolor(7);
_settextposition(25,30);
_outtext("640x200 16-color EGA mode");
return;
}
CGA_mode:
if (_setvideomode(_MRES4COLOR)==0)
{
goto abort_message;
}
else
{
x_res=320;
y_res=200;
C0=0;C1=3;C2=3;C3=3;C4=3;C5=3;C6=2;C7=3;C8=2;
C9=1;C10=3;C11=1;C12=3;C13=1;C14=3;C15=3;
mode_flag=4;
_settextcolor(3);
_settextposition(25,10);
_outtext("320x200 4-color CGA mode");
return;
}
abort_message:
<2 spaces> cout << "\n\nUnable to proceed.\n";
<2 spaces> cout << "Requires VGA,EGA, or CGA adapter\n";
<2 spaces> cout << "  with appropriate monitor.\n";
exit(0);
}
// SUBROUTINE: keyboard()
void keyboard(void)
{
union u_type
{
int a;
char b[3];
}
```

(continued)

Listing 8-3: *(continued)*

```
keystroke;
int get_keystroke(void);
do keystroke.a=get_keystroke();
while (keystroke.b[0]!=27);
}
int get_keystroke(void)
{
union REGS regs;
regs.h.ah=0;
return int86(0x16,&regs,&regs);
}
```

Note that although all three programs (2DCPLANE.EXE, 2DCP2.EXE, and 2DCP3.EXE) do the same things, because of their originating language, they do these three things differently. The operation and appearance of the Cartesian planes and the objects placed there are close to identical, but they are still different. Each language and each program that you use will place its own distinctive imprint on the finished product (which is why we asked you to do the same thing three times). The programming process and language structure the way you think, the way you program, and the way you create your worlds.

This "imprint" of the structure on your mind and your final product will become even more apparent as you make the move from two dimensions to three dimensions. In Chapter 4, we discuss some of the different PC programs that create VR environments. Some of those programs use a left-handed coordinate system, and others use a right-handed coordinate system. This is just a small example of the differences that exist between the languages and programs that you are going to be exposed to.

You can't get away from this structuring, but if you are aware of it, you can make efforts to keep it from ruling you indiscriminately. Don't allow yourself to be locked into one point of view.

Keeping in mind that languages and programming styles structure the way we think, we can move on to making the transition from two dimensions to three dimensions.

Making the Transition from 2D to 3D

So far you've placed points, drawn lines, and created boxes on the two-dimensional plane. In this part of the chapter, you learn to do the same things on a three-dimensional Cartesian coordinate system.

First, however, look at the program FVT.EXE in the \PROGRAMS\ subdirectory of the CD-ROM that accompanies this book. FVT is a program by Todd Porter that enables you to visualize various mathematical formulas in three-dimensional space. Run the program from the VR interface for the CD-ROM by clicking on the virtual building labeled FVT.

The first thing that you see after the program loads is a three-dimensional representation of a sine wave.

Compare this 3D sine wave to the sine wave in Figures 8-6 and 8-7, which are repeated from Chapter 4. Notice the similarities in how the sine wave is represented but also notice the differences.

These graphic images show how a visualization created with one language can differ from a visualization of the same formula that has been created with another language. They also show how a 2D visualization differs from a 3D visualization.

In addition to the formula for the sine wave, there are several other mathematical formulas built into FVT as well as the ability to visualize your own formula. Look at the other formulas and plug in your own formulas before moving on.

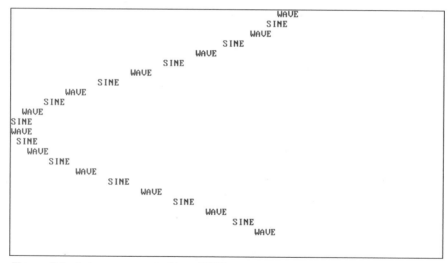

Figure 8-6: A sine wave created by a BASIC program.

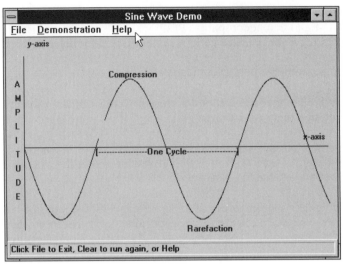

Figure 8-7: A sine wave created by a Visual Basic program.

How Many Coordinates Does It Take to Define a Point in 3D Space?

Before moving on to the software and virtual worlds that we cover in the remainder of this chapter, we need to point out some areas that can lead to problems when you are working in three dimensions.

As we said earlier in the chapter, on a two-dimensional plane, a third coordinate, identifying the location of the observer, is a hidden qualifier of what the point, line, or object looks like.

The placement of the origin, or the zero point, is completely at the discretion of the observer. For this reason, in most cases, no two observations are identical because each person tends to use his or her own location as the origin.

As a result, problems arise when people try to compare their observations. To solve the problem, they need to assign a third origin that is arbitrary, and both of them need to use that origin.

Another source of problems is the differences in the ways that programs create virtual worlds. They all define virtual worlds, but they define them in their own particular way. Some programs use a left-handed coordinate system (the x-axis grows larger on the right of the screen, the y-axis grows larger toward the top of the screen, and the z-axis grows larger into the screen).

Other programs use a right-handed coordinate system (the x-axis grows larger to the right, the z-axis grows larger toward the top of the screen, and the y-axis grows larger away from you into the screen).

Each system twists the coordinate axes in the programmer's own particular — and for the programmer's purposes necessary — ways. It's not important which way the virtual world is defined as long as you are fully aware of how the virtual world is defined and maintain that awareness while you are working with a particular system. Because most of us have worked with Cartesian planes, the left-handed coordinate system is easier to understand.

The point is to not get too confused or frustrated as you examine these systems. The particularities of any particular coordinate system are not important as long as you know what the systems are. Knowing this enables you to know where you are in the virtual world.

Building Your First 3D Object

It's time now to build your first three-dimensional object — a simple cube — using C/C++ to build it by hand and then using Todd Porter's 2Morrow World Builder to build it. Finally, you build it interactively by using Caligari's trueSpace2 and Virtus WalkThrough VRML.

Building a 3D cube with C/C++

Your first 3D project is to build the cube using C/C++. The code simply displays a wire frame cube floating in 3D space (See Figure 8-8).

The executable file for CUBE1.EXE is in the \C\PROGRAMS\ subdirectory of the CD-ROM. When you run the file, you see something similar to Figure 8-8 on your screen.

Type Listing 8-4. If you don't want to take the time to type the code and examine it as you type, the C code for CUBE1.C is in the \C\CODE\ subdirectory. You will miss the experience of the creation process, however, which is very important to your growth as a VR programmer.

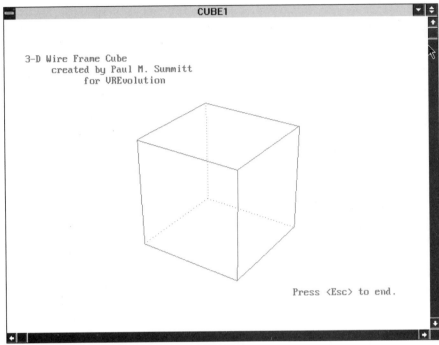

Figure 8-8: Your first 3D object, a cube as created with CUBE1.EXE.

Listing 8-4: CUBE1.C

```
/*<TAB>Program Name:<TAB>CUBE1.c */
/*<TAB>Purpose:<TAB>To Demonstrate how a simple cube can be
Lcreated */
/*<TAB><TAB>using C in a 3D coordinate system. */
/*<TAB>Compatibility:<TAB>Supports all graphics adapters and
Lmonitors. */
/*<TAB><TAB>The software uses the 640x480 16-color
Lmode */
/*<TAB><TAB>if a VGA is present, the 640x350 16-color mode */
/*<TAB><TAB>if an EGA and enhanced monitor are present, */
/*<TAB><TAB>the 640x200 16-color mode if an EGA and */
/*<TAB><TAB>standard monitor are present, and the 320x200 */
/*<TAB><TAB>4-color mode is a CGA is present. */
/*<TAB>Programmer:<TAB>Paul M. Summitt */
/*<TAB>Company:<TAB>VREvolution */
/*<TAB>Copyright Date:<TAB>August 8, 1995 */
/*<TAB>INCLUDE FILES<TAB>*/
```

```
#include <dos.h>
#include <stdio.h>
#include <graph.h>
#include <math.h>
/*<TAB>declare global variables<TAB>*/
struct videoconfig vc;
float x=0.0, y=0.0, z=0.0;
float sx=0.0,sy=0.0;
float xa=0.0,ya=0.0,za=0.0;
float sxa=0.0,sya=0.0,sxb=0.0,syb=0.0;
float sxs=0.0,sys=0.0;
float temp_swap=0.0;
float d=1200.0;
double r1=5.68319;
double r2=6.28319;
double r3=5.79778;
double sr1=0.0,sr2=0.0,sr3=0.0;
double cr1=0.0,cr2=0.0,cr3=0.0;
float mx=0.0,my=0.0,mz=-350.0;
int maxx=638,minx=1,maxy=198,miny=1;
float screen_x=639, screen_y=199;
float c=0.0;
float rx=0.0,ry=0.0;
int t1=0,t2=0;
int p1=0;
int array1[][3]={
30,-30,30, 30,-30,-30, -30,-30,-30, -30,-30,30, 30,-30,30,
30,30,-30, -30,30,-30, -30,-30,-30, 30,-30,-30, 30,30,-30,
-30,30,-30, -30,30,30, -30,-30,30, -30,-30,-30, -30,30,-30,
-30,30,30, 30,30,30, 30,-30,30, -30,-30,30, -30,30,30,
30,30,30, 30,30,-30, 30,-30,-30, 30,-30,30, 30,30,30,
-30,30,-30, 30,30,-30, 30,30,30, -30,30,30, -30,30,-30};
int C0=0,C1=1,C2=2,C3=3,C4=4,C5=5,C6=6,C7=7,C8=8,C9=9,C10=10,
<TAB>C11=11,C12=12,C13=13,C14=14,C15=15,mode_flag=0;
float sx1,sy1,sx2,sy2;
float x_res,y_res;
void keyboard(void);
void quit_prgm(void);
void calc_3d(void);
void rotation(void);
void window(void);
void viewport(void);
void graphics_setup(void);
void labels(void);
void coords(void);
/*M A I N   R O U T I N E*/
main()
{
```

(continued)

Listing 8-4: *(continued)*

```
graphics_setup();
_getvideoconfig(&vc);
_setcolor(C7);
sx=0;
sy=24;
coords();
sx1=sx;
sy1=sy;
sx=638;
sy=455;
coords();
sx2=sx;
sy2=sy;
rotation();
for (t2=1;t2<=6;t2++)
{
if (t2<4) _setlinestyle(0x8888);
else _setlinestyle(0xffff);
x=array1[p1][0];
y=array1[p1][1];
z=array1[p1][2];
calc_3d();
window();
sxa=sx;
sya=sy;
for (t1=1;t1<=4;t1++)
{
p1++;
x=array1[p1][0];
y=array1[p1][1];
z=array1[p1][2];
calc_3d();
window();
sxs=sx;
sys=sy;
sxb=sx;
syb=sy;
viewport();
_moveto(sxa,sya);
_lineto(sxb,syb);
sxa=sxs;
sya=sys;
}
p1++;
```

```
}
labels();
keyboard();
quit_prgm();
}
void rotation(void)
{
sr1=sin(r1);
sr2=sin(r2);
sr3=sin(r3);
cr1=cos(r1);
cr2=cos(r2);
cr3=cos(r3);
return;
}
/* SUBROUTINE: calc_3d() */
void calc_3d(void)
{
x=(-1)*x;
xa=cr1*x-sr1*z;
za=sr1*x+cr1*z;
x=cr2*xa+sr2*y;
ya=cr2*y-sr2*xa;
z=cr3*za-sr3*ya;
y=sr3*za+cr3*ya;
x=x+mx;
y=y+my;
z=z+mz;
sx=d*x/z;
sy=d*y/z;
return;
}
/* SUBROUTINE: window() */
void window(void)
{
sx=sx+399;
sy=sy+299;
rx=screen_x/799;
ry=screen_y/599;
sx=sx*rx;
sy=sy*ry;
return;
}
/* SUBROUTINE: viewport() */
void viewport(void)
{
if (sxa>sxb)
{
```

(continued)

Listing 8-4: *(continued)*

```
temp_swap=sxa;
sxa=sxb;
sxb=temp_swap;
temp_swap=sya;
sya=syb;
syb=temp_swap;
};
if (sxa<minx) if (sxb<minx) return;
if (sxa>maxx) if (sxb>maxx) return;
if (sya<miny) if (syb<miny) return;
if (sya>maxy) if (syb>maxy) return;
if (sxa<minx)
{
{
c=(syb-sya)/(sxb-sxa)*(sxb-minx);
sxa=minx;
sya=syb-c;
};
if (sya<miny) if (syb<miny) return;
if (sya>maxy) if (syb>maxy) return;
};
if (sxb>maxx)
{
{
c=(syb-sya)/(sxb-sxa)*(maxx-sxa);
sxb=maxx;
syb=sya+c;
};
if (sya<miny) if (syb<miny) return;
if (sya>maxy) if (syb>maxy) return;
};
if (sya>syb)
{
temp_swap=sya;
sya=syb;
syb=temp_swap;
temp_swap=sxa;
sxa=sxb;
sxb=temp_swap;
};
if (sya<miny)
{
c=(sxb-sxa)/(syb-sya)*(syb-miny);
sxa=sxb-c;
sya=miny;
```

```
};
if (syb>maxy)
{
c=(sxb-sxa)/(syb-sya)*(maxy-sya);
sxb=sxa+c;
syb=maxy;
;
return;
}
/* SUBROUTINE: keyboard() */
void keyboard(void)
{
union u_type
{
int a;
char b[3];
}
keystroke;
int get_keystroke(void);
do keystroke.a=get_keystroke();
while (keystroke.b[0]!=27);
}
int get_keystroke(void)
{
union REGS regs;
regs.h.ah=0;
return int86(0x16,&regs,&regs);
}
/* SUBROUTINE: quit_prgm() */
void quit_prgm(void)
{
  _clearscreen(_GCLEARSCREEN);
  _setvideomode(_DEFAULTMODE);
}
/* SUBROUTINE: graphics_setup() */
void graphics_setup(void)
{
VGA_mode:
if (_setvideomode(_VRES16COLOR)==0)
{
goto EGA_ECD_mode;
}
else
{
x_res=640;
y_res=480;
mode_flag=1;
```

Listing 8-4: *(continued)*

```
maxx=638;
minx=1;
maxy=478;
miny=1;
screen_x=639;
screen_y=479;
return;
}
EGA_ECD_mode:
if (_setvideomode(_ERESCOLOR)==0)
{
goto EGA_SCD_mode;
}
else
{
x_res=640;
y_res=350;
mode_flag=2;
maxx=638;
minx=1;
maxy=348;
miny=1;
screen_x=639;
screen_y=349;
return;
}
EGA_SCD_mode:
if (_setvideomode(_HRES16COLOR)==0)
{
goto CGA_mode;
}
else
{
x_res=640;
y_res=200;
mode_flag=3;
maxx=638;
minx=1;
maxy=198;
miny=1;
screen_x=639;
screen_y=199;
return;
}
```

```
CGA_mode:
if (_setvideomode(_MRES4COLOR)==0)
{
goto abort_message;
}
else
{
x_res=320;
y_res=200;
C7=3;
mode_flag=4;
maxx=318;
minx=1;
maxy=198;
miny=1;
screen_x=319;
screen_y=199;
return;
}
abort_message:
printf("\n\nUnable to proceed.\n");
printf("Requires VGA,EGA, or CGA adapter\n");
printf("  with appropriate monitor.\n");
exit(0);
}
/*1 space SUBROUTINE: coords()1 space*/
void coords(void)
{
sx=sx*(x_res/640);
sy=sy*(y_res/480);
return;
}
/* SUBROUTINE: labels() */
void labels(void)
{
_settextcolor(C7);
_settextposition(4,5);
_outtext("3D Wire Frame Cube");
_settextposition(5,10);
_outtext("created by Paul M. Summitt");
_settextposition(6,16);
_outtext("for VREvolution");
_settextposition(25,54);
_outtext("Press <Esc> to end.");
return;
}
```

This code creates the wireframe cube floating in black space. You've created a 3D cube using C/C++ now. It's time to create a cube using Todd Porter's 2Morrow World Builder.

Building a 3D cube in 2Morrow World Builder

In the preceding example, you created a cube by hand using C/C++. A cube, however, is simple enough that many of the software programs available today for building worlds include some form of a cube. The cube comes in the form of a specific file structure.

Many of these file structures are nothing more than descriptions that enable the specific software program to read the information that makes up the object and render this object in a three-dimensional environment. These descriptions are most often in the ASCII file format. In other words, these structures can be read by us humans as well as by the computer.

One such structure is the PLG format. PLG is a file extension that was used originally to designate the Hewlett-Packard graphics language format. The format is currently used to describe objects used with such DOS-based world renderers as REND386, VRBASIC, AVRIL, VR386, and 2Morrow World Builder.

Many CAD and 3D programs, such as NorthCad and trueSpace2, can produce PLG files or files that can be translated into the PLG format by the various conversion programs that are available. We walk through the steps involved in creating a cube by using trueSpace2 and WalkThrough VRML later in the chapter, but first you need to know the steps involved in creating a PLG file by hand.

The PLG format is quite easy to understand. Look at Listing 8-5 carefully. Descriptions of what the components of the format mean follow the listing.

Listing 8-5: CUBEALL.PLG

```
# a cube visible from the outside and inside, 10000x10000
cubeall 8 12

# vertices:
# X    Y    Z
       # front face
  -500  -500  -500  #VTX 0   # vertex 0
   500  -500  -500  #VTX 1   # vertex 1
   500   500  -500  #VTX 2   # vertex 2
  -500   500  -500  #VTX 3   # vertex 3
```

```
         # back face
 -500  -500   500   #VTX 4  # vertex 4
  500  -500   500   #VTX 5  # vertex 5
  500   500   500   #VTX 6  # vertex 6
 -500   500   500   #VTX 7  # vertex 7

# polygons: all cosine-lit, assorted colors
# color #verts vert1 vert2 ...

# these faces are derived from a shifted square
0x11ff   4 0 1 2 3 # front face: counterclockwise
0x12ff   4 7 6 5 4 # back face: clockwise

# these faces are facing us in the sketch, thus are CCW
0x13ff   4 2 6 7 3 # top
0x14ff   4 1 5 6 2 # right side

# these faces are away from us in the sketch, and thus CW
0x15ff   4 0 4 5 1 # bottom
0x16ff   4 0 3 7 4 # left side

# faces with vertex order reversed let cube be seen from the
inside

0x11ff   4 3 2 1 0 # front wall
0x12ff   4 4 5 6 7 # back wall

0x13ff   4 3 7 6 2 # top
0x14ff   4 2 6 5 1 # right side

0x15ff   4 1 5 4 0 # bottom
0x16ff   4 4 7 3 0 # left side
```

The PLG file format is normally composed of one or more object definitions. Each definition consists of a name, a vertex list, and a polygon list.

Some of this format's syntax is brought forward from the C language. As a result, the # sign alerts the compiler, or world renderer, that what follows it on the same line is a comment and is to be ignored. Another thing that is ignored in these files, as in C programs, is *whitespace*. Whitespace is the empty space left to create a pleasing aesthetic appearance to the file listing. The first line in CUBEALL.PLG, is, therefore, a comment telling you what this particular PLG file contains: a cube visible from the outside and inside with a size of 10000 x 10000.

The next line in the example file is the name line. This line must consist of a name, which can have no spaces or underscores, the number of *vertices* the object has, and the number of *polygons* in the object. A *vertex* (vertices is plural) is a point that marks the intersection of two or more edges of a particular polygon or graphic object. A *polygon* is a two-dimensional figure that consists of an ordered set of vertices connected in sequence by sides that don't intersect. In other words, the connection of these vertices forms a closed surface.

In the example PLG file, the name line is

```
cubeall 8 12
```

The name of the object is cubeall. It has 8 vertices and 12 polygons because it can be seen from both the inside and the outside.

Next is a group of comments that tell you that you are dealing with the vertex list and also help you interpret the meaning of the numbers that you are about to see. This vertex list supplies the x, y, and z coordinates of each of the vertices that describe the shape of the object that is being defined. In the example, the vertex list reads:

```
# vertices:
# X    Y    Z
        # front face
 -500  -500  -500  #VTX 0    # vertex 0
  500  -500  -500  #VTX 1    # vertex 1
  500   500  -500  #VTX 2    # vertex 2
 -500   500  -500  #VTX 3    # vertex 3

        # back face
 -500  -500   500  #VTX 4    # vertex 4
  500  -500   500  #VTX 5    # vertex 5
  500   500   500  #VTX 6    # vertex 6
 -500   500   500  #VTX 7    # vertex 7
```

With the exception of the three columns of numbers, everything else in this example is a comment, and as we explained before, is ignored. As indicated in the comment, the first column is the x-coordinate of the various vertices listed. The y- and z-coordinates for these vertices are provided in the second and third columns.

Another thing that you should notice is that the vertices are numbered and, although there are eight vertices, the numbers of the vertices run from 0 to 7. These numbers represent each vertex's specific identifying index number and can be used for more advanced programming applications.

Finally, here is the polygon list:

```
# polygons: all cosine-lit, assorted colors
# color #verts vert1 vert2 ...

# these faces are derived from a shifted square
0x11ff  4 0 1 2 3 # front face: counterclockwise
0x12ff  4 7 6 5 4 # back face: clockwise

# these faces are facing us in the sketch, thus are CCW
0x13ff  4 2 6 7 3 # top
0x14ff  4 1 5 6 2 # right side

# these faces are away from us in the sketch, and thus CW
0x15ff  4 0 4 5 1 # bottom
0x16ff  4 0 3 7 4 # left side

# faces with vertex order reversed let cube be seen from the
inside

0x11ff  4 3 2 1 0 # front wall
0x12ff  4 4 5 6 7 # back wall

0x13ff  4 3 7 6 2 # top
0x14ff  4 2 6 5 1 # right side

0x15ff  4 1 5 4 0 # bottom
0x16ff  4 4 7 3 0 # left side
```

The first number in the line describing each face is in hexadecimal format. This is the *surface specifier*. Basically, this number tells the renderer what type of texture the object is supposed to have on its surfaces.

The number that comes after this surface specifier tells how many points the polygon has. Because the example is a cube, each polygon has four points. The last four numbers in the example identify which vertex is to be used where.

That's really all there is to a PLG file. Now, you need to load 2Morrow World Builder (2MWB) so you can see how quickly you can create a cube in a program such as 2MWB.

Loading 2MWB

Installing 2Morrow World Builder (2MWB) is easy using the VisMenu user interface. Simply move through the town and choose the building that represents 2MWB by double-clicking on it. This action brings up the 2MWB installation program. Follow the directions in the installation program and load 2MWB onto your hard drive.

Remember, 2MWB is a DOS program and will take advantage of your system's specific memory capabilities. See the color insert for an example of a world created with 2MWB.

Creating a Cube with 2MWB

2MWB has an easy-to-use interface that enables users who have relatively little experience to create virtual worlds. When you run 2MWB, you see an opening screen that's similar to Figure 8-9.

Follow these steps to create a cube.

1. **Click on and pull down the Object menu and then double-click on the LOAD.OBJ option.**

   You see a directory of available subdirectories.

2. **Double-click on the OBJECTS subdirectory to bring up a list of files.**

3. **Select CUBEALL.PLG (the third file from the bottom) by double-clicking it.**

   The SCALE window appears.

4. **Type .2,.2,.2 and press Enter.**

   The entire screen changes, and you are in the center of the cube.

5. **Press the Esc key to clear the menu.**

6. **Press the down-arrow key (↓) to move through the cube's walls and outside the cube.**

   The screen should look similar to Figure 8-10.

Before you play around with the cube, examine the screen. In the upper-right corner of the screen, a display shows your x, y, and z position, and in the upper-left corner a display shows your exact x, y, and z coordinates.

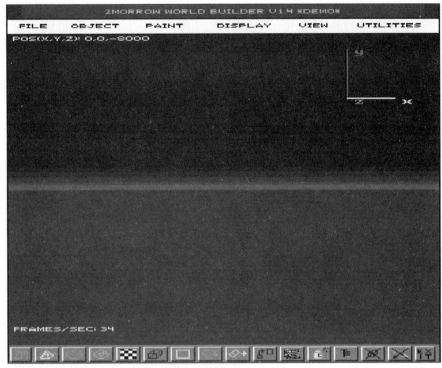

Figure 8-9: 2MWB's opening screen.

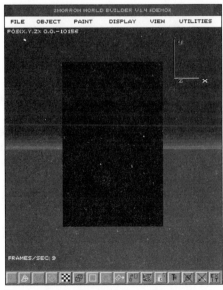

Figure 8-10: Although from this angle it looks like a 2D square, this is the cube you have created.

2MWB uses a left-handed system. Notice that you've moved down the z-axis in a negative direction. Under a right-handed system, coming back out of the cube by pushing ↓ as you did would bring you down the z-axis in a positive direction. In other words, under a right-handed system, positive x is to the right, positive y is up, and positive z is toward you, out of the screen. Under the left-handed screen, the x and y are still positive in the right and up directions, but the z is positive away from you, into the screen.

As we said earlier in the chapter, the main reason you need to notice what type of left- or right-handed coordinate system you are working with is so you can remain constantly aware of your position in 3D space. The only real difference between the left-handed and right-handed systems is the direction of the y- and z-axes. Later in the chapter, you see an example of working with a right-handed system.

Now, try rotating the cube.

1. **Click on the cube once to highlight it.**

2. **Click the Object Menu again, and then double-click the Rotate option.**

   You see the rotation window in the upper-left side of the screen.

   You have the choice of rotating on the x-, the y-, or the z-axis.

3. **Click on the y-axis.**

4. **Press the minus sign (–) twice.**

5. **Click the z-axis in the rotation window.**

6. **Press the minus sign twice again.**

   The result, as shown in Figure 8-11, is a cube standing on one corner with three faces toward the screen.

You've created a cube using 2Morrow World Builder. Save this as a .WLD file by choosing SAVE from the FILE menu and then choosing the .WLD option. In the SAVE WORLD dialog box, type CUBE.WLD and press Enter. The world will now be saved for you to work with in Chapter 11 when you convert it to VRML. In the next section of this chapter, you use Caligari's trueSpace2 to build the cube.

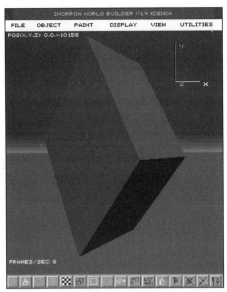

Figure 8-11: A cube in 2Morrow World Builder.

Building a 3D cube with trueSpace2

The first step in using the limited-use, full-featured version of Caligari trueSpace2 that is provided on the CD-ROM that accompanies this book is to click on the building in the CD-ROM VR user interface that's labeled "Caligari." You see two options: install trueSpace2 and install Fountain. Click on the install trueSpace2 option and the program, will install on your hard drive. Follow all of the on-screen directions.

The version of trueSpace2 provided on the CD-ROM is a regular, full-featured version of Caligari's product with a limit of 30 uses. In the back of this book is a coupon with a special offer from Caligari for the purchase of the full-featured, unlimited use version.

The minimum requirements for running trueSpace2 are an Intel 386 processor, 8MB of RAM, 8MB of free hard disk space, MS-DOS 6.0, Microsoft Windows 3.1, and a 640×480 8-bit color monitor. You need at least 800×600 8-bit video to run the demos that are included. The preferred system configuration includes at least a 486 DX2 processor, at least 16MB of RAM, at least 16MB of free hard drive space, a CD-ROM, MS-DOS 6.2 and Microsoft Windows 3.11, 1024×768 with 8-bit color graphics, and a Windows graphics acceleration board that supports Intel 3DR.

After trueSpace2 is installed on the hard drive, you can build a cube.

1. **Open the trueSpace2 Windows group and double-click on the trueSpace2 icon.**

   After the interesting opening screen is briefly displayed, you see a screen that looks much like Figure 8-12.

2. **Move the mouse pointer to the Libraries group and click the Primitives Panel (See Figure 8-13).**

   You can choose from a set of primitive objects (See Figure 8-14).

3. **Click on the cube to see a wireframe cube on trueSpace2's main display (See Figure 8-15 and the color insert).**

   Now you need to render the cube.

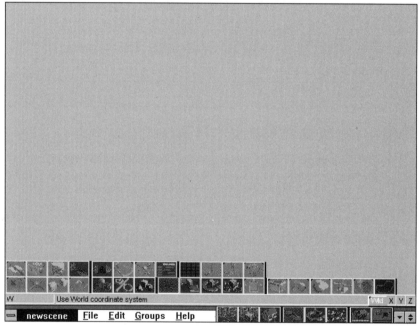

Figure 8-12: trueSpace2 is ready for you to create an object.

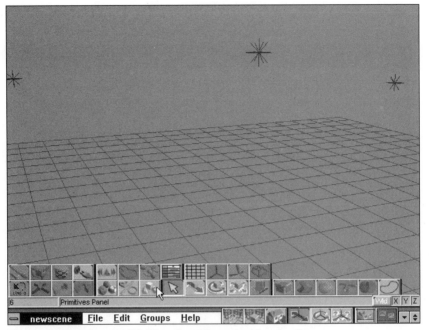

Figure 8-13: Select the Primitives Panel from the Libraries Group.

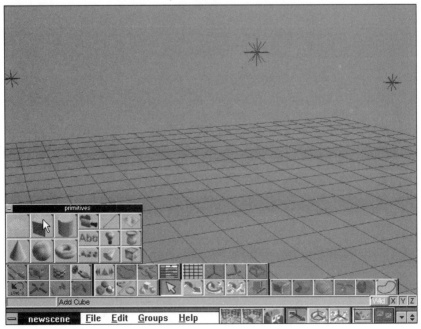

Figure 8-14: Your choices of primitive objects.

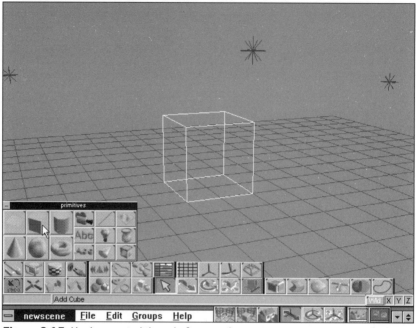

Figure 8-15: You've created the wireframe cube.

4. **Select the Render Current Object panel from the bottom row of options by clicking on it.**

    The program renders the object, and it looks similar to Figure 8-16.

    The last thing you need to do is save the cube in its own file.

5. **Choose Scene from the File menu at the bottom of the screen and then choose Save As (See Figure 8-17).**

    You need to save this file three times in three separate formats. The first format is the trueSpace2 .COB format.

6. **Name the file CUBE.COB and click OK.**

    The file is saved in the Caligari .COB format, which is not readable by humans.

7. **Choose Save As from the File menu again.**

8. **Choose the AutoCad .DXF format.**

9. **Name the file CUBE.DXF and click OK.**

    The file is saved in the AutoCad .DXF format. The .DXF format, like the .PLG format, is readable by humans. Listing 8-6 shows you what the DXF file for CUBE.DXF looks like.

Figure 8-16: You've now rendered your cube in trueSpace2.

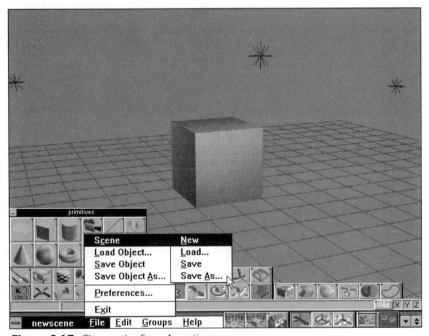

Figure 8-17: Choose the Save As option.

Listing 8-6: CUBE.DXF

```
0
SECTION
 2
HEADER
 0
ENDSEC
 0
SECTION
 2
TABLES
 0
TABLE
 2
LAYER
 70
   153
 0
LAYER
 2
Cube1
 70
 0
 62
15
 6
CONTINUOUS
 0
ENDTAB
 0
ENDSEC
 0
SECTION
 2
ENTITIES
 0
3DFACE
 8
Cube1
 10
1.000000
 20
-1.000000
 30
0.000000
 11
```

```
-1.000000
 21
-1.000000
 31
0.000000
 12
-1.000000
 22
-1.000000
 32
2.000000
 13
1.000000
 23
-1.000000
 33
2.000000
 62
0
  0
3DFACE
  8
Cube1
 10
-1.000000
 20
1.000000
 30
0.000000
 11
-1.000000
 21
-1.000000
 31
0.000000
 12
1.000000
 22
-1.000000
 32
0.000000
 13
1.000000
 23
1.000000
 33
```

(continued)

Listing 8-6: *(continued)*

```
0.000000
 62
0
 0
3DFACE
 8
Cube1
 10
1.000000
 20
1.000000
 30
0.000000
 11
1.000000
 21
-1.000000
 31
0.000000
 12
1.000000
 22
-1.000000
 32
2.000000
 13
1.000000
 23
1.000000
 33
2.000000
 62
0
 0
3DFACE
 8
Cube1
 10
1.000000
 20
1.000000
 30
2.000000
 11
1.000000
 21
```

```
-1.000000
 31
2.000000
 12
-1.000000
 22
-1.000000
 32
2.000000
 13
-1.000000
 23
1.000000
 33
2.000000
 62
0
 0
3DFACE
 8
Cube1
 10
-1.000000
 20
1.000000
 30
0.000000
 11
1.000000
 21
1.000000
 31
0.000000
 12
1.000000
 22
1.000000
 32
2.000000
 13
-1.000000
 23
1.000000
 33
2.000000
 62
0
 0
```

(continued)

Listing 8-6: *(continued)*

```
3DFACE
  8
Cube1
 10
-1.000000
 20
-1.000000
 30
0.000000
 11
-1.000000
 21
1.000000
 31
0.000000
 12
-1.000000
 22
1.000000
 32
2.000000
 13
-1.000000
 23
-1.000000
 33
2.000000
 62
0
  0
ENDSEC
  0
EOF
```

10.   Choose Save File As from the File menu one more time.

11.   Choose the 3dStudio ASCII .ASC format and click OK.

The file is saved in the 3dStudio .ASC format. Like .DXF format, .ASC format can be read by humans. Listing 8-7 shows what the .ASC file for CUBE.ASC looks like.

You look at these two files again later in the book when we discuss converting previously created object files to VRML.

Listing 8-7: CUBE.ASC

```
Ambient light color: Red=0.3 Green=0.3 Blue=0.3

Named object: "Cube1"
Tri-mesh, Vertices: 8    Faces: 12
Vertex list:
Vertex 0: X:-1.000000    Y:-1.000000    Z:0.000000
Vertex 1: X:-1.000000    Y:-1.000000    Z:2.000000
Vertex 2: X:1.000000     Y:-1.000000    Z:0.000000
Vertex 3: X:1.000000     Y:-1.000000    Z:2.000000
Vertex 4: X:-1.000000    Y:1.000000     Z:0.000000
Vertex 5: X:1.000000     Y:1.000000     Z:0.000000
Vertex 6: X:1.000000     Y:1.000000     Z:2.000000
Vertex 7: X:-1.000000    Y:1.000000     Z:2.000000
Face list:
Face 0:  A:2 B:3 C:1 AB:1 BC:1 CA:1
Material:"r210g210b210a0"
Smoothing: 1
Face 1:  A:2 B:1 C:0 AB:1 BC:1 CA:1
Material:"r210g210b210a0"
Smoothing: 1
Face 2:  A:4 B:5 C:2 AB:1 BC:1 CA:1
Material:"r210g210b210a0"
Smoothing: 1
Face 3:  A:4 B:2 C:0 AB:1 BC:1 CA:1
Material:"r210g210b210a0"
Smoothing: 1
Face 4:  A:6 B:3 C:2 AB:1 BC:1 CA:1
Material:"r210g210b210a0"
Smoothing: 1
Face 5:  A:6 B:2 C:5 AB:1 BC:1 CA:1
Material:"r210g210b210a0"
Smoothing: 1
Face 6:  A:6 B:7 C:1 AB:1 BC:1 CA:1
Material:"r210g210b210a0"
Smoothing: 1
Face 7:  A:6 B:1 C:3 AB:1 BC:1 CA:1
Material:"r210g210b210a0"
Smoothing: 1
Face 8:  A:6 B:5 C:4 AB:1 BC:1 CA:1
Material:"r210g210b210a0"
Smoothing: 1
Face 9:  A:6 B:4 C:7 AB:1 BC:1 CA:1
Material:"r210g210b210a0"
Smoothing: 1
Face 10:  A:1 B:7 C:4 AB:1 BC:1 CA:1
```

(continued)

Listing 8-7: *(continued)*

```
Material:"r210g210b210a0"
Smoothing: 1
Face 11:  A:1 B:4 C:0 AB:1 BC:1 CA:1
Material:"r210g210b210a0"
Smoothing: 1
```

---

12. Choose Exit from the File menu to exit trueSpace2.

     The program asks whether you want to save your file as it has been changed.

13. Click No.

Now, we finish up this chapter by creating this same cube with WalkThrough VRML.

Building a 3D cube with WalkThrough VRML

Notice from the beginning that Virtus WalkThrough VRML uses a right-handed coordinate system. WalkThrough VRML has an easy-to-use user interface, but knowing what kind of coordinate system you are dealing with helps you to know where you are in the virtual world.

Because the program is based on the top view as the default, the three dimensions of the virtual space are based on this top view rather than on a frontal view as with other 3D programs. As a result, the x-axis grows larger to the right, the z-axis grows larger toward the top of the screen, and the y-axis grows larger away from you into the screen (which fits the definition of a right-handed coordinate system).

Installing the software

As with trueSpace2, the first step in using the version of WalkThrough VRML that is provided on the CD-ROM is to find the Virtus building in the CD-ROM VR user interface and click on it. This action begins the WalkThrough VRML installation process that puts the program on your hard drive. Follow all of the on-screen directions.

Starting WalkThrough VRML

After the installation is complete, find the Virtus WalkThrough VRML Windows Group and click on it. Now, double-click on the WalkThrough VRML icon to start the program. After a brief identification screen, showing the copyright notice and the program version number, the WalkThrough VRML screens open, as seen in Figure 8-18.

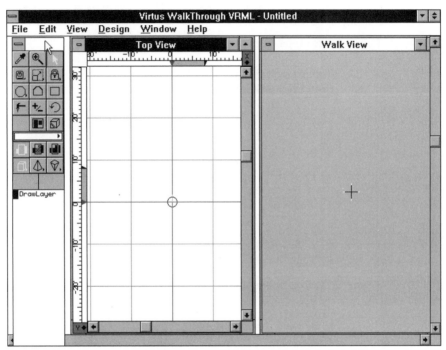

Figure 8-18: The Tools Pad, Top View, and Walk View as seen when WalkThrough VRML begins.

The screen now consists of three main parts: the Tools Pad, the Top View, and the Walk View. Only one of these three areas can be active at a time. You can tell which one is active by looking at the individual title bars. If the title bar is colored, that view is active. The program begins with the Top View active. You can change which part of the screen is active by clicking inside the view that you want.

The Top View is one of six Design views possible in that window. The others are Left, Right, Front, Back, and Bottom. You view and design your virtual world in these areas.

The Walk View shows the three-dimensional version of what you've created. You'll notice that it is blank. You are going to change that.

Creating the cube

Follow these steps to create the cube.

1. **In the Tools Pad to the left on the screen, click on the Square panel (See Figure 8-19).**

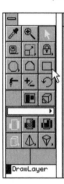

Figure 8-19: Click on the Square panel in the Tools Pad.

2. **Move the cursor to the Top View, just above the circle at the center of the axes.**

3. **Click and hold the left mouse button and move the cursor till you have drawn a square as in Figure 8-20.**

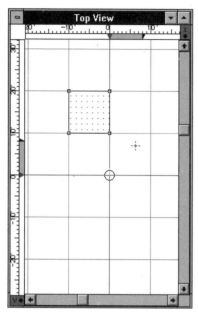

Figure 8-20: You have created a two-dimensional square in the Top View.

You've created a two-dimensional square in the Top View, but what have your created in the Walk View? Actually, what you see in the Walk View is a three-dimensional cube. The problem is your viewing position, which you can change with relative ease.

4. **Move the cursor into the Walk View and click once anywhere inside this window.**

   Next, use ↓ to move back to get a better view.

5. **Press ↓ 11 times, keeping your eyes on the Walk View.**

   Notice where the circle has moved in the Top View. This circle represents the viewer, or in this case, you.

   Your screen resembles Figure 8-21.

   In order to see the three dimensions of the cube, you have to change your viewing position again.

6. **Use the Shift and Ctrl keys, in conjunction with the ↑, ↓, ←, and → keys, to move to a point where your view looks like what you see in Figure 8-22 and in the color insert.**

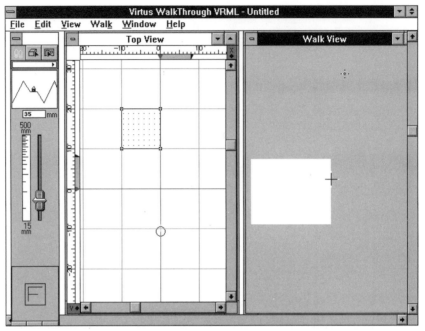

Figure 8-21: It still looks like a square, doesn't it?

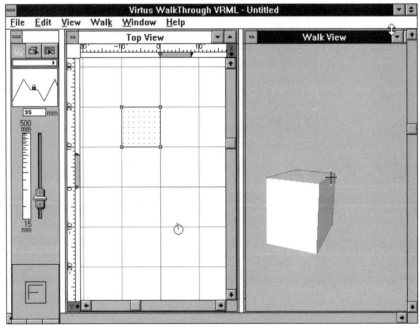

Figure 8-22: The cube in 3D using WalkThrough VRML.

Save the cube as a WalkThrough Pro .WTP file. In a later chapter, you save it again as a VRML .WRL file.

7. **Choose Save As from the File menu at the top of the screen.**

8. **Type CUBE.WTP for the filename and click OK.**

The file is saved. WTP files are not readable by humans.

That's all there is to it. You've created the cube using WalkThrough VRML. It's time to exit the program and move on. Simply choose the Exit option from the File menu to exit the program.

Moving On

In this chapter you've learned about placing points, drawing lines, and creating objects on both a two-dimensional plane and in three-dimensional space. You've used both DOS and Windows programming languages to perform these exercises. You've also created a three-dimensional cube using a variety of methods.

These simple exercises have provided you with background information that can make it easier to understand the next chapters and create virtual worlds with VRML.

VRML and Networking

In This Chapter

Learning how a network operates

Connecting networks

Using VRML for various tasks

Maintaining platform independence

C hapter 8 explains how to create simple three-dimensional applications using some of the tools available. Now you're ready to move onto the Internet and the Web.

In order to make this move, however, you need to have a general understanding of how the individual computers that are connected to the Internet and the Web communicate. We begin by looking at how a network works. We then look at how VRML is defined by the use you'll be placing on it. By this we mean that what you use VRML for defines the level of the platform required, as well as, in some cases, the specific hardware you need.

Network Connections

There are three basic designs for *network topology*. Network topology is the shape or geometric arrangement of the connected computers. These three methods are *star topology*, *ring topology*, and *bus topology*.

Star topology

In star topology, all the computers in the network are connected to a central computer. The central computer is connected to each of the other computers, but no individual computer in the network is connected to any other individual computer. All messages and information traveling on the network must first go through the central computer before being routed to the destination computer. Figure 9-1 shows an example of star topology.

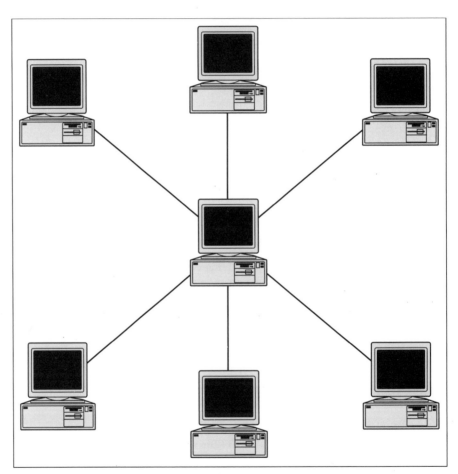

Figure 9-1: A network that uses star topology.

The major advantage of networks that use star topology is that a transmission breakdown between any individual computer and the central computer does not affect communication between the central computer and the other computers on the network. The major disadvantage is that if the central computer goes down, the entire network goes down. No communication can take place if the central computer is out of operation.

Another major advantage lies in the security that this topology provides. Because everything goes through the central computer, only the central computer has access to the information (data) that is being handled on the network.

Ring topology

In ring topology, the network is a continuous path that eventually returns to its origin. Data can travel in only one direction. Figure 9-2 shows an example of ring topology.

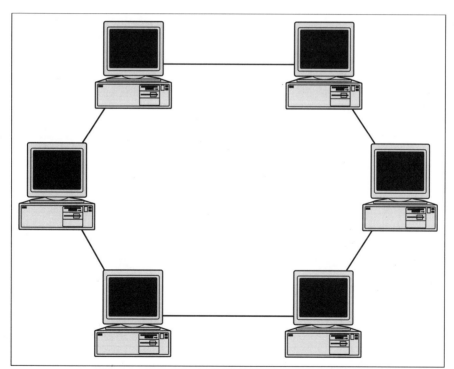

Figure 9-2: A network that uses ring topology.

If the connection between any two computers is broken or if any individual computer breaks down, the network goes down. Another disadvantage of ring topology is that all data passes every other computer on the network. Any individual computer on the network can, therefore, listen in on the data conversations of other computers on the network.

Bus topology

In bus topology, each computer is directly connected to a single transmission medium called a *bus,* and data can flow in either direction. Usually, a coaxial cable is the transmission medium. In many ways, bus topology resembles how cable television is transmitted into your home. Figure 9-3 shows an example of a network using bus topology.

Bus topology has similar disadvantages to those that plague ring topology: A breakdown anywhere in the network shuts down the entire network. Also, data security is a problem with this topology because data passes every computer on the network.

A Network of Networks

Many people think of the Internet as an individual network. This is not the case. Actually, the Internet could be called an *internetwork,* a system of interconnected networks. Although individual networks adhere to a specific topology, the Internet doesn't. It simply connects networks to networks, regardless of the networks' topologies.

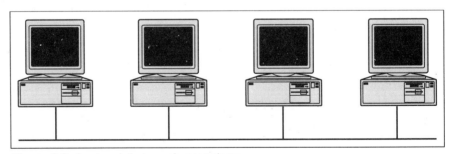

Figure 9-3: A network that uses bus topology.

Figure 1: *ABVBLW.WLD, created by Dennis McKenzie. This award-winning world, available for the first time to the public on the CD-ROM, enables you to explore both above and below this beautiful opening scene. Warning: Watch out for sharks.*

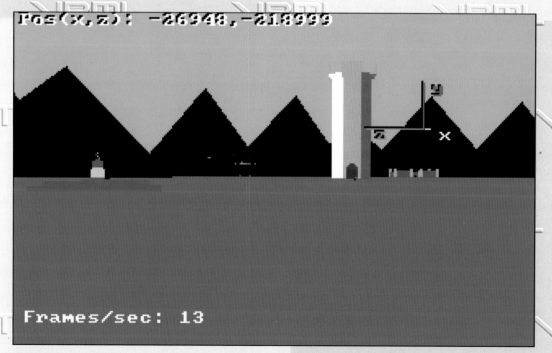

Pos(x,z): -26948,-218999

Frames/sec: 13

Figure 2: *KINGME.WLD, created by Dennis McKenzie. This world, also available to the public for the first time on the CD-ROM, is a fantasy world where, if you ever wanted to battle dragons, this is your chance. See Chapters 4 and 8 for a discussion of building worlds like these using 2Morrow World Builder.*

BANGEL1L.WRL

82POR91.WRL

AL.WRL

COW.WRL

P51MUSTA.WRL

WAIRBOAM.WRL

Figure 3: These worlds, made available by Viewpoint Datalabs, are just a few of the VRML sample worlds on the enclosed CD-ROM.

BEETOVEN.WRL

GALLEON.WRL

NIMITZ.WRL

TANK2.WRL

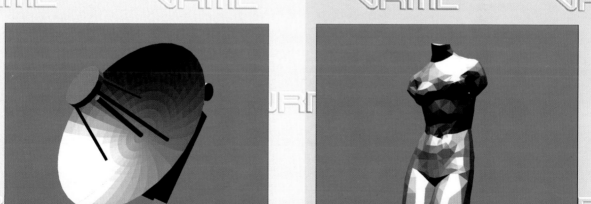

UPDISH.WRL

VENUS.WRL

Figure 4: A sample of the VRML worlds on the CD-ROM that were provided by Viewpoint Datalabs from the Avalon Net site.

Figure 5: VisMenu, from VisNet, provides the VR user interface for the enclosed CD-ROM. The programs on the CD-ROM become buildings in a city that you can walk or fly through. A version of VisMenu that you can use for creating your own virtual reality menu systems also is available on the CD-ROM.

Figure 6: The 2Morrow World Builder Demo that's provided on the CD-ROM and discussed in Chapters 4 and 8 enables you to build virtual worlds that can be converted to VRML.

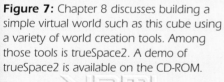

Figure 7: Chapter 8 discusses building a simple virtual world such as this cube using a variety of world creation tools. Among those tools is trueSpace2. A demo of trueSpace2 is available on the CD-ROM.

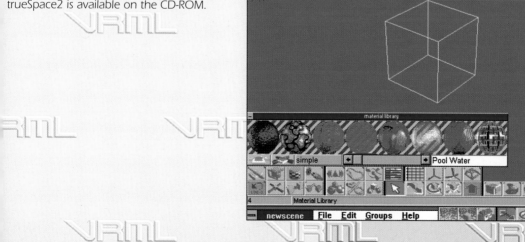

Figure 8: Virtual Reality Studio (Domark) is a DOS 3D creation tool that is discussed in Chapter 4.

Figure 9: Virtus WalkThrough VRML allows the creation and exploration of virtual worlds that can be saved as VRML.WRL files. Virtus WalkThrough VRML can be found on the CD-ROM and is discussed in Chapters 4 and 11.

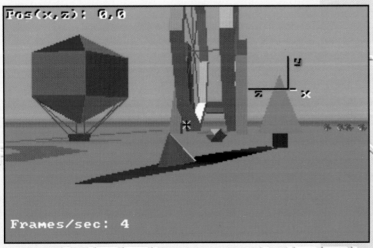

Figure 10: VR386 was written by Dave Stampe. The worlds created for this program can be converted to VRML .WRL files by using Bernie Roehl's WLD2VRML conversion utility that is included on the CD-ROM. VR386 is discussed in Chapter 4. WLD2VRML is discussed in Chapter 11.

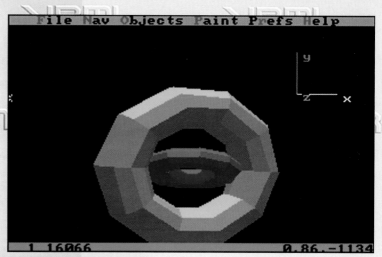

Figure 11: VRBASIC (White Group New Media) is another DOS-based virtual reality program that is discussed in Chapter 4. The worlds created by using this editor/viewer combination can be converted to VRML.WRL files by using WLD2VRML, which is included on the CD-ROM and discussed in Chapter 11.

Figure 12: VRCreator (VREAM) is a commercially available virtual reality creation tool. VRCreator is discussed in Chapter 4.

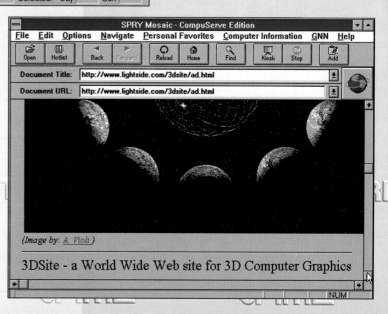

Figure 13: 3DSite. In addition to the worlds provided on the CD-ROM and those you create yourself, many more are available on the Web at locations such as the one for 3DSite. We tell you how to find this Web page and others in Chapters 4 and 15.

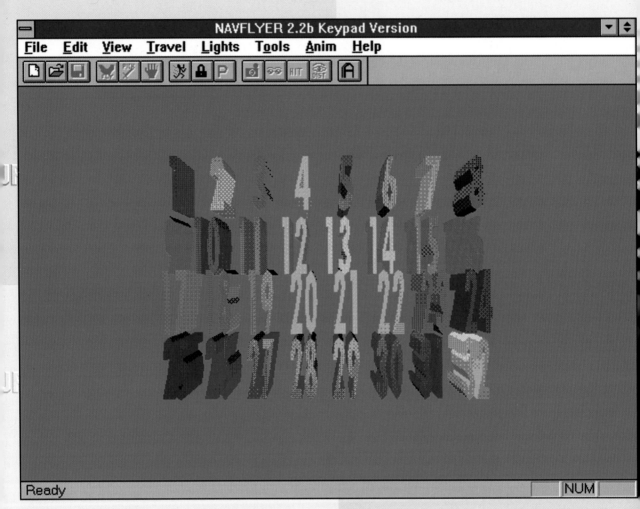

Figure 14: COLORS.DXF, as seen using NAVFlyer 2.2. Here, three-dimensional numbers are presented in a variety of colors. A demo of NAVFlyer is one of several VRML viewers that is on the CD-ROM and discussed in Chapter 10.

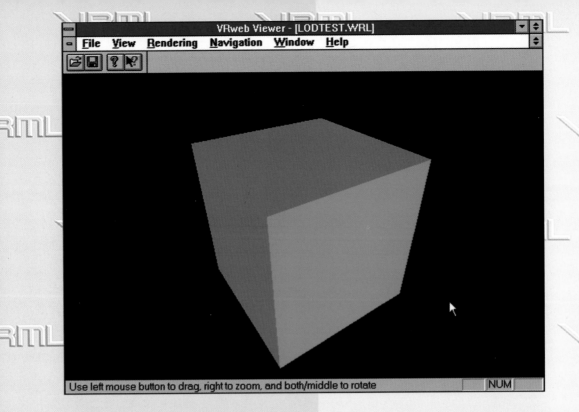

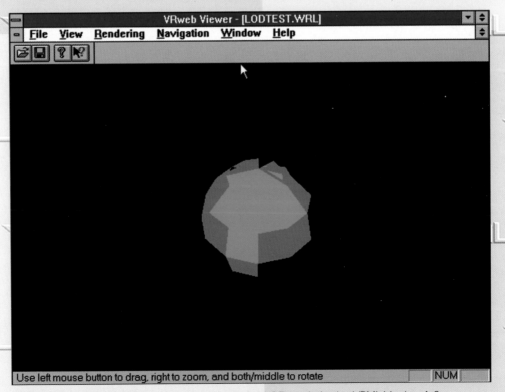

Figure 15: LODTEST.WRL demonstrates how the LOD node in the VRML Version 1.0 specification works. At close distances, the object is a cube. When you back away from it, the cube becomes a sphere. This world is discussed in Chapter 14.

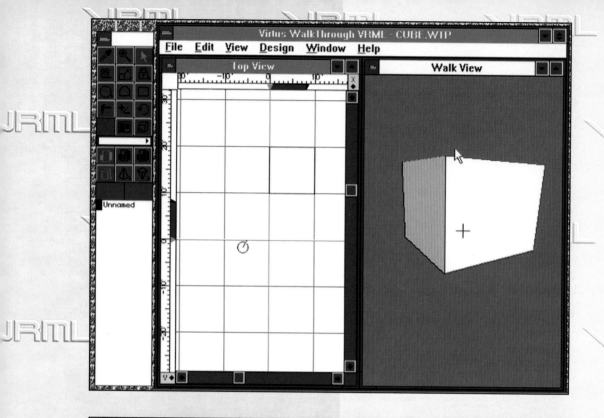

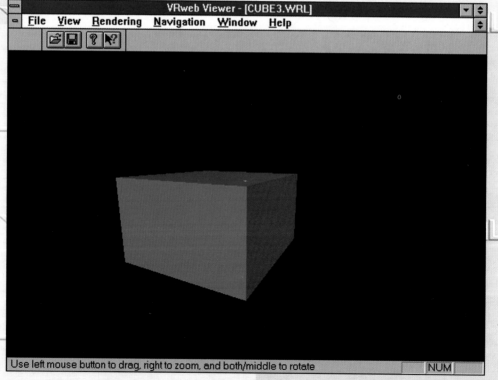

Figure 16: In Chapter 11, you build a virtual world with one of the VRML creation tools (as shown in the top figure) on the CD-ROM. You can then view that virtual world by using a VRML viewer. The VRML viewers discussed in Chapter 10 are on the CD-ROM.

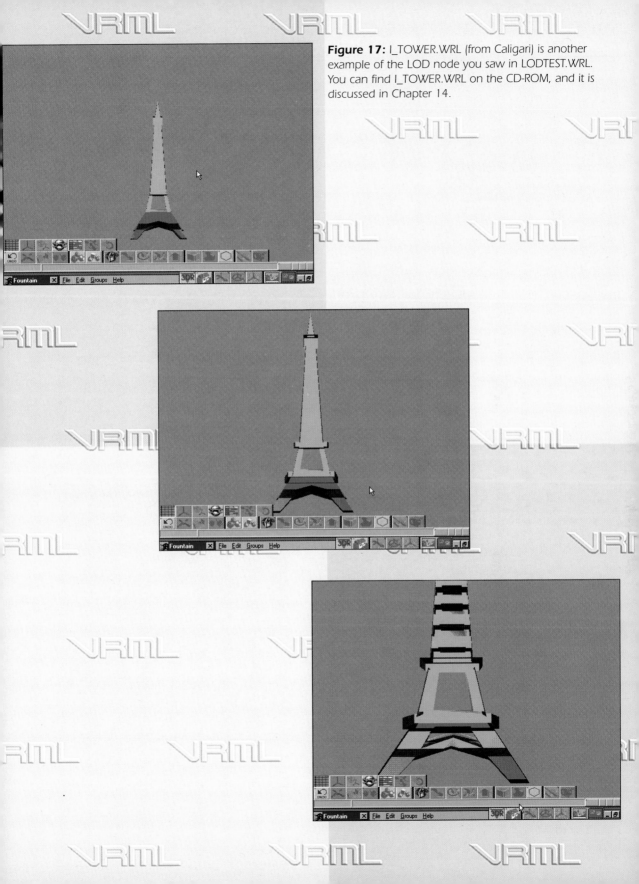

Figure 17: I_TOWER.WRL (from Caligari) is another example of the LOD node you saw in LODTEST.WRL. You can find I_TOWER.WRL on the CD-ROM, and it is discussed in Chapter 14.

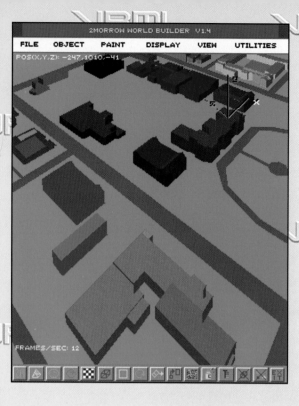

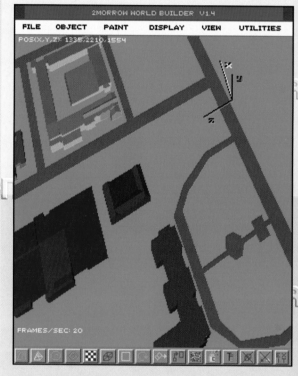

Figure 18: The Pittsburg State University campus in Pittsburg, Kansas. This world began as a project using VRBASIC, moved over to REND386, and then to VRML. PSU World is discussed in Chapters 11 and 14, and various forms of this world are available on the CD-ROM.

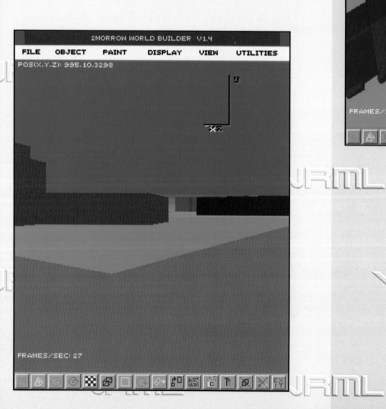

Figure 19: VirtualSOMA (part of Virtual San Francisco) by Planet 9 Studios, San Francisco - Copyright 1995, Planet 9 Studios. These screenshots of VirtualSOMA were not available during the writing of Chapter 10 and show how quickly the virtual worlds of the Web change and become more realistic every day.

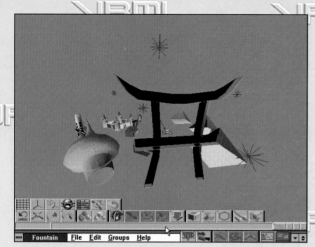

Figure 20: Caligari's Fountain, discussed in Chapters 11 and 14, is similar in use to Caligari's trueSpace2, discussed in Chapter 8. A version of trueSpace2 and a beta of Fountain are available on the CD-ROM.

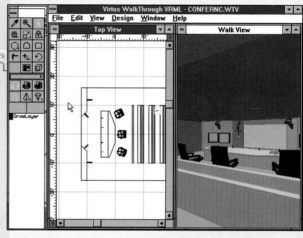

Figure 21: Virtus WalkThrough VRML is discussed in Chapters 8 and 11 and is available on the CD-ROM.

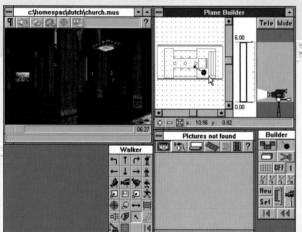

Figure 22: ParaGraph's Home Space Builder provides an easy-to-use interface and is discussed in Chapter 11. A beta of Home Space Builder is on the CD-ROM.

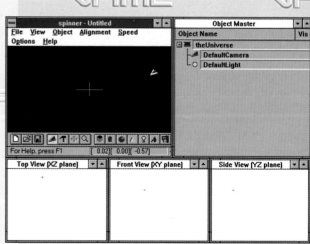

Figure 23: 3DWeb's Spinner is another of the easy-to-use VRML creation tools that are discussed in Chapter 11. A beta of Spinner is available on the CD-ROM.

Figure 24: PSU.WRL, as seen using NetScape and WebFX. Configuring NetScape and WebFX to work together is explained in Chapter 10. WebFX is on the CD-ROM.

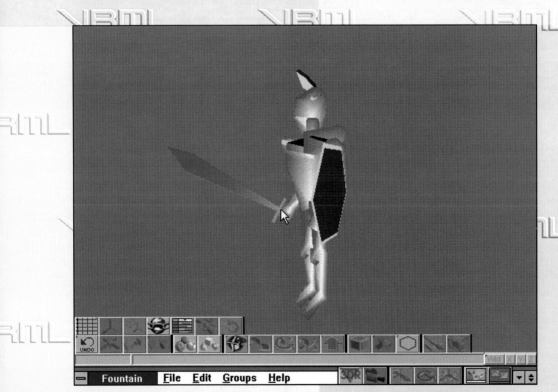

Figure 25: KNIGHT.WRL, as seen by using Caligari's Fountain. Fountain and KNIGHT.WRL are on the CD-ROM, and Fountain is discussed in Chapter 11.

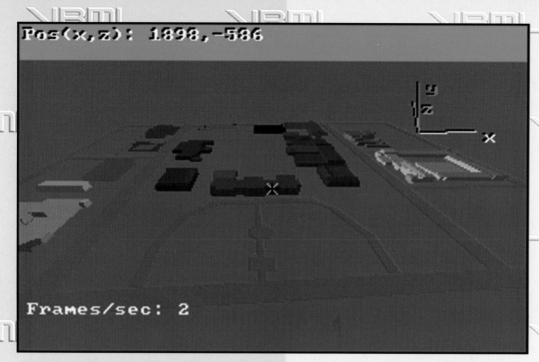

Figure 26: PSU.WRL, the original PSU World created for DOS on the PC using programs discussed in Chapter 4.

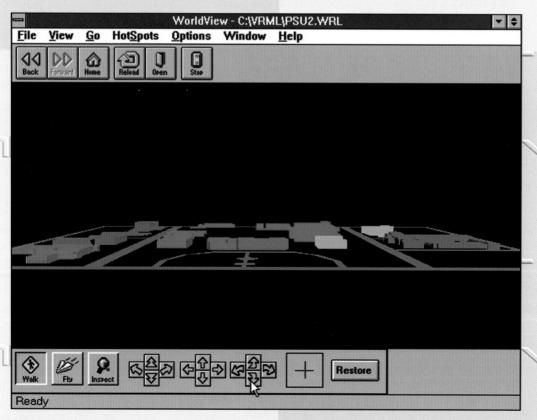

Figure 27: PSU2.WRL. After conversion and some modification in Chapter 14, this world is almost ready for the Web.

An important consideration is that each of these networks may consist of only one platform or it may consist of a variety of platforms. In Paul's office at the university, he has a 486 running Windows NT 3.51. Earlier in his teaching career, he had an Atari 130XE. Both platforms can provide access to the campus network, as well as the Internet, and they can be used to communicate with other faculty, both on campus and around the world.

Each specific platform has its own advantages and disadvantages for creating VRML worlds. VRML world creators need to choose the platform that maximizes the advantages and minimizes the disadvantages. For most of us, this platform is a PC with Windows 3.1 or 3.11. Over the next couple of years, Windows 95 will probably take the place of Windows 3.1. Currently, however, Windows 3.1 is the dominant computer platform in the world. For that reason, this book is geared toward Windows 3.1.

Different Requirements for VRML

One challenge for most computer languages and protocols is that they need to be distributable and usable over a variety of platforms. Another challenge is the user's expectations. These challenges have plagued VRML since its conception.

VRML is defined by the user's requirements — in other words, by what the user needs or wants to do with VRML. VRML will be what the user needs it to be. In the next few paragraphs, we look at some of the requirements that users place on VRML.

Science, engineering, and Hollywood

The question is, what does the user want to do with VRML? Some users may want to use VRML as a means for saving scientific visualizations so that they may be shared with other researchers.

For VRML to meet the requirements that some people in the sciences place on it, high-end platforms with accelerated graphics capabilities are needed. Current low-end platforms are not capable of high-level graphics with real-time display. Some scientific visualizations, engineering animations, and Hollywood special effects require many days to render, even on the high-end systems. On a 486, they take even longer.

This situation, however, is changing very quickly. Windows 95 has already brought a 32-bit operating system to the PC, and video acceleration cards such as 3Dlab's GLINT board will become more accessible in price within the next 12 months.

At the present time, VRML has many capabilities that science, math, engineering, and Hollywood can take advantage of. The 4×4 matrix node is one example. If, however, VRML were to emphasize these areas over other requirements, it would lose much of its platform independence and many of its multiplatform capabilities.

To some programmers, as you saw in the discussion of the birds-of-a-feather meeting at Siggraph 95 in Chapter 6, accessibility for the average user is of considerable importance. They would like both high-end users and low-end users to be able to use VRML.

A *scaleable format* could be the answer. By this we mean that VRML applications could be made intuitive and, based on the specific platform that is being used, adjust themselves for optimum operation.

The average user

For multiuser, multiplatform, three-dimensional display of graphical data, the 486 DX2 50 MHz running Windows 3.1 provides an acceptable display with VRML Version 1.0. VRML can be a scientific analysis tool if that's what the user wants it to be. It also can be accessible and usable by the average user who is running Windows 3.1 on a 486/66.

You can't create the special effects you've seen in the movies in real time on this platform, though. If that's what you want, you need to move up to a more powerful and expensive machine, different software, and a different protocol.

If, however, you are looking for a real-time, three-dimensional graphical user interface for communicating on the World Wide Web, then VRML running on a Windows 3.1 platform will suffice.

Platform Independence

For VRML to be what it was intended to be, it must remain platform independent. As the preceding paragraphs indicate, although specific needs are based, in a large part, on the user's specific hardware, VRML can, and will, be used for other applications. VRML must, to a certain degree, therefore, remain hardware nonspecific and platform independent.

In other words, many users may want to use VRML simply as a real-time, three dimensional graphical user interface for on-line Web communication using the hardware that they currently have. This is fine. At the same time, however, VRML must be usable for other applications on high-end hardware for specific applications.

A standard that can be used on multiple platforms will not take advantage of any hardware-specific capabilities. However, because VRML is a file format, not a program, individual platform browsers can display the format in any way, shape, or form that the platform and its users may require and are capable of.

The VRML file format, both in its current and future forms, should enable developers on specific platforms to create browsers specific to the individual platform that take advantage of that platform's capabilities. Discussions of future releases of VRML, therefore, should restrict themselves to VRML specifications and let the individual platform developers worry about implementation on their specific platform.

VRML is capable of serving business, scientific, and general consumer needs. It is up to you as a user and/or developer to define and develop VRML worlds and applications to meet the needs you have defined.

Moving On

In this chapter, you examined how networks work. Understanding how networks operate gives you a better understanding of how VRML and other Internet applications communicate. You also looked at how what you use VRML for defines VRML to a degree.

What we need to turn our attention to now is how you can look at VRML worlds on your PC. The next two chapters show you how you can do just that.

Setting Up the VRML Viewers

This is it! In this chapter, you choose a VRML viewer. Several viewers that run under Windows 3.1 are on the CD-ROM, and we tell you where you can download others that are available now or will be available in the near future.

We also tell you how to install VRML viewers, configure your software (in other words, make the necessary connections between the viewers and your Web browser), and then go for a cruise on the Net and look at some of the worlds that await you there.

In order to keep things simple, we deal with only one viewer at a time and show you how to connect everything. Then, after you choose the viewer that you want to use and are ready, you go online. The Windows 3.1 VRML viewers are discussed in alphabetical order.

NAVFlyer 2.2

NAVFlyer is a viewer for computer-generated 3D worlds from MicronGreen Inc. The software is a subset of MicronGreen's Virtual Environment Navigator. You can view VRML worlds both offline and online by using NAVFlyer in conjunction with a Web browser. It has features such as level of detail (LOD) control, adaptive viewing modes, and rudimentary collision detection that assist you in exploring the world of 3D simulations.

NAVFlyer, along with the latest in VRML browsing and development software, is on the San Diego Supercomputing Center (SDSC) VRML Resources page at http://www.sdsc.edu.

Hardware and software requirements

At a minimum, NAVFlyer requires a 486 with math coprocessor support and at least 16MB of RAM. You also need at least 10MB of free hard drive space to install the software.

The minimum operating system is Windows 3.1, but you need to install Win32s on your system also. (If you have installed VisMenu from the CD-ROM, the version of Win32s that's on the CD-ROM has already been installed.) Win32s provides 32-bit extensions and capabilities to Windows 3.1x. It includes a set of DLLs and a virtual device driver (VxD) that enables 32-bit applications to run on top of Windows or Windows for Workgroups.

You also need WinG, Microsoft's enhanced graphics library. For the most part, WinG handles bitmaps under Windows, providing the necessary tools to transfer these bitmaps quickly between memory and screen. This was something 16-bit Windows applications were not capable of doing before. Game developers and graphics applications developers have made use of this capability.

Current versions of Win32s and WinG are on the CD-ROM that's included with this book. In the "Finding Win32s and WinG" section, later in the chapter, we tell you how to get newer versions of Win32s and WinG free from Microsoft.

The version of NAVFlyer that you can download allows for both keyboard and mouse control of navigation. So you don't have to use a mouse, but it can come in handy.

Finally, you need a Windows 256-color display and driver. The Windows 3.1 default 16-color VGA driver just won't hack it.

Getting ready to install NAVFlyer 2.2

The first thing you need to do is determine whether WinG and Win32s are installed on your system.

1. Click the Main program group in the Program Manager.
2. Choose the File Manager by double-clicking on it.
3. Select the hard drive where Windows is installed and double-click on the WINDOWS subdirectory.

4.   Under the WINDOWS subdirectory, click on the SYSTEM
     subdirectory.

     If Win32s is present, you see it listed. If not, you need to install it.

5.   Before installing Win32s, check on your hard drive (or drives) to see
     whether you can find a subdirectory labeled WING.

     If it doesn't exist, you need to install it also.

Finding Win32s and WinG

You can obtain Win32s and WinG in a couple of different ways. We have
included the current versions of both programs on the CD-ROM. Probably
the best place to download newer versions is from Microsoft's FTP site
(ftp.microsoft.com). Both files are listed in the DEVELOPR\DRG
subdirectory as shown in Figure 10-1. They also are in the \SOFTLIB\
MSLFILES\ subdirectory.

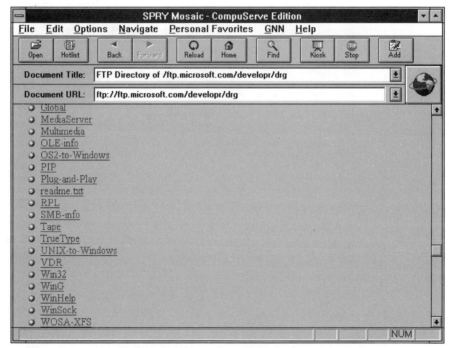

Figure 10-1: Finding the latest versions of Win32s and WinG at Microsoft's FTP site.

You also can download the files from the Microsoft Download Service, which is the Microsoft BBS. The phone number is 206-936-6735. The Win32s file, PW1118.EXE, does not include the OLE files that may be needed for browsers such as NCSA Mosaic. The WinG file is WING10.EXE.

Both files are also on CompuServe. Win32s Version 1.25 with OLE Version 2.3 is in PCFORUM; search for WIN32S.ZIP. You can find both files on other forums by using the PC File Finder or the search engine that's available on the CompuServeCD. In some locations, it is identified as PW1118.EXE.

These files are also available at the download sites for the viewers that require them. For example, as you can see in Figure 10-2, both Win32s and WinG are available at NAVFlyer's download site (`ftp://yoda.fdt.net/pub/users/m/micgreen`).

One other easy place to download Win32s is at the WebMaster site where you can download WorldView. Figure 10-3 shows what this site looked like in mid-August 1995.

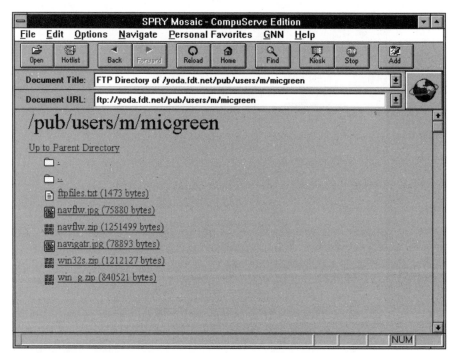

Figure 10-2: Both Win32s and WinG are available where you can download NAVFlyer.

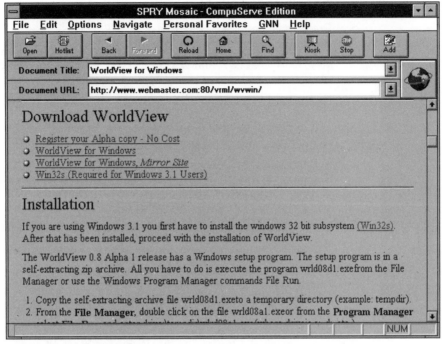

Figure 10-3: The WebMaster site.

Installing Win32s

When you installed Vis Menu from the CD-ROM, it should have installed the version of Win32s that's on the CD-ROM. If you need to install Win32s, PW1118.EXE is a self-executing file that decompresses into three files: LICENSE.TXT, README.TXT, and W32S125.EXE. The Win32s files are in the W32S125.EXE file in a compressed form. Clicking on this file decompresses the setup files for Win32s. Don't click on it yet, though. Follow these instructions for creating a temporary directory and then install Win32s:

1. Open the File Manager.

2. Make sure that you are at the top of the directory structure for the directory where you want to create a temporary directory.

3. Choose Create Directory from the File menu.

4. In the dialog box that appears, type TEMP in the Name box.

5. Click OK.

    A subdirectory named TEMP is created.

6. Click on the new TEMP subdirectory.

7.   Copy PW1118.EXE into this subdirectory.

8.   Double-click on PW1118.EXE.

This action causes the self-executing file to decompress into LICENSE. TXT, README.TXT, and W32S125.EXE, as mentioned earlier in the chapter.

9.   Delete PW1118.EXE.

You now have a subdirectory that contains the same files.

10.   Double-click on the file W32S125.EXE.

This self-extracting file decompresses the files that are needed to install Win32s. You end up with a TEMP subdirectory that contains the files.

11.   Double-click the SETUP.EXE file and then follow the directions.

The installation program installs Win32s on your system with little additional effort on your part.

12.   After the installation is complete and the setup program restarts Windows, go back to the File Manager and delete the entire TEMP subdirectory.

Win32s is now installed. Check it out by playing the FreeCell game (FREECELL.EXE) that was loaded by the installation program. If there are any errors in the way the game operates, the system will tell you, and you'll need to reinstall again. If you have to reinstall Win32s or if you later decide to update to a newer version, you need to do the following:

1.   Delete the WIN32S subdirectory, the WIN32APP subdirectory, and the W32SYS.DLL, W32S16.DLL, and WIN32S.EXE files from the hard drive.

2.   Edit the WIN32S.INI file on the hard drive by changing the line that reads SETUP=1 to SETUP=0.

3.   Exit Windows and reboot the computer.

4.   Reinstall Win32s as described in the preceding set of steps.

Installing WinG

Although WinG is easier to set up than Win32s, you only need to install WinG if the VRML viewer that you're using requires it.

WinG is provided on the CD-ROM that's included with this book and can be installed by double-clicking on the blue WinG setup building in VisMenu. Otherwise, follow these instructions:

1. Open the File Manager.

   No problem here. These first few instructions are the same as what you did to install Win32s.

2. Make sure that you are at the top of the directory structure for the directory where you want to create a temporary directory.

3. Choose Create Directory from the File menu.

4. In the dialog box opened by the Create Directory option, type TEMP.

5. Click OK to have a subdirectory created with the name TEMP.

6. Click on the new TEMP subdirectory.

7. Copy WING10.EXE into this new subdirectory.

8. Double-click on WING10.EXE.

   The self-executing file decompress into a large number of files.

9. Delete WING10.EXE.

10. Find the file SETUP.EXE, double-click on it, and then follow the directions.

    The installation program installs WinG on your system.

11. After the installation is complete, go back to the File Manager and delete the entire TEMP subdirectory.

WinG is now installed, so you're ready to install NAVFlyer.

Installing NAVFlyer 2.2

The installation procedure for NAVFlyer is a little bit different from the installation procedures that you've done previously in this chapter. You need a copy of PKUNZIP to decompress these files.

If you don't already have a copy of PKUNZIP, the most recent version at the time of this writing is Version 2.04. You can find this utility on many of the CompuServe Forums. The simplest way to find it is to use PC File Finder to search for PK204G.EXE. This self-executing file loads the necessary ZIP and UNZIP files onto your hard drive. We recommend that you place them in the \DOS\ subdirectory so that you can find them easily.

If you don't want to have to exit to DOS to use these files, download a copy of WINZIP from one of the CompuServe forums. Use the PC File Finder and search for WINZIP.EXE. WINZIP.EXE creates a Windows icon for the program and enables you to stay in Windows to unzip programs you may download.

Now, follow these directions to load NAVFlyer.

1. Load the File Manager again and create a TEMP subdirectory, using the same steps described earlier in the chapter.

2. If you are using the PKZIP DOS package, go to Step 3. If you're using WINZIP go to Step 8.

3. Exit the File Manager and Windows and wait for the DOS prompt.

4. Change to the NAVIGATR subdirectory by typing CD \TEMP.

5. Place the disk that you've placed NAVFLW.ZIP on in your disk drive.

6. Now, type X:PKUNZIP -D X:NAVFLW, where X represents the name of your floppy disk drive (usually either A or B).

   This action decompresses the NAVFlyer files onto your hard drive in the TEMP subdirectory.

7. Start Windows again and go to Step 16.

8. Using WINZIP, load the WINZIP program by double-clicking on its icon.

9. Click the Open button.

10. Change to the floppy drive where NAVFLW.ZIP is located.

11. Double-click on the file NAVFLW.ZIP.

   You see something similar to Figure 10-4.

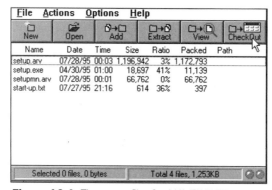

Figure 10-4: The setup files for NAVFLW.ZIP.

12. Click the Extract button.

   You are now asked where to extract the files to, as seen in Figure 10-5.

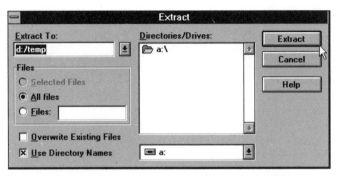

Figure 10-5: Indicate where you want to extract the files to.

13. In the Extract to text box, type X:/TEMP (where X represents the hard drive that you want the files placed on) and click Extract.

14. After WINZIP finishes extracting the files, choose Exit from the File menu in WINZIP and leave the program.

15. Re-enter the File Manager and go to the TEMP subdirectory.

16. Double-click on SETUP.EXE.

 The NAVFlyer installation program creates the NAVIGATR sub-directory and places the program's files in it. The installation program also asks you whether you want to set up a program group and icons for NAVFlyer and its accompanying files.

17. Answer yes.

Exploring NAVFlyer

The program is now installed, and you're ready to start exploring some of the virtual worlds available in the GEOMETRY subdirectory.

1. Open the Navigator program group and double-click on the NAVFlyer 2.2 icon.

2. Click the maximize button in the upper-right corner of the screen.

 Your screen looks similar to Figure 10-6.

3. Choose Open from the File menu to select a file, as in Figure 10-7.

 The GEOMETRY subdirectory contains several examples. In the default options of NAVFlyer, these examples are either in the AutoCad .DXF or 3DStudio .3DS formats. You also can change the type and choose either the Navigator .NAV or VRML .WRL format.

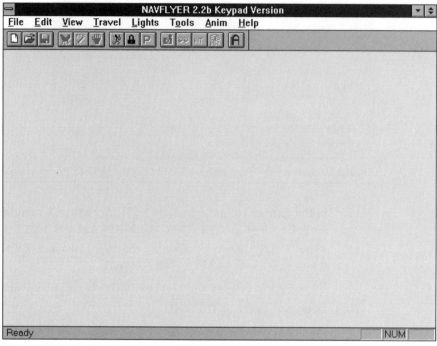

Figure 10-6: NAVFlyer 2.2b Keypad Version.

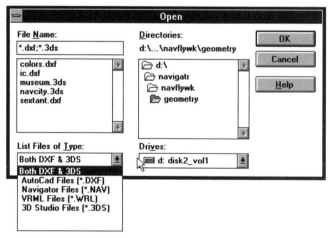

Figure 10-7: The List Files of Type drop-down list shows NAVFlyer's format options.

4. **Select the COLORS.DXF file and load it by clicking the OK button.**

The DXF File Options dialog box shown in Figure 10-8 appears.

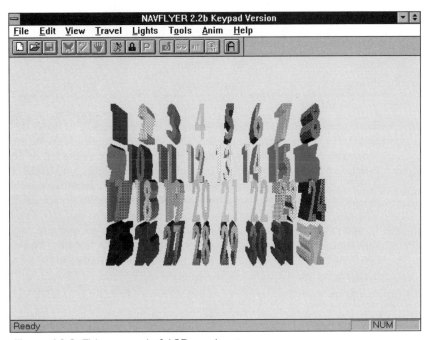

Figure 10-8: The DXF File Options dialog box.

5. **Click OK.**

The screen is filled with colorful numbers, as shown in Figure 10-9. This figure also appears in the color insert.

Figure 10-9: Thirty-two colorful 3D numbers.

In this version of NAVFlyer, you can use the mouse to open menus and such, but you cannot use it for navigation. To maneuver around in 3D space, you use the numeric keypad. Table 10-1 shows what each key does.

Table 10-1: Using the Numeric Keypad to Maneuver in NAVFlyer

Key	What It Does
NumLock	Toggles lock on/off
/	Translate IN
*	Translate OUT
-	Slower translation
+	Faster translation
1	Roll left
2	Translate down
3	Roll right
4	Translate left
5	Pitch up
6	Translate right
7	Yaw left
8	Translate up
9	Yaw right
0	Pitch down
Enter	Faster rotation
Delete	Slower rotation

Simply put, if you want to move toward the numbers, you press the / (forward slash) key on the keypad. If you want to move away from the numbers, you press the * (star) key. If you want to move in an arc to the left or right, you press 7 or 9, respectively. For up and down (translate), you press 8 and 2; for directly left and right (translate), you press 4 and 6. To move over or under, you press 5 and 0, and to spin to the left or to the right, you press 1 and 3.

To speed up your movements, you press the plus sign or Enter key, and to slow them down, you press the minus sign or the Delete key. You can become comfortable with moving around in the 3D space created in NAVFlyer in a few minutes.

A listing of the COLORS.DXF file would make this chapter more than 500 pages long. Take a look at it by opening it under a word processor such as Word 6.0 for Windows.

WebFX

WebFX is a product of Paper Software Inc. Currently two different versions of WebFX are available for Windows 3.1 Web browsers.

The first version available was designed to run only with QuarterDeck Mosaic. The second version, which is included on the CD-ROM that accompanies this book, was designed to run only with the 16-bit version of Netscape 1.1.

The third version, which should be available by the time you read this, can be configured to work with a variety of Web browsers. Check Paper Software's Web page (listed in Chapter 15) for the newest version.

Known bugs and unimplemented features

One of the things that we like most about this VRML viewer is that its creators are very up front right from the start about things that either don't work the way they are supposed to or haven't been implemented yet. Paper Software provides a list of bugs and unimplemented features with its product.

We worked with the beta 1 release of WebFX for NetScape. The color insert contains a screen shot of WebFX and Netscape working together. One of the first things that we noticed was that the NetScape animation looks different. Due to conflicts with the color palettes because of the use of WinG, the animation appears solarized.

WebFX, for the beta 1 release, did not save or print VRML files. Several other VRML 1.0 features weren't implemented, including level of detail, texture transformations, ASCII text, Orthographic cameras, and RGB and JPG texture support. Another difficulty is the inability of WebFX to work properly with multiple NetScape windows.

Installing WebFX

Two versions of WebFX are on the CD-ROM. One version is for QMosaic and the other for NetScape. You must have one of these Web browsers to use the versions of WebFX that are provided on the CD-ROM. We will discuss the installation of only the NetScape version. Installation instructions for the QMosaic version are available on the CD-ROM.

The installation of WebFX has been automated to a large extent by the CD-ROM's virtual reality user interface (VisMenu).

1. **Find the street that Paper Software Inc. is on and click on the WebFX building to start the WebFX startup program.**

   The first dialog box gives you the option of continuing or exiting. It also has a help button that you can use to get information about the setup procedure.

2. **Click the Continue button to bring up a dialog box that asks which path you want to install WebFX for Netscape in.**

3. **Choose a path or accept the default location, and click continue.**

   The setup program asks for the directory where your copy of NetScape is located.

4. **Type the correct location and click continue.**

WebFX is quickly installed onto your hard drive, and you see a dialog box saying that the setup was successful.

Running WebFX

WebFX has preinstalled itself with NetScape now so that when you go to a VRML .WRL file on the Web, WebFX will display the world for you. There is nothing else for you to do at this point. In the next section, we turn our attention to another VRML viewer, InterVista's WorldView.

WorldView

WorldView is a product of InterVista Software Inc., which was founded by the coauthor of VRML, Tony Parisi.

Hardware and software requirements

WorldView requires a minimum 486DX2 50 MHz with 8MB of RAM and a 256-color display driver and graphics card. It also requires either Windows 3.1 or Windows for Workgroups 3.11 and Win32s. If you haven't already installed Win32s, the installation program installs it for you.

The Windows 95 version of this program is also on the CD-ROM. You can find a screen shot of WorldView in the color insert.

Installing WorldView Version 0.9f Beta

WorldView Version 0.9f Beta is on the CD-ROM that accompanies this book. Just double-click the building with InterVista's name on it to start the installation program.

Next, the installation program asks whether you want to install WorldView. Again, click Yes. Follow the directions and answer the questions about where you want the program located. The program and the necessary program group and icons will be installed.

Running WorldView

To explore WorldView, click the WorldView Icon and run the program. After a few seconds, your screen looks something like Figure 10-10. Maximize the WorldView window for a better view of the virtual worlds that you are about to explore.

Loading VRML worlds into WorldView

Several example worlds are available in the \WORLDS\ subdirectory where you loaded WorldView. All of the worlds in this subdirectory are certified to be VRML 1.0 compliant. Not all of the 3D worlds on the Web are VRML 1.0 compliant. As a result, they have varying levels of viewability. Follow these steps to view the WorldView sample worlds:

1. Choose Open File from the File menu.

2. Highlight the \WORLDS\ subdirectory and click OK.

    You're presented with a list of .WRL files to choose from, as in Figure 10-11.

3. Double-click on CUBE.WRL.

    Your screen looks similar to Figure 10-12.

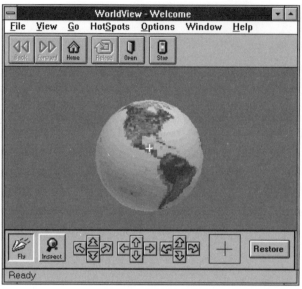

Figure 10-10: WorldView from InterVista Software Inc.

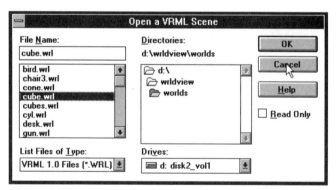

Figure 10-11: A partial list of the worlds that you can choose from.

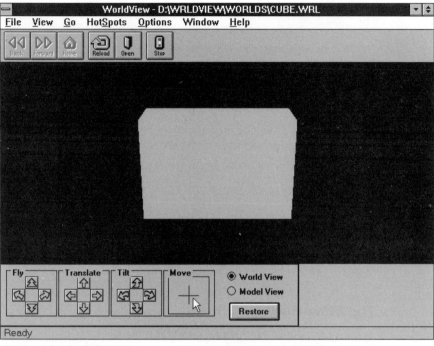

Figure 10-12: CUBE.WRL, as seen through an early version of WorldView.

Moving around in the virtual world

 When WorldView opens, along the bottom of the WorldView window, you see two buttons — Fly and Inspect — three groups of arrows, a Crosshair box, and a Restore button (see Figure 10-10).

Modes

WorldView has two navigation modes.

Fly Mode

This button is for the Fly Mode. The Fly Mode is the default mode when you load WorldView. It enables you to move around the virtual world. In other words, your point-of-view changes and the virtual world remains in one place.

Inspect Mode

 Pushing this button changes the way movement is handled. Changing to this mode enables you to move and tilt the 3D model. In other words, the objects in the world are moved, and your point of view remains static.

Arrow buttons

There are three groups of four arrow buttons along the bottom of the WorldView program window. These arrow buttons produce different results, depending on which of the modes you have chosen.

The first group of arrow buttons produces the following movements.

The Move Forward button

 In Fly Mode, the Move Forward button moves your point of view closer to the object. In the Inspect Mode it moves the model away from you.

The Move Backward button

 In Fly Mode, the Move Backward button moves your point of view farther away from the object. In Inspect Mode, it moves the model closer to you.

The Look Left button

 In Fly Mode, pressing the Look Left button moves your point of view to the left. This, in effect, moves the image of the object to the right. In Inspect Mode, this button tilts the top of the object toward the right of the screen. You can use the Alt or Ctrl keys as accelerators to simulate spinning.

The Look Right button

 In Fly Mode, the Look Right button moves your point of view to the right. The effect is to move the object to the left. In Inspect Mode, it tilts the top of the model to the left. You can use the Alt or Ctl keys as accelerators to simulate spinning.

The second group of buttons produces the following movements.

The Move Up button

 In Fly Mode, the Move Up button moves your point of view up, giving the appearance of moving the world down. In Inspect Mode, pressing the button moves the object up.

The Move Down button

In Fly Mode, pressing the Move Down button moves your point of view downward, giving the appearance of moving the object upward. In Inspect Mode, this same action moves the object down.

The Move Left button

In Fly Mode, pressing this button moves your point of view to the left. In Inspect Mode, this button moves the object to the left.

The Move Right button

In Fly Mode, the Move Right button moves your point of view to the right, and in Inspect Mode, it moves the object to the right.

The third group of arrow buttons produces the following movements.

The Tilt Left button

In Fly Mode, the Tilt Left button tilts your viewpoint to the right; in Inspect Mode, it tilts the top of the object to the left. The Alt or Ctrl keys act as accelerators to simulate spinning.

The Tilt Right button

In Fly Mode, the Tilt Right button tilts your viewpoint to the left, and in Inspect Mode, it tilts the top of the model to the right. The Alt or Ctrl keys act as accelerators to simulate spinning.

The Look Up button

In Fly Mode, the Look Up button tilts your point of view upward. In Inspect Mode, the top of the model tilts toward you.

The Look Down button

In Fly Mode, this button tilts your point of view downward, and in Inspect Mode, it tilts the top of the object away from you.

The Crosshair box

You activate this box by pressing and holding the left mouse button while the cursor is in the appropriate part of the box. When the cursor is above the crosshair, inside the box, your point of view moves forward. When the cursor is below the crosshair, inside the box, your point of view moves back. When the cursor is to the left of the crosshair, inside the box, your point of view rotates left. When the cursor is to the right of the crosshair, inside the box, your point of view rotates right. Holding down the Shift key with one of the above actions pans your point of view to the left or right or tilts your point of view up or down. Holding down the Ctrl key with these actions produces pitch and roll behaviors.

The Restore button

Pressing this button returns you to the first view you had when you started viewing the current world.

Try moving around in the world using the first group of arrow buttons. Clicking the up arrow, while in the Fly Mode, moves you deeper into the screen, closer to the object. You also can use the up arrow (↑) on the keyboard. The down arrow, both on the screen and on the keyboard (↓), pulls you out and away from the object. The right (→) and left (←) arrows move you to the right or to the left, respectively.

Now try moving around in the world using the second and third groups of arrow buttons.

Experiment with these controls for a few minutes, and then click the Restore button to return to the point of view that you had when you first started looking at this world.

CUBE.WRL

Once again, you need to look at how the cube is put together. Listing 10-2 is the VRML Version 1.0 ASCII code for CUBE.WRL.

Listing 10-2: CUBE.WRL

```
#VRML V1.0 ascii
DEF Root Separator {
    Cube {
```

```
        width      3
        height     2
        depth      1
    }
}
```

This extremely simple world file has only one node, the *cube node*. VRML files always begin with the statement #VRML V1.0 ascii.

Anything that begins with the # sign is a *comment*. The comment always continues to the end of the line that contains the # sign.

The next line describes the node in VRML syntax. The syntax for this line is

```
DEF objectname objecttype { fields children}
```

In this example, the programmer has given the objectname as Root and the objecttype as Separator. A node must have the objecttype specification and the curly braces, but the rest is optional.

The cube node is one of the *shape nodes* available in VRML. This node represents a cube aligned along the x, y, and z axes with a center of 0,0,0. It measures two units in each direction from +1 to –1.

The cube is changed and modified by the applied transformations. In this case, the width has been adjusted to 3, the height to 2, and the depth to 1. This means that the x-coordinates of the object now range from +1.5 to –1.5, the y-coordinates remain at +1 to –1, and the z-coordinates range from +0.5 to –0.5.

If no specifications are given for the material and texture, the object is drawn using the defaults. The defaults are used in this case.

Load some of the other worlds in this subdirectory. Try exploring them and getting comfortable with WorldView's user interface.

That's it for now for exploring the off-line .WRL files included with WorldView. It's time to configure WorldView and SPRY Air Mosaic to work together so that you can go surfing 3D VRML worlds on the Web.

If you decide to use a different Web browser, or a different viewer, be sure to set up the configuration for both the browser and the viewer before accessing the Web. The setup of the configuration is similar to what is discussed in the next section.

Setting up a Web browser to use with WorldView

WorldView comes preconfigured to work with NetScape. You need to run SPRY Air Mosaic in order to get SPRY Air Mosaic and WorldView to work together.

1. As SPRY Air Mosaic starts to make a connection, click on Cancel.

2. Choose the Options menu, as shown in Figure 10-13.

3. Choose the Configuration option.

   You see the Configuration dialog box, looking much like Figure 10-14.

   While you're in this dialog box, we suggest you take the *X* out of the check box labeled Load automatically at startup in the Home Page section of the dialog box so that you can load Mosaic without automatically connecting to the Web every time. Removing the *X* doesn't prevent you from accessing the Web. It just means that you'll only access the Web when you're ready.

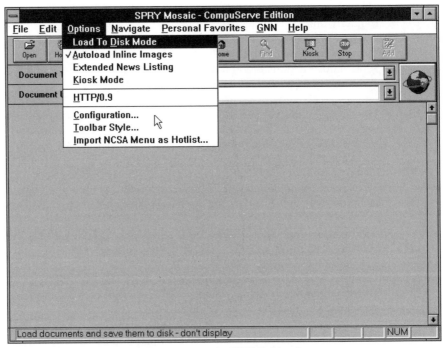

Figure 10-13: Choose the Options menu in SPRY Air Mosaic.

Configuration

☒ Show Toolbar ☒ Autoload inline images

☒ Show Status Bar ☒ Show URL in Status Bar

☒ Show Document Title ☒ Underline hyperlinks

☒ Show Document URL ☒ Animate logo

☒ Save last window position ☐ Use 8-bit Sound

When loading images, redraw every `1.5` seconds.

Home Page

URL: `http://www.compuserve.com`

☐ Load automatically at startup

Email Address: `76270.551@compuserve.com`

SMTP Server: `mail.compuserve.com`

News Server: `news.compuserve.com`

Cached Documents: `10`   Documents in dropdown: `5`

[Viewers...] [Link Color...] [Fonts...] [Proxy Servers...]

[OK] [Cancel] [Help]

Figure 10-14: The SPRY Air Mosaic Configuration dialog box.

4.   Click the Viewers button near the bottom of the Configuration dialog box to see the External Viewer Configuration dialog box.

It looks similar to Figure 10-15.

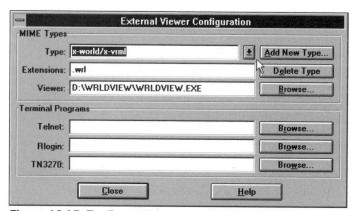

External Viewer Configuration

MIME Types

Type: `x-world/x-vrml` ▼ [Add New Type...]

Extensions: `.wrl` [Delete Type]

Viewer: `D:\WRLDVIEW\WRLDVIEW.EXE` [Browse...]

Terminal Programs

Telnet: [Browse...]

Rlogin: [Browse...]

TN3270: [Browse...]

[Close] [Help]

Figure 10-15: The External Viewer Configuration dialog box.

5. In the Type text box, type x-world/x-vrml.

6. In the Extensions text box, type .wrl.

7. In the Viewer text box, type the drive specification, the name of the subdirectory where you installed WorldView, and the program name.

   In this case, you type **wrldview.exe.**

8. Click the Add New Type button.

9. Click Close to exit the program.

   You've set SPRY Air Mosaic up to run WorldView when it encounters VRML worlds. But you're not done yet. You need to set WorldView up to run with SPRY Air Mosaic.

10. **Load Notepad and open the WRLDVIEW.INI file in your Windows subdirectory.**

    The file looks similar to Figure 10-16.

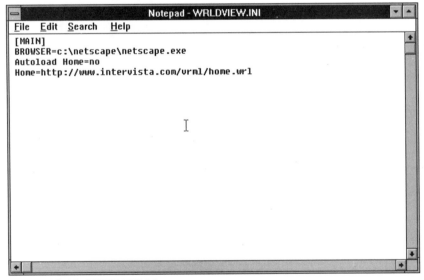

Figure 10-16: WRLDVIEW.INI.

WorldView comes preconfigured to work with NetScape. You need to edit this file so that it will work with SPRY Air Mosaic.

11. **Edit the line that reads**

    ```
    Browser=c:/netscape/netscape.exe
    ```

to read

```
Browser=X:\cserve\mosaic\airmos.exe.
```

where X represents the drive where SPRY Air Mosaic is located.

12.   Choose Exit from the File menu and click Yes when the program asks whether you want to save the file.

SPRY Air Mosaic and WorldView are ready for you to use to explore the Web. However, if you have configured a different Web browser and VRML viewer, you're still ready for the Web. In the next section, you tour an area that has plenty of VRML worlds to look at.

Putting What You've Learned into Practice

In this section, you visit three locations for a quick tour of some of the wondrous worlds that you can explore now in cyberspace. You can use any browser and VRML viewer, but we point out a few advantages and disadvantages to some of them during the tour.

Exercise #1: Testing your browser and viewer

First, check out how well your Web browser and VRML viewer work together. Point your browser at `http://www.vrml.com/models/test/cube.wrl`. As you can see in Figure 10-17, this is a simple world. For our purposes, a major point to this world is that it has hyperlinks. If a world has a hyperlink in it, the cursor appears as a hand when you move the cursor over the hyperlink.

If you click on the cube, the hyperlink takes you to another world file, such the one as shown in Figure 10-18.

Exercise #2: Exploring Virtual SOMA

The home of Virtual SOMA is next on your tour of virtual worlds on the Web. Aim your Web browser at the URL `http://www.planet9.com`. Your screen looks something like Figure 10-19.

Figure 10-17: CUBE.WRL is a world with hyperlinks.

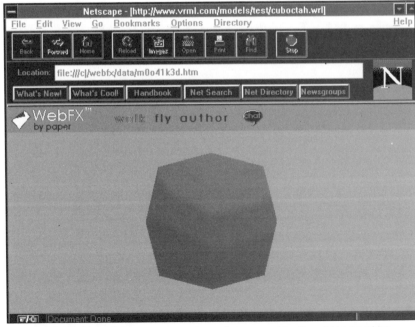

Figure 10-18: Hyperlinks can transport you from one virtual world to another.

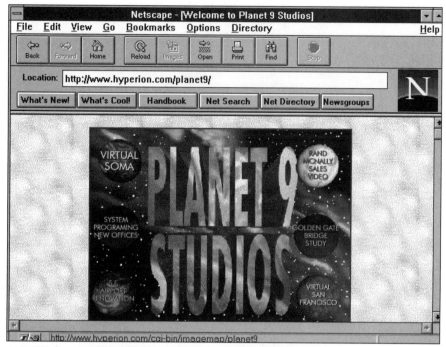

Figure 10-19: Planet 9 Studios: the home of Virtual SOMA.

Click on the Virtual SOMA icon to see the HTML page for Virtual SOMA, as shown in Figure 10-20.

This page describes how, where, and why Virtual SOMA was created. You move down the page to find the VRML hyperlink where you can view this world, as in Figure 10-21.

Click on the hyperlink to have your VRML viewer take over. The VRML world loads in the viewer window. Maximize this window to see something similar to what's shown in Figure 10-22.

If you're using WorldView, your view may start out below the ground level of this world. Use the navigation controls and move straight in toward this world. Maneuver yourself so that you can come down and straight in along the sidewalk as in Figure 10-23.

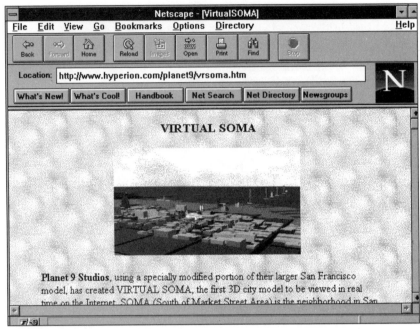

Figure 10-20: The Virtual SOMA Web Page.

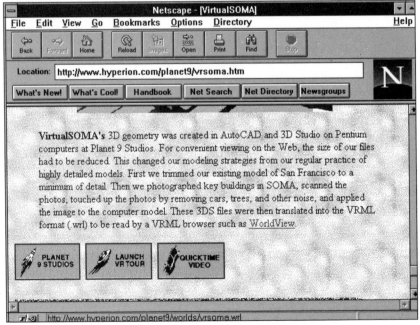

Figure 10-21: The VRML link from the HTML page to the SOMA virtual world is at the bottom of the Planet 9 Studios Web page.

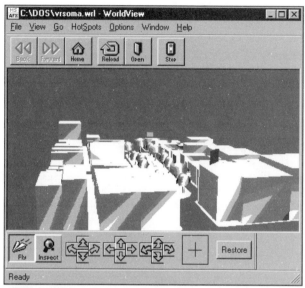

Figure 10-22: Virtual SOMA floating in space.

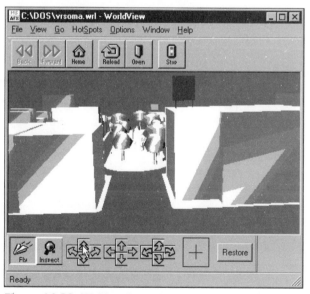

Figure 10-23: Walking down the sidewalk in Virtual SOMA.

If you're using WebFX, you can walk (or fly) farther down the street into the world, and you can click on buildings and enter them (See Figure 10-24).

Inside the buildings, you can view artwork, read about the company that inhabits the building, or experience other multimedia presentations, as in Figure 10-25. Check out the color insert for other screen shots of the new Virtual SOMA.

Exercise #3: Exploring WaxWeb

We mentioned WaxWeb earlier in the book. Now you can examine and explore it. Point your browser at `http://bug.village.virginia.edu/`, which is the home of WaxWeb. You see something similar to Figure 10-26 on your screen.

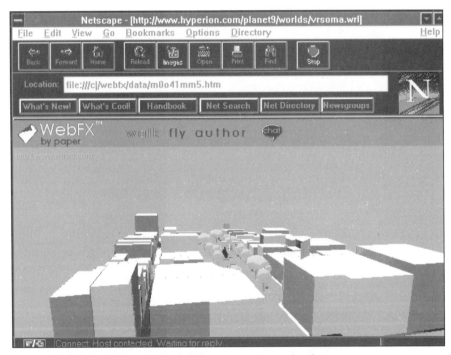

Figure 10-24: By clicking on the buildings, you can reach other information via hyperlinks.

Figure 10-25: An example of the kind of information that's inside the buildings.

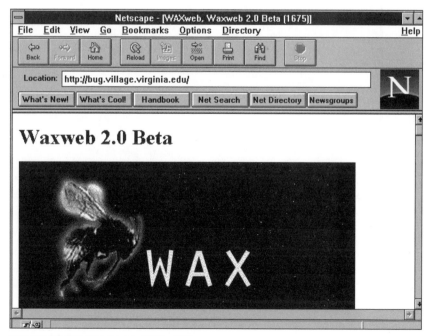

Figure 10-26: The home of WaxWeb.

Move down the Web page till you see an icon for guest. Click this icon and go about halfway down the next page till you come to something that looks similar to Figure 10-27. Click the blue underlined text, "see Wax in 3D."

Read the next page carefully. About halfway down the page, you see something that looks similar to Figure 10-28. Click on the graphic under the text, WHERE YOU GO NEXT. You'll find a multimedia version of the film here. Explore WaxWeb a little. It has many sights that are interesting viewing.

You may need to try several browser/viewer combinations before you can see anything on WaxWeb. Windows 3.1 browser/viewer combinations have some difficulty from time to time, but WaxWeb works fine with WebSpace on other platforms.

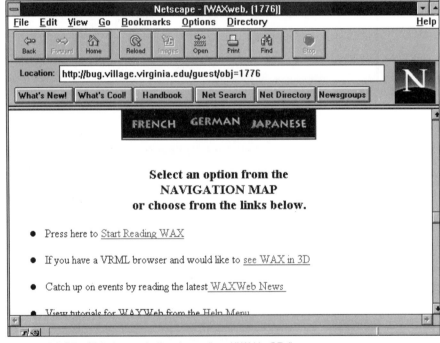

Figure 10-27: Click the underlined text, "see WAX in 3D."

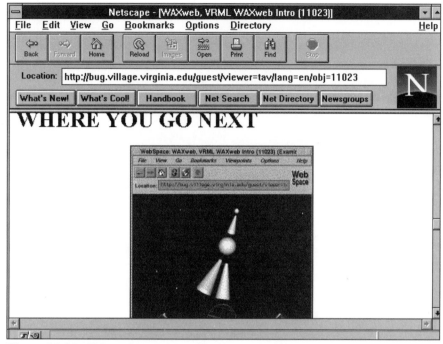

Figure 10-28: Click on the graphic.

Moving On

In this chapter you looked at a variety of VRML viewers and installed at least one of them on your computer. After that, you went surfing, looked at several worlds, and wandered around in one of them.

Several other worlds await your exploration, but we are saving them for Chapter 15. In the next chapter, you examine a few of the VRML editors and tools that you can use to build worlds. You also begin learning skills for creating a place in cyberspace that you can virtually call your own.

Setting Up and Using the VRML Editors

People have been using PCs to create artificial, or virtual, worlds for several years. In Chapter 4, we discuss some of the more popular programs used to create these worlds. In Chapter 8, you created a simple cube using 2Morrow World Builder. In this chapter, you learn how to use conversion utilities to convert a world created in the .WLD format to the VRML .WRL format.

You find out how to convert a simple program as well as a complex one. For the complex program, you open a world that Paul created in the .WLD format, explore it, and then convert it to VRML.

You also learn about several of the VRML editing and creation tools that you can use with Windows 3.1, beginning with the tools that are on the CD-ROM that accompanies this book. These tools enable you to save the worlds you create in the .WRL format without having to write one line of code yourself. After you learn how to install these editors, you begin creating your own worlds.

In the following discussion, we ask you to load a VRML viewer and look at the various worlds you'll be creating. Because you are using betas of some of the viewers, sometimes a world may not display in one viewer but will display in another. Before you give up, go into the Preferences of the specific viewer that you are using and change the options to display the scene on loading and to generate both normals and backfaces during rendering. We describe how to do this in Chapter 10. All of the virtual worlds in this chapter displayed for us in some form with the viewers provided on the CD-ROM.

Converting Files to the .WRL Format

The time that you put into creating virtual worlds with other programs and languages in earlier chapters has not been wasted. In the next few sections, you learn how to use programs that convert those worlds to VRML.

Converting a simple world with WLD2VRML

In Chapter 8, you created a file for a simple cube using 2Morrow World Builder. This file is in the .WLD format, which is the format used by files created with programs such as 2Morrow World Builder, AVRIL, REND386, VR386, and VRBASIC. You are now going to convert that file to the VRML .WRL format by using WLD2VRML by Bernie Roehl.

1. **Double-click the VRML CD-ROM icon.**

2. **Install the WLD2VRML software on the hard drive by clicking the WLD2VRML building and then following the directions.**

3. **Exit Windows.**

4. **Type** cd:\wld2vrml **at the DOS prompt.**

   The syntax for the WLD2VRML conversion program is as follows:

   ```
   wld2vrml inputfile >outputfile
   ```

   For *inputfile*, use the name and location of the file that you want to convert. For *outputfile*, use the name and location of the file that you want the conversion to be located in.

5. **Copy both the CUBE.WLD file and the PLG1.PLG file from the 2Morrow World Builder subdirectory to the WLD2VRML subdirectory.**

   WLD2VRML will convert any .PLG or .FIG file that is referenced by the .WLD file to the VRML .WRL format if the files are in the same subdirectory as the inputfile designated.

6. **Type** wld2vrml cube.wld >cube.wrl.

   The file is converted.

7. **Return to Windows and load your favorite VRML viewer.**

8. **Load CUBE.WRL.**

   You see a cube that looks like the one shown in Figure 11-1.

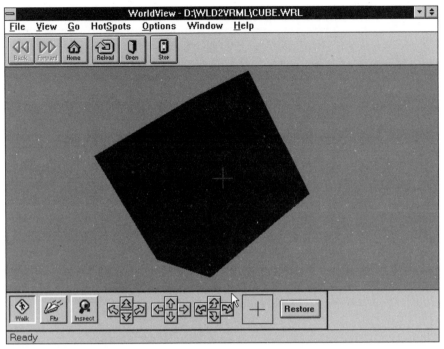

Figure 11-1: CUBE.WRL.

Listing 11-1 shows how the code from CUBE.WLD, which you saw in Chapter 8, looks after it has been converted into the VRML .WRL format.

Listing 11-1: CUBE.WRL

```
#VRML V1.0 ascii
#
# Converted from 'cube.wld' by WLD2VRML
#
Separator {
  MaterialBinding { value PER_FACE_INDEXED }
  ShapeHints { vertexOrdering CLOCKWISE }
DirectionalLight { }
Separator {
  Translation { translation 0.000000 0.000000 7.500000 }
  Material {
      emissiveColor [ 0.2 0.2 0.2 ]
```

(continued)

Listing 11-1 *(continued)*:

```
        ambientColor [ 0.500000 0.500000 0.500000 ]
        diffuseColor [
            0.359375 0.000000 0.000000,
            0.359375 0.171875 0.000000,
            0.359375 0.171875 0.171875,
            0.359375 0.265625 0.171875,
            0.359375 0.359375 0.171875,
            0.359375 0.359375 0.000000,
            ]
        shininess [
            0.0,
            0.0,
            0.0,
            0.0,
            0.0,
            0.0,
            ]
        transparency [
            0.0,
            0.0,
            0.0,
            0.0,
            0.0,
            0.0,
            ]
    }
    Coordinate3 { point [
        -0.500000 -0.500000 0.500000,
        0.500000 -0.500000 0.500000,
        0.500000 0.500000 0.500000,
        -0.500000 0.500000 0.500000,
        -0.500000 -0.500000 -0.500000,
        0.500000 -0.500000 -0.500000,
        0.500000 0.500000 -0.500000,
        -0.500000 0.500000 -0.500000,
        ]
    }
    IndexedFaceSet {
        coordIndex [
            0, 3, 7, 4, -1,
            0, 4, 5, 1, -1,
            1, 5, 6, 2, -1,
            2, 6, 7, 3, -1,
            7, 6, 5, 4, -1,
```

```
        0, 1, 2, 3, -1,
        4, 7, 3, 0, -1,
        1, 5, 4, 0, -1,
        2, 6, 5, 1, -1,
        3, 7, 6, 2, -1,
        4, 5, 6, 7, -1,
        3, 2, 1, 0, -1,
        ]
    materialIndex [
        5,
        4,
        3,
        2,
        1,
        0,
        5,
        4,
        3,
        2,
        1,
        0,
        ]
      }
   }
  }
 }
# End of file
```

Now, you are going to try something a little more complex.

Converting a more complex world with WLD2VRML

For this conversion, you use a world that Paul has worked on for a while, PSU.WLD. The world is in the \WLD\ subdirectory on the CD-ROM that accompanies this book.

Paul began work on this world shortly after he joined the faculty at Pittsburg State University. Its purpose is to enable potential students to explore the PSU campus in a virtual environment. PSU.WLD is available for download from the libraries in CyberForum on CompuServe as well as on America Online.

Paul used VRBASIC when he began to create this world, but soon the program's memory constraints forced him to continue building the world in REND386. As with the university itself, PSU.WLD is under construction. The football field, library, dorms, nursing building, physical fitness center, and new technology center have not yet been included in the virtual world. Screen shots from the original DOS-based PSU.WLD can be seen in the color insert.

Loading PSU.WLD into 2Morrow World Builder

Before you can convert PSU.WLD to a .WRL file, you need to load PSU.WLD into 2Morrow World Builder. If you did not transfer 2Morrow World Builder to your hard drive for the exercises in Chapter 8, turn back to that chapter and follow the directions for installing the software.

Follow these instructions to load PSU.WLD and explore the Pittsburg State University campus.

1. Start 2Morrow World Builder from the DOS prompt by changing to the subdirectory where it is stored and then typing 2MWB.

2. Choose Load .WLD from the File menu.

3. Select PSU.WLD from the directory.

   The world loads, and you see a screen that looks similar to Figure 11-2.

Grubbs Hall   Joplin Ave.

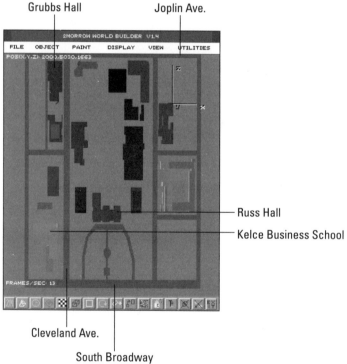

Russ Hall

Kelce Business School

Cleveland Ave.

South Broadway

Figure 11-2: PSU.WLD, view from camera one's position.

4. Use the Shift-↑ combination to climb higher into the sky above PSU.

   You are looking down on the campus. North is to your left on the screen, and east is toward the top of the screen.

   Paul programmed six cameras into this world. F1 is the original camera; your current view is from its position.

5. **Press F2 to change your view so that you are at the north end of South Broadway looking toward the southeast at the Kelce Business School, as in Figure 11-3.**

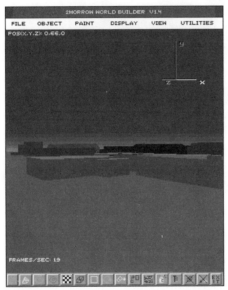

Figure 11-3: PSU from the north end of South Broadway looking back at the Kelce Business School building.

   This is the direction from which most people drive into the campus.

6. **Press F3 to change your viewpoint to the north end of campus looking off toward the southeast, as in Figure 11-4.**

Figure 11-4: View from the north looking off to the southeast.

The building on the left in the distance is Grubbs Hall, where Paul's office and the television studios are located.

7. **Press F4 to place your viewpoint back at the northwest corner of the campus above Broadway and at a higher altitude.**

    You're still looking off to the southeast, but this time you're looking down on the campus slightly. Kelce Business School is the building near the bottom of the screen (See Figure 11-5).

8. **Press F5 to change your viewpoint to directly above the center of the campus, looking down and off to the southwest.**

    The building with the circular drive at the bottom of the screen (See Figure 11-6) is Russ Hall. The registrar's office, the student affairs office, the financial aid office, and the university president's office are in this building.

9. **Press F6 to see the sixth, and final, camera position.**

    Now your viewpoint is on the corner of Joplin and Cleveland, as shown in Figure 11-7. You're facing the southwest. Behind you, although not added to the world yet, is the library. To your right is Grubbs Hall. To your left, although again not added to the world yet, is the football stadium.

Figure 11-5: PSU's campus from a higher altitude.

Figure 11-6: Russ Hall is at the bottom of the screen.

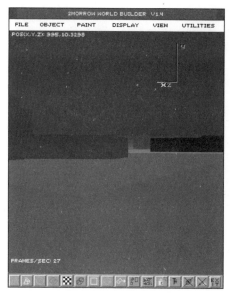

Figure 11-7: Looking to the southwest from the corner of Joplin and Cleveland.

Explore the campus for a few moments. Take the time to load the file into your Notepad or editor and look at how the world is constructed. Next, you convert PSU.WLD to the VRML .WRL file format, as you did with CUBE.WLD.

Converting PSU.WLD with WLD2VRML

Follow these steps to convert PSU.WLD to the .WRL format:

1. **Exit Windows and type** cd:\wld2vrml **at the DOS prompt.**

    Again, the syntax for the conversion program is as follows:

    ```
    wld2vrml inputfile >outputfile
    ```

2. **In this case, type** wld2vrml psu.wld >psu.wrl.

    This assumes that PSU.WLD, the input file, is in the WLD2VRML subdirectory. In this particular case, it is. It was installed with the converter.

You can check out the converted file by returning to Windows, entering your VRML browser, and loading the file. The world displays differently on different viewers. Figure 11-8 is what PSU.WRL looks like with WebFX and Netscape. This View is also available in the color insert.

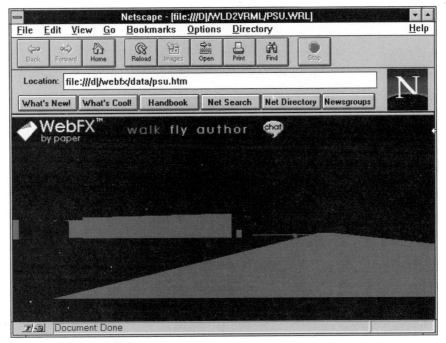

Figure 11-8: PSU.WRL.

Converting files with WCVT2POV

Suppose that you've created a great world using 3DStudio, AutoCAD, or trueSpace2, and you want to convert that world to the VRML .WRL format. What do you use? Keith Rule's WCVT2POV conversion program, which is on the CD-ROM that accompanies this book.

Installing WCVT2POV

You can install WCVT2POV from the CD-ROM's interface by clicking on the building labeled WCVT2POV. Again, as always, just follow the on-screen directions and you'll be able to transfer this Windows 3.1 program to your hard drive.

Using WCVT2POV

WCVT2POV can convert AOFF (*.GEO) files, AutoCAD (*.DXF) files, 3D Studio (*.3DS) files, Neutral File Format (*.NFF) files, RAW (*.RAW) files,

TrueType font (*.TTF) files, and Wavefront (*.OBJ) files to VRML (*.WRL) files. Follow these steps to convert the .DXF version of the cube file that you created using trueSpace2 in Chapter 8:

1. Click on the WCVT2POV icon to bring up the program window.

2. Choose Open from the File menu.

3. Choose the AutoCad (*.DXF) option.

4. Double-click on the CUBE.DXF file.

    The program loads the .DXF file into memory and onto the screen, and your screen looks similar to Figure 11-9.

5. Choose Save as from the File menu.

6. Choose the VRML V. 1.0 (*.WRL) option.

7. Name the file CUBE2.WRL and click OK.

    Saving the file under this name prevents this file from overwriting the CUBE.WRL file that you created earlier in the chapter. You now have two cube VRML files, the first converted from the .WLD format and the second converted from the .DXF format.

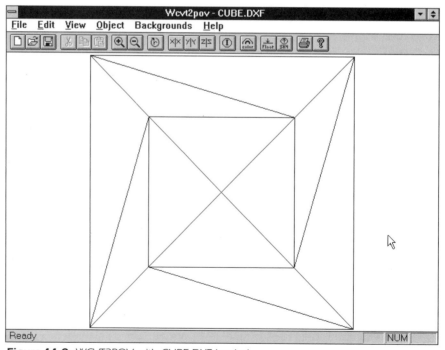

Figure 11-9: WCVT2POV with CUBE.DXF loaded.

8. Compare the program listing for CUBE2.WRL in Listing 11-2 with the program listing of CUBE.WRL provided in Listing 11-1.

Listing 11-2: CUBE2.WRL

```
#VRML V1.0 ascii
Separator {
  DEF SceneInfo Info {
   string "Converted by wcvt2pov v2.6"
  }
  PerspectiveCamera {
   position 0.000000 0.000000 -3.464102
   orientation 0 1 0 3.14
   focalDistance 5
   heightAngle 0.785398
  }
  PointLight {
   on      TRUE
   intensity     1.0
   color  1.0 1.0 1.0
   location 0.000000 0.866025 3.464102
  }
  PointLight {
   on      TRUE
   intensity     1.0
   color  1.0 1.0 1.0
   location 0.000000 0.866025 -3.464102
  }
  PointLight {
   on      TRUE
   intensity     1.0
   color  1.0 1.0 1.0
   location 0.000000 8.660254 0.000000
  }
  PointLight {
   on      TRUE
   intensity     1.0
   color  1.0 1.0 1.0
   location 0.000000 -8.660254 0.000000
  }
  DEF Cube1_Black Separator {
   Material {
         diffuseColor 0.000000 0.000000 0.000000
         ambientColor 0.000000 0.000000 0.000000
   }
```

(continued)

Listing 11-2 *(continued)*:

```
Coordinate3 {
        point [
                1.000000 -1.000000 1.000000,
                1.000000 -1.000000 -1.000000,
                -1.000000 -1.000000 -1.000000,
                -1.000000 -1.000000 1.000000,
                1.000000 1.000000 -1.000000,
                -1.000000 1.000000 -1.000000,
                -1.000000 1.000000 1.000000,
                1.000000 1.000000 1.000000
        ]
}
IndexedFaceSet {
        coordIndex [
                2, 1, 0, -1,
                2, 0, 3, -1,
                4, 1, 2, -1,
                4, 2, 5, -1,
                5, 2, 3, -1,
                5, 3, 6, -1,
                6, 3, 0, -1,
                6, 0, 7, -1,
                4, 5, 6, -1,
                4, 6, 7, -1,
                1, 4, 7, -1,
                1, 7, 0, -1
        ]
    }
  }
}
```

9. Exit WCVT2POV and load your VRML viewer.

10. Open CUBE2.WRL inside the VRML viewer.

    Your screen is similar to Figure 11-10. (We have moved the cube back and turned it slightly so that you can see that it is a cube.)

11. **Exit your viewer now and get ready for a new experience.**

    Your next stop is building worlds using some of the VRML tools provided on the CD-ROM.

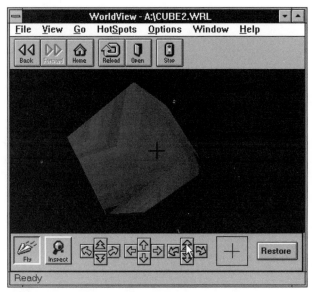

Figure 11-10: CUBE2.WRL seen in WorldView.

Building Some Simple Worlds

In the next several pages, we show you how to create a simple world that contains one cube, using the VRML creation tools on the CD-ROM. As you're working through these exercises, keep in mind that the tools you use to create a world and the tools you use to view it have an effect on the world that you're building.

We begin with Caligari's new VRML creation tool, Fountain. You can see one of the interesting worlds that can be created with this tool in the color insert.

Building a world with Fountain

Fountain is a new VRML world-building application from Caligari Corporation. The user interface is very similar to the interface for trueSpace2 in Chapter 8. In this section, you use Fountain to create a cube.

Installing Fountain

The first thing you need to do is load Fountain from the CD-ROM. Find the building in the CD-ROM VR user interface that's labeled Caligari and click on it, just as you did for the programs in Chapter 8. You have two options: install trueSpace2 and install Fountain. Click on the install Fountain option. VisMenu installs Fountain on the hard drive. Follow all of the on-screen directions.

After the program loads and creates its own program group, open the program group and double-click on the Fountain icon. You see an opening screen briefly, and then the screen looks similar to what you saw when you opened trueSpace2.

Creating a cube with Fountain

Follow these steps to create the cube in Fountain:

1. Choose Scene from the File menu and then choose New, as shown in Figure 11-11.

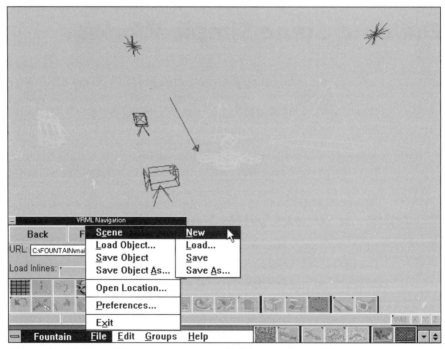

Figure 11-11: Clear Cyberspace so you can build your new world.

You now have an open grid on the screen to use in creating a cube.

2. **Click once on the Primitives Panel.**

    The Primitives group comes up, as shown in Figure 11-12.

3. **Click the Add Cube panel to have a wireframe of a cube appear on the screen (See Figure 11-13).**

4. **In the row of icons at the bottom of the screen, click the wireframe panel and hold down the mouse button (See Figure 11-14).**

    Two new options appear: wireframe at the top and 3DR on the bottom.

5. **Choose 3DR to transform the wireframe cube into a solid.**

6. **Choose Object Scale from the row of icons at the bottom of the screen, as shown in Figure 11-15.**

7. **Hold down both mouse buttons until the cube has shrunk to about half its original size.**

8. **Click the Object Move button at the bottom of the screen, as shown in Figure 11-16.**

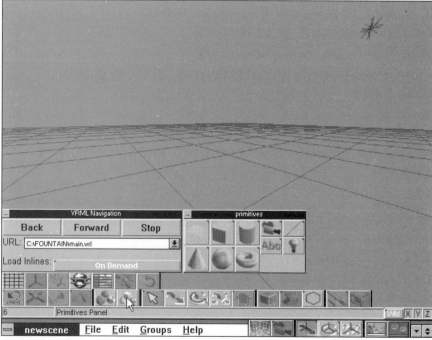

Figure 11-12: Fountain object tools are similar to those you worked with in trueSpace2.

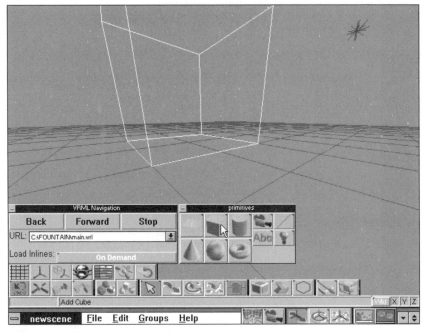

Figure 11-13: Add the wireframe cube by clicking Add Cube.

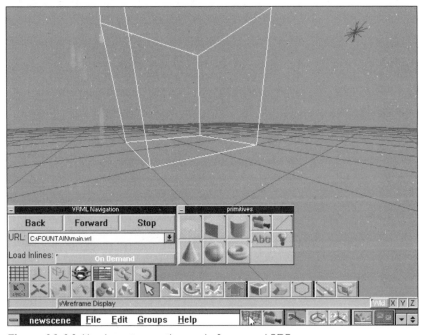

Figure 11-14: You have two options: wireframe and 3DR.

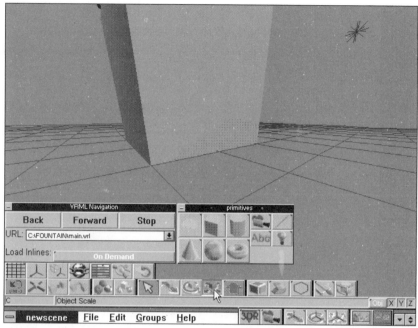

Figure 11-15: You need to scale the object now.

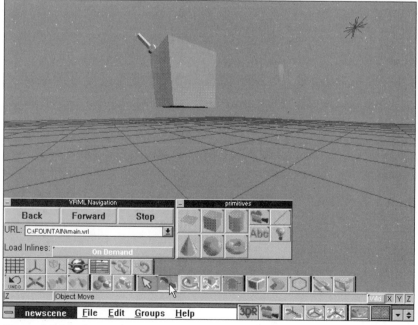

Figure 11-16: Click the Object Move button.

9. Click on the cube with the right mouse button.

10. Move the cube down to rest on the grid.

11. Choose Scene from the File menu and then choose Save As (See Figure 11-17).

12. Save the cube as CUBE_CAL.WRL.

13. Make sure that you remove the checks from all of the boxes and choose ASCII.

14. Exit Fountain.

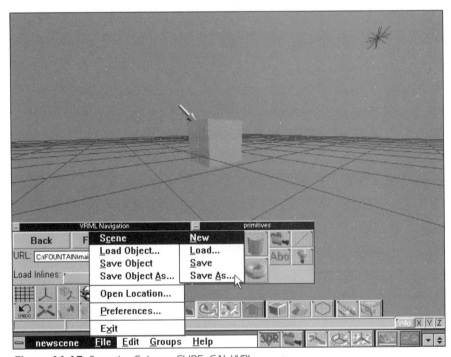

Figure 11-17: Save the Cube as CUBE_CAL.WRL.

Examining the code for CUBE_CAL.WRL

Load CUBE_CAL.WRL into Notepad. You see a VRML file that looks similar to Listing 11-3.

Listing 11-3: CUBE_CAL.WRL

```
#VRML V1.0 ascii
# created by Caligari Corp. Truespace (tm)
# copyright 1995 Caligari Corporation
Separator {
CALIGARISceneInfo {
fields [ SFVec3f background, SFVec3f environ,
SFVec3f fogColor, SFBool fog, SFLong fogNear,
SFLong fogFar, SFString envName, SFString backgroundName ]
background 0.502 0.502 0.502
environ 0.000 0.000 0.000
fogColor 0.502 0.502 0.502
fogNear 1
fogFar 500
fog FALSE
}
Switch { }
TransformSeparator {
MatrixTransform {
matrix
1.000 0.000 0.000 0
0.000 0.000 -1.000 0
0.000 1.000 0.000 0
4.827 4.089 1.121 1
}
DEF LocLight PointLight {
color 1.000 0.647 0.376
on TRUE
location 0.000 0.000 0.000
intensity 1.300
}
}
TransformSeparator {
MatrixTransform {
matrix
1.000 0.000 0.000 0
0.000 0.000 -1.000 0
0.000 1.000 0.000 0
-3.631 3.046 5.116 1
}
DEF LocLight_1 PointLight {
color 0.008 0.698 1.000
on TRUE
location 0.000 0.000 0.000
```

(continued)

Listing 11-3 *(continued)*:

```
intensity 1.300
}
}
TransformSeparator {
MatrixTransform {
matrix
1.000 0.000 0.000 0
0.000 0.000 -1.000 0
0.000 1.000 0.000 0
1.226 2.930 -5.390 1
}
DEF LocLight_2 PointLight {
color 0.800 0.800 0.800
on TRUE
location 0.000 0.000 0.000
intensity 1.300
}
}
Separator {
MaterialBinding {
value OVERALL
}
Material {
ambientColor [
0.100 0.100 0.100,
]
diffuseColor [
0.824 0.824 0.824,
]
specularColor [
0.100 0.100 0.100,
]
emissiveColor [
0.000 0.000 0.000,
]
shininess [
0.000,
]
transparency [
0.000,
]
}
MatrixTransform {
matrix
0.482 0.000 0.000 0
```

```
0.000 0.000 -0.335 0
0.000 0.402 0.000 0
1.000 0.000 0.000 1
}
Coordinate3 {
point [
-1.000 -1.000 -1.000,
-1.000 -1.000 1.000,
1.000 -1.000 -1.000,
1.000 -1.000 1.000,
-1.000 1.000 -1.000,
1.000 1.000 -1.000,
1.000 1.000 1.000,
-1.000 1.000 1.000,
]
}
ShapeHints {
creaseAngle 0.559
vertexOrdering COUNTERCLOCKWISE
shapeType SOLID
faceType UNKNOWN_FACE_TYPE
}
DEF Cube IndexedFaceSet {
coordIndex [
2, 0, 1, 3,
-1, 4, 0, 2,
5, -1, 5, 2,
3, 6, -1, 6,
3, 1, 7, -1,
4, 5, 6, 7,
-1, 0, 4, 7,
1, -1,  ]
}
}
}
```

Viewing CUBE_CAL.WRL

Load the CUBE_CAL.WRL file into one of the VRML viewers and examine it. You've done it again. Using Fountain, you've created your own VRML world containing a cube. But other tools are available out there. Next, you turn your attention to ParaGraph's Home Space Builder.

Building a world with Home Space Builder

Home Space Builder 1.0, which is on the CD-ROM that accompanies this book, is from ParaGraph International. The README file calls the program the "first inexpensive and powerful 3D+W3 [Web] authoring tool for middle and low-end computers." Home Space Builder is a very impressive VRML authoring tool. Look at the color insert to see how the program's interface compares with that of others.

Hardware and software requirements

At the very least, Home Space Builder requires a 386DX 33 MHz with 4MB of RAM and a color monitor that's capable of 256 colors. The program will run under Windows 3.1, Windows NT, or Windows 95. The files for Home Space Builder require about 1 1/2 MB of hard drive space.

Installing Home Space Builder

To start the program's installation procedure, click on the ParaGraph International building in the virtual city of the CD-ROM interface. As with most other programs on the CD-ROM, you just follow the directions. Be sure to read the README file for updates on this software.

Creating a cube with Home Space Builder

Using Home Space Builder to create an object is extremely simple, as you see when you create a three-dimensional cube.

Learning to use Home Space Builder

Open the program by clicking on the Home Space Builder icon. When the Open 3D Space File dialog box opens (See Figure 11-18), click the New 3D Space button.

The user interface (See Figure 11-19) for Home Space Builder includes six sections: the Viewer window, the Plane Builder window, the Image tool, the Walker toolbox, the Graphics Chooser window, and the Builder toolbox.

The Viewer window enables you to navigate through three-dimensional worlds by using your keyboard's arrow keys or, for more control, the Walker toolbox. The Viewer window is the window in the upper-left of the screen.

At the top of this window is the name of the .MUS, or museum, file that is loaded. The internal format of Home Space Builder saves the worlds that you create in these .MUS files. After you create a world, you can export it into the VRML format and save it as a .WRL file.

Figure 11-18: The Open 3D Space File dialog box.

Viewer window   Plane Builder window   Image tool

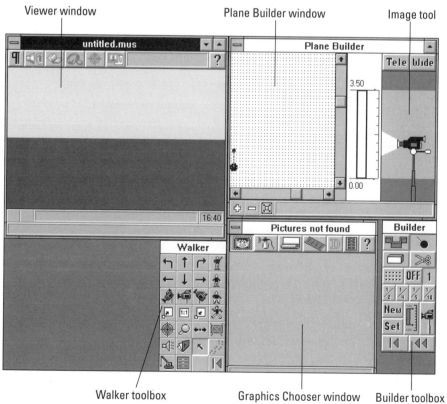

Walker toolbox   Graphics Chooser window   Builder toolbox

Figure 11-19: The Home Space Builder user interface.

The window to the right of the Viewer window is the Plane Builder window, where you design your worlds. You can use its Pinocchio button (the black circle with the long nose) to set the viewing positions of people who enter your world.

The three windows at the bottom of the screen are, from left to right, the Walker toolbox, which you use to control navigation through the virtual world; the Graphics Chooser window which enables you to control the color, picture, and wallpaper used on the objects in your world; and the Builder toolbox, which you use to build virtual worlds and adjust the height of objects in worlds.

Creating a cube

Follow these instructions to create a cube:

1. **Click on the Add 3D Box mode in the Builder toolbox.** (This looks like a 3-D rectangle. Also, as you move your mouse over the different tools, the names of these tools appears in the text line at the bottom of the Plane Builder window.)

2. **Click in the Plane Builder window.**

3. **Stretch the resulting rectangle into a small square.**

4. **Click again to make the square permanent.**

   Or if you aren't satisfied with the square, click on the Undo Last Operation button in the Walker toolbox to remove the square and start over. The Undo Last Operation button is a rectangle with an X through it.

5. **When you're happy with the square, look in the Viewer Window.**

   You see a rectangular, or cubic if you're really good, box sitting in the middle of the window. If you don't see it, move the Pinocchio button in the Plane Builder window, or use the Walker toolbox controls, to turn around until the box comes into view. Click on the arrow buttons in the Walker toolbox to turn the direction that you want.

6. **Click the paragraph symbol at the left end of the Viewer window control bar.**

   A menu appears.

7. **Choose the Save 3D Space option.**

   The Save 3D Space dialog box appears.

8. At the bottom of the dialog box, change the file type to Virtual Reality Modeling Language File (*.WRL).

9. Name the file CUBE3.WRL and select OK.

10. Activate the main menu by clicking on the reversed paragraph symbol in the upper-left corner of the Viewer window and click Exit to leave Home Space Builder.

Examining the code for CUBE3.WRL

Open CUBE3.WRL in the Notepad and look at the code. It is similar to Listing 11-4.

Listing 11-4: CUBE3.WRL

```
#VRML V1.0 ascii
Separator{
   ShapeHints {shapeType SOLID vertexOrdering COUNTERCLOCKWISE}
   SpotLight  {on FALSE}
   PerspectiveCamera{
       orientation 0 1 0 -2.51929
       position -9222 523 8729
       heightAngle 1.18843
   }
   Coordinate3{
       point[
       -7936 0 10035, -7936 0 11520, -7936 896 11520, -7936 896
       L10035, -6348 0 10035,
       -6348 896 10035, -6348 0 11520, -6348 896 11520,
       ] # 8 points
   }
   MaterialBinding {value PER_FACE_INDEXED}
   Material{
       ambientColor 0 0 0
       diffuseColor 0 0 0
       emissiveColor[
       0 0.501961 0, 0.611765 0 0, 0 0.501961 0.501961, 0.501961
       L0 0.501961, 0.360784 0.298039 0.0313726,
       ] # 5 colors
   }
   Separator{
       IndexedFaceSet{
           coordIndex[
```

(continued)

Listing 11-4 (continued):

```
          0, 1, 2, 3, -1, 4, 0, 3, 5, -1, 6, 4, 5, 7, -1, 1, 6,
          L7, 2, -1, 2, 7, 5, 3, -1,
          1, 0, 4, 6, -1,
          ] # 6 faces
          materialIndex[
          0, 1, 2, 2, 3, 4,
          ]
      }
    }
  }
#EOF
```

Compare the code of this cube with the code of the cubes created by Listings 11-1 and 11-2. We discuss these comparisons later in the chapter. Now exit the text editor.

Viewing CUBE3.WRL

Run one of the VRML viewers and load CUBE3.WRL. Move the cube around some. Your screen resembles what is shown in Figure 11-20.

In the next section, you look at another tool that you can use to create VRML worlds.

Building a world with Spinner

Spinner is a new VRML editing and world creation tool from 3D Web. This software is currently being released in the beta version that has been included on the CD-ROM that accompanies this book. You can see what this program looks like in the color insert.

Installing Spinner

As with previous installations, enter the CD-ROM virtual interface provided by VisMenu and find and double-click on the 3D Web building. The Spinner installation program begins. If you follow all of the directions, the program installs to your hard drive.

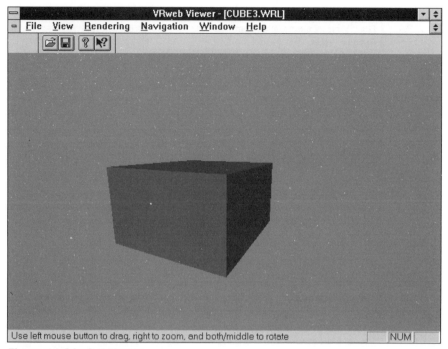

Figure 11-20: CUBE3.WRL.

Creating a cube with Spinner

When you start Spinner, you are presented with five windows: two along the top of the screen and three along the bottom. The three along the bottom are, from left to right, the top view showing you a two-dimensional view of the xz plane, the front view showing you a two-dimensional view of the xy plane, and the side view showing you a two-dimensional view of the yz plane. The window in the top right of the screen is called the Object Master, and it provides a listing of the hierarchy of the world's objects that you are creating. Finally, the window in the upper-left portion of the screen is the three-dimensional view of the world and the objects for it that you are creating.

Follow these instructions to create the cube:

1. **Click on the red cube at the bottom of the upper-left window as in Figure 11-21.**

    This action brings up the Create a New Block dialog box.

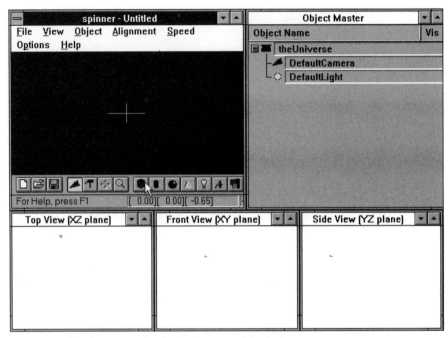

Figure 11-21: Click the red cube in the upper-left window.

2. **In the Create a New Block dialog box, type** CUBE_SPN.

   Leave the Size and Location as they are, as shown in Figure 11-22.

3. **Check the Backface check box.**

   You can make this cube slightly different from the ones you've previously created by adding color.

4. **Click the Color button to bring up the Color options dialog box, as in Figure 11-23.**

5. **Make this cube yellow by clicking the yellow box.**

6. **Click OK.**

7. **Click OK in the Create a New Block window.**

   The upper-left window is nearly filled with the yellow cube.

8. **Press the left button of your mouse and slowly move the cube back until it doesn't completely fill the window, as in Figure 11-24.**

   You can move the cube around by using the left and right buttons on the mouse.

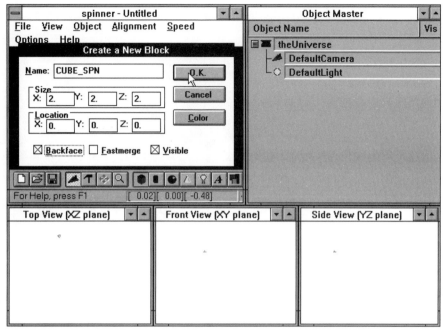

Figure 11-22: Name this object CUBE_SPN.

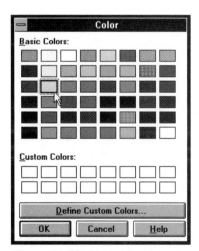

Figure 11-23: Make this cube yellow.

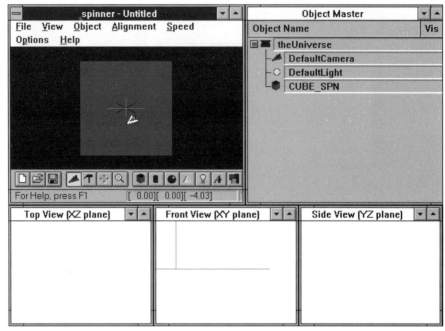

Figure 11-24: Move the yellow cube back to where you can see it better.

9. For now, save the file as a VRML file by choosing Export to WRL from the File menu.

   You see the Save As window as in Figure 11-25.

10. Under File Name, type CUBE_SPN.WRL and click OK.

11. Exit Spinner.

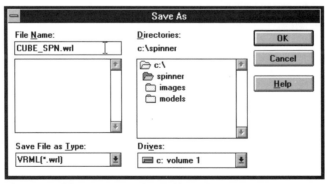

Figure 11-25: Save this as CUBE_SPN.WRL.

Examining the code for CUBE_SPN.WRL

To examine the code for CUBE_SPN.WRL, load the file into Notepad. You see a listing similar to that provided in Listing 11-5.

Listing 11-5: CUBE_SPN.WRL

```
#VRML V1.0 ascii

Separator {
Material { diffuseColor 1.000000 1.000000 1.000000 }
Group {
   DirectionalLight {
   intensity 0.400000
   direction 0.447214 0.000000 -0.894427
   }
   Separator {
   Material { diffuseColor 1.000000 1.000000 0.000000 }
   Cube {
   }
   } #sep
}
} #sep
```

Compare this listing with the previous VRML cube files you've created and notice the different methods used to create the same images.

Viewing CUBE_SPN.WRL

Exit the Notepad and load one of the VRML viewers. Load CUBE_SPN.WRL into it and examine how the world looks and feels. By now you should be getting an idea of how the different VRML tools use different methods to create the same images.

Your next task in this chapter is to create the cube by using Virtus WalkThrough VRML.

Building a world with Virtus WalkThrough VRML

Virtus WalkThrough VRML is a relatively new VR product from Virtus Corp. The program, which is on the CD-ROM that accompanies this book, is a scaled-down version of Virtus WalkThrough Pro. You can compare the interfaces for this and other VRML tools in the color insert.

Installing Virtus WalkThrough VRML

Installing this program is very similar to installing the other programs on the CD-ROM. In the virtual city interface, double-click the Virtus building. The Virtus WalkThrough VRML installation program begins. If you follow the directions, the program self-installs.

Creating a cube in Virtus WalkThrough VRML

Chapter 8 describes how to create a cube using Virtus WalkThrough Pro. If you don't have a copy of Virtus WalkThrough Pro and, therefore, didn't create the cube, go back and follow those directions, using Virtus WalkThrough VRML to create CUBE4.WRL.

Using the Virtus WalkThrough Pro File CUBE.WTP

If you don't want to take the time to create the cube, you can use the CUBE.WTP file in the \WORLDS\ subdirectory on the CD-ROM that accompanies this book.

1. **Double-click on the Virtus WalkThrough VRML icon.**

    The program loads, and you see a screen that's similar to Figure 11-26.

2. **Choose Open from the File menu.**

3. **Double-click on the file to load CUBE.WTP.**

    The screen looks similar to Figure 11-27.

4. **Choose Export from the File menu and then choose VRML.**

5. **Name the file CUBE4.WRL and click OK.**

6. **Exit Virtus WalkThrough VRML by choosing Exit from the File menu.**

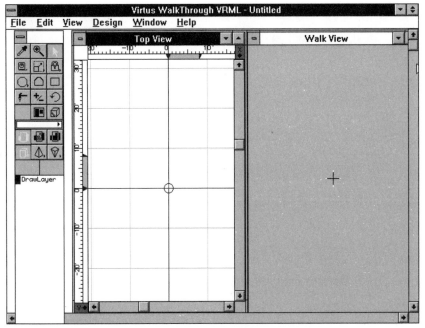

Figure 11-26: The opening screen of Virtus WalkThrough VRML.

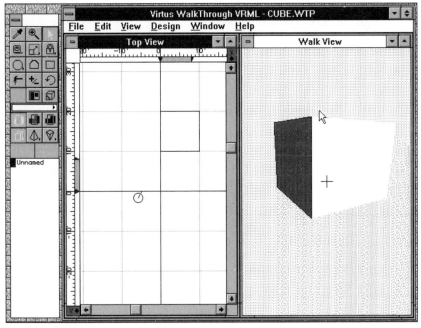

Figure 11-27: CUBE.WTP loaded in Virtus WalkThrough VRML.

Looking at CUBE4.WRL

Next, take a look at the code for CUBE4.WRL and then visit this virtual world.

Examining the code for CUBE4.WRL

Open your Notepad and load CUBE4.WRL. You see something similar to Listing 11-6.

Listing 11-6: CUBE4.WRL

```
#VRML V1.0 ascii

Separator {
   Info { string "Virtus WalkThrough VRML 1.0
   VRML Export Filter
   Virtus Corporation
   118 MacKenan Drive, Suite 250
   Cary, NC 27511
   919-467-9700"}

   ShapeHints {
      vertexOrdering     CLOCKWISE
      shapeType   SOLID
      }

   Transform {
      translation 0 0 0
      scaleFactor 1.0 1.0 1.0
      }

   Separator { #Polyhedron
      DEF COORD0 Coordinate3 {
         point [
         120.000000 96.000000 -240.000000 ,
         120.000000 96.000000 -120.000000 ,
         0.000000 96.000000 -120.000000 ,
         0.000000 96.000000 -240.000000 ,
         120.000000 0.000000 -240.000000 ,
         120.000000 0.000000 -120.000000 ,
         0.000000 0.000000 -120.000000 ,
         0.000000 0.000000 -240.000000 ]
      } #Coordinate3
```

```
USE COORD0
Material {
    ambientColor [ 0.249023 0.249023 0.249023,
    0.249023 0.249023 0.249023,
    0.249023 0.249023 0.249023,
    0.249023 0.249023 0.249023,
    0.249023 0.249023 0.249023,
    0.249023 0.249023 0.249023] #ambientColor
    diffuseColor [ 0.996094 0.996094 0.996094,
    0.996094 0.996094 0.996094,
    0.996094 0.996094 0.996094,
    0.996094 0.996094 0.996094,
    0.996094 0.996094 0.996094,
    0.996094 0.996094 0.996094] #diffuseColor
    transparency [ 0.996094,
    0.996094,
    0.996094,
    0.996094,
    0.996094,
    0.996094] #transparency
    } #Material

IndexedFaceSet {
    coordIndex [ 0,1,2,3,-1,
    0,3,7,4,-1,
    1,0,4,5,-1,
    2,1,5,6,-1,
    3,2,6,7,-1,
    7,6,5,4,-1]
    } #IndexedFaceSet
} #Polyhedron
}
```

Again, compare this listing with the previous listings and notice the different ways that a cube has been designed in VRML. Exit the Notepad and take a look at how this cube looks in a VRML viewer.

Viewing CUBE4.WRL

Run your VRML browser again and load CUBE4.WRL. After it loads, move around in it some. The screen should look similar to Figure 11-28. Play with it for a while before you exit.

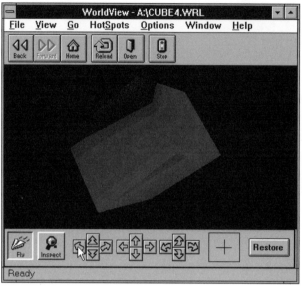

Figure 11-28: CUBE4.WRL.

Looking at the code

We've been having you compare the various listings of the cube codes as we've worked through these programs. One thing you should have noticed is that the various programs use different methods to display similar models. Even though we've worked with a simple cube in the entire chapter, each program has created that simple cube differently.

You should also have noticed that the viewers display each cube in different ways. It all depends on how the developers designed the viewer to work.

The point is that although VRML is a standard for virtual reality on the Internet, everything, from the platform on which you create or view the world to the specific viewer and creation tool that you use will affect what your world looks like and how it will behave.

Moving On

In this chapter, you learned how to convert virtual worlds created with other VR and 3-D creation programs to the .WRL format. You also looked at the software provided on the CD-ROM that enables you to create virtual worlds in VRML. Using these packages, you created some simple worlds. These programs enabled you to create virtual worlds without having to write the VRML code by hand. The next step is to get ready for the creation of more complex worlds.

In the next chapter, you look at the VRML Version 1.0 specification and the commands used to create virtual worlds using this language. Familiarize yourself with this specification. In Chapter 13, we go through each command, explain how to use the commands, and give examples.

The VRML Version 1.0 Specification

In this chapter, you examine the VRML Version 1.0 specification, which was finalized in May 1995. Chapter 13 explains each of the specification's components, using terms that laypersons can understand, and it gives an example of how each component is used. However, before going on to Chapter 13, you need to have at least a cursory understanding of the specification itself.

The original specification draft was written by Gavin Bell, Tony Parisi, and Mark Pesce. Mark Owen wrote the Internet version of the document, which is reproduced in this chapter.

The language specification is divided into the following sections:

➡ Language Basics

➡ Fields

➡ Nodes

➡ Instancing

➡ Extensibility

➡ isA Relationships

We begin by examining the basic syntax of the language. The following material is quoted directly from the VRML Version 1.0 specification. We have added a figure that shows the world produced by the sample code at the end of the quoted material.

Language Basics

At the highest level of abstraction, VRML is just a way for objects to read and write themselves. Theoretically, the objects can contain anything — 3D geometry, MIDI data, JPEG images, anything. VRML defines a set of objects useful for doing 3D graphics. These objects are called nodes.

Nodes are arranged in hierarchical structures called *scene graphs*. Scene graphs are more than just a collection of nodes; the scene graph defines an ordering for the nodes. The scene graph has a notion of *state* — nodes earlier in the scene can affect nodes that appear later in the scene. For example, a *Rotation* or *Material* node will affect the nodes after it in the scene. A mechanism is defined to limit the effects of properties (*Separator* nodes), allowing parts of the scene graph to be functionally isolated from other parts.

A node has the following characteristics:

➡ **What kind of object it is.** A node might be a cube, a sphere, a texture map, a transformation, etc.

➡ **The parameters that distinguish this node from other nodes of the same type.** For example, each *Sphere* node might have a different radius, and different texture maps nodes will certainly contain different images to use as the texture maps. These parameters are called *Fields*. A node can have 0 or more fields.

➡ **A name to identify this node.** Being able to name nodes and refer to them elsewhere is very powerful; it allows a scene's author to give hints to applications using the scene about what is in the scene, and creates possibilities for very powerful scripting extensions. Nodes do not have to be named, but if they are named, they have only one name.

➡ **Child nodes.** Object hierarchy is implemented by allowing nodes to contain other nodes. Parent nodes traverse their children in order during rendering. Nodes that may have children are referred to as **group nodes**. Group nodes can have zero or more children.

The syntax chosen to represent these pieces of information is straightforward:

```
DEF objectname objecttype { fields  children }
```

Only the object type and curly braces are required; nodes may or may not have a name, fields, and children.

Node names must not begin with a digit, and must not contain spaces or control characters, single or double quote characters, backslashes, curly braces, or the plus character.

For example, this file contains a simple scene defining a view of a red cone and a blue sphere, lit by a directional light:

```
#VRML V1.0 ascii
Separator {
DirectionalLight {
direction 0 0 -1  # Light shining from viewer into scene
}
PerspectiveCamera {
position -8.6 2.1 5.6
orientation -0.1352 -0.9831 -0.1233  1.1417
focalDistance    10.84
}
Separator {    # The red sphere
Material {
diffuseColor 1 0 0   # Red
}
Translation { translation 3 0 1 }
Sphere { radius 2.3 }
}
Separator {  # The blue cube
Material {
diffuseColor 0 0 1  # Blue
}
Transform {
translation -2.4 .2 1
rotation 0 1 1  .9
}
Cube {}
}
}
```

General Syntax

For easy identification of VRML files, every VRML file must begin with the following characters:

```
#VRML V1.0 ascii
```

Any characters after these on the same line are ignored. The line is terminated by either the ASCII newline or carriage-return characters.

The '#' character begins a comment; all characters until the next newline or carriage return are ignored. The only exception to this is within string fields, where the '#' character will be part of the string.

Note: Comments and whitespace may not be preserved; in particular, a VRML document server may strip comments and extraneous whitespace from a VRML file before transmitting it. Info nodes should be used for persistent information like copyrights or author information.

Blanks, tabs, newlines and carriage returns are whitespace characters wherever they appear outside of string fields. One or more whitespace characters separates the syntactical entities in VRML files, where necessary.

After the required header, a VRML file contains exactly one VRML node. That node may, of course, be a group node, containing any number of other nodes.

Fields

There are two general classes of fields: fields that contain a single value (where a value may be a single number, a vector, or even an image), and fields that contain multiple values. Single-valued fields all have names that begin with "SF," multiple-valued fields have names that begin with "MF." Each field type defines the format for the values it writes.

Multiple-valued fields are written as a series of values separated by commas, all enclosed in square brackets. If the field has zero values, then only the square brackets ("[]") are written. The last may optionally be followed by a comma. If the field has exactly one value, the brackets may be omitted and just the value written. For example, all of the following are valid for a multiple-valued field containing the single integer value 1:

```
1
[1,]
[ 1 ]
```

SFBitMask

A single-value field that contains a mask of bit flags. Nodes that use this field class define mnemonic names for the bit flags. So SFBitMasks are written to file as one or more mnemonic enumerated type names, in this format:

```
( flag1 | flag2 | ... )
```

If only one flag is used in a mask, the parentheses are optional. These names differ among uses of this field in various node classes.

SFBool

A field containing a single Boolean (true or false) value. SFBools may be written as 0 (representing FALSE), 1, TRUE, or FALSE.

SFColor

A single-value field containing a color. SFColors are written to file as an RGB triple of floating point numbers in standard scientific notation, in the range 0.0 to 1.0.

SFEnum

A single-value field that contains an enumerated type value. Nodes that use this field class define mnemonic names for the values. SFEnums are written to file as a mnemonic enumerated type name. The name differs among uses of this field in various node classes.

SFFloat

A field that contains one single-precision floating point number. SFFloats are written to file in standard scientific notation.

SFImage

A field that contains an uncompressed 2-dimensional color or greyscale image.

SFImages are written to file as three integers representing the width, height, and number of components in the image, followed by width * height hexadecimal values representing the pixels in the image, separated by whitespace. A one-component image will have one-byte hexadecimal values representing the intensity of the image. For example, 0xFF is full intensity, 0x00 is no intensity. A two-component image puts the intensity in the first (high) byte and the transparency in the second (low) byte. Pixels in a three-component image have the red component in the first (high) byte, followed by the green and blue components (so 0xFF0000 is red). Four-component images put the transparency byte after red/green/blue (so 0x0000FF80 is semi-transparent blue). A value of 1.0 is completely transparent, 0.0 is completely opaque. Note: each pixel is actually read as a single unsigned number, so a three-component pixel with value "0x0000FF" can also be written as "0xFF" or "255" (decimal).

For example,

```
1 1 1 0xFF 0x00
```

is a 1 pixel wide by 2 pixel high greyscale image, with the bottom pixel white and the top pixel black. And:

```
2 4 3 0xFF0000 0xFF00 0 0 0 0 0xFFFFFF 0xFFFF00
```

is a 2 pixel wide by 4 pixel high RGB image, with the bottom left pixel red, the bottom right pixel green, the two middle rows of pixels black, the top left pixel white, and the top right pixel yellow.

SFLong

A field containing a single long (32-bit) integer. So SFLongs are written to file as an integer in decimal, hexadecimal (beginning with '0x') or octal (beginning with '0') format.

SFMatrix

A field containing a transformation matrix. SFMatrices are written to file in row-major order as 16 floating point numbers separated by whitespace. For example, a matrix expressing a translation of 7 units along the X axis is written as:

```
1 0 0 0  0 1 0 0  0 0 1 0  7 0 0 1
```

SFRotation

A field containing an arbitrary rotation. SFRotations are written to file as four floating point values separated by whitespace. The four values represent an axis of rotation followed by the amount of right-handed rotation about that axis, in radians. For example, a 180° rotation about the Y axis is:

```
0 1 0 3.14159265
```

SFString

A field containing an ASCII string (sequence of characters). SFStrings are written to file as a sequence of ASCII characters in double quotes (optional if the string doesn't contain any whitespace). Any characters (including newlines) may appear within the quotes. To include a double-quote character within the string, precede it with a backslash. For example:

```
Testing
"One, Two, Three"
"He said, \"Immel did it!\""
```

are all valid strings.

SFVec2f

Field containing a two-dimensional vector. SFVec2fs are written to file as a pair of floating point values separated by whitespace.

SFVec3f

Field containing a three-dimensional vector. SFVec3fs are written to file as three floating point values separated by whitespace.

MFColor

A multiple-value field that contains any number of RGB colors. MFColors are written to file as one or more RGB triples of floating point numbers in standard scientific notation. When more than one value is present, all of the values must be enclosed in square brackets and separated by commas. For example:

```
[ 1.0 0.0 0.0, 0 1 0, 0 0 1 ]
```

represents the three colors red, green, and blue.

MFLong

A multiple-value field that contains any number of long (32-bit) integers. MFLongs are written to file as one or more integer values, in decimal, hexadecimal or octal format. When more than one value is present, all the values are enclosed in square brackets and separated by commas; for example:

```
[ 17, -0xE20, -518820 ]
```

MFVec2f

A multiple-value field that contains any number of two-dimensional vectors. MFVec2fs are written to file as one or more pairs of floating point values separated by whitespace. When more than one value is present, all of the values are enclosed in square brackets and separated by commas; for example:

```
[ 0 0, 1.2 3.4, 98.6 -4e1 ]
```

MFVec3f

A multiple-value field that contains any number of three-dimensional vectors. MFVec3fs are written to file as one or more triples of floating point values separated by whitespace. When more than one value is present, all of the values are enclosed in square brackets and separated by commas; for example:

```
[ 0 0 0, 1.2 3.4 5.6, 98.6 -4e1 212 ]
```

Nodes

VRML defines several different classes of nodes. Most of the nodes can be classified into one of three categories: shape, property or group. Shape nodes define the geometry in the scene. Conceptually, they are the only nodes that really draw anything. Property nodes affect the way shapes are drawn. And grouping nodes gather other nodes together, allowing collections of nodes to be treated as a single object. Grouping nodes can also control whether or not their children are drawn.

Nodes may contain zero or more fields. Each node type defines the type, name, and default value for each of its fields. The default value for the field is used if a value for the field is not specified in the VRML file. The order in which the fields of a node are read is not important; for example, "Cube { width 2 height 4 depth 6 }" and "Cube { height 4 depth 6 width 2 }" are both valid.

Here are the 36 nodes grouped by type.

Shape nodes

The shape nodes specify geometry:

- AsciiText
- Cone
- Cube
- Cylinder
- IndexedFaceSet
- IndexedLineSet
- PointSet
- Sphere

Property nodes

Next are the properties. These can be further grouped into properties of the geometry and its appearance, matrix or transform properties, cameras, and lights:

Geometry and appearance group

➡ Coordinate3

➡ FontStyle

➡ Info

➡ Material

➡ MaterialBinding

➡ Normal

➡ NormalBinding

➡ Texture2

➡ Texture2Transform

➡ TextureCoordinate2

➡ ShapeHints

Matrix or transform group

➡ MatrixTransform

➡ Rotation

➡ Scale

➡ Transform

➡ Translation

Camera group

➡ OrthographicCamera

➡ PerspectiveCamera

Lights group

➡ DirectionalLight

➡ PointLight

➡ SpotLight

Group nodes

These are the group nodes:

➡ Group

➡ LOD

➡ Separator

➡ Switch

➡ TransformSeparator

➡ WWWAnchor

Unclassified nodes

➡ WWWInline

AsciiText

This node represents strings of text characters from the ASCII coded character set. The first string is rendered with its baseline at (0,0,0). All subsequent strings advance y by – (size * spacing). See FontStyle for a description of the size field. The justification field determines the placement of the strings in the x dimension. LEFT (the default) places the left edge of each string at x=0. CENTER places the center of each string at x=0. RIGHT places the right edge of each string at x=0. Text is rendered from left to right, top to bottom in the font set by FontStyle. The width field defines a suggested width constraint for each string. The default is to use the natural width of each string. Setting any value to 0 indicates that the natural width should be used for that string.

The text is transformed by the current cumulative transformation and is drawn with the current material and texture.

Textures are applied to 3D text as follows. The texture origin is at the origin of the first string, as determined by the justification. The texture is scaled equally in both S and T dimensions, with the font height representing one unit. S increases to the right. The T origin can occur anywhere along each character, depending on how that character's outline is defined.

JUSTIFICATION

LEFT	Align left edge of text to origin
CENTER	Align center of text to origin
RIGHT	Align right edge of text to origin

FILE FORMAT/DEFAULTS

```
AsciiText {
    string            ""      # MFString
    spacing           1       # SFFloat
    justification     LEFT    # SFEnum
    width             0       # MFFloat
}
```

Cone

This node represents a simple cone whose central axis is aligned with the y-axis. By default, the cone is centered at (0,0,0) and has a size of –1 to +1 in all three directions. The cone has a radius of 1 at the bottom and a height of 2, with its apex at 1. The cone has two parts: the sides and the bottom.

The cone is transformed by the current cumulative transformation and is drawn with the current texture and material.

If the current material binding is PER_PART or PER_PART_INDEXED, the first current material is used for the sides of the cone, and the second is used for the bottom. Otherwise, the first material is used for the entire cone.

When a texture is applied to a cone, it is applied differently to the sides and bottom. On the sides, the texture wraps counterclockwise (from above) starting at the back of the cone. The texture has a vertical seam at the back, intersecting the yz-plane. For the bottom, a circle is cut out of the texture square and applied to the cone's base circle. The texture appears right side up when the top of the cone is rotated toward the –Z axis.

PARTS

SIDES	The conical part
BOTTOM	The bottom circular face
ALL	All parts

FILE FORMAT/DEFAULTS

```
Cone {
    parts           ALL     # SFBitMask
    bottomRadius    1       # SFFloat
    height          2       # SFFloat
}
```

Coordinate3

This node defines a set of 3D coordinates to be used by a subsequent IndexedFaceSet, IndexedLineSet, or PointSet node. This node does not produce a visible result during rendering; it simply replaces the current coordinates in the rendering state for subsequent nodes to use.

FILE FORMAT/DEFAULTS

```
Coordinate3 {
   point        0 0 0          # MFVec3f
}
```

Cube

This node represents a cuboid aligned with the coordinate axes. By default, the cube is centered at (0,0,0) and measures 2 units in each dimension, from –1 to +1. The cube is transformed by the current cumulative transformation and is drawn with the current material and texture.

If the current material binding is PER_PART, PER_PART_INDEXED, PER_FACE, or PER_FACE_INDEXED, materials will be bound to the faces of the cube in this order: front (+Z), back (–Z), left (–X), right (+X), top (+Y), and bottom (–Y).

Textures are applied individually to each face of the cube; the entire texture goes on each face. On the front, back, right, and left sides of the cube, the texture is applied right side up. On the top, the texture appears right side up when the top of the cube is tilted toward the camera. On the bottom, the texture appears right side up when the top of the cube is tilted toward the –Z axis.

FILE FORMAT/DEFAULTS

```
Cube {
   width       2          # SFFloat
   height      2          # SFFloat
   depth       2          # SFFloat
}
```

Cylinder

This node represents a simple capped cylinder centered around the y-axis. By default, the cylinder is centered at (0,0,0) and has a default size of –1 to +1 in all three dimensions. You can use the radius and height fields to create a cylinder with a different size.

The cylinder is transformed by the current cumulative transformation and is drawn with the current material and texture.

If the current material binding is PER_PART or PER_PART_INDEXED, the first current material is used for the sides of the cylinder, the second is used for the top, and the third is used for the bottom. Otherwise, the first material is used for the entire cylinder.

When a texture is applied to a cylinder, it is applied differently to the sides, top, and bottom. On the sides, the texture wraps counterclockwise (from above) starting at the back of the cylinder. The texture has a vertical seam at the back, intersecting the yz-plane. For the top and bottom, a circle is cut out of the texture square and applied to the top or bottom circle. The top texture appears right side up when the top of the cylinder is tilted toward the +Z axis, and the bottom texture appears right side up when the top of the cylinder is tilted toward the –Z axis.

PARTS

SIDES	The cylindrical part
TOP	The top circular face
BOTTOM	The bottom circular face
ALL	All parts

FILE FORMAT/DEFAULTS

```
Cylinder {
    parts      ALL      # SFBitMask
    radius     1        # SFFloat
    height     2        # SFFloat
}
```

DirectionalLight

This node defines a directional light source that illuminates along rays parallel to a given 3-dimensional vector.

A light node defines an illumination source that may affect subsequent shapes in the scene graph, depending on the current lighting style. Light sources are affected by the current transformation. A light node under a separator does not affect any objects outside that separator.

FILE FORMAT/DEFAULTS

```
DirectionalLight {
    on              TRUE        # SFBool
    intensity       1           # SFFloat
    color           1 1 1       # SFColor
    direction       0 0 -1      # SFVec3f
}
```

FontStyle

This node defines the current font style used for all subsequent AsciiText. Font attributes only are defined. It is up to the browser to assign specific fonts to the various attribute combinations. The size field specifies the height (in object space units) of glyphs rendered and determines the vertical spacing of adjacent lines of text.

FAMILY

SERIF	Serif style (such as TimesRoman)
SANS	Sans Serif Style (such as Helvetica)
TYPEWRITER	Fixed pitch style (such as Courier)

STYLE

NONE	No modifications to family
BOLD	Embolden family
ITALIC	Italicize or Slant family

FILE FORMAT/DEFAULTS

```
FontStyle {
    size        10              # SFFloat
    family      SERIF           # SFEnum
    style       NONE            # SFBitMask
}
```

Group

This node defines the base class for all group nodes. Group is a node that contains an ordered list of child nodes. This node is simply a container for the child nodes and does not alter the traversal state in any way. During traversal, state accumulated for a child is passed on to each successive child and then to the parents of the group (Group does not push or pop traversal state as Separator does).

FILE FORMAT/DEFAULTS

```
Group {
}
```

IndexedFaceSet

This node represents a 3D shape formed by constructing faces (polygons) from vertices located at the current coordinates. IndexedFaceSet uses the indices in the coordIndex field (from IndexedShape) to specify the polygonal faces. An index of –1 indicates that the current face has ended and the next one begins.

The vertices of the faces are transformed by the current transformation matrix.

Treatment of the current material and normal binding is as follows: The PER_PART and PER_FACE bindings specify a material or normal for each face. PER_VERTEX specifies a material or normal for each vertex. The corresponding _INDEXED bindings are the same, but use the materialIndex or normalIndex indices (see IndexedShape). The DEFAULT material binding is equal to OVERALL. The DEFAULT normal binding is equal to PER_VERTEX_INDEXED; if insufficient normals exist in the state, vertex normals will be generated automatically.

Explicit texture coordinates (as defined by TextureCoordinate2) may be bound to vertices of an indexed shape consecutively (if the texture coordinate binding is PER_VERTEX) or by using the indices in the textureCoordIndex field (if the binding is PER_VERTEX_INDEXED). As with all vertex-based shapes, if there is a current texture but no texture coordinates are specified, a default texture coordinate mapping is calculated using the bounding box of the shape. The longest dimension of the bounding box defines the S coordinates, and the next longest defines the T coordinates. The value of the S coordinate ranges from 0 to 1, from one end of the bounding box to the other. The T coordinate ranges between 0 and the ratio of the second greatest dimension of the bounding box to the greatest dimension.

Be sure that the indices contained in the coordIndex, materialIndex, normalIndex, and textureCoordIndex fields are valid with respect to the current state, or errors will occur.

FILE FORMAT/DEFAULTS

```
IndexedFaceSet {
    coordIndex          0       # MFLong
    materialIndex       -1      # MFLong
    normalIndex         -1      # MFLong
    textureCoordIndex   -1      # MFLong
}
```

IndexedLineSet

This node represents a 3D shape formed by constructing polylines from vertices located at the current coordinates. IndexedLineSet uses the indices in the coordIndex field to specify the polylines. An index of –1 indicates that the current polyline has ended and the next one begins.

The coordinates of the line set are transformed by the current cumulative transformation.

Treatment of the current material and normal binding is as follows: The PER_PART binding specifies a material or normal for each segment of the line. The PER_FACE binding specifies a material or normal for each polyline. PER_VERTEX specifies a material or normal for each vertex. The corresponding _INDEXED bindings are the same, but use the materialIndex or normalIndex indices. The DEFAULT material binding is equal to OVERALL. The DEFAULT normal binding is equal to PER_VERTEX_INDEXED; if insufficient normals exist in the state, the lines will be drawn unlit. The same rules for texture coordinate generation as IndexedFaceSet are used.

FILE FORMAT/DEFAULTS

```
IndexedLineSet {
    coordIndex          0       # MFLong
    materialIndex      -1       # MFLong
    normalIndex        -1       # MFLong
    textureCoordIndex  -1       # MFLong
}
```

Info

This class defines an information node in the scene graph. This node has no effect during traversal. It is used to store information in the scene graph, typically for application-specific purposes, copyright messages, or other strings.

```
Info {
    string      "<Undefined info>"      # SFString
}
```

LOD

This group node is used to allow applications to switch between various representations of objects automatically. The children of this node typically represent the same object or objects at varying levels of detail, from highest detail to lowest.

The specified center point of the LOD is transformed by the current transformation into world space, and the distance from the transformed center to the world-space eye point is calculated. If the distance is less than the first value in the ranges array, then the first child of the LOD group is drawn. If between the first and second values in the ranges array, the second child is drawn, etc. If there are N values in the ranges array, the LOD group should have N+1 children. Specifying too few children will result in the last child being used repeatedly for the lowest levels of detail; if too many children are specified, the extra children will be ignored. Each value in the ranges array should be less than the previous value, otherwise results are undefined.

FILE FORMAT/DEFAULTS

```
LOD {
    range   [ ]     # MFFloat
    center  0 0 0   # SFVec3f
}
```

Material

This node defines the current surface material properties for all subsequent shapes. Material sets several components of the current material during traversal. Different shapes interpret materials with multiple values differently. To bind materials to shapes, use a MaterialBinding node.

FILE FORMAT/DEFAULTS

```
Material {
    ambientColor      0.2 0.2 0.2      # MFColor
    diffuseColor      0.8 0.8 0.8      # MFColor
    specularColor     0 0 0            # MFColor
    emissiveColor     0 0 0            # MFColor
    shininess         0.2              # MFFloat
    transparency      0                # MFFloat
}
```

MaterialBinding

This node specifies how the current materials are bound to shapes that follow in the scene graph. Each shape node may interpret bindings differently. The current material always has a base value, which is defined by the first value of all material fields. Since material fields may have multiple values, the binding determines how these values are distributed over a shape.

The bindings for faces and vertices are meaningful only for shapes that are made from faces and vertices. Similarly, the indexed bindings are only used by the shapes that allow indexing.

When multiple material values are bound, the values are cycled through, based on the period of the material component with the most values. For example, the following table shows the values used when cycling through (or indexing into) a material with 2 ambient colors, 3 diffuse colors, and 1 of all other components in the current material. (The period of this material cycle is 3):

Material	Ambient color	Diffuse color	Other
0	0	0	0
1	1	1	0
2	1	2	0
3 (same as 0)	0	0	0

BINDINGS

DEFAULT	Use default binding
OVERALL	Whole object has same material
PER_PART	One material for each part of object
PER_PART_INDEXED	One material for each part, indexed
PER_FACE	One material for each face of object
PER_FACE_INDEXED	One material for each face, indexed
PER_VERTEX	One material for each vertex of object
PER_VERTEX_INDEXED	One material for each vertex, indexed

FILE FORMAT/DEFAULTS

```
MaterialBinding {
    value       DEFAULT      # SFEnum
}
```

MatrixTransform

This node defines a geometric 3D transformation with a 4 by 4 matrix. Note that some matrices (such as singular ones) may result in errors.

FILE FORMAT/DEFAULTS

```
MatrixTransform {
    matrix      1 0 0 0      # SFMatrix
                0 1 0 0
                0 0 1 0
                0 0 0 1
}
```

Normal

This node defines a set of 3D surface normal vectors to be used by vertex-based shape nodes (IndexedFaceSet, IndexedLinedSet, PointSet) that follow it in the scene graph. This node does not produce a visible result during rendering; it simply replaces the current normals in the rendering state for subsequent nodes to use. This node contains one multiple-valued field that contains the normal vectors.

FILE FORMAT/DEFAULTS

```
Normal {
   vector        0 0 1         # MFVec3f
}
```

NormalBinding

This node specifies how the current normals are bound to shapes that follow in the scene graph. Each shape node may interpret bindings differently.

The bindings for faces and vertices are meaningful only for shapes that are made from faces and vertices. Similarly, the indexed bindings are only used by the shapes that allow indexing. For bindings that require multiple normals, be sure to have at least as many normals defined as are necessary; otherwise, errors will occur.

BINDINGS

DEFAULT	Use default binding
OVERALL	Whole object has same normal
PER_PART	One normal for each part of object
PER_PART_INDEXED	One normal for each part, indexed
PER_FACE	One normal for each face of object
PER_FACE_INDEXED	One normal for each face, indexed
PER_VERTEX	One normal for each vertex of object
PER_VERTEX_INDEXED	One normal for each vertex, indexed

FILE FORMAT/DEFAULTS

```
NormalBinding {
   value        DEFAULT         # SFEnum
}
```

OrthographicCamera

An orthographic camera defines a parallel projection from a viewpoint. This camera does not diminish objects with distance, as a PerspectiveCamera does. The viewing volume for an orthographic camera is a rectangular parallelepiped (a box).

By default, the camera is located at (0,0,1) and looks along the negative z-axis; the position and orientation fields can be used to change these values. The height field defines the total height of the viewing volume.

A camera can be placed in a VRML world to specify the initial location of the viewer when that world is entered. VRML browsers will typically modify the camera to allow a user to move through the virtual world.

Cameras are affected by the current transformation, so you can position a camera by placing a transformation node before it in the scene graph. The default position and orientation of a camera is at (0,0,1) looking along the negative z-axis.

FILE FORMAT/DEFAULTS

```
OrthographicCamera {
    position          0 0 1          # SFVec3f
    orientation       0 0 1 0        # SFRotation
    focalDistance     5              # SFFloat
    height            2              # SFFloat
}
```

PerspectiveCamera

A perspective camera defines a perspective projection from a viewpoint. The viewing volume for a perspective camera is a truncated right pyramid.

By default, the camera is located at (0,0,1) and looks along the negative z-axis; the position and orientation fields can be used to change these values. The heightAngle field defines the total vertical angle of the viewing volume.

FILE FORMAT/DEFAULTS

```
PerspectiveCamera {
    position          0 0 1          # SFVec3f
    orientation       0 0 1 0        # SFRotation
    focalDistance     5              # SFFloat
    heightAngle       0.785398       # SFFloat
}
```

PointLight

This node defines a point light source at a fixed 3D location. A point source illuminates equally in all directions; that is, it is omni-directional.

A light node defines an illumination source that may affect subsequent shapes in the scene graph, depending on the current lighting style. Light sources are affected by the current transformation. A light node under a separator does not affect any objects outside that separator.

FILE FORMAT/DEFAULTS

```
PointLight {
   on            TRUE      # SFBool
   intensity     1         # SFFloat
   color         1 1 1     # SFColor
   location      0 0 1     # SFVec3f
}
```

PointSet

This node represents a set of points located at the current coordinates. PointSet uses the current coordinates in order, starting at the index specified by the startIndex field. The number of points in the set is specified by the numPoints field. A value of –1 for this field indicates that all remaining values in the current coordinates are to be used as points.

The coordinates of the point set are transformed by the current cumulative transformation. The points are drawn with the current material and texture.

Treatment of the current material and normal binding is as follows: PER_PART, PER_FACE, and PER_VERTEX bindings bind one material or normal to each point. The DEFAULT material binding is equal to OVERALL. The DEFAULT normal binding is equal to PER_VERTEX. The startIndex is also used for materials, normals, or texture coordinates when the binding indicates that they should be used per vertex.

FILE FORMAT/DEFAULTS

```
PointSet {
   startIndex    0         # SFLong
   numPoints     -1        # SFLong
}
```

Rotation

This node defines a 3D rotation about an arbitrary axis through the origin. The rotation is accumulated into the current transformation, which is applied to subsequent shapes.

FILE FORMAT/DEFAULTS

```
Rotation {
   rotation        0 0 1 0        # SFRotation
}
```

Scale

This node defines a 3D scaling about the origin. If the components of the scaling vector are not all the same, this produces a non-uniform scale.

FILE FORMAT/DEFAULTS

```
Scale {
   scaleFactor        1 1 1        # SFVec3f
}
```

Separator

This group node performs a push (save) of the traversal state before traversing its children and a pop (restore) after traversing them. This isolates the separator's children from the rest of the scene graph. A separator can include lights, cameras, coordinates, normals, bindings, and all other properties. Separators are relatively inexpensive, so they can be used freely within scenes.

Separators can also perform render culling. Render culling skips over traversal of the separator's children if they are not going to be rendered, based on the comparison of the separator's bounding box with the current view volume. Culling is controlled by the renderCulling field. These are also set to AUTO by default, allowing the implementation to decide whether or not to cull.

CULLING ENUMS

ON	Always try to cull to the view volume
OFF	Never try to cull to the view volume
AUTO	Implementation-defined culling behavior

FILE FORMAT/DEFAULTS

```
Separator {
   renderCulling        AUTO       # SFEnum
}
```

ShapeHints

The ShapeHints node indicates that IndexedFaceSets are solid, contain ordered vertices, or contain convex faces.

These hints allow VRML implementations to optimize certain rendering features. Optimizations that may be performed include enabling back-face culling and disabling two-sided lighting. For example, if an object is solid and has ordered vertices, an implementation may turn on back-face culling and turn off two-sided lighting. If the object is not solid but has ordered vertices, it may turn off back-face culling and turn on two-sided lighting.

The ShapeHints node also affects how default normals are generated. When an IndexedFaceSet has to generate default normals, it uses the creaseAngle field to determine which edges should be smooth shaded and which ones should have a sharp crease. The crease angle is the angle between surface normals on adjacent polygons. For example, a crease angle of .5 radians (the default value) means that an edge between two adjacent polygonal faces will be smooth shaded if the normals to the two faces form an angle that is less than .5 radians (about 30°). Otherwise, it will be faceted.

VERTEX ORDERING ENUMS

UNKNOWN_ORDERING	Ordering of vertices is unknown
CLOCKWISE	Face vertices are ordered clockwise (from the outside)
COUNTERCLOCKWISE	Face vertices are ordered counterclockwise (from the outside)

SHAPE TYPE ENUMS

UNKNOWN_SHAPE_TYPE	Nothing is known about the shape
SOLID	The shape encloses a volume

FACE TYPE ENUMS

UNKNOWN_FACE_TYPE   Nothing is known about faces

CONVEX   All faces are convex

FILE FORMAT/DEFAULTS

```
ShapeHints {
    vertexOrdering    UNKNOWN_ORDERING      # SFEnum
    shapeType         UNKNOWN_SHAPE_TYPE    # SFEnum
    faceType          CONVEX                # SFEnum
    creaseAngle       0.5                   # SFFloat
}
```

Sphere

This node represents a sphere. By default, the sphere is centered at the origin and has a radius of 1. The sphere is transformed by the current cumulative transformation and is drawn with the current material and texture.

A sphere does not have faces or parts. Therefore, the sphere ignores material and normal bindings, using the first material for the entire sphere and using its own normals. When a texture is applied to a sphere, the texture covers the entire surface, wrapping counterclockwise from the back of the sphere. The texture has a seam at the back on the yz-plane.

FILE FORMAT/DEFAULTS

```
Sphere {
    radius    1    # SFFloat
}
```

SpotLight

This node defines a spotlight style light source. A spotlight is placed at a fixed location in 3D space and illuminates in a cone along a particular direction. The intensity of the illumination drops off exponentially as a ray of light diverges from this direction toward the edges of the cone. The rate of drop-off and the angle of the cone are controlled by the dropOffRate and cutOffAngle fields.

A light node defines an illumination source that may affect subsequent shapes in the scene graph, depending on the current lighting style. Light sources are affected by the current transformation. A light node under a separator does not affect any objects outside that separator.

FILE FORMAT/DEFAULTS

```
SpotLight {
    on              TRUE        # SFBool
    intensity       1           # SFFloat
    color           1 1 1       # SFVec3f
    location        0 0 1       # SFVec3f
    direction       0 0 -1      # SFVec3f
    dropOffRate     0           # SFFloat
    cutOffAngle     0.785398    # SFFloat
}
```

Switch

This group node usually traverses only one, none, or all of its children. One can use this node to switch on and off the effects of some properties or to switch between different properties.

The whichChild field specifies the index of the child to traverse, where the first child has index of 0.

A value of –1 (the default) means do not traverse any children. A value of –3 traverses all children, making the switch behave exactly like a regular Group.

FILE FORMAT/DEFAULTS

```
Switch {
    whichChild      -1          # SFLong
}
```

Texture2

This property node defines a texture map and parameters for that map. This map is used to apply texture to subsequent shapes as they are rendered.

The texture can be read from the URL specified by the filename field. To turn off texturing, set the filename field to an empty string ("").

Textures can also be specified in memory by setting the image field to contain the texture data. Specifying both a URL and data inline will result in undefined behavior.

WRAP ENUM

REPEAT	Repeats texture outside 0–1 texture coordinate range
CLAMP	Clamps texture coordinates to lie within 0–1 range

FILE FORMAT/DEFAULTS

```
Texture2 {
    filename      ""          # SFString
    image         0 0 0       # SFImage
    wrapS         REPEAT      # SFEnum
    wrapT         REPEAT      # SFEnum
}
```

Texture2Transform

This node defines a 2D transformation applied to texture coordinates. This affects the way textures are applied to the surfaces of subsequent shapes. The transformation consists of (in order) a non-uniform scale about an arbitrary center point, a rotation about that same point, and a translation. This allows a user to change the size and position of the textures on shapes.

FILE FORMAT/DEFAULTS

```
Texture2Transform {
    translation    0 0        # SFVec2f
    rotation       0          # SFFloat
    scaleFactor    1 1        # SFVec2f
    center         0 0        # SFVec2f
}
```

TextureCoordinate2

This node defines a set of 2D coordinates to be used to map textures to subsequent vertex-based PointSet, IndexedLineSet, or IndexedFaceSet objects. It replaces the current texture coordinates in the rendering state for the shapes to use.

Texture coordinates range from 0 to 1 across the texture. The horizontal coordinate, called S, is specified first, followed by the vertical coordinate, T.

FILE FORMAT/DEFAULTS

```
TextureCoordinate2 {
    point      0 0     # MFVec2f
}
```

Transform

This node defines a geometric 3D transformation consisting of (in order) a (possibly) non-uniform scale about an arbitrary point, a rotation about an arbitrary point and axis, and a translation.

FILE FORMAT/DEFAULTS

```
Transform {
    translation       0 0 0          # SFVec3f
    rotation          0 0 1 0        # SFRotation
    scaleFactor       1 1 1          # SFVec3f
    scaleOrientation  0 0 1 0        # SFRotation
    center            0 0 0          # SFVec3f
}
```

TransformSeparator

This group node is similar to the Separator node in that it saves state before traversing its children and restores it afterwards. However, it saves only the current transformation; all other states are left as is. This node can be useful for positioning a camera, since the transformations to the camera will not affect the rest of the scene, even through the camera will view the scene. Similarly, this node can be used to isolate transformations to light sources or other objects.

FILE FORMAT/DEFAULTS

```
TransformSeparator {
}
```

Translation

This node defines a translation by a 3D vector.

FILE FORMAT/DEFAULTS

```
Translation {
    translation    0 0 0     # SFVec3f
}
```

WWWAnchor

The WWWAnchor node loads a new scene into a VRML browser when one of its children is chosen. Exactly how a user "chooses" a child of the WWWAnchor is up to the VRML browser; typically, clicking on one of its children with the mouse will result in the new scene replacing the current scene. A WWWAnchor with an empty ("") name does nothing when its children are chosen. The name is an arbitrary URL.

The WWWAnchor's map field is an enumerated value that can be either NONE (the default) or POINT. If it is POINT then the object-space coordinates of the point on the object the user chose will be added to the URL in the name field, with the syntax "?x,y,z".

FILE FORMAT/DEFAULTS

```
WWWAnchor {
    name     ""       # SFString
    map      NONE     # SFEnum
}
```

WWWInline

The WWWInline node reads its children from anywhere in the World Wide Web. Exactly when its children are read is not defined; reading the children may be delayed until the WWWInline is actually displayed. A WWWInline with an empty name does nothing. The name is an arbitrary URL.

The effect of referring to a non-VRML URL in a WWWInline node is undefined.

If the WWWInline's bboxSize field specifies a non-empty bounding box (a bounding box is non-empty if at least one of its dimensions is greater than zero), then the WWWInline's object-space bounding box is specified by its bboxSize and bboxCenter fields. This allows an implementation to view-volume cull or LOD switch the WWWInline without reading its contents.

FILE FORMAT/DEFAULTS

```
WWWInline {
    name            ""        # SFString
    bboxSize        0 0 0     # SFVec3f
    bboxCenter      0 0 0     # SFVec3f
}
```

Instancing

A node may be the child of more than one group. This is called "instancing" (using the same instance of a node multiple times; called "aliasing" or "multiple references" by other systems), and is accomplished by using the "USE" keyword.

The DEF keyword both defines a named node, and creates a single instance of it. The USE keyword indicates that the most recently defined instance should be used again. If several nodes were given the same name, then the last DEF encountered during parsing "wins." DEF/USE is limited to a single file; there is no mechanism for USE'ing nodes that are DEF'ed in other files.

A name goes into scope as soon as the DEF is encountered, and does not go out of scope until another DEF of the same name or end-of-file is encountered. Nodes cannot be shared between files (you cannot USE a node that was DEF'ed inside the file to which a WWWInline refers).

For example, rendering this scene will result in three spheres being drawn. Both of the spheres are named 'Joe;' the second (smaller) sphere is drawn twice:

```
Separator {
   DEF Joe Sphere { }
   Translation { translation 2 0 0 }
   Separator {
       DEF Joe Sphere { radius .2 }
       Translation { translation 2 0 0 }
   }
   USE Joe          # radius .2 sphere will be used here
}
```

Extensibility

Extensions to VRML are supported by supporting self-describing nodes. Nodes that are not part of standard VRML must write out a description of their fields first, so that all VRML implementations are able to parse and ignore the extensions.

This description is written just after the opening curly-brace for the node, and consists of the keyword 'fields' followed by a list of the types and names of fields used by that node, all enclosed in square brackets and separated by commas. For example, if *Cube* was not a standard VRML node, it would be written like this:

```
Cube {
    fields [ SFFloat width, SFFloat height, SFFloat depth ]
    width 10
    height 4
    depth 3
}
```

Specifying the fields for nodes that ARE part of standard VRML is not an error; VRML parsers must silently ignore the specification.

isA relationship

A new node type may also be a superset of an existing node that is part of the standard. In this case, if an implementation for the new node type cannot be found, the new node type can be safely treated as the existing node it is based on (with some loss of functionality, of course). To support this, new node types can define an MFString field called 'isA' containing the names of the types of which it is a superset. For example, a new type of Material called "ExtendedMaterial" that adds index of refraction as a material property can be written as:

```
ExtendedMaterial {
   fields [ MFString isA, MFFloat indexOfRefraction,
       MFColor ambientColor, MFColor diffuseColor,
       MFColor specularColor, MFColor emissiveColor,
       MFFloat shininess, MFFloat transparency  ]
 isA     [ "Material" ]
 indexOfRefraction .34
 diffuseColor      .8   .54  1
 }
```

Multiple isA relationships may be specified in order of preference; implementations are expected to use the first for which there is an implementation.

An Example

The following code is a longer example of a VRML scene. It contains a simple model of a track-light consisting of primitive shapes, plus three walls (built out of polygons) and a reference to a shape defined elsewhere, both of which are illuminated by a spotlight. The shape acts as a hyperlink to some HTML text (See Figure 12-1).

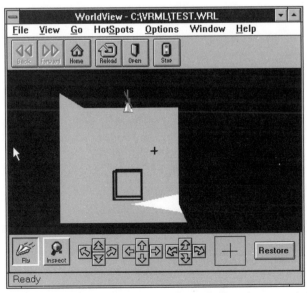

Figure 12-1: This is what the test file looks like when seen in WorldView.

```
#VRML V1.0 ascii

Separator {
  Separator {        # Simple track-light geometry:
Translation { translation 0 4 0 }
Separator {
  Material { emissiveColor 0.1 0.3 0.3 }
  Cube {
width 0.1
height   0.1
depth 4
  }
}
Rotation { rotation 0 1 0  1.57079 }
Separator {
  Material { emissiveColor 0.3 0.1 0.3 }
  Cylinder {
radius    0.1
height    .2
  }
}
Rotation { rotation -1 0 0  1.57079 }
Separator {
  Material { emissiveColor 0.3 0.3 0.1 }
  Rotation { rotation 1 0 0  1.57079 }
  Translation { translation 0 -.2 0 }
  Cone {
height    .4
bottomRadius .2
  }
  Translation { translation 0 .4 0 }
  Cylinder {
radius    0.02
height    .4
  }
}
  }
  SpotLight {        # Light from above
location 0 4 0
direction 0 -1 0
intensity 0.9
cutOffAngle        0.7
  }
  Separator {        # Wall geometry; just three flat polygons
Coordinate3 {
  point [
  -2 0 -2, -2 0 2, 2 0 2, 2 0 -2,
```

```
   -2 4 -2, -2 4 2, 2 4 2, 2 4 -2]
}
IndexedFaceSet {
   coordIndex [ 0, 1, 2, 3, -1,
0, 4, 5, 1, -1,
0, 3, 7, 4, -1
]
}

   }
   WWWAnchor {    # A hyperlinked cow:
name "http://www.foo.edu/CowProject/AboutCows.html"
Separator {
   Translation { translation 0 1 0 }
   WWWInline {    # Reference another object
name "http://www.foo.edu/3DObjects/cow.wrl"
      }
   }
   }
}
```

Moving On

In this chapter, you looked at the current VRML specification, Version 1.0. In Chapter 13 you take everything you've read in this chapter and everything you've learned so far in this book and start putting it into practice. You begin by learning to use each statement that you've been exposed to. You'll then have the basic knowledge required to build a space. It can be any space, but, most importantly, it will be your space.

Learning VRML
Version 1.0
Specification
Basics

In This Chapter

Expanding on the specification definitions

Understanding the VRML file syntax

In Chapter 12, you looked at the specification for VRML Version 1.0 as it has been published. In this chapter, we explain how each and every component of the specification works and provide examples of how each command and component is used.

We begin by looking at the section in both the specification and in Chapter 12 labeled "Language Basics." Here the discussion concerns what makes up the virtual world that is created using VRML.

General VRML File Syntax

In the highest abstraction of the VRML format, the VRML ASCII formatted file would be the top of the format structure. This file must contain all the information about the three-dimensional world that's being created.

All VRML files must begin with the following characters:

```
#VRML V1.0 ascii
```

These characters make it easy to identify the VRML files. Anything after these characters on the same line is ignored.

Keep in mind that the # character signifies the beginning of a comment. Any characters after the # sign are ignored until the end of the line. The only time this is not true is when the # sign is contained within a string field. (A *string field* is the characters that are between two quotes when you are working with text.)

The Scene Database

Each three-dimensional world created in VRML can be thought of as consisting of a *scene database.* This scene database is the file that makes up the 3D world. It contains at least one scene graph.

The scene graph

The scene graph is the ordered collection of nodes that make up the 3D world and represent the geometry, properties, and grouping of the objects in the world. The scene graph consists of at least one node. The scene graph is more than just a collection of nodes, however. It also defines the order of the nodes contained within it.

The order of the nodes is important because a node can affect each and every node that comes afterward in the scene graph. The Separator node enables you to prevent this interaction.

Nodes

VRML defines several different classes of nodes, with a total of 36 nodes in all. We begin by discussing the nodes in general terms, and then we discuss each of them in detail.

The node groupings include three general categories into which most of the nodes can be classified: Shape, Property, and Group nodes. There is also one unclassified node.

➡ The nodes in the first major node grouping, *Shape nodes,* create the objects that you see in 3D worlds. This is how things get drawn. There are eight Shape nodes: AsciiText, Cone, Cube, Cylinder, IndexedFaceSet, IndexedLineSet, PointSet, and Sphere. Basically, these nodes define what the object to be drawn is.

➡ The second major grouping of nodes is the *Property nodes.* Property nodes affect the way the objects in the 3D world are drawn. This grouping has four subgroups: Geometry and Material, Transformation, Cameras, and Lights. Basically, these nodes define how the object looks.

  ➡ Within the Geometry and Material subgroup, there are 11 nodes: Coordinate3, FontStyle, Info, Material, MaterialBinding, Normal, NormalBinding, Texture2, Texture2Transform, TextureCoordinate2, and ShapeHints.

  ➡ Within the Transformation subgroup, there are five nodes: MatrixTransform, Rotation, Scale, Transform, and Translation.

  ➡ There are two nodes in the Cameras subgroup: OrthographicCamera and PerspectiveCamera.

  ➡ Finally, in the Lights subgroup, there are three nodes. These nodes are DirectionalLight, PointLight, and SpotLight.

➡ The third major grouping is the *Group nodes.* Group nodes group, or collect, other nodes together so that these groups, or collections, of nodes can be handled as single objects. These Group nodes also control when child nodes within them are drawn.

Only Group nodes have *child nodes,* which are basically nodes within the node. The parent node extends over the children in the order that the children are listed during rendering. In other words, the parent node will affect all of its children. The parent can have no children or many.

The six Group nodes are Group, LOD, Separator, Switch, TransformSeparator, and WWWAnchor.

➡ The one unclassified node is WWWInline.

Before we begin discussing each node and its specifics, we want to explain the general format, or *syntax,* for a node.

Node Syntax

The following examples are from worlds that are either provided on the CD-ROM that's included with this book or available on the Internet.

The basic format, or syntax, of a node has the following form:

```
DEF objectname objecttype { fields  children }
```

Only the objecttype and curly braces are required, so the following node syntax from FWORLD1.WRL is acceptable:

```
Sphere {}
```

FWORLD1.WRL can be found at `ftp://ftp.portal.com/pub/fredness/VRML`.

Nodes can, but don't have to, have names, fields, or children. The following example code syntax from BLDGF.WRL is also acceptable:

```
DEF bldgf Separator {   # Object: bldgf Created by LightWave3D
    ... }
```

BLDGF.WRL is in the WorldView Worlds subdirectory on the CD-ROM that's included with this book.

The node name must begin with a letter. It cannot begin with a digit, and it must not contain a space, a control character, single or double quotation marks, backslashes, curly braces, or the plus character.

Fields

As the specification states, there are two classes of fields: fields containing a single value and fields containing multiple values.

A *single value field* may contain a single number, a single vector, or a single image. The names of these fields always begin with the letters *SF*.

A *multiple-value field* contains multiple values. The names of these fields always begin with the letters *MF*. These fields are written as a series of values separated by commas, all of which are enclosed by brackets. If a particular field has no values in it, then only the brackets are written. If the field contains only one value, and one value exactly, you can forget about using the brackets and just write the value. The last value in a multiple-value field can be followed by a comma but does not have to be. For example, all of the following code fragments are valid representations of a multiple-value field that contains a single integer value of 2.

```
2
[2,]
[2]
```

Node and field descriptions

In this section, we discuss each of the nodes and fields in detail, explaining their purpose, syntax, and defaults, giving examples of how they are used, and mentioning other nodes or fields that you should examine in context with the node being discussed. These nodes and fields are listed in alphabetical order.

————————————————— **AsciiText** —————————————————

Purpose   This node is one of the eight Shape nodes. Use this node to display text in the VRML world. This node allows the representation of text string characters from the ASCII coded character set to be displayed on the screen.

Syntax   **JUSTIFICATION**

LEFT   Align left edge of text to origin. LEFT (the default) places the left edge of each string at x=0.

CENTER   Align center of text to origin. CENTER places the center of each string at x=0.

RIGHT   Align right edge of text to origin. RIGHT places the right edge of each string at x=0.

FILE FORMAT/DEFAULTS

```
AsciiText {
        string          " "     # MFString
        spacing         1       # SFFloat
        justification   LEFT    # SFEnum
        width           0       # MFFloat
}
```

Explanation   **string:** This is the group of characters you want to be displayed.

spacing: The first string, or group of characters, is rendered with its baseline at (0,0,0). All of the strings that follow are advanced along the y-axis by the formula –(size × spacing). Size is specified by the height (in object space units) of the character images rendered. Spacing determines the vertical spacing of the adjacent lines of text.

justification: This field determines where the strings will be placed along the x-axis. The character string is rendered from left to right, top to bottom, in the font set by FontStyle.

width: This field defines a suggested width constraint for each string. The default, 0, is to use the natural width of each string.

The character string is transformed according to the current cumulative transformation of the parent node. The string is drawn with the current material and texture.

Textures are applied to 3D text in the following way. The texture begins at the origin of the first string, as determined by the current justification. The texture is then scaled in both S and T dimensions equally. S represents the horizontal aspects of the character, and T represents the vertical aspects. The font height represents one unit. S increases to the right. The origin of T can occur anywhere along each character of the string, depending on how that specific character's outline is defined.

Example Use   The following code fragment is from ALLNODES.WRL:

```
AsciiText {
    string    [ "Hello", "there" ] # MFString
    spacing  1
    justification        LEFT
    width    0
}
```

ALLNODES.WRL is included with the QvLib files on the CD-ROM that's included with this book. The Windows 3.1 port of QvLib was made available by Paper Software Inc.

See Also   FontStyle

Cone

Purpose   This Shape node creates a simple cone to use in your worlds. The central axis of this node is aligned along the y-axis. The default location for the cone is centered at $(0,0,0)$. The cone has a size of -1 to $+1$ in all three directions. The cone has a radius of 1 at the bottom and a height of 2, with its apex at 1 and its bottom at -1. The cone has two parts: the side and the bottom.

Syntax   PARTS

SIDES   The conical part

BOTTOM   The bottom circular face

ALL   All parts

FILE FORMAT/DEFAULTS

```
Cone {
    parts         ALL     # SFBitMask
    bottomRadius  1       # SFFloat
    height        2       # SFFloat
}
```

Explanation   This node is transformed by the parent's current cumulative transformation. It is also drawn with the parent's current texture and material.

Unless the current material binding is PER_PART or PER_PART_INDEXED,
the first current material is used for the entire cone. Under these circum-
stances, the first current material is used for the sides of the cone, and the
second is used for the bottom.

If a texture is applied to a cone, the texture is applied differently to the
sides and bottom. For the sides, the texture wraps counterclockwise,
starting at the back of the cone. This counterclockwise direction is
determined by looking at the cone from above. The texture has a vertical
seam along the back of the cone and intersects the yz-plane. The base
of the cone is covered by a circle that is cut out of the texture square
and applied to the base. When the top of the cone is rotated toward the
–z axis, the texture appears right side up.

Example Use   The following code fragment is from CONE.WRL:

```
Cone {
    parts          ALL
    bottomRadius   1
    height         3
}
```

CONE.WRL is in the WorldView Worlds subdirectory on the CD-ROM that
is included with this book.

See Also   PER_PART, PER_PART_INDEXED

Coordinate3

Purpose   This node belongs to the Geometry and Material subgroup of the Property
nodes. It defines a set of 3D coordinates to be used by a subsequent
IndexedFaceSet, IndexedLineSet, or PointSet node.

Syntax   FILE FORMAT/DEFAULTS

```
Coordinate3 {
    point  0 0 0    # MFVec3f
}
```

Explanation   This node doesn't produce any immediately visible result during scene rendering. Instead, it replaces the current coordinates and provides new coordinates for subsequent nodes to use.

Example Use   The following code fragment is from BIRD.WRL:

```
Coordinate3 {
    point { 0.0  0.0  0.4,
            1.8  0.0  0.3,
            1.8  0.0 -0.3,
            0.0  0.0 -0.4,
            0.2 -1.0  0.0,
            1.7 -0.8  0.0}
    }
```

BIRD.WRL is in the NAVFlyer directories on the CD-ROM that's included with this book.

See Also   IndexedFaceSet, IndexedLineSet, PointSet

Cube

Purpose   This Shape node provides a cube aligned with the coordinate axes. The default for the cube node centers it at (0,0,0) and measures two units in each dimension, from –1 to +1.

Syntax   FILE FORMAT/DEFAULTS

```
Cube {
    width    2      # SFFloat
    height   2      # SFFloat
    depth    2      # SFFloat
    }
```

Explanation   You can change the width, height, and depth variables to achieve different sized objects.

As with some of the previously discussed nodes, transformation of the cube node is performed by the scene graph's current cumulative transformation. It is also drawn with the scene graph's current material and texture.

In the scene graph, if the current material binding is PER_PART, PER_PART_INDEXED, PER_FACE, or PER_FACE_INDEXED, materials are bound to the individual faces of the cube in the following order: front (+z), back (–z), left (–x), right (+x), top (+y), and bottom (–y). If you have trouble visualizing this, remember how the left-handed coordinate system works: +z is into the screen, –z is out of the screen toward you, –x is to the left, +x is to the right, +y is toward the top of the screen, and –y is toward the bottom.

In much the same way, textures are applied individually to each face of the cube. Keep in mind that the entire texture is applied on each face. On the front (–z), back (+z), right (+x), and left (–x) sides of the cube, the texture is applied right side up. On the top (+y), the texture appears right side up if you tilt the top of the cube toward your viewpoint. On the bottom (–y), the texture appears right side up when the top of the cube is tilted toward the –z axis, or away from your viewpoint. Please keep in mind that these material, texture, and material binding transformations are applied to the object at its initial 3D coordinate location.

Example Use

The following code fragment is from one of the many CUBE.WRL files available:

```
Cube  {
    width    3
    height   2
    depth    1
}
```

CUBE.WRL can be found in the WorldView Worlds subdirectory on the CD-ROM that's included with this book.

See Also

PER_PART, PER_PART_INDEXED, PER_FACE, PER_FACE_INDEXED

Cylinder

Purpose

This Shape node creates a primitive object known as simple capped cylinder. The cylinder is centered around the y-axis. The default for this node has the cylinder centered at (0,0,0) with a size of -1 to +1 in all three dimensions. You can change the radius and height field variables to create cylinders with different sizes.

Syntax

PARTS

    SIDES   The cylindrical part

    TOP   The top circular face

    BOTTOM   The bottom circular face

    ALL   All parts

FILE FORMAT/DEFAULTS

```
Cylinder {
    parts    ALL    # SFBitMask
    radius   1      # SFFloat
    height   2      # SFFloat
}
```

Explanation

As with other nodes of this type, the cylinder is transformed by the current cumulative transformation and drawn with the current material and texture.

If the current material binding is not PER_PART or PER_PART_INDEXED, the first material is used for the entire cylinder. If the material binding is one of these two, the first current material is used for the side of the cylinder, the second is used for the top, and the third is used for the bottom.

Texture is applied in different ways to the sides, the top, and the bottom of a cylinder. For the sides, the texture wraps in a counterclockwise direction, as you look at it from above, starting at the back of the cylinder. The texture has a vertical seam along the back of the cylinder, intersecting the yz-plane.

For the top and bottom, as with the cone node, a circle is cut out of the texture square and applied to the top or bottom circle. The top texture appears right side up when the top of the cylinder is tilted toward the +z axis, or away from your viewpoint. The bottom texture appears right side up when the top of the cylinder is tilted toward the –z axis, or toward your viewpoint.

Example Use

The following code fragment is from CYL.WRL:

```
Cylinder {
    parts    ALL
    radius   0.8
    height   3
}
```

CYL.WRL can be found in the WorldView Worlds subdirectory on the CD-ROM that's included with this book.

See Also   PER_PART, PER_PART_INDEXED

DEFAULT

Purpose   This bindings setting instructs the node to use the default binding.

DirectionalLight

Purpose   This node is one of the three nodes in the Lights subgroup of the Property nodes. It defines a directional light source that illuminates objects falling inside rays that are parallel to a given three-dimensional vector.

Syntax   FILE FORMAT/DEFAULTS

```
DirectionalLight {
    on              TRUE      # SFBool
    intensity       1         # SFFloat
    color           1 1 1     # SFColor
    direction       0 0 -1    # SFVec3f
}
```

Explanation

DirectionalLight nodes, like other Lights nodes, define an illumination source that may affect subsequent shapes in the scene graph. This node is affected by the current transformation. Note that a DirectionalLight node under a separator does not affect any objects that are outside that separator.

Example Use   The following code fragment is from ALLNODES.WRL:

```
DirectionalLight {
    on              True
    intensity       0.8
    color           1 1 1
    direction       0 0 -1
}
```

ALLNODES.WRL can be found in the QvLib subdirectory on the CD-ROM that's included with this book. The Windows 3.1 port of QvLib was made available by Paper Software Inc.

See Also   PointLight, SpotLight

FontStyle

Purpose
This node is one of the 11 Geometry and Material subgroup nodes in the Property node group. It defines the font style to be used for all subsequent AsciiText.

Syntax

FAMILY

SERIF	Serif style (such as TimesRoman)
SANS	Sans Serif Style (such as Helvetica)
TYPEWRITER	Fixed pitch style (such as Courier)

STYLE

NONE	No modifications to family
BOLD	Embolden family
ITALIC	Italicize or slant family

FILE FORMAT/DEFAULTS

```
FontStyle {
    size    10      # SFFloat
    family  SERIF   # SFEnum
    style   NONE    # SFBitMask
}
```

Explanation
Keep in mind that only the font attributes are defined. The specific browser you are using is expected to assign specific fonts to the various attribute combinations. As explained earlier, the size field specifies the height (in object space units) of glyphs rendered and the vertical spacing of any adjacent lines of text.

Example Use
The following code fragment is from ALLNODES.WRL:

```
FontStyle {
    Size      10
    family    SERIF
    style     NONE
}
```

ALLNODES.WRL can be found in the QvLib subdirectory on the CD-ROM that's included with this book.

See Also   AsciiText

Group

Purpose   As one of the grouping nodes, this node defines the base class for all Group nodes. This node contains an ordered list of child nodes.

Syntax   FILE FORMAT/DEFAULTS

```
Group {
}
```

Explanation   The Group node provides a container for the child nodes included within it. It does not alter the traversal state in any way, shape, or form. The state accumulated for a child during the traversal is passed on to each successive child and then to the parents of the Group. Keep in mind that Group does not push or pop traversal state in the same manner as Separator does. For an explanation of *push* and *pop,* see the "Separator" description, later in this chapter.

Definitions for both *traversal* and *state* are provided in the Glossary. In general, however, what is meant by traversal state is the orderly addressing and processing of the current image environment, from the first image information to the last.

Example Use   The following code fragment is from 1RIBBONS.WRL:

```
Group {
   Separator {
          MaterialBinding {
          value    OVERALL
          }
   Material {
          ambientColor   0.2 0.2 0.2 ~
          diffuseColor   1 0.327273 0
          specularColor  0 0 0 ~
          shininess      0.2 ~
          transparency   0 ~
          }
   Coordinate4 {  ...
          }
   }
}
```

**CD-
ROM**

The 1RIBBONS.WRL file is in the NAVFlyer subdirectory on the CD-ROM that's included with this book.

See Also   Separator

IndexedFaceSet

Purpose   This Shape node provides a 3D shape formed by constructing faces, or polygons, from vertices located at the current coordinates.

Syntax   FILE FORMAT/DEFAULTS

```
IndexedFaceSet {
    coordIndex           0      # MFLong
    materialIndex        -1      # MFLong
    normalIndex          -1      # MFLong
    textureCoordIndex    -1      # MFLong
}
```

Explanation   This node uses the indices in the coordIndex field to specify the polygonal faces. An index of –1 means that the current face is finished and the next face is beginning.

The vertices of these polygons, or the faces, are transformed by the current transformation matrix.

The current material and normal binding are treated in the following way: The material or normal for each face is determined by the PER_PART and PER_FACE bindings. The material or normal for each vertex is determined by PER_VERTEX. The corresponding INDEXED bindings are the same, but they use the materialIndex or normalIndex indices. In regard to default values, the DEFAULT material binding is equal to OVERALL, and the DEFAULT normal binding is equal to PER_VERTEX_INDEXED. If there aren't enough normals in the world's state, vertex normals will be created automatically.

You can bind explicit texture coordinates to vertices of an indexed shape either one after another, if the texture coordinate binding is PER_VERTEX, or by using the indices in the textureCoordIndex field, if the binding is PER_VERTEX_INDEXED. Explicit texture coordinates are defined in the discussion of TextureCoordinate2 later in this chapter. A default texture coordinate mapping is created using the bounding box of the shape if a current texture is declared but no texture coordinates are specified. The S and T coordinates are created in the following manner:

The longest dimension of the bounding box defines the S coordinates. The second longest dimension of the bounding box defines the T coordinates. The S coordinate can be between 0 and 1, ranging the length of the bounding box. The T coordinate can be between 0 and the ratio of the second greatest dimension of the bounding box to the greatest dimension.

You need to make sure that the indices listed in the coordIndex, materialIndex, normalIndex, and textureCoordIndex fields are valid in relationship to the current state. If you don't, it is probable that you'll have errors.

Example Use   The following code fragment is from RELIANT.WRL:

```
IndexedFaceSet { coordIndex [
    1224, 1276, 1364, -1,
    1120, 1134, 1364, -1,
    1276, 1361, 1397, -1,
    1162, 1224, 1276, -1,
    1162, 1361, 1276, -1,
    1035, 1162, 1224, -1,
     951, 1035, 1166, -1,
    1035, 1166, 1224, -1,
    1166, 1224, 1364, -1,
     951, 1134, 1166, -1,
    1276, 1397, 1364, -1,
    1134, 1166, 1364, -1,
    ...
    ]
}
```

RELIANT.WRL can be found at URL http://www.vrml.com.

See Also   IndexedShape, MFLong, PER_PART, PER_FACE, PER_VERTEX, PER_VERTEX_INDEXED, TextureCoordinate2

IndexedLineSet

Purpose   This node is another of the nodes that make up the Shape nodes group. It represents a 3D shape created by constructing polylines from vertices located at the currently specified coordinates. The indices in the coordIndex field are used to specify the polylines. An index of –1 tells when the current polyline has ended and the next one is beginning.

Syntax

FILE FORMAT/DEFAULTS

```
IndexedLineSet {
    coordIndex           0      # MFLong
    materialIndex       -1      # MFLong
    normalIndex         -1      # MFLong
    textureCoordIndex   -1      # MFLong
}
```

Explanation

The current cumulative transformation is used to transform the coordinates of the line set.

The current material and normal binding are treated in the following ways: The material or normal for each segment of the line is specified by the PER_PART binding. The material or normal for each polyline is specified by the PER_FACE binding. The material or normal for each vertex is specified by PER_VERTEX. The corresponding _INDEXED bindings are the same. You need to use the materialIndex or normalIndex indices, though. The DEFAULT material binding is equal to OVERALL, and the DEFAULT normal binding is equal to PER_VERTEX_INDEXED. If there aren't enough normals defined in the world state, the lines are drawn unlit. The same rules are used for texture coordinate generation as for IndexedFaceSet, explained previously.

Example Use

The following code fragment is from ALLNODES.WRL:

```
IndexedLineSet {
    coordIndex           [ 0 ]
    materialIndex        [ -1 ]
    normalIndex          [ -1 ]
    textureCoordIndex    [ -1 ]
}
```

ALLNODES.WRL is in the QvLib subdirectory on the CD-ROM that's included with this book.

See Also

IndexedFaceSet, MFLong, PER_PART, PER_FACE, PER_VERTEX, PER_VERTEX_INDEXED

─────────────────────── **Info** ───────────────────────

Purpose

This Geometry and Material Property node defines an information node in the scene graph.

Syntax

```
Info {
    string  "<Undefined info>"   # SFString
}
```

Explanation

The Info node has no effect on any subsequent nodes or objects during traversal. This node is used primarily to supply information concerning the scene graph for the user. Typically, this information can be stored for application-specific purposes, copyright messages, or other character strings.

Example Use

The following code fragment is from 767.WRL:

```
Info {
    string  "Created at Silicon Graphics using MultiGen.
This is an inefficient scene graph—
NEEDS OPTIMIZATION.
Public domain.
"
}
```

The 767.WRL file is in the WebFX subdirectory on the CD-ROM that's included with this book.

———————————————————— **LOD** ————————————————————

Purpose

One of the six Grouping nodes, LOD allows the worlds you build to change from one representation of an object to another, automatically. The child nodes specified in this node usually represent the same object or objects at varying levels of detail, from highest detail to lowest. But this is not always the case. Keep in mind that viewers moving in your world will see the representations change as they move closer to and farther away from the object.

Syntax

FILE FORMAT/DEFAULTS

```
LOD {
    range   [ ]     # MFFloat
    center  0 0 0   # SFVec3f
}
```

Explanation

The LOD's center, as defined in the preceding file format syntax, is changed by the current transformation of your VRML world. The distance from this newly transformed center to the viewpoint is calculated. If this distance is less than the first value in the ranges array, then the first child of the LOD Group is drawn. If the distance is between the first and second values in the ranges array, the second child is drawn. This continues as long as there are ranges in the ranges array and there are children to be drawn.

There is an important consideration to keep in mind when using this technique. If you have placed N values in your ranges array, your LOD Group should have N+1 children. If you specify too few children, the last child will be used repeatedly for the lowest levels of detail. On the other hand, if you specify too many children, these extra children will be ignored. Each value in the ranges array should be less than the preceding value. If they aren't, the results of this technique will be undefined. In other words, if you were to declare range[8, 14, 12, 34], the results would be unpredictable and probably not be visualizable.

Example Use   The following code fragment is from I_TOWER .WRL:

```
LOD {
            range[8, 14, 22, 34]
      Separator {
            MaterialBinding {
                  value OVERALL
            }
            Material { ...
}
```

I_TOWER.WRL is in the Caligari Fountain subdirectories on the CD-ROM that's included with this book.

———————————————— Material ————————————————

Purpose   This node is one of the 11 Geometry and Material nodes in the Property node group. The Material node determines the current surface material properties for all shapes that follow in the 3D scene.

Syntax   FILE FORMAT/DEFAULTS

```
Material {
    ambientColor    0.2 0.2 0.2    # MFColor
    diffuseColor    0.8 0.8 0.8    # MFColor
    specularColor   0 0 0          # MFColor
    emissiveColor   0 0 0          # MFColor
    shininess       0.2            # MFFloat
    transparency    0              # MFFloat
}
```

Explanation   This node declares several of the components of the current material during the traversal stage. Remember that different shapes interpret materials with multiple values differently. In order to bind materials to shapes, you need to use a MaterialBinding node, which is discussed next.

Example Use   The following code fragment is from CALIG4.WRL:

```
Material {
  ambientColor [
        0.100 0.100 0.100,
        0.100 0.100 0.100,
        0.100 0.100 0.100,
  ]
  diffuseColor [
        0.773 0.529 0.125,
        0.149 0.098 0.671,
        0.020 0.020 0.027,
  ]
  specularColor [
        0.100 0.100 0.100,
        0.100 0.100 0.100,
        0.100 0.100 0.100,
  ]
  emissiveColor [
        0.000 0.000 0.000,
        0.000 0.000 0.000,
        0.000 0.000 0.000,
  ]
  shininess [
        0.000,
        0.000,
        0.000,
  ]
  transparency [
        0.000,
        0.000,
        0.000,
  ]
}
```

CALIG4.WRL is in the Caligari Fountain subdirectories on the CD-ROM that's included with this book.

See Also   MaterialBinding, MFColor

--------------------- **MaterialBinding** ---------------------

Purpose   This node is another of the 11 Geometry and Material Property nodes.
Material Binding specifies how the current materials are bound to shapes
that follow the node in the scene graph.

Syntax   **BINDINGS**

DEFAULT	Use default binding
OVERALL	Whole object has same material
PER_PART	One material for each part of object
PER_PART_INDEXED	One material for each part, indexed
PER_FACE	One material for each face of object
PER_FACE_INDEXED	One material for each face, indexed
PER_VERTEX	One material for each vertex of object
PER_VERTEX_INDEXED	One material for each vertex, indexed

FILE FORMAT/DEFAULTS

```
MaterialBinding {
   value   DEFAULT      # SFEnum
   }
```

Explanation   Shape nodes may interpret bindings differently from one another.
The way that materials are handled is relatively simple. The current
material always has a base value that is defined by the first value of all
material fields. Because material fields can have multiple values, this
MaterialBinding node determines how these values are distributed over a
3D object.

Keep in mind that bindings for faces and vertices are meaningful only for
shapes made from faces and vertices. In the same manner, indexed
bindings are used only by shapes allowing indexing.

When indexed bindings are used with multiple material values, these
values are cycled through. The cycle is based on the period of the
material component with the most values. For example, Table 13-1
shows the values used when cycling through, or indexing into, a material
with two ambient colors, three diffuse colors, and one of all other components in the current material. This material has a period cycle of three.

Table 13-1: Material Values

Material	Ambient Color	DiffuseColor	Other
0	0	0	0
1	1	1	0
2	1	2	0
3 (same as 0)	0	0	0

Example Use   The following code fragment is from CALIG4.WRL:

```
MaterialBinding {
   value PER_FACE_INDEXED
}
```

CALIG4.WRL is in the Caligari Fountain subdirectories on the CD-ROM that's included with this book.

See Also   Material

MatrixTransform

Purpose   This node is one of the five Transformation Property nodes. MatrixTransform defines a geometric 3D transformation with a 4 × 4 matrix.

Syntax   FILE FORMAT/DEFAULTS

```
MatrixTransform {
   matrix  1 0 0 0   # SFMatrix
           0 1 0 0
           0 0 1 0
           0 0 0 1
}
```

Explanation   Some matrices, such as singular ones, can produce errors. Care should be taken when using this node.

Example Use The following code fragment is from CHAIR3.WRL:

```
MatrixTransform {
   matrix 1 0 0 0
          0 -3.69549e-06 -1 0
          0 1 -3.69549e-06 0
          0 0 0 1
   }
```

 CHAIR3.WRL is in the WorldView Worlds subdirectory on the CD-ROM that's included with this book.

MFColor

Purpose This is a multiple-value field found in the Material node. This field can contain any number of RGB colors. A full description of multiple-value fields is in the "Fields" section, earlier in this chapter.

Syntax

```
[ 1.0 0.0 0.0, 0 1 0, 0 0 1 ]   # where each triplet
⌐represents a red, green, and blue value
```

Explanation MFColors are written as one or more RGB triplets. These RGB triplets represent floating point numbers and are always presented in standard scientific notation. As discussed earlier in the chapter, if more than one value is present, all of the values must be enclosed in square brackets and the triplets separated by commas.

Example Use The following code fragment is from CALIG4.WRL:

```
ambientColor [
   0.100 0.100 0.100,
   0.100 0.100 0.100,
   0.100 0.100 0.100,
   ]
```

 CALIG4.WRL is in the Caligari Fountain subdirectories on the CD-ROM that's included with this book.

See Also Material

MFLong

Purpose   This is a multiple-value field found in the IndexedFaceSet and
              IndexedLineSet nodes. MFLong contains any number of long (32-bit)
              integers.

Syntax

```
[ 17, -0xE20, -518820 ]
```

Explanation   MFLong fields are written as one or more integer values. These values
              may be written in decimal, hexadecimal, or octal format. As with all
              multiple-value fields, when more than one value is present, all values
              must be enclosed in square brackets and separated by commas.

Example Use   The following code fragment is from ALLNODES .WRL:

```
IndexedLineSet {
    coordIndex          [ 0 ]
    materialIndex       [ -1 ]
    normalIndex         [ -1 ]
    textureCoordIndex   [ -1 ]
}
```

              ALLNODES.WRL is in the QvLib subdirectory on the CD-ROM that's
              included with this book.

See Also   IndexedFaceSet, IndexedLineSet

MFVec2f

Purpose   This is a multiple-value field found in TextureCoordinate2. MFVec2f can
              contain any number of two-dimensional vectors.

Syntax

```
[ 0 0, 1.2 3.4, 98.6 -4e1 ]
```

Explanation   The MFVec2f field is written as one or more pairs of floating point values
              separated by whitespace. Again, as with other multiple-valued fields,
              when more than one value is present, all of the values are enclosed in
              square brackets and separated by commas.

Example Use   The following code fragment is from NONAME_7.WRL:

```
TextureCoordinate2  {
   Point[   0.000 0.000,
            0.000 0.000,
            1.000 0.000,
            ...
   ]
}
```

NONAME_7.WRL is in the NAVFlyer subdirectory on the CD-ROM that's included with this book.

See Also   TextureCoordinate2

—————————————————————— **MFVec3f** ——————————————————————

Purpose   This is a multiple-value field found in Coordinate3 and Normal. MFVec3f can contain any number of three-dimensional vectors.

Syntax

```
[ 0 0 0, 1.2 3.4 5.6, 98.6 -4e1 212 ]
```

Explanation   The MFVec3f field is written as one or more triplets of floating point values separated by whitespace. Again, as with other multiple-valued fields, when more than one value is present, all of the values are enclosed in square brackets and separated by commas.

Example Use   The following code fragment is from NONAME_4.WRL:

```
Coordinate3  {
   Point  [
            -1.000 -1.000 0.000,
            -1.000  1.000 0.000,
             1.000 -1.000 0.000,
             1.000 -1.000 0.000,
             0.000  0.000 1.481,
          ]
}
```

NONAME_4.WRL is in the NAVFlyer subdirectory on the CD-ROM that's included with this book.

See Also   Coordinate3, Normal

───────────────────────────── **Normal** ─────────────────────────────

Purpose   This node is another of the 11 Geometry and Material Property nodes. Normal defines a set of three-dimensional surface normal vectors to be used by vertex-based Shape nodes such as IndexedFaceSet, IndexedLinedSet, or PointSet, that may follow the Normal node in the scene graph.

Syntax   FILE FORMAT/DEFAULTS

```
Normal {
    vector 0 0 1   # MFVec3f
}
```

Explanation   The Normal node doesn't produce any visible results during the rendering. The Normal node does replace the current normals in the rendering state for other nodes that follow this node to use. The Normal node contains one multiple-valued field that contains the normal vectors.

Example Use   The following code fragment is from SIMPLE~1.WRL:

```
Normal {  vector [
            1.000000 0.000000 0.000000,
            1.000000 0.000000 0.000000,
           -1.000000 0.000000 0.000000,
           -1.000000 0.000000 0.000000,
            0.000000 -1.000000 0.000000,
            0.000000 0.000000 1.000000,
            . . .
            ]
}
```

SIMPLE~1.WRL is in the NAVFlyer subdirectory on the CD-ROM that's included with this book.

See Also   IndexedFaceSet, IndexedLinedSet, MFVec3f, PointSet

—————————— **NormalBinding** ——————————

Purpose   The NormalBinding node is another of the 11 Geometry and Material
Property nodes. This node determines how the current normals are bound
to shapes that follow this node in the scene graph. Keep in mind that
each Shape node may interpret bindings differently.

Syntax   **BINDINGS**

DEFAULT	Use default binding
OVERALL	Whole object has same normal
PER_PART	One normal for each part of object
PER_PART_INDEXED	One normal for each part, indexed
PER_FACE	One normal for each face of object
PER_FACE_INDEXED	One normal for each face, indexed
PER_VERTEX	One normal for each vertex of object
PER_VERTEX_INDEXED	One normal for each vertex, indexed

FILE FORMAT/DEFAULTS

```
NormalBinding {
    value    DEFAULT    # SFEnum
}
```

Explanation   Bindings for faces and vertices are meaningful only for shapes made from

faces and vertices. In the same way, indexed bindings are used only by
shapes that allow indexing. If you have bindings that require multiple
normals, make sure that you have defined at least as many normals as
are necessary. If you don't, you will have errors in your world.

Example Use   The following code fragment is from one of the many CUBE.WRL files
available:

```
NormalBinding { value PER_FACE }
```

CUBE.WRL is in the WorldView Worlds subdirectory on the CD-ROM
that's included with this book.

See Also   SFEnum

─────────── **OrthographicCamera** ───────────

Purpose

This node is one of the two Cameras nodes in the Property group. The OrthographicCamera node produces a parallel projection, with no distortions for distance. As such, these cameras are extremely useful in design work, where visual distortions can interfere with exact measurements. The OrthographicCamera node is similar to the SoOrthographicCamera in Open Inventor.

Syntax

FILE FORMAT/DEFAULTS

```
OrthographicCamera {
    position         0 0 1        # SFVec3f
    orientation      0 0 1  0     # SFRotation
    focalDistance    5            # SFFloat
    height           2            # SFFloat
}
```

Explanation

The default position of the camera is $(0,0,1)$, and it looks back along the –z axis when using the OrthographicCamera node. You can use the position and orientation fields, however, to change these values. Altering the value of the height field changes the total height of the viewing volume. *Viewing volume* can be thought of as what can be seen from a specific point of view.

The viewing volume for an OrthographicCamera node, when visualized, looks very much like a long, rectangular box. The width of this box is determined by multiplying the height field by the aspect ratio of the screen image.

You can use this node to define the initial location from which a viewer enters the VRML world. A VRML browser, however, usually modifies the camera, allowing you to move through the virtual world.

Remember that both Cameras nodes will be affected by the current transformation. This means that you can position a camera by placing a transformation node in front of it in the scene graph.

Example Use

The following code fragment is from ALLNODES.WRL:

```
OrthographicCamera {
    position         0 0 1
    orientation      0 0 1  0
    focalDistance    5
       height        2
}
```

ALLNODES.WRL is in the QvLib subdirectory on the CD-ROM that's included with this book.

See Also   PerspectiveCamera, SFFloat, SFRotation, SFVec3f

OVERALL

Purpose   This bindings settings defines the whole object as having the same material.

PER_FACE

Purpose   This bindings setting defines one material for each face of an object.

PER_FACE_INDEXED

Purpose   This bindings setting defines one material for each part of an object. The materials are indexed.

PER_PART

Purpose   This bindings setting defines one material for each part of an object.

PER_PART_INDEXED

Purpose   This bindings setting defines one material for each part of an object. The materials are indexed.

PER_VERTEX

Purpose   This bindings setting defines one material for each vertex of an object.

PER_VERTEX_INDEXED

Purpose   This bindings setting defines one material for each vertex of an object. The materials are indexed.

PerspectiveCamera

Purpose   PerspectiveCamera is one of the two Cameras nodes in the Property nodes group. The PerspectiveCamera node produces a perspective projection from a given viewpoint. This node is similar in context to the SoPerspectiveCamera in Open Inventor.

Syntax   FILE FORMAT/DEFAULTS

```
PerspectiveCamera {
    position         0 0 1         # SFVec3f
    orientation      0 0 1 0       # SFRotation
    focalDistance    5             # SFFloat
    heightAngle      0.785398      # SFFloat
}
```

Explanation   The default values for this node place the camera at (0,0,1). Like the OrthographicCamera node, this node looks back along the –z axis in the default, but the view can be changed by altering the values of the position and orientation fields.

The viewing volume for the PerspectiveCamera node is a truncated right pyramid. The heightAngle field defines the total vertical angle of the viewing volume. At the same time, the widthAngle of the viewing volume is determined by multiplying the heightAngle by the aspect ratio.

As with the OrthographicCamera node, you can use this node to define the initial location from where a viewer will enter the VRML world. A VRML browser, however, usually modifies the camera, allowing you to move through the virtual world.

Remember that both Cameras nodes are affected by the current transformation. As a result, you can position a camera by placing a transformation node in front of it in the scene graph.

Example Use   The following code fragment is from CASTLE.WRL:

```
DEF Courtyard PerspectiveCamera
  {
          position       20 5 -10
          orientation    0 1 0 -4
  }
```

CASTLE.WRL is in the WebFX subdirectories on the CD-ROM that's included with this book.

See Also   OrthographicCamera, SFFloat, SFRotation, SFVec3f

---------------------------------- **PointLight** ----------------------------------

Purpose   This node is one of the three Lights nodes in the Property group. PointLight defines a point light source at a fixed and stationary three-dimensional location. This light source is omnidirectional. In other words, it illuminates the virtual world equally in all directions.

Syntax   FILE FORMAT/DEFAULTS

```
PointLight {
    on              TRUE      # SFBool
    intensity       1         # SFFloat
    color           1 1 1     # SFColor
    location        0 0 1     # SFVec3f
}
```

Explanation   Basically, any of the three Lights nodes define an illumination source that may affect any shapes or objects coming later in the scene graph. This, of course, depends on the current lighting style. Keep in mind that light sources are affected by the current transformation. Also, any Lights node under a separator does not affect any objects outside that separator.

Example Use   The following code fragment is from CALIG4.WRL:

```
DEF LocLight PointLight {
    color           1.000 0.647 0.376
    on              TRUE
    location        0.000 0.000 0.000
    intensity       1.300
}
```

CALIG4.WRL is in the Caligari Fountain subdirectories on the CD-ROM that's included with this book.

See Also   DirectionalLight, Separator, SFBool, SFColor, SFFloat, SFVec3f, SpotLight

---------------------------------- **PointSet** ----------------------------------

Purpose   This node is one of the eight Shape nodes that specify the geometry of the object. PointSet creates a set of points located at the current coordinates. The node uses the current coordinates in order, beginning at the index specified by the startIndex field.

Syntax   FILE FORMAT/DEFAULTS

```
PointSet {
   startIndex    0      # SFLong
   numPoints    -1      # SFLong
}
```

Explanation   The number of points in the set defined by the PointSet node is deter-
                  mined by the value in the numPoints field. If you place a value of –1 in
                  this field, it indicates that all remaining values in the current coordinates
                  are to be used as points.

                  The current cumulative transformation transforms the coordinates of the
                  point. The points in the set are drawn with the current material and
                  texture.

                  The current material and normal binding are treated in the following
                  ways. One material or normal is bound to each point by PER_PART,
                  PER_FACE, and PER_VERTEX bindings. OVERALL is the DEFAULT
                  material binding. PER_VERTEX is the DEFAULT normal binding. Materi-
                  als, normals, or texture coordinates use the startIndex when the binding
                  indicates that they are to be used per vertex.

Example Use   The following code fragment is from ALLNODES.WRL:

```
PointSet {
   startIndex    0
   numPoints    -1
}
```

                  ALLNODES.WRL is in the QvLib subdirectory on the CD-ROM that's
                  included with this book.

See Also   DEFAULT, OVERALL, PER_FACE, PER_PART, PER_VERTEX, SFLong

---

Rotation

Purpose   This node is one of the five Transformation Property nodes. Rotation
                  defines a three-dimensional rotation about an arbitrary axis through the
                  origin located at $(0,0,0)$.

Syntax   FILE FORMAT/DEFAULTS

```
Rotation {
   rotation     0 0 1 0       # SFRotation
}
```

Explanation   The rotation becomes part of the current transformation. The transformation is then applied to subsequent shapes following in the scene graph.

Example Use   The following code fragment is from ALLNODES.WRL:

```
Rotation {
   rotation        0 0 1  0
}
```

ALLNODES.WRL is in the QvLib subdirectory on the CD-ROM that's included with this book.

See Also   SFRotation

Scale

Purpose   This node is another of the five Transformation Property Group nodes. Scale defines a three-dimensional scaling around the origin.

Syntax   FILE FORMAT/DEFAULTS

```
Scale {
   scaleFactor     1 1 1  # SFVec3f
}
```

Explanation   When you make the individual variables of the scaling vector all different — in other words, not all the same value — you won't get a uniform scale.

Example Use   The following code fragment is from CUBES.WRL:

```
Scale { scaleFactor 4 4 4 }   # Make everything bigger
```

CUBES.WRL is in the WorldView Worlds subdirectory on the CD-ROM that's included with this book.

See Also   SFVec3f

Separator

Purpose

The Separator node is one of the six Group nodes. This node performs a push, or save, of the traversal state before traversing the children. It then performs a pop, or a restore, after traversing them. This action isolates, or separates, the separator's children from the rest of the objects in the scene graph.

Syntax

CULLING ENUMS

ON   Always try to cull to the view volume

OFF   Never try to cull to the view volume

AUTO   Implementation-defined culling behavior

FILE FORMAT/DEFAULTS

```
Separator {
    renderCulling  AUTO    # SFEnum
}
```

Explanation

A Separator node can include other nodes such as the ones for lights, cameras, coordinates, normals, bindings, and all other properties. Separators can be used freely within scenes because they take up little memory in the VRML file.

These nodes also perform render culling. *Render culling* is a method that allows the node to skip over the traversal of the separator's children if they are not going to be rendered. This is determined by comparing the separator's bounding box with the current view volume. Culling itself is then controlled by the renderCulling field. These fields are set to AUTO by default. This allows you to determine whether the implementation should decide whether or not to cull.

What *render culling* means in simpler terms is that if the object is not going to show in the view of the user, it will be culled or passed without being drawn. Very simply, if it's not seen in the view of the user, it's not drawn in memory.

Example Use

The following code fragment is from CUBES.WRL:

```
Separator {
    Transform {
            translation   -0.01 0.016 -0.069
            scaleFactor   1 1 0.89
    }
```

```
Material {
        ambientColor  0.08 0.1 0.06
        diffuseColor  0.3 0.5 0.25
        shininess     0.51
}
Cube {

        width  0.42
        height 0.47
        depth  0.42

}
}
```

CUBES.WRL is in the WorldView Worlds subdirectory on the CD-ROM that's included with this book.

See Also   SFEnum

SFBitMask

Purpose   SFBitMask is a single-value field found in the Cone, Cylinder, and FontStyle nodes. This field contains a mask of bit flags. Nodes that use this field class define mnemonic names for the bit flags. SFBitMasks are written as one or more mnemonic enumerated type names.

What this means is that a word is used as a symbol representing another word, function, or code segments. These symbolic words are also enumerated as you can see in the syntax example.

Syntax

```
( flag1 | flag2 | ... )
```

Explanation   If only one flag is used, the parentheses are optional. The mnemonic enumerated type names in the example syntax differ among uses of this field in various node classes.

SFBool

Purpose   SFBool is a single-value field found in the DirectionalLight, PointLight, and SpotLight nodes. This field contains a single Boolean value.

Explanation   Remember that Boolean values are either true or false therefore it can be written either as 0 (representing FALSE), 1 (representing TRUE), TRUE, or FALSE.

SFColor

Purpose   SFColor is a single-value field found in the DirectionalLight and PointLight nodes. This node contains a color.

Explanation   The SFColor field is written as an RGB triplet of floating point numbers. These floating point numbers are written in standard scientific notation. They range in value from 0.0 to 1.0.

SFEnum

Purpose   SFEnum is a single-value field found in the AsciiText, MaterialBinding, NormalBinding, Separator, ShapeHints, Texture2, and WWWAnchor nodes. This field contains an enumerated type value.

Explanation   As with SFBitmask, nodes that use this field class define mnemonic names for the values. These values are written mnemonic enumerated type names. Again, the names differ among uses of this field in the various nodes.

SFFloat

Purpose   SFFloat is a single-value field found in the AsciiText, Cone, Cube, Cylinder, DirectionalLight, FontStyle, OrthographicCamera, PerspectiveCamera, PointLight, ShapeHints, Sphere, SpotLight, and Texture2Transform nodes. SFFloat contains one single-precision floating point number. These fields are written in standard scientific notation.

SFImage

Purpose   SFImage is a single-value field that is found in the Texture2 node. This field contains an uncompressed two-dimensional color or gray-scale image.

Explanation   This field is written as three integers representing the width, height, and number of components in the image. This is followed by a number of hexadecimal values representing the pixels in the image. This number of hexadecimal values is determined by the formula width × height. The values are all separated by whitespace.

A one-component image has a one-byte hexadecimal value representing the intensity of the image. For example, 0xFF represents full intensity while 0x00 signifies no intensity.

A two-component image puts the intensity in the first, or high, byte and the transparency in the second, or low, byte.

Pixels in a three-component image have the red component in the first byte, followed by the green and blue components. Red would therefore be 0xFF0000.

Four-component images put the transparency byte after the red/green/blue. A semi-transparent blue would be 0x0000FF80.

A value of 1.0 is completely transparent, and a value of 0.0 is completely opaque. Keep in mind that each pixel is read as a single unsigned number. This means that a 3-component pixel with the value 0x0000FF can also be written as 0xFF or 255.

Examples

```
1 1 1 0xFF 0x00
```

This represents a one pixel wide by two pixel high gray-scale image, with the bottom pixel white and the top pixel black.

```
2 4 3 0xFF0000 0xFF00 0 0 0 0 0xFFFFFF 0xFFFF00
```

This represents a two pixel wide by four pixel high RGB image, with the bottom left pixel red, the bottom right pixel green, the two middle rows of pixels black, the top left pixel white, and the top right pixel yellow.

——————————— SFLong ———————————

Purpose   SFLong is a single-value field found in the PointSet and Switch nodes. The SFLong field contains a single long (32-bit) integer. These fields are written as an integer in decimal, hexadecimal, or octal format. Remember that hexadecimal format begins with 0x and octal begins with 0.

——————————— SFMatrix ———————————

Purpose   SFMatrix is a single-value field found in the MatrixTransform node. This field contains a transformation matrix. These fields are written in row-major order as 16 floating point numbers separated by whitespace.

Example

```
1 0 0 0  0 1 0 0  0 0 1 0  7 0 0 1
```

This represents a matrix expressing a translation of seven units along the x-axis.

SFRotation

Purpose   SFRotation is a single-value field found in the OrthographicCamera, PerspectiveCamera, Rotation, and Transform nodes. This field contains an arbitrary rotation. The SFRotation field is written as four floating point values separated by whitespace. These four floating point values represent the axis of rotation followed by the amount of right-handed rotation about that axis, in radians.

Example

```
0 1 0  3.14159265
```

This example describes a 180° rotation about the y-axis.

SFString

Purpose   SFString is a single-value field found in the AsciiText and Info nodes. SFString contains a sequence of characters known as an ASCII string. The SFString field is written as a sequence of ASCII characters in double quotes. The quotes are optional if the string doesn't contain any whitespace. Any type of character, including newlines (the character that you see when you press Enter), may appear within the quotes. You can even include a double quote character within the string by preceding it with a backslash.

Example

```
Testing
"One, Two, Three"
"He said, \"Immel did it!\""
```

All three of the preceding examples are valid strings.

SFVec2f

Purpose   SFVec2f is a single-value field found in the Texture2Transform node. SFVec2f contains a two-dimensional vector. The SFVec2f field is written as a pair of floating point values separated by whitespace.

SFVec3f

Purpose   SFVec3f is a single-value field found in the DirectionalLight, LOD, OrthographicCamera, PerspectiveCamera, PointLight, Scale, SpotLight, Transform, Translation, and WWWInline nodes. This field contains a three-dimensional vector. The SFVec3f field is written as three floating point values separated by whitespace.

ShapeHints

Purpose   ShapeHints node determines whether IndexedFaceSets are solid, contain ordered vertices, or contain convex faces.

Syntax   **VERTEX ORDERING ENUMS**

UNKNOWN_ORDERING	Ordering of vertices is unknown
CLOCKWISE	Face vertices are ordered clockwise (from the outside)
COUNTERCLOCKWISE	Face vertices are ordered counter-clockwise (from the outside)

SHAPE TYPE ENUMS

UNKNOWN_SHAPE_TYPE	Nothing is known about the shape
SOLID	The shape encloses a volume

FACE TYPE ENUMS

UNKNOWN_FACE_TYPE	Nothing is known about faces
CONVEX	All faces are convex

FILE FORMAT/DEFAULTS

```
ShapeHints {
   vertexOrdering   UNKNOWN_ORDERING      # SFEnum
   shapeType        UNKNOWN_SHAPE_TYPE    # SFEnum
   faceType         CONVEX                # SFEnum
   creaseAngle      0.5  # SFFloat
}
```

Explanation   The ShapeHints node provides information that enables VRML to optimize certain rendering features. These optimizations include enabling backface culling and disabling two-sided lighting. For example, if an object is solid and has ordered vertices, this node may turn on backface culling and turn off two-sided lighting. On the other hand, if the object is not solid but has ordered vertices, the node may turn off backface culling and turn on two-sided lighting.

This node also affects how default normals are generated. When an IndexedFaceSet is required to generate default normals, it will use the creaseAngle field to determine which edges should be smooth-shaded and which ones should have a sharp crease. A *crease angle* is the angle between surface normals on adjacent polygons. For example, a crease angle of 0.5 radians means that an edge between two adjacent polygonal faces is smooth-shaded if the normals to the two faces form an angle that is less than 0.5 radians. Otherwise, the edge between the two adjacent polygonal faces will be faceted. (The default value for the crease angle is 0.5 radians or about 30°.)

Example Use   The following code fragment is from ALLNODES.WRL:

```
ShapeHints {
   vertexOrdering   UNKNOWN_ORDERING
   shapeType        UNKNOWN_SHAPE_TYPE
   faceType         CONVEX
   creaseAngle      0.5
}
```

ALLNODES.WRL is in the QvLib subdirectory on the CD-ROM that's included with this book.

See Also   IndexedFaceSet, SFEnum, SFFloat

———————— Sphere ————————

Purpose   This node is another of the eight Shape nodes. It provides a representation of a sphere. The node's default values create a sphere centered at the origin of (0,0,0) and having a radius of 1. This node, as with other Shape nodes, is transformed by the current cumulative transformation and is drawn with the current material and texture.

Syntax   FILE FORMAT/DEFAULTS

```
Sphere {
   radius    1    # SFFloat
}
```

Explanation   This node doesn't have any faces or parts. The node, therefore, ignores material and normal bindings. Instead, Sphere uses the first material for the entire sphere. It also uses its own normals. When you apply a texture to the sphere, the texture covers the entire surface. The texture is wrapped counterclockwise from the back of the sphere and, therefore, has a seam along the back on the yz-plane.

Example Use   The following code fragment is from LODTEST.WRL:

```
Sphere    { }    # for [3, 5)
```

LODTEST.WRL is in the VRWeb subdirectories on the CD-ROM that's included with this book.

See Also   SFFloat

SpotLight

Purpose   This node is another of the three Light Property nodes, and it defines a spotlight style light source. A spotlight can be placed at any fixed location in three-dimensional space. It will then provide a cone-shaped illumination in a specific direction.

Syntax   FILE FORMAT/DEFAULTS

```
SpotLight {
    on             TRUE        # SFBool
    intensity      1           # SFFloat
    color          1 1 1       # SFVec3f
    location       0 0 1       # SFVec3f
    direction      0 0 -1      # SFVec3f
    dropOffRate    0           # SFFloat
    cutOffAngle    0.785398    # SFFloat
}
```

Explanation   When you use the SpotLight node, keep in mind that the intensity of the illumination drops off as the light gets farther from the source. The rate of this drop-off is controlled by the dropOffRate field. The angle of the cone of light is controlled by the cutOffAngle fields.

The Lights nodes define illumination sources that may affect any following objects in the scene graphs. These effects depend, of course, on the current lighting style. Light sources are affected by the current transformation. Keep in mind, also, that a Lights node under a separator does not affect any objects outside that separator.

Example Use The following code fragment is from ALLNODES.WRL :

```
SpotLight {
    on            TRUE
    intensity     1
    color         1 1 1
    location      0 0 1
    direction     0 0 -1
    dropOffRate   0
    cutOffAngle   0.785398
}
```

ALLNODES.WRL is in the QvLib subdirectory on the CD-ROM that's included with this book.

See Also DirectionalLight, PointLight, SFFloat

Switch

Purpose This node is another of the six Group nodes. Switch usually traverses only one, none, or all of its children. You may use this node to switch on and off the effects of some properties or to switch between different properties.

Syntax FILE FORMAT/DEFAULTS

```
Switch {
    whichChild    -1     # SFLong
}
```

Explanation Which child will be traversed is determined by the whichChild field. This field specifies the index of the child to traverse. The first child has an index of 0.

The default value for the whichChild field is -1. This value means that none of the children will be traversed. If the value is set to -3, the switch behaves just like a regular Group, traversing all children.

Example Use The following code fragment is from ALLNODES.WRL:

```
Switch {
    whichChild    -1
}
```

ALLNODES.WRL is in the QvLib subdirectory on the CD-ROM that's included with this book.

See Also   Group, SFLong

Texture2

Purpose

This node is another of the 11 Geometry and Material Property nodes. The Texture2 node determines a texture map and then defines parameters for that map. All subsequent shapes are referred to this map as they are being rendered.

Syntax   **WRAP ENUM**

     REPEAT   Repeats texture outside 0-1 texture coordinate range

     CLAMP   Clamps texture coordinates to lie within 0-1 range

FILE FORMAT/DEFAULTS

```
Texture2 {
    filename      ""         # SFString
    image         0 0 0      # SFImage
    wrapS         REPEAT     # SFEnum
    wrapT         REPEAT     # SFEnum
}
```

Explanation

Using this node, a texture can be read from the URL listed by the filename field. Setting the filename field to an empty string ("") turns off the texturing.

Another way to specify a texture is to set the image field to contain the texture data. Make sure that you don't specify both a URL and data inline. This will result in undefined behavior in your world.

Example Use   The following code fragment is from I_TOWER.WRL:

```
Texture2 { filename "tex27.bmp" }
```

I_TOWER.WRL is in the Caligari Fountain subdirectories on the CD-ROM that's included with this book.

See Also   SFEnum, SFImage, SFString

Texture2Transform

Purpose

This node is another of the Geometry and Material Property nodes. Texture2Transform sets up a two-dimensional transformation applied to texture coordinates.

Syntax

FILE FORMAT/DEFAULTS

```
Texture2Transform {
    translation     0 0     # SFVec2f
    rotation        0       # SFFloat
    scaleFactor     1 1     # SFVec2f
    center          0 0     # SFVec2f
}
```

Explanation

The Texture2Transform node changes the way textures are applied to the surfaces of shapes that will come later in the scene graph. Possible changes include a nonuniform scale about an arbitrary center point, a rotation about that same point, and a translation. These three possible transformations are listed in the order in which they can occur. This node enables you to change the size and position of the textures on shapes.

Example Use

The following code fragment is from ALLNODES.WRL:

```
Texture2Transform {
    translation     0 0
    rotation        0
    scaleFactor     1 1
    center          0 0
}
```

ALLNODES.WRL is in the QvLib subdirectories on the CD-ROM that's included with this book.

See Also

SFFloat, SFVec2f

TextureCoordinate2

Purpose

This node is another of the 11 Geometry and Material Property nodes. This node defines a set of two-dimensional coordinates that will be used to map textures to any vertex-based PointSet, IndexedLineSet, or IndexedFaceSet objects that follow it in the scene graph.

Syntax   FILE FORMAT/DEFAULTS

```
TextureCoordinate2 {
    point  0 0     # MFVec2f
}
```

Explanation   TextureCoordinate2 replaces the current texture coordinates in the
                    rendering state with new ones for the shapes to use.

                    Texture coordinates are between 0 and 1 and range across the texture.
                    The horizontal coordinate is always specified first, followed by the vertical
                    coordinate. The horizontal coordinate is named S. The vertical coordinate
                    is named T.

Example Use   The following code fragment is from FLOOR.WRL:

```
TextureCoordinate2 {
    point  [ 25 25, 25 0, 0 0, 0 25 ]
}
```

                    FLOOR.WRL is in the WebFX subdirectories on the CD-ROM that's
                    included with this book.

See Also   MFVec2f

─────────────────────────── **Transform** ───────────────────────────

Purpose   This node is one of the five Transformation Property nodes. Transform
                    describes three geometric three-dimensional transformations.

Syntax   FILE FORMAT/DEFAULTS

```
Transform {
    translation         0 0 0       # SFVec3f
    rotation            0 0 1 0     # SFRotation
    scaleFactor         1 1 1       # SFVec3f
    scaleOrientation    0 0 1 0     # SFRotation
    center              0 0 0       # SFVec3f
}
```

Explanation   The three possible transformations that this node can initiate are a
                    nonuniform scale about an arbitrary point, a rotation about an arbitrary
                    point and axis, and a translation. These three possibilities are in the order
                    in which they might be called. Also keep in mind that the nonuniform
                    scale about an arbitrary point is a possibility. The scale doesn't have to
                    be nonuniform.

Example Use   The following code fragment is from CORNER.WRL:

```
Transform
  {
  translation   5 5 0
  rotation      1 1 0 3.14
  scaleFactor   10 1 10
  }
```

CORNER.WRL is in the WebFX subdirectories on the CD-ROM that's
included with this book.

See Also   SFRotation, SFVec3f

TransformSeparator

Purpose   This node is one of the six Group nodes. The TransformSeparator node is
similar to the Separator node.

Syntax   FILE FORMAT/DEFAULTS

```
TransformSeparator {
  }
```

Explanation   The TransformSeparator node is similar to the Separator node in that it
also saves state before traversing its children, and it restores state
afterwards. However, TransformSeparator saves only the current transformation. The rest of the state condition is left as is.

You can use this node for positioning a camera in a world. The transformations to the camera do not affect the rest of the scene. You can also
use this node to isolate transformations to light sources or other objects.

Example Use   The following code fragment is from CORNER.WRL:

```
TransformSeparator {
  }
```

CORNER.WRL is in the WebFX subdirectories on the CD-ROM that's
included with this book.

See Also   Separator

Translation

Purpose

This node is the last of the five Transformation Property nodes. It defines a translation by a three-dimensional vector.

Syntax

FILE FORMAT/DEFAULTS

```
Translation {
   translation   0 0 0   # SFVec3f
}
```

Example Use

The following code fragment is from ALLNODES.WRL:

```
Translation {
   translation   0 0 0
}
```

ALLNODES.WRL is in the QvLib subdirectory on the CD-ROM that's included with this book.

See Also

SFVec3f

WWWAnchor

Purpose

One of the most valuable nodes available for cyberspace navigation, the WWWAnchor node loads a new scene into a VRML browser when one of the node's children is chosen.

Syntax

FILE FORMAT/DEFAULTS

```
WWWAnchor {
   name    ""      # SFString
   map     NONE    # SFEnum
}
```

Explanation

Exactly how you "choose" a child of the WWWAnchor is up to the VRML browser. Typically, the method involves clicking on one of the node's children with the mouse. The new scene then replaces the current scene. Choosing a WWWAnchor with an empty (" ") name does nothing. The WWWAnchor name field is an arbitrary URL.

The WWWAnchor's map field is an enumerated value. You have two choices for this value, either the default, NONE, or POINT. If POINT is chosen the object-space coordinates of the point on the object the user chooses is added to the URL in the name field. The syntax for this addition is ?x,y,z.

Example Use   The following code fragment is from FWORLD1.WRL:

```
WWWAnchor {
    name "http://www.sd.tgs.com/~template/vrml/stuff.wrl"
    ...
}
```

FWORLD1.WRL can be found at `ftp://ftp.portal.com/pub/fredness/VRML`.

See Also   SFVec3f

WWWInline

Purpose   This node is the other unclassified node in the specification. The WWWInline node reads its children from anywhere in the World Wide Web.

Syntax   FILE FORMAT/DEFAULTS

```
WWWInline {
    name           ""        # SFString
    bboxSize       0 0 0     # SFVec3f
    bboxCenter     0 0 0     # SFVec3f
}
```

Explanation   Exactly when WWWInLine's children are read is not defined. The reading of the children may be delayed until the WWWInline is actually displayed. A WWWInline with an empty name ("") does nothing. The WWWInLine name field is an arbitrary URL.

The effect of referring to a non-VRML URL in a WWWInline node is undefined. In common terms, if you refer to a non-VRML URL in the WWWInline node, what will happen depends on how the user has the Web browser and VRML viewer configured with one another.

If the WWWInline's bboxSize field specifies a nonempty bounding box, then the node's object-space bounding box is determined by its bboxSize and bboxCenter fields. Keep in mind that a bounding box is nonempty when at least one of its dimensions is greater than zero. This allows an implementation to view-volume cull or LOD switch the WWWInline without reading its contents. In other words, the VRML viewer can skip over the WWWInline.

Example Use   The following code fragment is from FWORLD1.WRL:

```
DEF NoName_1 WWWInline {
    name            "main000.wrl"
    bboxSize        5.425 3.401 3.223
    bboxCenter      2.713 1.662 0.599
}
```

FWORLD1.WRL can be found at `ftp://ftp.portal.com/pub/fredness/VRML`.

See Also   SFString, SFVec3f

Moving On

In this chapter and in Chapter 12, you examined the VRML Version 1.0 specification and the nodes and fields that make virtual worlds on the Internet possible. To help you understand the specification, we've provided explanations and example code fragments for each of the nodes and most of the fields.

In the next chapter, you see some actual VRML worlds. You look at each line of code and learn what it does in that virtual world.

VRML Sample Worlds

Examining some of the sample worlds on the CD-ROM

Editing a sample world

I n this chapter, you learn more about how VRML worlds work by closely examining the code for some of the sample worlds that are on the CD-ROM that accompanies this book. In Chapter 12, you looked at the VRML Version 1.0 specification, and in Chapter 13, you learned more about how each node affects the virtual world that it helps to create. Now you look at some virtual worlds and the code that creates them to see the effects that various parts of the code have when you are creating a virtual world. You'll probably want to look back at the preceding two chapters from time to time as you work through the following exercises.

You can look at the code for two of the VRML worlds discussed in this chapter by using the Notepad application that comes with Windows. To examine the code for larger worlds, you may need to use your word processor, but if you do, always remember to resave the world in straight ASCII format if you make any changes.

Examining the Code for the Eiffel Tower

The first world you look at is I_TOWER.WRL in Caligari's FOUNTAIN sub-directory. This world is a representation of the Eiffel Tower. Open Notepad and load I_TOWER.WRL into it. We're going to go through this file line by line and node by node.

VRML identification and comment lines

The first thing you see at the top of this file is

```
#VRML V1.0 ascii
```

As you know by now, this comment line identifies the file as a VRML Version 1.0 file. The next line is empty, or whitespace, and it is there for cosmetic purposes. After that comes

```
# created by Caligari Corp. Truespace (tm)
# copyright 1995 Caligari Corporation
```

These two comment lines are ignored, as is white space, by the VRML browser. These lines identify how the world was created and provide the copyright information concerning this world.

Identifying how and when the world was created is an excellent idea. Not only should each world be identified in a manner that's similar to this, but the name of the author, an e-mail address, and the name of the world should also be included here in comment lines. This identifying information will help to identify worlds that might be varying from the VRML standard. It will also give credit to companies and individuals that have worked hard to create these worlds. Good virtual worlds deserve credit and admiration.

The scene graph

The line after these three lines is whitespace. After that, you see the first node, a Separator node. This represents the beginning of the scene graph.

```
Separator {
```

As you learned in Chapters 12 and 13, a Separator node is one of the six Group nodes, so it can include other nodes. These nodes can include lights, cameras, coordinates, normals, bindings, and all other properties. The format and default for the Separator node are as follows:

```
Separator {
   renderCulling  AUTO   # SFEnum
}
```

An important consideration is that this node also performs render culling. Render culling is controlled by the renderCulling field. This field is set by default to AUTO, which is a setting that allows the implementation to decide whether to cull. The renderCulling field can also be set to On (always try to cull to the view volume) or OFF (never try to cull to the view volume).

The next line in this world is

```
CALIGARISceneInfo {
```

This node, which was created by the author of this world, takes advantage of the extensibility of the VRML language. (Extensibility is discussed in Chapter 12 in the VRML Version 1.0 specification.) CALIGARISceneInfo is a self-describing node. Self-describing nodes are supported by Version 1.0 of the specification and are discussed fully in the Extensibility section of Chapter 12.

Extensibility and self-describing nodes work by forcing nodes that are not part of standard VRML to begin with a description of the node's fields so that all VRML implementations will be able to parse and ignore these extensions. The next three lines of this world are descriptions of the fields that are used to describe this node.

```
fields [ SFVec3f background, SFVec3f environ,
    SFVec3f fogColor, SFBool fog, SFLong fogNear,
    SFLong fogFar, SFString envName, SFString backgroundName ]
```

This description of the fields is written just after the opening curly brace for the node. As stated in the specification, this description consists of the keyword *fields* followed by a list of the types and names of fields used by the node. The list of fields is enclosed in square brackets and separated by commas. These fields are not part of the VRML specification, but are allowed under the Extensibility of VRML.

Notice that three of the field names are of the SFVec3f type. This kind of field contains a three-dimensional vector and is written as three floating-point values separated by whitespace.

One of the field names is of the SFBool type. This field type contains a single Boolean value that can be written either as 0 (representing FALSE), 1 (representing TRUE), TRUE, or FALSE.

Two of the field names are of the SFLong type. This kind of field contains a single long (32-bit) integer and is written as an integer in decimal, hexadecimal or octal format.

Finally, the last two field names are of the SFString type. This kind of field contains a sequence of characters in double quotes. The quotes are optional if the string doesn't contain any whitespace, and any type of character, including newlines, may appear within the quotes.

These field names for the new node are then listed in the world, making up the rest of the node description and the next seven lines.

```
background 0.463 0.753 0.847
environ 0.000 0.000 0.000
fogColor 0.502 0.502 0.502
fogNear 1
fogFar 500
fog FALSE
}
```

The last two field names, envName and backgroundName, are not listed and used in this world.

The Switch node

The next line in the world file is the Switch node.

```
Switch {
  }
```

Switch allows the traversal of only one, none, or all of its children. The syntax and defaults for the Switch node are

```
Switch {
   whichChild  -1 # SFLong
  }
```

The whichChild field determines the child to be traversed. The default value for this field is -1, meaning that none of the children are traversed. In this world, the Switch node contains nothing between the two braces, so the node is using the default, and none of the children will be traversed.

The first TransformSeparator node

The next lines in the world are

```
TransformSeparator {
  MatrixTransform {
```

```
       matrix
            1.000 0.000 0.000 0
            0.000 0.000 -1.000 0
            0.000 1.000 0.000 0
            6.597 1.899 -0.329 1
  }
  DEF LocLight PointLight {
       color 1.000 0.325 0.071
       on TRUE
       location 0.000 0.000 0.000
       intensity 1.650
  }
 }
```

The TransformSeparator node is similar in use to the Separator node. It saves the state before traversing its children and restores the state afterwards. Remember, the TransformSeparator node saves only the current transformation.

In this particular situation, this node is being used to isolate the transformation of a light source. The node has two children; a MatrixTransform node and a PointLight node.

The MatrixTransform node defines a geometric, three-dimensional transformation with a 4 × 4 matrix. The PointLight node, named LocLight, is then affected by this matrix.

The PointLight node defines the light source at a fixed and stationary three-dimensional location, in this case at the location 0.000, 0.000, 0.000. This light source is omnidirectional with a color of 1.000, 0.325, 0.071 and an intensity of 1.650.

The light source is created and transformed within the TransformSeparator, not affecting anything else in the world, and then the file goes on to the next node.

The second TransformSeparator node

```
TransformSeparator {
   MatrixTransform {
       matrix
            1.000 0.000 0.000 0
            0.000 0.000 -1.000 0
            0.000 1.000 0.000 0
            -3.631 3.046 5.116 1
   }
```

(continued)

```
DEF LocLight_1 PointLight {
    color 0.008 0.698 1.000
    on TRUE
    location 0.000 0.000 0.000
    intensity 1.300
}
}
```

This node is also a TransformSeparator. In this case, it has another MatrixTransform node and another PointLight node. This time the PointLight node is named LocLight_1. This TransformSeparator changes the location, the color, and the intensity of the second light source in this virtual world.

The third TransformSeparator node

A third TransformSeparator follows in the file. The code for this node is

```
TransformSeparator {
    MatrixTransform {
        matrix
            1.000 0.000 0.000 0
            0.000 0.000 -1,000 0
            0.000 1.000 0.000 0
            1.226 2.930 -5.390 1
    }
    DEF LocLight_2 PointLight {
        color 1.000 0.522 0.412
        on TRUE
        location 0.000 0.000 0.000
        intensity 1.770
    }
}
```

This TransformSeparator contains another MatrixTransform node and another PointLight node. This time the PointLight node is named LocLight_2. This TransformSeparator changes the location, the color, and the intensity of the third light source in this virtual world.

The LOD node

The next node in this world is the LOD node.

```
LOD {
    range[8, 14, 22, 34]
```

This kind of node allows the worlds you build to change automatically from one representation of an object to another representation of the same object. The LOD's center, as defined in the format syntax, is changed by the current transformation of the VRML world. The distance from this newly transformed center to the viewpoint is calculated, and if this distance is less than the first value in the ranges array, then the first child of the LOD group is drawn. This process continues as long as there are ranges in the ranges array and there are children to be drawn. Don't forget that if you place X number of values in the ranges array, the LOD group should have X+1 children. What this means very simply is that you should have one more child node than you have ranges in the LOD node.

This LOD node contains several other nodes. The first is

```
Separator {
```

The object created and transformed by this node is displayed by the LOD node when the range is between the LOD's center and the first value in the range values. This first value is 8 units.

The other nodes within this Separator node create the object to be displayed by the LOD node. The first node inside this separator is a MaterialBinding node.

```
MaterialBinding {
   value OVERALL
}
```

Remember that this node specifies how the current materials, within this particular separator, are bound to shapes that follow this node in the scene graph. In this particular case, the binding is specified as OVERALL. This means that the objects within this separator will be made of the same material.

Following this in the scene graph is a Material node.

```
Material {
   ambientColor [
       0.150 0.150 0.150,
   ]
   diffuseColor [
       0.824 0.824 0.824,
   ]
   specularColor [
       1.000 1.000 1.000,
   ]
```

(continued)

```
    emissiveColor [
        0.000 0.000 0.000,
    ]
    shininess [
        0.000,
    ]
    transparency [
        0.000,
    ]
}
```

This is where the material that the objects will be made up of is defined. The Material node determines the current surface material properties for all shapes that follow in the three-dimensional scene within this scene graph.

This Material node is followed by a MatrixTransform node:

```
MatrixTransform {
    matrix
        0.653 0.000 0.000 0
        0.000 0.000 -0.653 0
        0.000 0.076 0.000 0
        0.000 0.710 0.000 1
}
```

Again, the MatrixTransform node defines the geometric, three-dimensional transformation with a 4 × 4 matrix for the nodes within this separator.

A Coordinate3 node follows in the scene graph.

```
Coordinate3 {
    point [
        -1.000 -1.000 -1.000,
        -1.000 -1.000 1.000,
        . . .
    ]
}
```

In order to conserve space, we haven't included the entire node description in this code fragment. Take the time to examine it carefully inside your text editor.

Remember that the Coordinate3 node defines a set of three-dimensional coordinates that will be used by any IndexedFaceSet, IndexedLineSet, or PointSet nodes that may follow in the scene graph. Also keep in mind that this node doesn't produce any immediately visible result during the scene rendering.

Instead, it replaces the current coordinates and provides new coordinates for subsequent nodes to use.

This node is followed by a ShapeHints node.

```
ShapeHints {
    creaseAngle 0.559
    vertexOrdering COUNTERCLOCKWISE
    shapeType SOLID
    faceType UNKNOWN_FACE_TYPE
}
```

This kind of node determines whether IndexedFaceSets are solid, contain ordered vertices, or contain convex faces. The ShapeHints node provides information that enables VRML to optimize certain rendering features. Keep in mind that this node also affects how default normals are generated. In this particular object, the shape is solid and consists of an unknown face type.

The last node in this Separator node is an IndexedFaceSet node. The node is named Cube_7. This node is defined here.

```
DEF Cube_7 IndexedFaceSet {
    coordIndex [
        1, 3, 2, 0,
        . . .
    ]
}
```

To save space, we have not listed the entire node description here, but you can examine the particulars of this node with your text editor.

The IndexedFaceSet node creates a three-dimensional shape that is formed by constructing faces, or polygons, from vertices located at the current coordinates. The indices in the coordIndex field are used to specify the polygonal faces. Keep in mind that the vertices of these polygons, or the faces, will be transformed by the current transformation matrix.

Next, another Separator node is defined in the file.

```
Separator {
```

This node creates and transforms the object displayed by the LOD node when the range is between 8 and 14 units. The first node in this Separator node is again a MaterialBinding node.

```
MaterialBinding {
   value OVERALL
}
```

This node does the same thing that the MaterialBinding node in the first Separator node in the LOD node did. It's followed by another Material node.

```
Material {
   ambientColor [
      0.150 0.150 0.150,
   ]
   diffuseColor [
      0.824 0.824 0.824,
   ]
   specularColor [
      1.000 1.000 1.000,
   ]
   emissiveColor [
      0.000 0.000 0.000,
   ]
   shininess [
      0.000,
   ]
   transparency [
      0.000,
   ]
```

This Material node is identical to the Material node in the first Separator node in the LOD node. The differences between the two Separators occur in the MatrixTransform and Coordinate3 nodes (although the short listing we've included here looks identical to the previous listings).

```
MatrixTransform {
   matrix
      0.653 0.000 0.000 0
      0.000 0.000 -0.653 0
      0.000 0.076 0.000 0
      0.000 0.710 0.000 1
}
Coordinate3 {
   point [
      -1.000 -1.000 -1.000,
      -1.000 -1.000 1.000,
      . . .
   ]
}
```

To conserve space, we have not listed the entire Coordinate3 node. Make sure that you examine the entire code in your text editor. The MatrixTransform and Coordinate3 nodes begin the drawing and transformation of the object created here.

The last two child nodes in this Separator node are

```
ShapeHints {
    creaseAngle 0.559
    vertexOrdering COUNTERCLOCKWISE
    shapeType SOLID
    faceType UNKNOWN_FACE_TYPE
}
DEF Cube_4 IndexedFaceSet {
    coordIndex [
        0, 1, 3, 2,
        . . .
    ]
}
```

The ShapeHints node is identical to that in the preceding Separator. The IndexedFaceSet node is named Cube_4. Closely examining the Cube_4 node in your text editor (such as Notepad or your favorite word processor) should enable you to see the differences between Cube_4 and the preceding Cube_7.

The third Separator takes effect and displays its object when the LOD range is between 14 and 22. Most of the code for this Separator follows:

```
Separator {
    MaterialBinding {
        value OVERALL
    }
    Material {
        ambientColor [
            0.150 0.150 0.150,
        ]
        diffuseColor [
            0.824 0.824 0.824,
        ]
        specularColor [
            1.000 1.000 1.000,
        ]
        emissiveColor [
            0.000 0.000 0.000,
        ]
```

(continued)

```
        shiniess [
            0.000,
        ]
        transparency [
            0.000,
        ]
    }
    MatrixTransform {
        matrix
            0.187 0.000 0.000 0
            0.000 0.000 -0.187 0
            0.000 0.134 0.000 0
            0.000 4.140 0.000 1
    }
    Coordinate3 {
        point [
            -1.000 -1.000 -1.000,
            -1.000 -1.000 1.000,
            . . .
        ]
    }
    ShapeHints {
        creaseAngle 0.559
        vertexOrdering COUNTERCLOCKWISE
        shapeType SOLID
        faceType UNKNOWN_FACE_TYPE
    }
    DEF Cube_3 IndexedFaceSet {
        coordIndex [
            0, 1, 3, 2,
            . . . .
        ]
    }
}
```

Make sure that you examine the Coordinate3 and IndexedFaceSet nodes of this Separator in your text editor. As before, you will find slight modifications in the child nodes of this Separator that make the displayed and transformed object slightly different and the detail of the image sharper, the closer you get to the object.

The next Separator node in the file displays and transforms the object when the range is between 22 and 34. Only part of the Coordinate3 and IndexedFaceSet nodes are listed here.

```
Separator {
  MaterialBinding {
     value OVERALL
  }
  Material {
     ambientColor [
          0.150 0.150 0.150,
     ]
     diffuseColor [
          0.824 0.824 0.824,
     ]
     specularColor [
          1.000 1.000 1.000,
     ]
     emissiveColor [
          0.000 0.000 0.000,
     ]
     shininess [
          0.000,
     ]
     transparency [
          0.000,
     ]
  }
  MatrixTransform {
     matrix
          1.000 0.000 0.000 0
          0.000 0.000 -1.000 0
          0.000 1.000 0.000 0
          0.000 0.000 0.000 1
  }
  Coordinate3 {
     point [
          -0.129 -0.129 4.102,
          -0.129 0.129 4.102,
          . . .
     ]
  }
  ShapeHints {
     creaseAngle 0.559
     vertexOrdering COUNTERCLOCKWISE
     shapeType SOLID
     faceType UNKNOWN_FACE_TYPE
  }
```

(continued)

```
DEF Plane_1 IndexedFaceSet {
    coordIndex [
        16, 2, 0, -1,
        . . . ]
    }
}
}
}
```

This node is the fourth Separator node listed in this file. However, there should be one more child node than there are ranges in the LOD. Here there are four ranges and four child nodes, so the last, and lowest, level of detail, is used again at ranges greater than 34 units.

Putting it all together

Load the file into one of the VRML browsers and examine its behavior. Moving toward the tower enhances the level of detail. Moving away from the tower detracts from the level of detail.

You can find color screen shots of the I_TOWER.WRL as seen in Caligari's Fountain in the color insert of this book.

The LOD node is not supported in several of the VRML viewer and creation tool betas that are on the CD-ROM that is included with this book. It is supported in WebSpace, VRWeb, Spinner, and Fountain, and it will be supported in versions of WorldView andWebFX that will be available at their Web sites soon after the publication of this book. Be sure and download the most current versions of these software applications from their Web sites.

Examining the Code for LODTEST.WRL

In the Eiffel Tower world, you saw how minor changes can be produced by using the LOD node. In this section, you take a closer look at the LOD node in the test file LODTEST.WRL .

VRML identification and comments

Load LODTEST.WRL from the CD-ROM that accompanies this book into your text editor (Notepad or your word processor). The first line of the code, as usual, is the VRML identification information.

```
#VRML V1.0 ascii
# test file for LOD (level of detail)
```

The comment line that follows the VRML identification states the purpose of this world. Adding comment lines with the author's name and the date of the world's creation is a good programming practice.

The Material node

The first node in this file is the Material node.

```
Material { diffuseColor 0 1 0 }
```

Material nodes determine the current surface material properties for all shapes that follow in the 3D scene. How many shapes exist in this world? That's something you can determine by looking at the code.

The LOD node

The next node in the file is the LOD node itself.

```
LOD {
   center 0 0 0   # center of children
   range [ 5, 10 ]# increasing ranges
   # for n ranges there should be n+1 children
   # too few children: use last one
   # too many children: ignored
Cube { } # for [0, 3)
Sphere { }# for [3, 5)
Cone { } # for [5, inf)
# Cylinder { }
}
```

As you can see, the center is defined at 0,0,0, and two ranges are defined; from the origin to 5 units, and from 5 units to 10 units. Because two ranges are defined, at least three children need to be defined. The children are defined by the Cube, Sphere, and Cone nodes. In all three cases, the braces are empty, so the nodes use their default values.

Keep in mind that the LOD node usually defines different representations of the *same* object. Here, however, three different objects are defined so that the change from one representation to the next is obvious in this example.

Now that you've had some experience interpreting VRML nodes, you can see that the comments after the Cube, Sphere, and Cone nodes are incorrect. The Cube node will be displayed at distances from the origin to 5 units, not from 0 to 3. The Sphere node will be displayed at ranges from 5 units to 10 units, not from 3 to 5. Finally, the Cone node will be displayed at all distances greater than 10 units, not from 5 to infinity. The Cylinder node has been commented out by the # sign and won't be displayed at all.

You can find color screen shots of the LODTEST.WRL as seen in VRWeb in the color insert located near the center of the book.

Putting What You've Learned into Practice

You've looked at two individual worlds and examined how nodes and fields are used to display and transform the objects and shapes that make up the virtual world. In the last part of this chapter, you work with PSU.WRL to make it display correctly in a VRML viewer.

What's wrong with PSU.WLD?

The first thing that you need to determine is how the world is being displayed currently. When you load PSU.WRL into one of the VRML viewers and look at it, the world is colorless.

Originally, Paul began creating PSU world using VRBASIC. VRBASIC has its own built-in text editor that allows for easy switching from the world's code to the displayed world. As Paul built PSU.WLD, the PSU.WLD file and the VRBASIC program quickly outgrew the DOS 640K limit. Paul had to switch to the DOS text editor, Edit, and use REND386 to continue.

A square area of the central campus was chosen to make up the world because of memory limitations at the beginning. The world was usable from within PC programs that read the .WLD format. When Bernie Roehl released his WLD2VRML converter, Paul used this program to convert PSU.WLD to PSU.WRL.

Looking at PSU.WRL

The first step that you need to take to make sure that PSU.WRL displays the way it should in a VRML viewer is to load it into one of the VRML viewers that's on the CD-ROM and see what PSU.WRL looks like. We loaded it into WorldView (see Figure 14-1). All of the buildings are the same color.

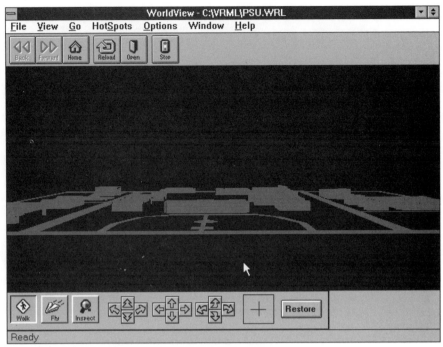

Figure 14-1: PSU.WRL, as seen in WorldView.

If WorldView does not display PSU.WRL at all, enter the Options menu and make the following changes: Select Preferences and, under Rendering, make sure that the check boxes for Generate polygon back faces and Generate normals when not specified are both checked. Under Viewpoint choose Always look at scene on load. Next, click OK and choose Save Options from the Options menu. Reload PSU.WRL to see something resembling Figure 14-1.

Using 2Morrow World Builder to view PSU.WLD (see Figure 14-2), the buildings in PSU.WLD do have different colors. Because the VRML .WRL file is not showing the colored buildings as in the .WLD file, we know that there is an error in the VRML .WRL file.

First, you need to figure out why colors are not being displayed for PSU.WRL in your VRML viewer. Load PSU.WRL into your text editor (use your word processor because of the size of PSU.WRL) and take a look at the file.

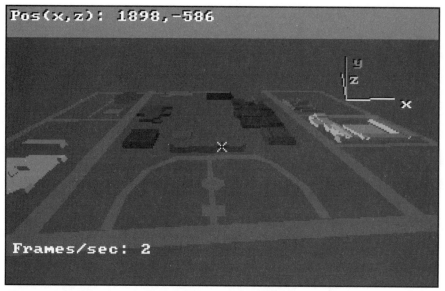

Figure 14-2: PSU.WLD, as seen in 2Morrow World Builder.

The first changes to make are in the comment lines at the beginning of the file. You need to identify the world, its purpose, how it was created, when it was created, who created it, and who may have modified it. In this case, you need to change the following lines of code:

```
#VRML V1.0 ascii
#
# Converted from '\temp\psu\psu.wld' by WLD2VRML
#
```

Change the lines so they look like this:

```
#VRML V1.0 ascii
# PSU.WRL - The Virtual Pittsburg State University Campus
# Originally Converted from 'psu.wld' by WLD2VRML
# WRL file Created by Paul M. Summitt, August 1995
# Cameras and Colors Modified by Paul M. Summitt, September 1995
```

Now, anyone accessing this file will have information about what this world is, who created it, and who changed it.

Next, turn your attention to the Cameras defined in the original file. Highlight all the Cameras with the exception of the first and use the Edit/Cut function of your text editor to delete these lines of code.

Next, you need to get the buildings to be displayed in different colors. A total of 478 individual Separator nodes are inside the Separator node that makes up PSU.WRL. Each of these Separator nodes contains an emersiveColor field that currently contains the RGB values of 0.2, 0.2, and 0.2.

One method you can use to change these values is to use your text editor's Search and Replace function to find each instance of the emersiveColor [0.2 0.2 0.2] and replace each instance with emersiveColor [1 0 0]. Save the VRML world file, exit the text editor, and reload the world into your VRML viewer. You now have something resembling Figure 14-3 on your screen. This time, however, you have color! At least for some of the buildings. There are still errors in the code that need to be tracked down but we'll not worry about that here. (Paul will fix it before he puts it on the Web.) The important thing to notice here is that small changes in the code can affect the entire world.

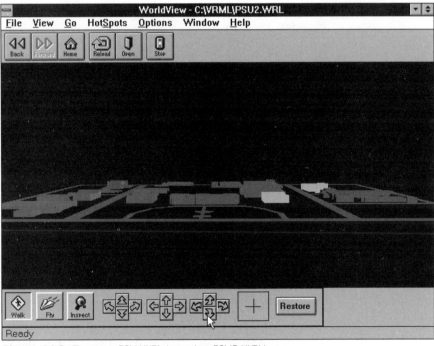

Figure 14-3: The new PSU.WRL (saved as PSU2.WRL).

As we said earlier in the book, PSU.WRL, like the campus itself, is very much under construction. Paul has plans to add the football stadium, the library, the sports complex, the nursing building, and the new technology center in the near future. Check out Pittsburg State University's Web page (`http://www.PittState.edu`), and some time in the future, maybe you'll be able to walk the virtual campus.

This brings up the question of how to access the VRML world from the Web page. In Chapter 3, we discussed adding the VRML world to the home page that you created there. Now you can do just that.

1. **Open Word for Windows and load HOMEPAGE.HTM.**

    This is the home page that you worked on in Chapter 3.

2. **Go to the bottom of the document and insert another picture by choosing Picture from the Insert menu and then selecting a .GIF file.**

    We used the screen capture of PSU.WRL that you saw earlier in this chapter. We saved it as a .GIF file named 041402.GIF. Remember, HTML accepts only .GIF or .JPG graphics for many Web Browsers.

    The picture is placed on the Web page, and you're ready to create the hyperlink to PSU.WRL.

3. **Choose Hyperlink from the Insert menu.**

4. **In the Text to display box, type** Visit PSU.

5. **Select the document by typing PSU.WRL in the local document box.**

6. **Press Enter or click OK to see Visit PSU highlighted in blue and underlined below the .GIF file that you just placed on the page.**

    That's all there is to it.

Save the file as HOMEPG2.HTM and view it with a Web Browser that is configured for a VRML viewer. You can now create a Web page that has hyperlinks to VRML worlds.

Moving On

In this chapter you examined how two worlds operate. You then modified a world that wasn't working properly and began making the changes that would make this world display correctly.

Chapters 12 and 13 cover the VRML Version 1.0 specification. The VRML specification is in a constant state of flux, and by the time this book is in your hands, VRML Version 1.1 may have been agreed upon and be available. The question, then, is how do you keep up with current information on VRML? That's what the next chapter is all about.

PART IV
WHERE TO GO FROM HERE

File   Edit   View   Go   Bookmarks   Options   Directory   Help

VRML On-Line Sources

The number of locations where you can find VRML information and VRML worlds grows every day. In previous chapters, you learned about some of these locations, and this chapter lists some of the other ones. Please keep in mind that because of VRML's expansion and the growing acceptance of it as the Internet standard for 3D graphics, any list such as this one is outdated the day that it is created. Therefore, some of the URLs we have listed may be gone by the time you read this, and others will have been created. Happy surfing!

The Virtual VRML List

The following list is in alphabetical order by URL location. After each location, we have provided a short description of what you can find there. The list includes everything from discussions of virtual reality, interactivity, and behaviors, to information on the people involved with VRML and the software and hardware that make 3D on the Web possible.

Please remember that this is not a complete list of everything that is out there. No such list could ever exist, given the constant changeability of the Internet. Also remember that new subdirectories are constantly being added and directories are being changed, so new information may be available. Be sure and drop us e-mail at 76270.551@CompuServe.com if you find additions for this list.

`majordomo@wired.com`

Send an e-mail message to this address if you want to subscribe to the VRML mailing list. Paul lurks on this list.

`worldbuilders-request@caligari.com`

This relatively new mail list provides an area where individuals can discuss world building and the tools involved, especially Caligari products such as trueSpace, trueSpace2, Fountain, and upcoming products. Again, Paul lurks on this list and occasionally contributes to the discussions. To be added to the list, send a message with the contents "subscribe" to this address.

`ftp://ftp.netscape.com`

This site is one of many Netscape FTP locations. You can download various versions of Netscape here. Before you download a program, make sure that you use the BINARY command.

`ftp://ftp.portal.com/pub/fredness`

You'll find subdirectories for 3Dlabs and VRML at this ftp site.

`ftp://ftp.portal.com/pub/fredness/VRML`

This subdirectory of the `ftp.portal.com` connection contains three VRML .WRL files: FWORLD1.WRL, FWORLD2.WRL, and FWORLD3.WRL. You can download these worlds and use your VRML viewer to view them.

`ftp://ftp.webmaster.com`

WebMaster's FTP site has several subdirectories that contain many programs and applications that may be useful to you. Among the programs available is the latest version of WorldView.

`ftp://ftp.webmaster.com/Internet_Apps`

This subdirectory of WebMaster's FTP site contains a variety of Internet programs and applications that you can use to improve your access to the Internet.

`ftp://ftp.webmaster.com/VRML`

The three subdirectories here are MODELS, SOFTWARE, and SPECIFICA-TIONS. The MODELS subdirectory contains three subdirectories: BASIC, WORLDVIEW, and MISC, which hold a variety of VRML .WRL files that you can download and use for testing your VRML viewer. The SOFTWARE subdirectory under VRML contains three subdirectories also: BROWSERS, CONVERTERS, and MODELERS.

`ftp://ftp.webmaster.com/Windows`

You can download the latest version of Win32s here, as well as other NT, 95, or 3.11 assistance files.

`http://alex-immersion.army.mil/vr.html`

This is the Army Research Institute (ARI) Virtual Reality Research home page. At this location, you will find information on several areas of research on topics such as cognitive tracking, PC-based virtual reality, and immersive training programs.

`http://bug.village.virginia.edu/vrml`

This site is the VRML site for WaxWeb.

`http://dis.pica.army.mil`

Everything you ever wanted to know about DIS (Distributed Interactive Simulation) is available at this URL. This system is used for massive military conflict simulations.

`http://earth.path.net/mitra`

This site is Mitra's home page. Mitra, a programmer with Worlds Inc., is involved in VRML world creation and contributes often to the VRML mailing list mentioned earlier in this chapter. Worlds Inc. is the originator of WorldChat and VRML+.

```
http://home.netscape.com
```

This site is Netscape's home page, where you can download the most recent version of Netscape and learn interesting information about such topics as how to find things on the Internet.

```
http://home.netscape.com/assist/net_sites/index.html
```

This site has information on creating your own Web page. It has documents on beginning to use HTML, composing with HTML, adding extensions to HTML, and writing HTML. It also has software to use when creating Web pages.

```
http://home.netscape.com/assist/helper_apps/index.html
```

At this site you will find a list of archive sites of documents and applications that are useful in setting up your software; configuration advice; and advanced geek information, such as MIME documentation and advanced graphics capabilities.

```
http://www.intervista.com/worldview.html
```

From this Web page, you can download the most current version of WorldView.

```
http://java.sun.com
```

This home page is for Sun's HotJava. HotJava is a Web browser written in Java, which is Sun's Internet programming language.

```
http://nemo.nscl.nist.gov
```

This is the home page for the Systems and Software Technology Division of the National Institute of Standards and Technology. The main thrust of this page is the discussion of the open systems environments standards.

```
http://nemo.ncsl.nist.gov/~sressler
```

On this Open Virtual Reality Testbed home page, you'll find a list of other virtual reality locations on the Net, as well as the House of Immersion, a VRML world written as part of an immersion study.

http://private.worlds.net/mitra/papers/behaviors.html

This is Mitra's proposal for a VRML behaviors API.

http://sunee.uwaterloo.ca/~broehl

This is Bernie Roehl's home page. Roehl, author of *Playing God* and coauthor of *Virtual Reality Creations*, has personal information here, as well as information concerning the various virtual reality software packages and tools he is working with. Among those tools is the WLD2VRML conversion utility that's available on the CD-ROM that's included with this book. Information concerning future improvements on this tool will be available at this location.

http://sunee.uwaterloo.ca/~broehl/avril.html

This page describes Bernie Roehl's AVRIL, A Virtual Reality Interface Library.

http://uvacs.cs.virginia.edu/~rws2v

Richard Stoakley's research into user interface design for 3D environments is on his home page. It makes for interesting reading.

http://uvacs.cs.virginia.edu/~rws2v/wim

Here you will find hyperlinks to Richard Stoakley's Worlds in Miniature research. Download this page for directions to some extremely interesting reading.

http://vr-atlantis.com

This is Atlantis Cyberspace. With more than 250 pages and 30MB of pictures and movies to download, this area is definitely worth looking at. Of special interest are the Home VR and What is VR areas.

http://vrml.wired.com

This is the VRML forum. You'll find the archives of previous mail list discussions as well as other locations where you can find VRML related materials.

```
http://vrml.wired.com/arch/1107.html
```

This archive in the VRML forum contains a discussion of using QvLib and C++ to create a parser for reading VRML files.

```
http://www.access.digex.net/~starfyr/index.html
```

Check this out if you are interested in adventure games. This example of the beginnings of interactivity on the Internet is not specifically VRML, but you'll be surprised at what you may find by rummaging around in this area.

```
http://www.austin.ibm.com
```

IBM's Austin, Texas, location has software and technology areas that deal primarily with the AIX operating system and applications.

```
http://www.besoft.com
```

On this home page for the BE Software Company, you may want to check out the section that discusses the behavior engine (BE) and VRML. This document discusses a possible VRML extension for behaviors.

```
http://www.ccs.neu.edu/home/nop/mudwww.html
```

This page provides information about *MUD* implementations on the Web. (MUD stands for *Multi-User Dungeon.* See also Chapter 16.) Its value is in describing how MUDs have dealt with behaviors in the past.

```
http://www.chaco.com
```

This is the home page for Chaco Communication Inc., creators of the Pueblo and VRScout software. You'll find information on upgrading the software on the CD-ROM on this page.

```
http://www.chaco.com/pueblo
```

From this site, you can download a beta version of the Pueblo software. The most current version of Pueblo, as of September 1995, is on the CD-ROM that accompanies this book.

`http://www.cis.ohio-state.edu/hypertext/faq`

At this site, you can find specific documents concerning hypertext applications and implementations.

`http://www.comdex.com`

COMDEX is the world's largest information technology (IT) trade show, conference, and exhibition. This site provides for on-line registration to attend these events.

`http://www.compuserve.com`

This is CompuServe's Internet home page. Information concerning services available on CompuServe is available here, as well as notices concerning updated software.

`http://www.cruz.com:80/~hughes`

This home page for Peter J. Hughes, who has been involved with VRML since 1994, has some interesting papers dealing with VRML. This page has hyperlinks to a few worlds, including the following one.

`http://www.cruz.com:80/~hughes/tree/tropical_forest.wrl`

Peter J. Hughes likes trees. His home page shows this, and this VRML world file presents a forest of virtual trees for you to visit and enjoy.

`http://www.cs.tu-berlin.de/~jutta/toast.html`

This page provides a discussion of a sound compression application that future VRML extensions might emulate.

`http://www.cs.tu-berlin.de/~ki/engines.html`

This up-to-date listing of more than 100 3D graphics engines includes hyperlinks to the source code for DOOM and Wolfenstein type games engines.

`http://www.cs.uidaho.edu/lal/cyberspace/VR.VR.html`

This is Luke Sheneman's virtual reality page. Sheneman is another of the many people in cyberspace who work with virtual reality. This page includes a VR primer, information concerning creating your own virtual realities (sometimes referred to as *homebrew* or *garage VR*), and a cyberpunk area (for those of you for which this book is your first exposure to virtual reality and cyberspace, *cyberpunk* refers to a style of science fiction and to a lifestyle).

`http://www.csh.rit.edu/~airwick/dist.html`

The title of this page is Distributed Virtual Reality Resources. It provides access to many documents discussing the viability of distributed virtual realities. VRML is one form of distributed virtual reality.

`http://www.csl.sony.co.jp/project/VS`

This page is the Virtual Society information booth, and it includes a proposed extension to VRML. If you're interested in what the Virtual Society is, this is an excellent place to start.

`http://www.dimensionx.com`

Dimension X is a high-end Web-site development company, which uses IcedJava, its own extension to Java, and recommends the use of the HotJava browser for accessing the Web.

`http://www.division.com`

This is the home page of Division, Limited, which is one of the world's leading virtual reality applications companies. Through this page's hyperlinks to other pages, you can check the price of Division's stock and visit an entertainment area.

`http://www.divelabs.com`

This is the home page for Dive Laboratories Inc. Dive Labs is currently in the process of releasing Amber, a 3D virtual reality development system for Windows NT, Windows 95, and Windows 3.1.

http://www.europa.com/~keithr/

This is the home page for Keith Rule, who created WCVT2POV. You can down-load WCVT2POV here, but it's on the CD-ROM that accompanies this book. Rule has said that there will be no new versions of this program, so the one on the CD-ROM should be the most up-to-date version available. Check this site from time to time to see what Rule is up to.

http://www.fourmilab.ch/documents/hacklinks.html

This document describes a method for the exchange of sound information between two sites tied together with URLs.

http://www.ftech.net/~anywhere/bio

At this location, you can read the autobiography of David Galbraith, who is one of the founders of Realtime Anywhere, a multimedia design agency in London.

http://www.geom.umn.edu:80/software/geomview

This page describes one of the software projects at the Geometry Center at the University of Minnesota. Geomview is a program for use on an SGI system, but the source code is available here and can be examined and studied for other applications.

http://www.geom.umn.edu:80/software/Weboogl

Here you'll find a discussion of WebOOGL, another "semi-VRML compliant" Web browser created at the Geometry Center at the University of Minnesota. Again, the source code is available for study, but the software is for use on an SGI or Sun system.

http://www.hhcl.com

This is the home page of the Howell, Henry, Chaldecott, and Lury advertising agency in London. The agency now refers to itself as doing 3D marketing. There is some interesting material here: Take the time to look at their favorite places list.

http://www.hyperion.com/intervista

Intervista Software Inc. makes its home on this page. Tony Parisi, one of the cocreators of VRML, is the president of this company. You can download the latest version of WorldView and several test worlds from this site.

http://www.hyperreal.com/~mpesce/circle.wrl

Here is one of the many worlds available on the Web. This one, however, was created by Mark Pesce, one of the cocreators of VRML.

http://www.ibm.com

This is IBM's home page. You can find out what's happening with Big Blue in this virtual news magazine.

http://www.intsim.com/~isigen

This is the home page of Interactive Simulations Inc., San Diego, California. This company deals primarily with biotechnological and pharmaceutical industries. SCULPT is the SGI platform software package that the company uses and sells for scientific visualization projects.

http://www.intervista.com/worldview.hmtl

This is another way to access Tony Parisi's company, Intervista Inc. This location provides easy access to the current version of WorldView.

http://www.magnet.com/~jah/index.html

This is the home page of Jeffrey Holmes at Magnet Interactive Studios. This page has a great deal of material, and some of it even has something to do with VRML. Check out the VRML Test Bed.

http://www.media.mit.edu

This is the home page of the Media Lab at MIT. Current research in visualization as well as other topics is presented and described. In some cases, demonstrations are available.

http://www.merl.com

At this location, you will find the site for Mitsubishi Electronic Research Laboratories (MERL), which is located in Cambridge, Massachusetts. Check out the demonstration of an Interactive Multimedia Environment. There is a hyperlink to the next site that is listed.

http://www.merl.com/merle

This is MERL's Interactive Multimedia Environment, which is called Merle's Virtual Adventure.

http://www.netpower.com

This is the home page for NeTpower Inc. in Sunnyvale, California. This company home page deals with Windows NT and offers Open Inventor for Windows NT, a 3D graphics toolkit for Visual C++ 4.0, and several other software packages.

http://www.newcollege.edu/vrmLab

This page is maintained by Jeff Sonstein at the New College of California. It includes many areas of interest, two of which are listed below.

http://www.newcollege.edu/vrmLab/Packages

This site has a fairly comprehensive list of downloadable Web product packages, ranging from browsers to editors.

http://www.newcollege.edu/vrmLab/Warehouse

This site has an extensive library of VRML objects, including creatures, airplanes and spacecraft, computer equipment, and household objects.

http://www.ncsa.uiuc.edu

This is the URL for the National Center for SuperComputing Applications (NCSA) at the University of Illinois at Champaign. This is an excellent place to start exploring when in search of what computers can make possible.

http://www.ncsa.uiuc.edu/General/VRML

Clicking the Multimedia Exhibits icon on the NCSA home page and then selecting VRML in the list of exhibits takes you to the VRML at NCSA page. Entering the URL into the Location window of your browser will also get you here. Applications include VRML examples from fields such as cosmology and numerical relativity and a VRML navigator through a variety of texture examples.

http://www.northnet.org/VisNet

 This is the home page for John Gwinner's VisNet Inc. For the CD-ROM that's included with this book, VisNet provided the VisCIS demo and the VisMenu program that was used for the user interface.

http://www.oki.com/people/jch

This home page for Jan C. Hardenbergh has information about Jan and some of his personal observations. Jan taught a course at Siggraph 95 on VRML.

http://www.oki.com/vrml

Here you will find four .WRL files that are linked together, as well as a link to Jan Hardenbergh's Siggraph 95 course slides and the VRML FAQ.

http://www.paperinc.com

 At this home page for Paper Software Inc., you can get the most recent version of WebFX, which is on the CD-ROM that accompanies this book.

http://www.paragraph.com

 This is the home page for ParaGraph International, which brought you Home Space Builder. There are several very good software packages here that you may find useful. You can arrange to purchase them as well as the updated version of Home Space Builder at this site.

http://www.radiance.com/~radiance

Here you will find a description of Ez3d graphics software for the SGI platform.

`http://www.sd.tgs.com/~template`

At this home page for Template Graphics Software Inc. (TGS), you'll find information about Open Inventor, WebSpace, and many other VRML related topics.

`http://www.sd.tgs.com/~template/WebSpace`

This page takes you directly to TGS's WebSpace download area. Currently, versions are available for many platforms, including Windows NT and Windows 95 but not Windows 3.1.

`http://www.sdsc.edu`

This site is the home page for the San Diego SuperComputing Center. Established in 1985 by the National Science Foundation, SDSC is a national laboratory for computational science and engineering. Several other pages, including the next five sites in this list, are available via hyperlink from this page.

`http://www.sdsc.edu/EnablingTech/Visualization/Behaviors`

Here is a discussion of VRBS, the virtual reality behavior system, proposed by SDSC as an extension to VRML.

`http://www.sdsc.edu/Events/vrml95`

Here are some of the papers to be presented at the VRML symposium, which will be held at the University of California at San Diego in December 1995.

`http://www.sdsc.edu/SDSC/Partners/vrml`

This is the VRML Repository at SDSC. You can learn about events, applications, and software, as well as many other topics from the considerable amount of information that's available here.

`http://www.sdsc.edu/SDSC/Partners/vrml/examples.html`

This site is a list of sample applications using VRML.

http://www.sdsc.edu/SDSC/Partners/vrml/repos_software.html

This site is a list of software and utilities for creating and viewing VRML.

http://www.sgi.com/Products/WebFORCE/WebSpace

This is the Silicon Graphics page on WebSpace. From here you can find tools, utilities, and libraries of software for the SGI platform.

http://www.sgi.com/Technology/Inventor

Here you will find all sorts of information on Open Inventor. There's even a Free Stuff area.

http://www.ssec.wisc.edu/~billh/vis.html

This page describes the visualization project of the Space Science and Engineering Center of the University of Wisconsin at Madison. You'll find two visualization systems (Vis5D and VisAD) and the Mesa 3D graphics library API, which is very similar to that of OpenGL.

http://www.tc.cornell.edu/Visualization/Contrib/cs490-94to95/ckline/dx2vrml/dx2vrml.html

This page presents a student project at Cornell University that translates Data Explorer files to VRML. These files are workstation files.

http://www.ee.washington.edu/UWWeb.html

This site is the University of Washington WWW Developer's Group home page. Its virtual library is worth examining.

http://www.worldserver.pipex.com/3Dlabs

At this home page, you can get information about GLINT, one of the most interesting, inexpensive, and usable 3D graphics accelerator cards on the market today.

http://www.virtpark.com/theme

Here you'll find the home page for Scott Virtual Theme Parks. It includes an on-line area for the creation of VRML worlds online.

http://www.virtus.com

This site is the home page for Virtus Corporation, the makers of Virtus Walk-Through Pro and WalkThrough VRML.

http://www.vrml.com

Here is the home page of Infinite Light Inc., distributors of InterVista Software's WorldView.

http://www.w3.org

This home page of the WWW Consortium has a great deal of information about Web projects and the various versions of HTML.

http://www.webmaster.com

The first thing you see at this site is an option for high or low bandwidth. You need a 28.8 or higher connection for the high bandwidth, so if you're connecting through a 14.4 CompuServe connection, go the low route. This site is WebMaster's home page. You'll find a hyperlink to Mark Owen's home page here, as well as information on downloading the latest versions of WorldView.

http://www.well.com/www/jack

This is the home page of Inner Action Corporation, the company that is developing a VRML world-building tool that is code named PORTAL. You can get information about PORTAL here.

http://www.worlds.net

This site, which is the home page for Worlds Inc., has information on Worlds Chat and VRML+.

```
http://www.ziff.com/~pcmag
```

At this *PC Magazine* Web site, you can download all sorts of Internet software for free.

```
http://www-dsed.llnl.gov/documents/WWWtest.html
```

This test page contains a variety of movie, image, and sound file formats that you can use to test your browser to make sure that it's working properly with the installed viewers.

```
http://xanadu.net/the_project
```

This is an open hypermedia publishing experiment. Explore this to see what is going on in the area of Web publishing.

Virtual First Steps

This chapter has brought us full circle. In Chapters 1 and 2, we began our search for VRML and Internet 3D graphics. In this chapter we have returned again to the Web.

VRML is a constantly changing, ever-evolving, growing entity, and the people who were involved in its conception are still involved in its evolution. No printed media, such as this book, could ever hope to be the last word on VRML. In fact, this book may very well be a historical artifact almost as soon as it reaches your hands.

Windows 3.1 is still the dominant user platform at the time of this writing, but Windows 95 has just been released and will very definitely move toward platform domination. Many of you may have already made the change. You may be forced to upgrade hardware and software as support for the 16-bit platform fades into memory. Already, IBM and other vendors have made marketing decisions based on not supporting or releasing future 16-bit applications.

The result is that we will probably be revising this book in the very near future simply to provide you with Windows 95 versions of VRML viewers and other software. Interestingly enough, VRML Version 1.1, building on what you've learned in this book, will be released about the same time that this book reaches your book store. Within a year, perhaps, we will have VRML Version 2.0, with all of the behaviors (the ability to interact with objects in the virtual world) that so many of us want and need for our applications.

Interactive 3D graphical interfaces on the Internet are almost here. This book is just one of the first virtual steps that you need to make toward becoming a VRML guru. Learn from this book and then build those virtual worlds and let us know where they are so that we can include their locations on the next book's CD-ROM. Again, our e-mail address is 76270.551@CompuServe.com.

Moving On

The next chapter is a glossary of terms used in virtual reality and Internet programming. As with any glossary, some words change meaning on almost a daily basis. These definitions can help you understand where the Internet, the Web, VR, and VRML stand today.

We've had fun writing this book and met a large group of interesting and dedicated people in the process. We hope that reading about them and their work has been fun for you. We also hope that next time you'll be one of those people we meet.

See you in cyberspace.

Glossary

2Morrow World Builder

A program written by Todd Porter to create and view virtual worlds. The shareware version of this program is on the CD-ROM that's included with this book.

3D coordinate system

The three-dimensional equivalent of the Cartesian coordinate system. See also *Cartesian coordinate system.*

3D interface

A three-dimensional interface between the user and the software.

3DR

Intel's three-dimensional graphics tool-kit for Microsoft Windows. 3DR gives Windows graphics applications a standard, device-independent programming interface for the rendering of three-dimensional functions.

3DS

The 3DStudio file extension. 3DStudio is a graphics program made by AutoCad. You can use trueScape2 to save graphics files in this format.

algorithm

A formula, well-defined rules, or a procedure for solving a problem. A series of steps is used, usually via mathematical equations, to accomplish a logical or mathematical process in a clear, concise manner.

aliasing

1. A visual representation resulting from producing an image by sampling the image at a sample frequency lower than the highest spatial frequencies contained in the image. Aliasing occurs when a real scene is reduced to the number of samples dictated by the available pixels on a display screen. Undesirable effects include the stair-stepping of surface edges, the breaking up of thin lines into dots, and moiré patterns in finely detailed areas. 2. To use the same instance of a node multiple times (a node may be the child of more than one group).

ambient color

Color with no direct light.

anti-aliasing/antialiasing

In the generation of images, any technique that is used to remove undesirable effects, such as staircasing and line breakup, that are caused by aliasing. Techniques that are applied before the sampling prevent aliasing rather than removing it. Several filters are commonly used for anti-aliasing.

API

The acronym for *application program interface*. It defines the interface standards for an application: how an application should appear to the user, how input should be requested and obtained, and how output should be done.

Archie

A method for searching the entire world's FTP servers for files. Much like another service called Veronica, Archie makes it easier to find the files you are looking for. Because of the number of files on the Internet, a search through this service can take a long time and provide a long list of results.

ARPA

The Advanced Research Projects Administration, the arm of the U.S. Department of Defense that created the ARPANET.

ARPANET

This network was begun during the late 1960s by the Advanced Research Projects Administration (ARPA). Its purpose was to connect several research institutions and laboratories. It

had two goals: to coordinate research among the various labs and to create a completely decentralized network.

array

A collection of individual data items organized so that the entire collection can be treated as a single piece of data. The individual elements of the array have like data types, thus enabling them to be addressed individually or as a group.

ASCII

The acronym for the *American Standard Code for Information Interchange*. It refers to the character coding system most commonly used by computer systems to convert numeric values to humanly understandable characters and digits. It also works in the reverse.

asynchronous communication

The transmission of information between two devices in which intercharacter timing is not synchronized. Rather, the beginning and end of data packets is indicated by start and stop bits.

AT

A 286 or above PC or IBM clone.

AVRIL

An acronym for *A Virtual Reality Interface Library*. Created by Bernie Roehl, AVRIL is a PC-based VR application that contains a polygon-based rendering engine and support routines. It is free for noncommercial use.

B-spline

Basis spline. A method specifying control points to determine the shape of a curve that is very similar to the Bezier curve, but allows additional control of shape and continuity.

base 10

The normal counting system, which is based on the use of ten digits.

beta

A new software that's being tested by users prior to its commercial release. Beta testing provides for the discovery of problems before software is marketed to the general public.

binary

The numeric system used by computers that's based on the powers of 2. The digits 0 and 1 are used exclusively.

bitmap

A representation of the characters or graphics in a display by individual pixels. These are usually arranged in order of a row of pixels horizontally, and then additional similar rows follow to make up all the rows in the display. Monochrome data can be represented by one bit per pixel, but color displays may require up to 32 bits per pixel.

BMP

The abbreviation and file extension for *bitmap*. See *bitmap*.

bounding box

Used to simplify ray tracing, it is a rectangular polyhedron that encompasses one or more primitive objects. If the ray doesn't intersect the bounding box, it doesn't intersect the enclosed primitive objects, so no more testing is required. However, if the ray intersects the bounding box, more complex tests are needed to determine whether the ray intersects any of the enclosed objects. Using the bounding box approach reduces the amount of computer time required for intersect testing.

browser

A computer program used to view World Wide Web pages. Different browsers offer different Internet tools, but most offer, at the very least, gopher, FTP, and telnet. A browser is an intuitive graphical program that sends specific commands to the computer site that you are accessing and then displays the information contained in the page you are viewing. The basic types of browsers are line-mode browsers and graphical browsers.

bus

A set of lines on which signals are entered for use by many devices that are connected together.

bus topology

The computer network topology in which a single transmission medium, called a *bus,* is used to connect each computer in the network. Usually a coaxial cable is the transmission medium in networks using bus topology, resulting in the coaxial cable's actually being the bus. See also *bus.*

CAD

The acronym for Computer-Aided (or-Assisted) Design (or Drafting).

Cartesian coordinate system

The common rectangular coordinate system, consisting of three mutually perpendicular axes known as x, y, and z, from which all points in a volume are referenced.

case sensitive

Differentiating between uppercase and lowercase letters. That is, the letter *a* is treated differently from the letter *A*.

Cello

One of the first graphical browsers available, Cello is a 16-bit application. Developed at the Cornell University Law School, it is available for download by anonymous FTP.

CERN

The French acronym for the *European Center for Particle Physics*. In 1989, it became the birthplace of the Web, a collaborative effort to enable scientists to publish hypertext documents and make them available over the Internet.

CGI

An acronym for *computer generated images, Computer Graphics Interface,* or *Common Gateway Interface*. A Common Gateway Interface is a set of conditions that are guaranteed by the server and a set of rules that programs must follow; the CGI can be written in any language that can create console programs.

Chameleon

A commercial Web browser that uses a 16-bit application. It includes both Windows and HTML on-line help files, as well as printed documentation.

compiler

A program that translates the source code of an entire file into native machine code prior to execution.

compress

To use a software or hardware technique to reduce the storage space required for a set of data.

console program

A program whose interface is nongraphical and like a teletype. Contains a very simple, "stripped down" user interface. The most common languages used for console programs are UNIX, Shell, and Perl.

CU_HTML.DOT

A template that enables you to create HTML documents from inside Word for Windows. It is copyrighted by the Computer Services Centre of the Chinese University of Hong Kong, and it may be downloaded through FTP. This program and its URL are discussed in Chapter 2.

culling

Eliminating data from graphics processing by using tests to isolate objects that will ultimately be invisible in the finished image.

culling, backface

Testing faces of a convex polygonal object and eliminating faces that are not visible (as identified by the fact that the normal to the face is pointed away from the screen) so that they don't have to be processed in order to display.

cyberspace

William Gibson has been given credit for coining this term in his novel *Neuromancer*. Perhaps the simplest definition is the location of all electronic mediated communication.

Cyberspace Protocol

Allows for the visualization and maintenance of uniform definitions of objects, scene arrangements, and spatio-locations that would be consistent across the Internet. This was presented as a paper by Mark Pesce and is not an official protocol.

data bit

The character being transmitted.

decompress

To restore a compressed block of data to the original data state, thus reversing the compression.

Descent

Game from Parallax. Fly your Pyro-GX space fighter through mines and underground military installations. Has support for some HMD's.

diffuse color

The general color of an object.

DIS

Acronym for *Distributed Interaction Simulation*. This protocol is heavily used in U.S. military simulation systems. The system, which was created by John Locke, David R. Pratt, and Michael J. Zyda of the Department of Computer Science at the Naval Postgraduate School in Monterey, California, is mostly used to simulate battles.

DLL

Acronym for *dynamic link library* (Microsoft). DLLs are loaded into memory by an application when you run it. They enable you to create a library (file) of functions that can be called by the program's executable file. Using DLLs is a handy way to package usable functions without having to put them all together in one extremely large file. DLLs can be called by other programs and shared by different programs while stored in memory.

DMF

Acronym for *Distribution Media Format*. Microsoft's method of storing more data on 3½-inch disks. This results in the formatted disks' being 1.7MB.

Doom

Game from id. By manipulating the DOOM.WAD file, you can alter almost any aspect of the game yourself.

DXF

The standard file format of the 3-D universe. Most commonly used by AutoCad, it is also supported by many other software packages.

electronic publishing

Various texts and graphics published on the Net. Includes some magazines, newspapers, newsletters, and artwork.

emulator

A software package that enables one platform to behave or function in the same way as another platform.

Enhanced Mosaic 2.0

See *Mosaic.*

European Center for Particle Physics

See *CERN.*

extensibility

The capability to add new features to a node class without modifying existing code that uses that class.

eye point or eyepoint

Viewpoint. See also *POV.*

FAQ

The acronym for *frequently asked questions.* Many topics on the Web have FAQ pages that answer commonly asked questions about that particular topic.

field

1. An individual item of information in a database. A set of data elements (fields) describes the parameters of a node. 2. Data that makes up one vertical scan of a cathode-ray tube.

File Transfer Protocol

See *FTP.*

fixed-point number

The term *point* refers to the decimal point. In a fixed-point number, the decimal point is fixed in one position. Generally, this position is to the right of the number, making the number a whole number. As a result, the number is stored without a decimal point. See *floating-point number.*

floating-point number

In general, a number that contains a decimal point. The decimal point can be in any location. Floating-point numbers are suitable for representing values that contain fractional components. A floating-point number can be either a whole number or a fractional number. See *fixed-point number.*

FTP

The acronym for File Transfer Protocol, which is one of the de facto Internet standards that is used to transmit files over the Internet. Specific FTP servers contain specific types of files. FTP is often used as a verb, as in "to ftp a file to your computer."

G Web

The VRML-compatible, 3D graphics Web toolkit from Virtual Presence Ltd, London.

GEO

One of many polygon file formats. This format can be found at the FTP site `avalon.chinalake.navy.mil` and can be converted to VRML using WCVT2POV.

GERNET forum

A CompuServe forum for German-speaking participants.

GIF

Graphics interchange format. It is a file format developed by CompuServe for compressing and storing graphics image data. It is also the file extension given to files in this format.

glyphs

Basically, pictures or images. Typically, a character or a symbol.

gopher

A menu-driven search application on the Net that enables users to find a wide variety of information. This application, which was developed at the University of Minnesota, is a text-only service.

gray scale

The use of various shades from black to white to produce numerous shades of gray.

group node

A node that gathers other nodes into a group that can be treated as a single object by the browser.

GUI

The acronym for *graphical user interface*. A user interface system for either an operating system or a program that utilizes pictures and objects to communicate information. Contrasts with traditional text-based interfaces, which are menu driven or command driven.

GVU

The Graphics, Visualization, and Usability Center, which is affiliated with Georgia Tech's College of Computing. The center has performed WWW user surveys to obtain important information about Web demographics. Copies of both the surveys and the results are available for download through http.

```
http://www.cc.gatech.edu/
gvu/user_surveys/
User_Survey_Home.html
```

hacker

1. Basically, someone who builds their own hardware/software from ground zero, knowing the technology inside out. 2. The media uses the term to refer to persons who illegally crack their way into computer systems.

Hayes-compatible

A modem's compatibility with the modem command language that was developed by Hayes Microcomputer Products.

heading

Generally found at the beginning of a file. May include such information as title, date, program name, column headings, and so on.

head-mounted display

See *HMD*.

hexadecimal

Sometimes abbreviated as *hex*, it is a numerical system in which 16 digits are used instead of 10. In this system, the digits 0–9 are used as in a decimal system, and the letters A through F are used to represent counts of 10 through 15 in the decimal system. As a result, higher order numbers in the hexadecimal system have a different meaning than in the decimal system. For example, 10 in the hexadecimal system is the same as 16 in the decimal system. When running out of available symbols, the next count is represented by the first symbol with a 0 at its right. So, in the decimal system, you can count to 9 with the available symbols, and the next count is 10. However, in the hexadecimal system, you can count to F (equal to 15 in decimal), and the next count is 10.

HMD

The acronym for *head-mounted display*. A complex helmet-type device that includes position/orientation tracking, imaging devices, and optics for exploring virtual environments. It may also include sound technology. Many newer versions of HMDs are less bulky than their predecessors and look like an exaggerated pair of eyeglasses.

home page

The top-level document in a series of hyperlinked pages. The linked pages are secondary documents. See also *page*.

HotJava

An extensible Web browser from Sun that provides "executable content." Currently in alpha release.

HoTMetal

An SGML tool that beginners can use to learn how to create HTML documents. Requires Windows 3.1 and comes in both free and commercial versions.

HTML

The acronym for *HyperText Markup Language*. It acts as a source code for the Web.

HTML Assistant

Basically, a text editor with additions that assist the user in creating Web pages. Created in Visual Basic, it comes in both commercial and free versions.

HTML Writer

Created by Kris Nosack with Visual Basic, HTML Writer is a text-based editor created for building and editing Web pages using HTML.

http

The acronym for *Hypertext Transfer Protocol*. The http prefix on a URL means that the address is for a document containing hypertext and hyperlinks to other documents.

hyperlink

Pertaining to a hypertext system. A link is established between a word or phrase in one document and another document that further explains that word or phrase or has information on a related issue.

hypermedia

All media, audiovisual or textual, that contains connections to other media.

hypertext

Text that contains connections to other text. For example, if a hypertext system contains an article about dogs and it mentions that dogs are mammals, the reader may be able to use the word *mammals* to find another article in the system on mammals.

IICM

Information Processing and Computer Supported New Media located at Gratz University of Technology, Austria.

ImageView graphics utility

Included in the Mosaic in a Box 1.0 commercial version of Mosaic. This utility allows you to view graphic images.

inline/inlining

These terms refer to the practice of including directions for the inclusion of a separate file in the file that's currently being worked on. For C and C++ programmers, the #include statement is an example of this type of practice. For VRML, the WWWInline statement does the same thing. Inlining enables a given program or file to include other files while not having to either type or cut and paste the code from these files into the current project.

inputfile

In some programs, such as conversion applications, you need to tell the program what file to convert. This would be the inputfile. See also *outputfile*.

input/output

The process of moving data to a place where the computer can use it (input) or to another place after the computer has processed it (output).

instance

1. Object that belongs to some class. Class is a C++ keyword and structure that defines objects. 2. An occurrence of a graphical entity in a drawing.

instancing

1. Using the same instance of a node multiple times. 2. In 2D and 3D modeling, using multiple occurrences of the same object at different locations in the drawing. See also *instance*.

instantiation

Defining a graphics object in such a way that it may be used repeatedly at different locations in an image without completely redescribing it each time it is used.

interactive

The ability of a program and a user to interact with each other during execution of the program's action.

Internet

The world's largest computer internetwork.

Internet Protocol (IP) packet

Information sent over IP networks is broken up into these bite-sized pieces. The information contained within a packet is usually between 1 and 1,500 characters long.

internetwork

A system of interconnected networks.

InternetWorks

A commercial Web browser.

I/O

Acronym for input/output. See *input/output*.

ISDN

Acronym for *Integrated Services Digital Network*. An international telecommu-nications standard that allows the transmission of data, voice, and video over the same communications channel.

iteration

A single, complete repetition of a sequence of instructions.

Java

An object-oriented programming language developed by Sun to address the problems associated with distributing platform-independent code in an insecure and widely distributed network.

JPEG

Developed by the Joint Photographic Experts Group, JPEG is a proposed standard for image compression. It is sanctioned by the International Standards Organization (ISO) and the Comité Consultatif Internationale de Télégraphique et Téléphonique (CCITT).

JPG

Abbreviated form of *JPEG*. Is used as a file extension. See *JPEG*.

Kermit

Developed at Columbia University, this asynchronous communication protocol can be used on many dissimilar computer systems. Kermit does tend to be slower than other types of protocols however, because traditional versions use a 7-bit data format.

lag time

The time delay between two successive events. Usually refers to the delay between when a command is issued by the user and when the computer reacts to the command.

LAN

Acronym for *local area network*. Two or more computers connected in an arrangement that enables them to share data or other resources. A LAN will not extend across a public right-of-way, such as a telephone system.

level of detail

Node included in Open Inventor 2.0 that switches between models based on the screen area occupied by the model.

library

A set of commonly used routines that a program can call.

list

A collection of data items that are to be processed in a particular order.

LOD

A node included in Open Inventor 2.1 and VRML that switches models based on the distance that the specified center point is from the camera. This Group node enables applications to switch between various representations of objects automatically, showing various levels of detail of the same object perceived from different distances.

Manchester Scene Description Language

Created at the University of Manchester, in England, this language enables the user to specify 3D objects.

mask

A pattern of bits which are logically, using Boolean logic, ANDed with incoming data to determine which bits will survive and be further acted upon.

MF

In VRML, a multiple-valued field.

Microsoft Internet Assistant

Enables the use of Word for Windows 6.0 to create and view Web pages. It includes a built-in browser that uses Word as its viewing screen. It will allow creation of a document without entering a title field that is required by all browsers.

MID

Abbreviation and acronym for *Metafile for Interactive Documents*. Can also be used as the extension for MIDI files.

MIDI

Acronym for *Music Instrument Digital Interface*.

mirror site

An alternate Web site that contains copies of files, Web pages, and so on that are located at an original Web site. Mirror sites can be helpful when access to the original Web site is limited due to mass usage.

mnemonic

Refers to a word or code that is symbolic of another function, word, or code.

Mosaic

A browser that comes in several versions, both commercial and free. NCSA Mosaic 2.009a is a free version that's downloadable by anonymous FTP. Enhanced Mosaic 2.0 is a Spyglass, commercial version of Mosaic. Mosaic in a Box 1.0 is another commercial version; this package contains a default service provider (CompuServe), and the Imageview graphics utility. SPRY Air Mosaic is a commercial version by CompuServe, and it is included on the CD-ROM that accompanies this book.

Mosaic in a Box 1.0

See _Mosaic_.

MUD

A multiuser game.

multimedia

Hypertext-based systems that combine text, graphics, video, and sound with traditional data. Also referred to as _hypermedia_.

NAVFlyer 2.2

This viewer for 3D worlds from MicronGreen Inc. can be used in conjunction with a Web browser to view VRML worlds both online and offline. NAVFlyer 2.2 is on the CD-ROM that accompanies this book.

NCSA

An acronym for the National Center for Supercomputing Applications at the University of Illinois.

NCSA Mosaic 2.009a

See _Mosaic_.

Net

An abbreviation for the Internet. See _Internet_.

NetCruiser Plus 1.52

A commercial Web browser that works only in conjunction with Netcom.

Netscape Navigator

According to surveys, the most-used browser on the Web. It comes in both commercial and free versions for academic, nonprofit, and evaluation purposes.

network

Basically, a communications path between computers and computer peripherals. See also _LAN_.

network topology

The shape or geometric arrangement of the connected computers in a network. The three basic methods of network topology are star topology, ring topology, and bus topology. See also *star topology, ring topology,* and *bus topology.*

nibble

Four binary bits, or half of a byte. Also spelled *nybble.*

node

A fundamental part of a scene graph. A node contains data and methods that define some specific 3D shape, property, or grouping. A node is composed of a set of data elements, called *fields,* that describe the parameters of the node. See also *scene graph* and *field.*

noise

In communications, the interference taking place during the communication of the message.

NURB

Acronym for nonuniform rational B-spline. A mathematical description of a curved surface where the surface is specified as a ratio of two polynomials for each region of the spline.

OBJ

The file extension for an object in such programs as 2Morrow World Builder, AVRIL, REND386, VRBasic, VR386, and others.

object-oriented

1. Graphics operations dealing directly with primitive geometric figures instead of bit-mapped representations. 2. Computer programming in which collections of related data are formed into objects that are acted upon by sending and receiving messages to the objects.

object oriented programming

See *OOP.*

OLE

Abbreviation for *object linking and embedding.* A method for enhancing the interoperability between applications for Windows.

OOGL

Acronym for *object oriented geometry language.* Developed at the Geometry Center at the University of Minnesota, OOGL is a nonproprietary language that includes sophisticated graphics and support for hyperbolic geometry.

OOP

Acronym for *object oriented programming.* It is a programming technique that's based upon objects consisting of data structures that associate these structures with the operations upon them. The focus of the programming style is on the data instead of processes.

origin

The arbitrarily designated point of zero on the x-,y-, and z-axis.

orthogonal

Mutually perpendicular.

outputfile

In some programs, such as conversion applications, the program needs to be told where to place the converted material. This would be the outputfile. See also *inputfile*.

page

1. A hyperlinked document consisting of various combinations of text, graphics, digitized sounds, video animation, and virtual environments; its top-level document being its home page.
2. A screen of graphics.

parity

Used for error detection, it is an additional bit that is added to a block of data. Parity can be EVEN, ODD, NONE, MARK, or SPACE. In all instances, the setting of the parity bit will depend on the number of ones in the data bits. In EVEN parity, the parity bit is set to EVEN if the number of data bits set to 1 is odd. In ODD parity, if the number of data bits set to 1 is even, then the parity bit is set to ODD. If the parity is set to NONE, the parity bit is either ignored or not transmitted. MARK parity results in the parity bit's being set to 1. In SPACE parity, the parity is always set to 0.

parse

The process of analyzing a series of words in order to determine their collective meaning. Basically, every program that accepts user input, via commands, must perform some sort of parsing before acting upon the commands.

parser

The portion of a program that performs the parsing. See also *parse*.

PC FileFinder

The CompuServe search engine that searches CompuServe for PC files; part of CompuServe's on-line services.

PCI

Acronym for *peripheral component interconnect*.

PCX

Originated by Z-Soft Corporation and first used in the PC Paintbrush program, it is a file format that uses run-length encoding to store bitmapped graphics in compressed form.

PDF

Portable Document Format from Adobe. Enables a formatted document to be read by a large number of computers, using a PDF reader.

PHIGS

Acronym for *Programmer's Hierarchical Interface for Graphics System*. This software interface standard for graphics includes data structures for high-level three-dimensional applications.

Pinocchio button

In Home Space Builder, the image that represents the location of the user in the 3D world is called the Pinocchio button. It gets its name from the fact that a line, representing a nose or the direction that the eyes are looking, is located on the circle that represents the user. The line is rather long, like Pinocchio's nose in the children's story.

PKZIP

A file compression utility program from PKWARE Inc. that's available in a commercial version and as shareware.

PKUNZIP

A file decompression utility program from PKWARE Inc. that's available in a commercial version and as shareware.

platform

The particular hardware system on which a program will run.

PLG

Abbreviation for *polygon object.*

polygon

A two-dimensional figure that consists of an ordered set of vertices connected in sequence by sides that don't intersect.

polygon back faces

Those sides of a polygon that are not visually seen on the screen, the backside.

polygonally rendered objects

An object rendered through the use of polygons.

portable

The ability of a program or application to be translated or converted to another computer platform environment with a minimal amount of coding.

POV

The acronym for *point of view.* It usually refers to camera angles.

PowerGlove

Developed in a joint arrangement between VPL and Abrams-Gentile Entertainment, and manufactured by Mattel, this glove was originally sold as a game controller for the Nintendo. Because of its low cost, the PowerGlove was quickly adapted to use in virtual reality applications. Each glove has two ultrasonic transmitters on the back, pointing out toward the tips of the fingers. Receivers that have been placed around a television or monitor will pick up the ultrasonic signals and translate them into a position in space.

protocol

A formal set of conventions defining the format and control of I/O between the programs or devices.

QvLib

This is the library for QV, a quick VRML parser created by Paul Strauss of SGI. Versions of this library are available for Windows NT and Windows 3.x, as well as for other platforms.

radian

Unit of angle measure. The measure of a central angle of a circle whose intercepted arc is equal in length to the radius of the circle.

RAW

This relatively primitive graphics format supports only descriptions of triangles. No color or texture information is supported. The extension for this format is .RAW.

ray tracing

A technique used to create a realistic image by tracing light rays. Forward ray tracing entails tracing all rays of light that illuminate a scene, from the light source to the object they intersect, and then if there are reflections or refractions, continuing the tracing until the ray leaves the scene. Backward ray tracing results in the rays' being traced from the observer to the display screen and back to the scene objects and light source. Therefore, all reflections and shadows appear in the image without being specifically described in the scene description.

real-time

Actual time during which an event occurs.

REND386

A program written by Bernie Roehl and Dave Stampe to enable users to create virtual worlds on the PC. Version 5.0 includes support for head-mounted displays (HMDs), the PowerGlove, and greater keyboard, joystick, and mouse controls.

render

The process of converting a graphics image into an array of pixel colors for display.

rendering engine

That part of the code in a program or application that performs the conversion of the graphics image into the array of pixel colors for display.

RenderWare

Commercial software available from Criterion Software Ltd., in England, for building 3D applications on several platforms including DOS, Windows, and Sparc.

RGB

The primary colors, red, green, and blue, which are combined at various intensities in an additive color system to produce all intermediate shades.

ring topology

A network using ring topology has no end connections. The network is a continuous path that eventually returns to its origin. Data can travel in only one direction. Ring topology requires an unbroken connection between all computers.

scaleable format

This refers to the capability of a program to be usable and accessible to a wide range of platforms having a range of graphics capabilities, memory, and CPU speeds.

scene graph

An ordered collection of nodes. See also *node*.

scroll

To shift text either up, down, left, or right from its current on-screen position. In GUI environments, such as Microsoft Windows or the Macintosh, the arrows located at the right side or bottom of the display areas control the scrolling of the on-screen image or text.

SDSC

The acronym for the *San Diego Supercomputer Center*.

self-executing file

Generally refers to an installation program of some sort. This program will, upon execution, perform the functions of installation with little or no other input from the user.

sensory breadth

In an electronic or mechanically mediated communication, this concept refers to the number of human senses that are involved in the mediation. See also *sensory depth* and *vividness*.

sensory depth

In an electronic or mechanically mediated communication, this concept refers to the level of resolution, or quality, of the perceptual channel through which the communication is taking place. See also *sensory breadth* and *vividness*.

server

In reference to a computer network, a device that is dedicated to serving other nodes attached to the network.

service provider

The organization that provides the connection from your computer to the Internet system.

SGML

Standard Generalized Markup Language. Found mainly on high-end workstations. HTML is a subset.

shareware

Software distributed free of charge, but for which a user "donation" is requested. A user who likes a program is asked to send a suggested amount to the author of the software, who then may provide service, updates, or enhancements to the user.

SIGGRAPH

An annual computer graphics conference organized by the Special Interest Group, Graphics, of the American Association of Computing Machinery, an association of computing companies.

signal

In communications, the original message of the sender.

SlipKnot

A Web browser that's designed to work with slower modem connections without needing SLIP, PPP, or TCP/IP services from the service provider. It is available for download on CompuServe's Internet Resources forum.

SMTP

The acronym for *Simple Mail Transfer Protocol*. A common protocol that enables dissimilar computers to send mail to each other via the Net.

source code

Written by humans, this code is the programming instructions that cause a computer to execute a series of functions in an organized manner. An assembler or compiler translates the source code into object code that the computer can recognize and act upon.

spam

Any material sent to any particular "list" (such as a newsgroup, mail thread, list server, or mail list), that appears in other persons' mail boxes, and so on, is off the subject or considered worthless by the receiver. The term can be used as a noun, as in "That was certainly spam" or as a verb, as in "Watch it. I'll spam you!"

spline

A curve that is mathematically defined so as to provide a smooth path from one point to another, with a shape controlled by a number of control points. See also *B-spline*.

sprite

Often used in video game animation, it is a small movable graphics pattern on a display.

SPRY Air Mosaic

See *Mosaic*.

standard generalized markup language

See *SGML*.

star topology

A network configuration in which all of the computers in the network are connected to a central computer. Though the central computer is connected to each of the individual computers in the network, no individual computer in the network is connected to any other individual computer. Thus, all data traveling on the network must first go through the central computer before being routed to the individual destination computer.

start bit

In asynchronous communication, a bit that precedes the data bits and signals to the receiving computer that data is to follow.

state

The current condition or environment.

stop bit

In asynchronous communication, a bit that follows the data and parity bits, signaling to the receiving computer that the character is complete.

straw man

Generally refers to a proposal or plan that is put "out in the field" to see whether it generates comments or controversy.

string

A series of alphanumeric characters. The contents of a string are treated as though they were text, even if the string contains numbers.

Superscape VRT (Virtual Reality Toolkit)

A commercial VR creation package available for the PC.

surface specifier

Basically, denotes to the renderer what type of texture an object is supposed to have on its surfaces.

surfing

Refers to "cruising" the Web, visiting various Web sites.

TCP/IP

Transmission Control Protocol/Internet Protocol. Developed at the University of California for the U.S. Department of Defense, this is the standard for communications between internetworked computers. This relatively slow protocol provides communication between different computer platforms.

telnet

A remote log-in service for the Internet that allows the user to access another Internet site as if the two sites were directly connected. It is a wide-area packet-switched network service. The upside is that log-ins can be made with no long-distance fees. Unfortunately, the downside is that telnet is notoriously slow.

TIFF

The acronym for *tagged image file format*. It is a common file format used to store bitmapped graphics images. The common file extension for this type of file is .TIF.

toolkit

A set of utility programs. Normally furnished along with the main program to enable performance of applications not included in the main program.

topology

The layout scheme for a network. It is a set of geometric properties related to connectivity — in particular, the definition of nodes and their interconnection and constraints on the pathways of interconnected networks. See also *star, ring,* and *bus topology.*

Tpoly

This graphics file format is a slight variation of the RAW file format. The extension for this format is .TPO.

traversal

The process of sequentially addressing and processing the elements of a display. In other words, the information provided in the data file, starting at the first element and continuing through to the last, is identified, given a location on the display, and processed so as to provide the image that is seen.

ttf

TrueType font file.

URL

Acronym for *Uniform Resource Locator.* It specifies the exact location for a specific Internet resource.

uudecode

A method that converts uuencoded files back to binary format for use on the receiving system. See also *uuencode.*

uuencode

A widely used encoding scheme on the Internet that converts binary files to text so that they can be transmitted over the system. See also *uudecode.*

VeRGe

The San Francisco Bay area virtual reality group named Virtual Reality Educational Foundation.

vertex

A point which denotes the intersection of two or more edges of a polygon or some other graphics object.

vertices

The plural of vertex. See also *vertex.*

virtual reality

See *VR.*

Virtual Reality Studio

A PC-based VR software package created by Domark. Versions 1.0 and 2.0 are available. It can be used to create self-executing demos and games with a 286 or higher PC.

Virtus WalkThrough Pro 2.0

A commercial package produced by Virtus Corporation for creating virtual worlds on the PC.

Virtus WalkThrough VRML

A VRML creation tool from Virtus Corporation for creating virtual worlds on the PC.

Vistapro

A commercial three-dimensional landscape-simulation program for the PC.

vividness

A measure of the degree to which a technology, an electronic or mechanical system, can produce a sensorially rich mediated environment — in other words, how close the technology can come to the "real" experience of an environment without mediation. The electronic or mechanical system must extend the human senses. See also *sensory breadth* and *sensory depth*.

VPL (Research)

A company founded by Jaron Lanier, who coined the term *virtual reality*. VPL's DataGlove and EyePhones are now widely used in the VR research community.

VR

The acronym for virtual reality. A mediated electronic environment that exists only within the confines of the program that's executing the environment and disappears from existence when no longer in use.

VR386

Written by Dave Stampe, this program is an expansion of the REND386 software written by Dave Stampe and Bernie Roehl. VR386 provides for the use of extended memory in creating VR worlds on the PC. It is sometimes referred to as REND386 Version 6.0. It can be downloaded, and the location where it can be found is discussed in Chapter 4.

VRBasic

A commercial software package for creating virtual worlds for the PC, from Waite Group Press. The program was written by Zane Thomas.

VR Creator

A commercial software package for creating virtual worlds that's available from VREAM, Inc.

VREAM

The name of a company as well as a virtual reality development system available from that company.

VRML

The acronym for *Virtual Reality Modeling Language*. Mark Pesce describes VRML as "a language for describing multi-user interactive simulations — virtual worlds networked via the global Internet and hyperlinked within the World Wide Web."

VRWeb 0.53 Beta

A VRML browser that runs under Windows using Win32s. Versions are also available for Windows 95 and Windows NT.

VT100 emulator

A popular and widely used terminal type that was originally developed by Digital Equipment Corporation (DEC).

W3 Consortium

An industry consortium led by the Laboratory for Computer Science at the Massachusetts Institute of Technology. Its goal is to promote standards and to strive for interoperability between Web products.

WAIS

An acronym for *Wide-Area Information Server's.* It provides for the retrieval of information from Internet databases, though it is textually based. Everything is either an index or a document returned from an index.

WaxWeb

An Internet-based, distributed, interactive and intercommunicative 3D narrative environment. Based on David Blair's feature film, *WAX or the discovery of television among the bees,* it contains approximately 25,000 hyperlinks, 5,000 color stills, 85 minutes of digital video, and more than 250 3D VRML scenes.

Web

Abbreviation for World Wide Web. See also *World Wide Web.*

Web browser

See *browser.*

WebFX

VRML viewer by Paper Software Inc. Three different versions of WebFX are available for Windows 3.1 Web browsers.

Web publishing

Electronic publishing occurring on the Web portion of the Net. See also *electronic publishing.*

WebSpace

A commercial VRML browser/viewer from Silicon Graphics Inc. and Template Graphics Software.

Web Weaver

An editor that assists with the creation and editing of HTML documents through automation. Requires Windows 3.1 and is downloadable. The location is provided in Chapter 3.

whitespace

1. Characters such as spaces, tabs, and new-lines that appear outside of the string field. 2. Related to typography, it is the white space left on a page in order to give the page a pleasing appearance.

Wide-Area Information Server

See *WAIS.*

wide area network

A method of networking or connecting computers separated by long distances by using modems to send and receive signals. Communication is, therefore, independent of the computers using the network.

Win32s

Software that provides 32-bit extensions and capabilities to Windows 3.1. It includes a set of DLLs and a virtual device driver (VxD) that enables 32-bit applications to run on top of Windows or Windows for Workgroups. Provided on the CD-ROM that accompanies this book.

WinCIM

CompuServe's Information Manager for Windows.

WinG

An enhanced graphics library from Microsoft.

winWeb

A browser that's available in both commercial and free versions. Can be downloaded through anonymous FTP or is available as shareware. See Chapter 2 for more information.

WinZip

The Windows file compression utility.

WLD

The virtual world file format used by 2Morrow World Builder, REND 386, AVRIL, VR Basic, and VR 386.

word

A word is a basic unit of data manipulation and storage. It is generally equal to 2 bytes or 16 bits. Values ranging from 0 to 65,536 can be contained in a word. On some computer systems, a word may more aptly be defined as the number of bits that can be processed at a single time.

world parser

A software engine that reads the VRML file and converts the geometry definitions and the visualized geometry to produce a set of objects that can be manipulated by the computer.

WorldView

A VRML browser/viewer by InterVista Software Inc. Provided on the CD-ROM that accompanies this book.

World Wide Web

A system or method for accessing information on the Internet. The World Wide Web consists of a multitude of documents, graphics, videos, and other multimedia resources that are scattered throughout the Internet. These resources, which are linked together through hypertext, exist in a collection of computers that are located in many geographical locations around the world.

WRL

The file extension (meaning world) for VRML files.

WWW

Acronym for *World Wide Web*. See also *World Wide Web*.

The Creating Cool 3D Web Worlds with VRML CD-ROM

Appendix

Credits

Although we have acknowledged the contributions of many people earlier in this book, we want to stress here that this CD-ROM represents the creative efforts of many people, who, as we came closer and closer to the final deadline, lived off mugs of coffee and looked at their computer screens through bleary eyes as they pulled these software applications and examples together for you to use. From New York to California, from Florida to Alaska, from all over North America, the CD-ROM you have with this book is the product of the efforts of many people who believe in the future of VRML, of virtual reality, and of 3D graphics and virtual reality on the Internet. We sincerely appreciate those efforts. The VRML community is better for having these people as citizens, and we are better human beings for knowing them and counting them as our friends.

Installing the User Interface

If you're using Windows 95, when you access your CD-ROM drive a file named AUTORUN.INF automatically runs and installs the necessary files for the CD-ROM user interface.

If you're using Windows 3.1*x*, choose Run from the File menu and type **X:\setup** where X represents the drive designation of your CD-ROM. The user interface setup program begins. Follow the directions to install the necessary files.

Starting the CD-ROM User Interface

After installation is complete, double-click on the VisMenu icon in the Creating Cool 3D Web CD subdirectory. VisMenu will load, and you'll see a VisMenu opening title screen while the program loads. When the program is loaded, you'll find yourself in the middle of a plaza with a newsstand on your left and a blue building with the word "Setup" on your right. You'll see billboards behind these, the VRML background on the left, and a man with his back to you and his arms raised on the right.

If you have problems at this point, choose options from the File menu. You should have a window labeled General Options. In the Directories section of this window, make sure that the first text box, VisCIS (if installed), includes the hard drive that you installed the program to, followed by the directory. For instance, if you installed the program to your C drive, it would read C:\VISMENU.

The next text box, VRML Files, should then read C:\VISMENU\SUPPORT (or whatever drive you loaded the program on). Finally, make sure that the CD-ROM Location textbox correctly identifies the letter of your CD-ROM drive. Now click OK at the bottom of this window and exit the VisMenu program. Double-click on the VisMenu icon again and the program should run more smoothly.

Moving Around in the CD-ROM City

Movement is easy. Simply hold down the left button on your mouse and move the mouse. Your view will move in the direction that you have moved the mouse. The up, down, left, and right arrow keys will move you around the world, also.

Try moving over to one of the nearby newsstands. Release the left button, and in the lower-left corner of the VisMenu window you'll see the name of the area. Each area of the city is identified in this way.

Click on the Help menu for more assistance in moving around the city, editing buildings, and adding programs. You'll also find assistance for the menu commands here.

What's in the CD-ROM City?

Each program on the CD-ROM has at least one building associated with it, and in most cases, several buildings. The newsstand that sits in front most often is a README file associated with the specific program. Green buildings are most often documentation files for the program; gold buildings are help files for the program; and the big blue buildings, with the word *setup* on the side, are the setup and installation procedures for the program. Double-clicking on any of the buildings runs the specific application that the building represents.

The CD-ROM user interface includes buildings that provide access to and installation of the following programs and files:

➠ Over 200 VRML .WRL files to examine and explore from 3DWeb, Caligari Corpor., Chaco Communication Inc., InterVista Inc., MicronGreen Inc., Paper Software Inc., ParaGraph International, Viewpoint Datalabs, Virtus Corp., and VisNet Inc.

➠ 3DWeb's Spinner, an easy-to-use VRML world creation tool.

➠ A demo of Caligari's trueSpace2, a product that provides powerful, usable 3D graphics and animation for Windows.

➠ A demo of Todd Porter's 2morrow World Builder. This program enables you to create virtual reality worlds (.WLD format) from DOS. Included in the demo is a program that enables you to convert these worlds to VRML.

➠ A demo of VisNet's VisCIS, the virtual reality interface for CompuServe.

➠ Caligari's Fountain, a VRML creation tool and viewer that provides for both the creation of VRML worlds and the viewing of VRML worlds on the Web.

➠ Caligari's ViewSpace for Windows for viewing 3D graphics created with trueSpace2.

➠ Chaco's VRScout, a VRML viewer that works with your Web browser for viewing virtual worlds on the Internet.

➠ CompuServe's service and Internet connection software. This includes a Web Browser. Not only can you access CompuServe's full member services, but you have a direct connection to the Internet and the World Wide Web.

➠ Conversion programs from Keith Rule and from Bernie Roehl that enable you to convert a variety of different 3D graphic file formats to VRML .WRL format.

➠ Dennis McKenzie's award winning Above and Below, a virtual vacation experience.

➠ Dennis McKenzie's King Me world. A virtual world where even you can fight dragons.

➡ Examples and demonstration programs written by one of the authors using a variety of 16-bit programming languages.

➡ MicronGreen's NavFlyer keypad version of its VRML viewer.

➡ InterVista's WorldView, a VRML viewer from one of the original authors of the VRML specification.

➡ Microsoft's Internet Assistant for Word for Windows 6.0. Now you can create your own Web page while using Word for Windows.

➡ Paper Software's WebFX, a VRML viewer that works seamlessly with NetScape 1.1 and 1.2.

➡ ParaGraph's Home Space Builder, which provides an easy to use, VRML world creation tool.

➡ The QvLib files ported to Windows 3.1 and provided for inclusion here by Paper Software, Inc.

➡ Virtus WalkThrough VRML, which enables you to create great looking virtual worlds and save them in the VRML format.

➡ VisNet's VisMenu, the software that provides the virtual reality interface for this CD-ROM.

➡ Windows 95 versions of several of the programs and applications in this list as well as some not yet available for Windows 3.1.

Visit the virtual city provided on the CD-ROM and install the software that will kickstart your abilities to create your own cool 3D Web worlds with VRML.

Symbols & Numbers

(continued)